Time-Tested Plants

Time-Tested Plants

Thirty Years
in a Four-Season Garden

PAMELA J. HARPER

TIMBER PRESS
Portland, Oregon

Published in 2000 by

Timber Press, Inc.
The Haseltine Building
133 S.W. Second Avenue, Suite 450
Portland, Oregon 97204, U.S.A.

Library of Congress Cataloging-in-Publication Data

Harper, Pamela.
    Time-tested plants: thirty years in a four-season garden/Pamela J. Harper.
        p.   cm.
    Includes bibliographical references (p.)
    ISBN 0-88192-486-5
    1. Plants, Ornamental. 2. Plants, Ornamental—Pictorial works. I. Title.

SB407 H282 2000
635.9—dc21   00-026990

HALF TITLE PAGE: *Zephyranthes candida* (rain lily), with fernlike yellow-leaved *Rubus cockburnianus* 'Golden Vale'.

TITLE PAGE: *Rosa* 'Pink Pet' in center row, with *Pennisetum* 'Tall Tails' and *Arundo donax* 'Variegata'. In front row, left to right, *Achillea* 'Oertel's Rose' (pale pink), with *Nepeta* 'Six Hills Giant' behind it; *Hemerocallis* 'Little Business' (red); *Hemerocallis* 'Corky' (bright yellow) at far end. In back row, *Tamarix* (pink and feathery); coppery young leaves of *Lagerstroemia* 'Prairie Lace'; *Vitex agnus-castus* and a solitary spire of hollyhock. Trees at far end are *Magnolia stellata* 'Pink Stardust' and *Cornus florida*.

DEDICATION: *Oxalis regnellii* 'Triangularis' at right, with silvery-spotted *Pulmonaria longifolia* (lungwort) and *Athyrium niponicum* 'Pictum' (Japanese painted fern).

PAGE 6, OPPOSITE CONTENTS: *Ligularia tussilaginea* at right, with white-striped *Acorus gramineus* 'Variegatus' and autumnal foliage of *Itea virginica* 'Henry's Garnet'.

All photographs by Pamela J. Harper

Designed by Susan Applegate

Printed in Hong Kong

To Patrick,
for 47 years the rock on which my life stood firm

CONTENTS

ACKNOWLEDGMENTS

The gardener's world is a chain forged of many links that connects the past with the present and extends into the future. Acknowledging the kinship of contemporary and younger links would fill many pages. These colleagues know who they are, and I thank them all for their gifts of hospitality, plants, advice, and friendship. Here I would like to pay homage to earlier links, some of them dropped out of sight in their retirement and some no longer with us.

Remembered with particular affection are those who welcomed me at a time when my enthusiasm greatly exceeded my knowledge: Harold and Joan Bawden, whose Surrey and Devon gardens were for many years a fixture in that indispensable guide to private British gardens, the "yellow book" (*Gardens of England and Wales Open for Charity*), and Henry Fuller, a Heather Society contact who welcomed me to America. From Harold came *Chrysanthemum* 'Mei Kyo', and from Henry the plant that bears his name, *Phlox divaricata* 'Fuller's White'. A dwarf rhododendron is a reminder of Jim Cross of Environmentals Nursery, whose infectious enthusiasm lifted my spirits when, as a new transplant, they were at a low ebb, and *Phlox* 'Millstream Jupiter' a remembrance of Linc and Timmy Foster, whose enchanting garden brought recognition that American gardens could be as beautiful as any in England. During my short sojourn in Maryland, Henry Hohman answered my questions about unfamiliar plants at his Kingsville Nursery, showed me how to graft maples, and later sent me the white *Prunus mume* that still graces my garden.

Arthur Hellyer published my first article ("Bulbs in a Beginner's Garden") in England's *Amateur Gardening*, and a decade later Rachel Snyder of *Flower and Garden* Americanized my English spelling, pointing out that my *ss* and *zs* were all in the wrong places. Peter Healing instigated my interest in co-ordinated garden color, a topic further explored and sometimes argued about with Harland Hand, friend of many years, who also shared with me on several trips the wild beauty that inspired his garden artistry.

A stroll around my garden is a bit like the telling of a rosary, with each bead a friend remembered by a plant they gave me: *Veronica* 'Waterperry Blue' from Harold and Winifred Bevington; *Galanthus* and *Brunnera macrophylla* 'Langtrees' (named for their Devon garden) from Tony and Marney Rogerson; *Iris unguicularis* 'Walter Butt' and *Mahonia* 'Arthur Menzies' from Joe Witt of Seattle; *Hosta* 'Halcyon' and an exquisite white poppy from John Treasure's English garden; *Xanthoceras sorbifolium* from Bob Talley of the old Gulfstream Nursery on Virginia's Eastern Shore, where I also ate my first ever kiwi.

Faith Mackaness gave me the seed for *Habranthus texanus* and was an inspired guide to Oregon's Columbia Gorge, a trip made all the more memorable by the scrumptious picnic packed by her husband, Frank. Polly Hill of Martha's Vineyard sent me cuttings and seed of her azalea introductions, and Fred Galle a start of the evergreen azalea 'Primitive Beauty'. *Paeonia tenuifolia* came from John Wurdack of the Smithsonian Institution in Washington, D.C., and his gentle wife, Marie; *Chrysanthemum* 'Bronze Elegance' from botanical artist Kevin Nicolay of Seattle, who died too young; *Adonis amurensis* from Alan Bloom of Bressingham; *Ranunculus ficaria* 'Primrose' from Terry Jones of Devon; and my best form of *Arum italicum* 'Pictum' from Bill and Joan Baker in England. In 1976 heather expert Dorothy Metheny of Seattle gave me a low-growing stransvaesia (*Photinia davidiana*) and, as if blessed by friendship, it lives on where fireblight has taken other stransvaesias. *Anemone nemorosa* 'Robinsoniana' came from Jane Platt, whose Oregon garden has been a source of inspiration and remains so under the stewardship of her husband, John.

I still turn constantly to the books of Elizabeth Lawrence, my friend and mentor when I was coming to grips with gardening in Virginia, and seeing what Fred Heutte had accomplished at nearby Norfolk Botanical Garden got me off to a good start.

Returning to the present. Credit is given to *Horticulture* magazine for those portions of my text on celandines (*Ranunculus ficaria*), winter iris (*Iris unguicularis*), and hardy cyclamen first published there in similar form.

And finally, my grateful thanks to friend and garden helper Don McKelvey who, in an occasional day, accomplishes more than I get done in a week, while sharing my delight in beautiful plants, helping to right failures, and discussing such matters of the moment as whether box turtles can rebuild portions of broken shell. (They can.)

INTRODUCTION

In the course of more than four decades of playing with plants (for, no matter how seriously one may take oneself, that is what it amounts to) I must have read or browsed through thousands of gardening books, and from few have I failed to learn something. At first, not recognizing authors' names and unable to assess merit, I followed a trail from books I found helpful through others recommended in their bibliographies. Because I then lived in England, most of these were by English authors, but not all. I still recall the impression made by *The Carefree Garden* by Jean Hersey, an American writer ahead of her time in advocating a more relaxed gardening style at a time when unbroken sweeps of manicured suburban lawn were socially more or less mandatory.

If the information a book imparts is to be interpreted in the light of one's own regional conditions, it is important to know the basis from which the author writes. I have watched with dismay a growing tendency for publishers to disguise the origin of a book. Although the desire to garner sales nationally and internationally is understandable, it is not playing fair to handicap readers in this way and may set them up for disappointments.

It behooves me, then, to outline my own experience. I gardened avidly in England from 1955 to 1968, when my husband's work brought us to North America where, after brief sojourns in Connecticut and Maryland, we came to live in the coastal plain of Virginia in 1971. Most of my hands-on gardening has been in England and Virginia, similar hardiness zones yet different in many respects, not the least of them that in England I gardened on clay, in Virginia on sand. For the rest, there have been books, catalogs (the latter containing much useful regional or specialized information), travel, and plant chat with gardening friends, in person or by mail, in many faraway places.

What has struck me over the years is how versatile most plants are. England has a limited native flora, and most of its garden plants are natives of other lands. Although knowing the habitat of a plant makes it easier to assess the likelihood of its accepting what one has to offer, my way has been less scholarly: if I wanted a plant and could get it, I would try it. A pattern does emerge. Many plants in my present garden, including such splendid and little-known species as *Erythrina herbacea*, *Spigelia marilandica*, amsonias, and baptisias, are from the rich flora of southeastern North America, but equally many are from Asia, with smaller contingents from other parts of North and South America, from Europe, and from such far-flung and diverse regions as South Africa, Russia, Australia, and New Zealand.

Setting the Scene

My 2-acre garden is a long, flat oblong on a sheltered tidal creek off the Chesapeake Bay. Rural when we came, the area is now the typical ugly suburban sprawl of uncontrolled development, in stark contrast with breathtaking natural beauty. Behind the house, which is 350 feet from the road, is a water-girt apron of land left natural, strewn with loblolly pines (*Pinus taeda*), oaks (*Quercus falcata*), tupelo (*Nyssa sylvatica*), holly (*Ilex opaca*), and thickets of wax myrtle (*Myrica cerifera*). On the marshy fringe, partly or entirely under water at high tide, are marsh grasses (including *Panicum virgatum*), seashore mallow (*Kosteletzyka virginica*), sea ox-eye (*Borrichia frutescens*), and the salt-bush or groundsel-bush (*Baccharis halimifolia*) that becomes white clouds of silky seedheads in autumn. One indigenous native returning in growing numbers through the carpet of tawny pine needles, which was lawn before I came, is spotted wintergreen (*Chimaphila maculata*) with white-striped, hollylike evergreen leaves and nodding white waxy flowers in late spring. This plant occupies a specialized niche in the low fertility soils of dry thin woodlands, and my attempts to transplant it to the "better" conditions of the cultivated garden have repeatedly failed.

Most of the land lies in front of the house and is densely planted, mostly informally. A graveled drive, regraded every other year, runs down the middle of the lot and encircles a large island in front of the house. Although hard-surfacing the drive would reduce both work and cost, water could not then percolate through to the roots of large trees. Long paths run along both boundaries, and others, some mulch, some paving slabs, curve off from the drive and sweep back further along. There is no lawn.

The soil is basically an easily dug acid sand (most now much enriched with years of mulch and manure) without so much as a pebble to be found, just the occasional oyster shell. All is not as it seems; there is blue clay under the sand and the water table is high, resulting in temporary waterlogging after prolonged or heavy rain. Much of the garden is therefore banked, bermed, or raised. One section lies low, with heavy soil, part in sun, part in light shade, and there I can grow such moisture lovers as astilbes, *Primula japonica*, and *Lobelia cardinalis*, which thrive here and nowhere else in the garden. The sand of another section has been covered with a deep layer of gravel for the benefit of plants needing sharp drainage and not tolerating water round their necks, notably dianthus. About half the area is under the high canopy of forest-size oaks and pines, so there is both sun and shade. Some parts dry out rapidly, while others are more moisture retentive.

With what weather conditions must plants contend? Annual rainfall averages 45 inches. Although summer drought is all too common, there usually is periodic rain. Not, however, Shakespeare's "gentle rain from heaven." Short gully-washer thunderstorms dump down water too fast for the soil to absorb it, with much of it lost to run-off, leaving herbaceous plants looking like soufflés kept waiting too long. This rain precludes the xeriscape gardening practiced in regions where summers are consistently dry. The difference in rain patterns misleads many into supposing that England gets more rain than the East Coast of North America, when the reverse is the case. It rains more often in England but less heavily.

When heat is so intense that just-washed hair dries on the few-minute stroll to the mailbox and back, 2 weeks without rain constitutes a drought. I can and do water during summer, from two wells and sometimes also city water. Could I not do so the range of plants that flourish would be considerably reduced. Overhead sprinklers are used and soaker hoses are permanently placed beneath a layer of mulch on straight runs. Because summers are unremittingly hot, plants need much more water, and usually more shade, than they do in cooler regions.

Were it not for winter freezes and constant pruning and cutting back, my 2 acres would be a jungle. Plants, especially woody plants, grow so fast that seldom does a month go by without a large truckload of brush and branches going off for shredding into the mulch I can buy at modest cost. The quintessential tool of suburban gardening here is the pickup truck. Mulch breaks down rapidly in the moist heat, and an average of 15 cubic yards is spread on beds and paths each year, as well as quantities of leaves, both my own and the sacks put out for collection by my neighbors.

The average winter low is 15°F, seldom enduring long enough to freeze the ground more than an inch or two. The average last frost date is 15 April, but in fact frost is uncommon after the end of March, so I am usually spared the late spring frosts that called for careful positioning of some plants, especially azaleas, in my English garden. Damage more often occurs at the other end of the year. The first frost of autumn seldom comes before the end of October, and sometimes not until December. Sudden temperature plunges sometimes then occur, damaging woody plants not hardened off by gradual cooling. Ice storms are common, creating a magical, glittering crystalline world, with plants as vulnerable as glass to breakage. There is little wind, but tornadoes and lightning strikes are constant threats.

Spring, from March through May, is glorious, mostly sunny and warm without being hot and humid. June is variable, sometimes spring and sometimes summer. The 3 summer months are a Turkish bath of heat and humidity, day and night. They would be intolerable were it not for air-conditioned cars and buildings: 75°F is a cool day, 90°F and higher more typical. Autumn is usually a long Indian summer, often lasting to Christmas. Winter is short, with widely fluctuating temperatures, occasionally as high as 80°F or as low as 0°F, sometimes with a snowfall or two, usually light.

On sandy soil in a hot, moist climate, many plants trustable in cooler regions or heavier soil become too invasive, by root or seed. The worst offenders have been *Houttuynia cordata*, trumpet vine (*Campsis radicans*), *Pinellia ternata*, cross vine (*Bignonia capreolata*), *Eomecon chionantha*, and *Disporum sessile* 'Variegatum'. The herbicide Roundup (glyphosate) is my standby for eliminating or controlling these and such other ever-present, bird-sown local weeds as smilax, poison ivy, and the pokeweed (*Phytolacca americana*) and dog fennel (*Eupatorium capillifolium*) sometimes grown as ornamentals in England but here far too invasive.

As for pests and diseases, name it and it probably occurs in this region. My willow-leaf pear (*Pyrus salicifolia* 'Pendula') and two stransvaesias (*Photinia davidiana*) were lost to fire blight; many cherries, plums, and apricots to borer; and several large shrubs or trees to root rots. To refrain from growing a plant because it is subject to this or that would be akin to rejecting medications after reading the warning labels. When, however, the warnings become reality I do not usually replace that plant, though there are always exceptions for particular favorites. Chemical preventatives or cures are infrequently used. Where I do resort to them (dormant oil for *Euonymus*, for instance), I say so. My general approach is to seek those plants that live healthily without such intervention. Getting them in the right place is an important part of this approach: many azaleas, for instance, suffer from spider mite or petal blight in sun but not in shade.

Birds (including hummingbirds and the great pileated woodpecker) and such creatures as possums, raccoons, squirrels, black snakes, box turtles, bees, and butterflies share the garden and bring more pleasure than problems. I have so far been spared deer. I do, sadly, wage war on voles and rabbits, for few plants would survive were these pests not controlled.

How the Plants Were Selected

I grow many more plants than those mentioned here and which to pick out for mention has often been hard to decide. Some plants have been in and out umpteen times as the manuscript proceeded. Nearly all the finalists have proved their long-term worth in beauty and adaptability for a decade or more. In a few cases success of an attractive newcomer was predicated on the long-term survival of a similar plant: *Physocarpus opulifolius* 'Diabolo', for instance, is not likely to fail where *P. opulifolius* 'Dart's Gold' has long proved invincible. Conversely, few hypericums have been top rankers in the long run, so *Hypericum androsaemum* 'Albury Purple' was omitted despite its fine performance through two of the hottest, driest summers on record, awaiting the test of a harsh winter. Sometimes, of course, it is entirely a matter of personal preference. "Now that," said a friend standing in front of *Buddleia* 'Lochinch', "is a good buddleia—if there is such a thing." I feel the same way, so buddleias got short shrift, though in general they thrive.

Hardiness

All the plants described have survived cold and heat for many years in USDA Zone 7. Beyond this, suggested cold hardiness is approximate, which is all it ever can be with so many variables. Both heat and cold hardiness often can be pushed a zone in favorable microclimates within a garden, and there are many inconsistencies. A largish patch of *Salvia leucantha* has been in the same spot in my garden for two decades, yet this species has quickly been killed everywhere else I have tried it. *Lantana camara* 'Miss Huff' has gone through many winters in a friend's Raleigh, North Carolina, garden, also Zone 7, but never survived one in mine, while *Ceratostigma willmottianum* is weedlike in its self-sufficiency for me yet does not survive for my friend. All the plants mentioned in this book survive summer heat to Zone 8. Beyond that heat hardiness cannot be tied down to a zone number, as there is little similarity between, for example, Zone 9 California and Zone 9 Florida.

The Photographs

While I fully understand the reasons for it (which of us would buy a gardening publication with mediocre photographs?), I consider it a flaw that pictures in books and magazines are seldom closely related to the text, having usually been taken elsewhere than in the writer's garden, often in another region, and frequently another country. I have therefore resisted the temptation to use prettier pictures taken far away and, with two exceptions (*Syringa* 'Miss Kim' and *Aralia elata* 'Variegata'), used only those taken in my own garden, most of them in the same year. The other two photos were taken in the nearby garden of my friend Ellen Penick, who displays those plants more effectively than I have so far managed to do.

Botanical Nomenclature

If we do not speak the language, we cannot converse. I have always been a staunch advocate of botanical nomenclature, the language of plants and, living my life among plantspeople, it has come easily to me. Regrettably, plant names are now being changed with such frequency, often only temporarily, that scientific names are ceasing to be a practical means of communication for gardeners. More influential voices than mine are being raised in protest, and it seems likely that compromises will be reached that will enable the language to serve equally the needs of taxonomists and gardeners.

Meantime it is my practice to avoid new

names until they seem to have taken hold, staying, for example, with *Sedum* 'Autumn Joy' rather than *Hylotelephium* 'Autumn Joy'. In this I am generally guided by the names being used in nursery catalogs. A recent telephone conversation with one of North America's leading plantsmen makes my point. We were discussing the hardiness of *Chrysanthe-mum* 'Bronze Elegance', and I pointed out that a northeastern wholesale nursery listed it, so it was, presumably, hardy there. There followed a riffling of catalog pages and then, "It's not here." "Are you looking," I asked, "under *Dendranthema*?"

Gardeners cannot take refuge in popular names, which in the main are even more confusing and seldom well known. I have tried to include those most commonly used. As a photographer I frequently get calls from book and magazine editors who know only the common name of what they seek. *Hortus Third* comes to the rescue with an extensive list that includes such "common" names as angel's eye, Arab's turban, and cathedral windows.

Spring

BULBS

Every year end I am frustrated anew as I leaf through the latest batch of desk diaries and find the same assumption that life ceases abruptly on the last day of December and starts afresh next day. The business of life makes no such demarcation, nor does nature, and a plant that flowers in winter one year may, if held back by a cold snap, cross the calendar's seasonal dividing line in the ensuing year.

Usually, though, in Zone 7, the weather and the calendar are in accord by the last week of March. It is spring, though it may briefly regress with an April frost that nips perennials pushing through the ground and scorches the tender unfurling leaves of trees and shrubs. Putting out before the end of April the tender annuals already appearing outside the supermarkets is tempting fate. Bulbs and shrubs by the dozen are now vying for attention.

Ranunculus ficaria
CELANDINE

Among the first bulbous plants to flower is the English celandine. When using popular names, gardeners don't all speak the same language. To some "celandine" means *Chelidonium majus*, also called greater celandine, while to others it means celandine poppy, *Stylophorum diphyllum*. These belong to the poppy family, but what I call celandine, *Ranunculus ficaria* (Zone 5), belongs with the buttercups. Some call it lesser celandine. Lesser! In size? Yes! In numbers? No! In beauty and diversity? Absolutely not!

As a child I ate first from my plate what I liked least, leaving the best for last. Adopting

LEFT *Cornus florida* (dogwood) underplanted with *Helleborus orientalis* (Lenten rose)

Ranunculus ficaria 'Wisley Double Cream' (celandine, English celandine)

perhaps eliminated, by growing only double-flowered forms, which seldom if ever set seed.

While low-lying, boggy places are lesser celandine's natural habitat, wet soil is not essential. The plants need moisture while above ground, but the tubers aren't harmed by drought during their summer dormancy. In my garden, growth starts around the turn of the year, when rosettes of burnished leaves appear, prettily and variously patterned and snuggled flat against the ground. They begin to flower when the weather warms up, continuing for 6 weeks or more and peaking in April. The petals, typically bright yellow, are as highly polished as those of their buttercup relations. When their flowering is done, celandines seem almost to melt away, so quickly and neatly do they disappear. This pattern of early growth and summer dormancy enables them to tolerate overplanting with herbaceous plants. I have them under painted ferns (*Athyrium niponicum* 'Pictum') and hardy orchids (*Bletilla striata*). There they increase less rapidly than those with less competition, which is not altogether a bad thing.

My collection began with a single-flowered white form, a gift from the late Elizabeth Lawrence. That the best way to keep a plant is to give it away is sage advice. I was later to return the white celandine to the new owner of

now the same approach with this little celandine, I'll dispose first of the distasteful part, then the rest can be relished. In its wild form it spreads rapidly, both by seed and by proliferation of the tiny tubers. If you can't stomach that, keep it off your garden plate.

I grow the wildling in a roadside ditch beyond the fence. Within the garden, sundry selected forms bring incalculable pleasure during the early months of the year. Most of these are not unduly invasive given a reasonably watchful eye. They may not be suitable for the rock garden, but they are a joyful sight under and among shrubs, where control amounts to little more than removing seedlings that don't resemble their parent and aren't worth preserving in their own right. I don't find this chore tiresome, but it could be reduced, and

Elizabeth's garden. Elizabeth didn't know its name, but *Ranunculus ficaria* 'Randall's White' and 'Salmon's White' are as nearly the same as to make no difference if you don't concern yourself with such minutiae as whether petals are slate-flushed on the reverse. *Ranunculus ficaria* 'Primrose', 'Citrina', and 'Limelight' also resemble each other: their single flowers open lemon yellow, paling as they age. One of these is tucked under a winter hazel (*Corylopsis pauciflora*) with flowers of matching yellow. The other is in front of *Epimedium grandiflorum* 'Lilafee', with flowers of complementary pale purple, and *E. ×versicolor* 'Sulphureum', with creamy yellow flowers.

My next acquisition was *Ranunculus ficaria* 'Flore Pleno', widely disseminated in my area as marsh marigold. Superficially it resembles the double-flowered marsh marigold (*Caltha palustris* 'Flore Pleno'), but no one familiar with the two could possibly confuse them: the celandine is more compact and smaller in all its parts. It makes its way up through a mat of a dusky purple periwinkle (*Vinca minor* 'Atropurpurea'), a captivating combination that leaves no bare ground when the celandine goes dormant. Because it is too hard to control, the periwinkle is, nonetheless, on my eviction list.

There have been no seedlings from *Ranunculus ficaria* 'Flore Pleno', nor from another double, the neat and compact *R. ficaria* 'Collarette', which has leaves reminiscent of cyclamen in shape and patterning and flowers as precisely crafted as the cogs in a watch, with stubby petals evenly spaced around a green-eyed hub. Its warm orange-yellow color harmonizes nicely with tufts of the little yellow-bladed sweet flag (*Acorus gramineus* 'Minimus Aureus'). A short row of 'Collarette' edging a mulched path leaves no obvious gap when it goes dormant; the path just looks a bit wider.

Single-flowered *Ranunculus ficaria* 'Cupreus', with light orange petals shading into copper at the base, grows around and among *Epimedium ×warleyense*, which is shorn in late winter of its wiry-stemmed leaves, shabby by then, to better display its flame-colored flowers rising over those of the celandine. This epimedium is a thinly-wandering grower; most other species are too dense to permit underplanting. Fresh new epimedium leaves later fill the space left vacant by the celandine. In my sandy soil black mondo grass (*Ophiopogon planiscapus* 'Nigrescens') runs thinly, allowing an interplanting of this orange celandine, a stunning combination.

Ranunculus ficaria 'Brazen Hussy', found and named by Christopher Lloyd, is such a knockout that few can resist it. Even wary rock gardeners have been known to risk it. Scintillating buttercup yellow flowers are set against burnished leaves of a dark chocolate brown that shows particularly well against golden gravel or chartreuse foliage.

When I was growing up in England, "coppernob" was a term used for people with auburn hair. Adults used the term affectionately, children often tauntingly. The celandine so named, *Ranunculus ficaria* 'Coppernob', attracts only favorable comment. A child of 'Brazen Hussy' and 'Cupreus', it combines dark foliage with coppery orange flowers that fade to banana yellow and finally to white.

Mankind and nature continue to experiment, and there has been quite a rush of new celandines. I have not yet found a double white to rival the double bloodroot (*Sanguinaria canadensis*) that blooms at the same time, but if the flowers of one I christened "Ivory Buttons"—before I knew that its proper name was 'Wisley Double Cream' (also acquired as 'Wisley Double Mud')—are neither as large nor as snowily white as those of the bloodroot, they are much longer lasting. Newly opened when I left, these flowers were still there to greet me 3 weeks later, flattened pompoms of gentle, poised appeal with petals of ivory flushed with slate. *Ranunculus ficaria* 'Green Petal', by contrast, is a clown, raising a

Ipheion uniflorum 'Wisley Blue' (starflower) at base of *Magnolia stellata*

smile from those who find pleasure in the quaint and curious. A conglomeration of green and yellow paddle-shaped petals forms a scrambled semi-double flower that looks as if it had been stirred with a fork. Celandines are addictive, and I'll try any that come along.

Ipheion uniflorum

STARFLOWER

A blue ribbon goes to a blue starry flower of starring quality. Having produced a sprinkling of flowers since January, *Ipheion uniflorum* (Zone 5) reaches its zenith shortly before Easter, when it seems to reflect the blue of the sky—a somewhat overcast sky in the case of the milky blue species, light azure in 'Wisley Blue', and a deeper blue in 'Rolf Fiedler'.

Years ago I bought a dozen bulbs of *Ipheion uniflorum* 'Wisley Blue'. Today, despite the depredations of that bulb-gobbling varmint the pine vole, there are thousands of bulbs. Starflower's prolificacy, by bulb increase and seed, makes it a fine naturalizer. Winter cold is its Achilles' heel, with Zone 6 its limit of certain survival. Otherwise it is adaptable provided it gets moisture while in growth. It can take full sun, but in hot regions the flowers last longer with afternoon shade.

The challenge is to find a place for starflower where its absence is not noticed during its summer dormancy. Under a spreading star magnolia (*Magnolia stellata* 'Pink Stardust') it is a pool of blue. Here it is deeply shaded and often dry in summer, but moist and open to sun during the magnolia's leafless months. Starflower's leaves emerge as those of the magnolia fall and are briefly submerged, soon growing through to the light.

In a moister part of my garden a sheet of starflowers surrounds early daffodils. As these go dormant, a spreading Japanese anemone (*Anemone tomentosa* 'Robustissima'; Zone 5) grows up to take their place, so the ground is never bare. Starflower can be combined with many, but not all, perennials and other bulbs. I moved it out from among primroses (*Primula vulgaris*; Zone 5) when it began to engulf them. Two taller, robust perennials in the same east-facing bed spear up easily through patches of starflower, in mutually enhancing combinations of color, form, and texture—a creamily variegated Solomon's seal (*Polygonatum odoratum* 'Variegatum'; Zone 4) and the less-well-known, equally sturdy *Disporum uniflorum* (Zone 5), with nodding clusters of waxy lemon-yellow bells.

When starflower is grown in quantity, spontaneous variations occur. One of these, selected by Norman Beal of Raleigh, North Carolina, and named 'Graystone White', is the best white form I've seen. It has pure white petals that are full and rounded. I planted it towards the front of a moist and lightly shaded bed among the stoloniferous stems of Virginia sweetspire (*Itea virginica* 'Henry's Garnet'; Zone 5), which has not yet leafed out when starflower blooms. In a drier place there is a strong color combination from *Camellia japonica* 'Ville de Nantes Red' (Zone 7), a dark red semi-double, underplanted with *Ipheion uniflorum* 'Froyle Mill', an English introduction with white-eyed purple flowers.

Narcissus

DAFFODIL, JONQUIL

Until I came to write about them I had never tried to identify two robust daffodils of early spring that were on the property when my husband and I bought it. The previous owners were not gardeners, and the survival of these two heirloom varieties in barren, acid sand testifies to their toughness. Brent Heath,

a near neighbor, came to my rescue. His family has grown daffodils for three generations, and Brent had no hesitation in naming my two. The first to bloom is the primrose and lemon-yellow *Narcissus* 'Sir Watkin' (Zone 5), which usually starts halfway through March and goes on for about 3 weeks, overlapped by *N.* 'Queen of the North' (Zone 4). In their book *Daffodils for American Gardens*, Brent and Becky Heath picture 'Queen of the North' massed on a hillside at Winterthur Gardens in Delaware, where it has been growing for almost 100 years. Although placed in Division 3, for short-cupped daffodils of garden origin, this yellow-cupped white narcissus has the dancing, butterfly grace of poeticus narcissus such as the old pheasant's-eye, *Narcissus* 'Actaea' (Zone 3), one of the last daffodils to bloom and another long-term survivor.

Narcissus 'W. P. Milner' (Zone 5), which follows 'Queen of the North', was introduced in 1869 and in my opinion has not been improved on since. It bears close resemblance to the wild Lent lily (*N. pseudonarcissus*; Zone 5) and is an equally good doer. The flowers are pale silvery yellow, nodding a little, and perfectly proportioned to the 8-inch height. 'W. P. Milner' usually straddles winter and spring, blooming along with one of the first perennials, *Euphorbia myrsinites* (Zone 5). This dainty

daffodil is too small and pale to be effective way back in a border or competing with such resplendent hybrids as *N.* 'Ice Follies' (Zone 3), a much larger, very reliable daffodil that blooms at the same time. Evergreen ferns such as autumn fern (*Dryopteris erythrosora*; Zone 5) make a good background for 'W. P. Milner', and the similar, slightly larger, old *N.* 'Queen of Spain' (Zone 5), which needs rechristening with a name suggesting elfin charm, not grandeur. Ferns and daffodils alike are comfortable in their east-facing bed, along with primroses. *Narcissus* 'W. P. Milner' increases rapidly, so I'm always looking for new places for divisions. I've got my eye on a spot under *Corylopsis pauciflora* (Zone 6), the smallest winter hazel, which flowers at the same time. There the daffodil would join *Ranunculus ficaria* 'Primrose' in a triple color echo: same pale primrose yellow, but different forms, sizes, and levels.

Narcissus bulbocodium var. *conspicuus* (Zone 6), a hoop-petticoat daffodil, has leaves so fine, dense, and floppy that the warm yellow flower megaphones seem to rise over a carpet of flood-flattened grass. On the dry bank of a ditch, bulb increase is so prodigious that I lift each clump when the flowers have gone, tease it into two pieces, and replant them separately. Compensation for less than 2

Ornithogalum nutans

weeks of bloom comes in the quick, neat way this daffodil then goes dormant.

Muscari armeniacum
GRAPE HYACINTH

Countless books and catalogs have featured grape hyacinth (*Muscari armeniacum*; Zone 4) massed in Dutch bulb fields. Inherent in those lakes of blue and in the modest price is a warning: this bulb increases fast. That was exactly what I wanted to compete on equal terms alongside starflower (*Ipheion uniflorum*) in ground sunny and bare during the dormancy of deciduous shrubs, perennials, and grasses. Starflower gets a head start, then its bloom time overlaps with grape hyacinth in a blue echo, with ample contrast from the deeper blue and spikelike form of the muscari. This autumn I shall be adding *Muscari armeniacum* 'Valerie Finnis', a recent introduction with flowers of a luminous pale blue.

Chionodoxa
GLORY-OF-THE-SNOW

In late March or early April chionodoxas (Zone 3) bloom under *Magnolia ×soulange-ana*. I've yet to see them blooming through the snow, but in the few years when the magnolia flowers are not ruined by frost, fallen petals make a pink carpet around the bulb's blue flowers. Planted here were *Chionodoxa luciliae*, *C. siehei*, *C. tmolusi*, and *C. sardensis*. Differences between the first three are so subtle that I'd rather not be asked just which is which, and their identities may in any case be confused in the trade. Only bulb connoisseurs need venture beyond the first and least expensive of the three. There's a good white form as well as the blue. *Chionodoxa sardensis* has smaller flowers of a brighter blue and would benefit from being moved out and given a spot of its own.

Chionodoxa nana (synonym *C. cretica*) is a collector's item sized for the rock garden. It has small starry milky blue flowers. Planted under the outer branches of *Deutzia* 'Rosealind', it has hung in there for many years without increasing much. It flowers before the deutzia leafs out.

Ornithogalum nutans

Frail ghost of a flower though it seems in its white-edged greeny gray, this Balkan native is very much at home in southeastern North America and an excellent naturalizer in sun, or preferably dappled shade. The flowers, ranged down one side of a spikelike raceme, open around Easter time. *Ornithogalum nutans* is hardy to Zone 6.

Anemone nemorosa

WOOD ANEMONE

The plump little tubers of *Anemone blanda* (Zone 5) make tasty morsels for rodents. It self-sows for me, and there is always some around, but for drifts I've turned to *A. nemorosa* (Zone 5) with twiglike rhizomes seemingly too small to make a meal. Only a few inches high, the foliage, just pushing through when *A. blanda* blooms, is delicately divided yet dense, the flowers are beguilingly simple in form, the vigor all that one could ask, and the tidy way it dies away commendable. A woodland plant in nature, yet able to take considerable sun if the soil is moist, it makes a delightful early blooming carpeter among deciduous shrubs or well-spaced herbaceous perennials such as hostas and arisaemas. Flowers may be white, pink, or blue, single or double. Among my favorites are *A. nemorosa*

Anemone nemorosa 'Blue Eyes' (wood anemone)

'Robinsoniana', with large pale lavender-blue flowers, white 'Vestal', shaggy white, blue-eyed 'Blue Eyes', and green and white 'Bracteata'.

Leucojum

SNOWFLAKE

Snowdrops (*Galanthus nivalis*) fail for many southern gardeners, but prosper for me. I have no explanation. The other side of the coin is that few southerners fail with summer snowflake (*Leucojum aestivum*; Zone 4), but I got a D grade, at best, for many years. "Easily grown in damp rich soil," advises *The Bulb Book* by Martyn Rix and Roger Phillips. "The robust flowers merrily chiming out spring in every southern dooryard are those of the summer snowflake," says Scott Ogden in *Garden Bulbs for the South*. I gave my plants damp, rich soil, and they multiplied at prodigious speed, but the flowering chime was only the faintest ting-a-ling. I know gardens where summer snowflake has grown untouched for years and still blooms abundantly, but in gardening there's no one-size-fits-all and for me the winning recipe is full sun, moist soil, and—the key—frequent division.

That summer snowflake is often confused with both spring snowflake (*Leucojum vernum*; Zone 4) and snowdrops (*Galanthus nivalis*) is understandable. Snowdrops and spring snowflake are often in bloom together, and summer snowflake follows closely behind. To further confuse, Dutch bulbs sold as spring snowflake have for years been summer snowflake more often than not. Once the real thing is seen, confusion dissipates. The chubby flowers of snowflakes resemble little Tiffany lampshades fringed in green (yellow in one form of spring snowflake), and two or more dangle from the tip of each stalk where snowdrops have only one. The leaves of snowflakes are longer, broader, and brighter green than the gray-green leaves of snowdrops. Spring snowflake is barely 9 inches high, while summer snowflake is more than twice as tall and much more substantial. Spring snowflake is uncommon. The best display I've seen in North America is at Winterthur Gardens,

Delaware, where it grows on a wooded slope with snowdrops, glory-of-the-snow (*Chionodoxa*), and yellow-flowered, ferny-leaved *Adonis amurensis* (Zone 4), a sight that amply rewarded a long, late winter drive.

Tulipa clusiana
LADY TULIP

Think spring, think tulips—and I have, feeding thousands of tulip bulbs to voles over the years. Even without the rodent problem, hybrids seldom endure in my garden. Many species do endure, if they are not eaten, including the graceful, scarlet-flowered *Tulipa sprengeri* (Zone 7), which survives for me in plunged pots, while the drifts I long for remain a dream. Only two kinds of tulips have persisted in the open ground. The lady tulip (*T. clusiana*; Zone 6), with red-striped buds and white opened flowers, has self-sown among *Iris unguicularis* in a hot dry spot. Its scarlet and yellow counterparts, *T. clusiana* var. *chrysantha* and such similar forms such as 'Cynthia' and 'Tubergen's Gem', flourish on a sunny bank with lots of gravel dug in.

Hyacinthoides hispanica
SPANISH BLUEBELL

Scilla hispanica, *Scilla campanulata*, *Endymion hispanicus*, and *Hyacinthoides hispan-*

ica (Zone 3). Poor thing! This species has to be good to remain in demand through so many rechristenings, and it is. Although it has the same shortcoming as daffodils—the leaves are substantial and take a long time dying—this is not a conspicuous flaw in the places to which it is best suited, naturalized among shrubs or under trees. Spanish bluebell flowers at the same time as evergreen azaleas, so I have it surrounding 'Hampton Beauty'. This azalea's buds are deep coral, paling as they open, a similarly winsome combination to that of apple blossom. At Winterthur Gardens in Delaware, Spanish bluebells flow in a blue river between scarlet azaleas (*Rhododendron kaempferi*). There's a wishy-washy pink form of Spanish bluebell and white forms of varying flower size and color purity. Long ago I learned the wisdom of potting up new bulbs, plunging the pots, and waiting until they flower before putting them out. This method is easier than digging up and relocating bulbs that turn out not to be what was ordered, a regrettably frequent occurrence.

Allium

I am wary of ornamental onions. The genus contains more than one overly fecund species, including my most ineradicable weed, *Nothoscordum inodorum* (synonym *Allium fra-*

Leucojum aestivum (summer snowflake) at left, with heirloom daffodil *Narcissus* 'Sir Watkin' in right foreground, and *Ipheion uniflorum* in left foreground under *Corylopsis sinensis*

Allium triquetrum

when the glossy onion leaves reappear in autumn. Loose umbels of up to ten starry, green-striped white bells tip sturdy triangular stalks for almost 2 months from late March into May, both flowers and leaves remaining pristine throughout this time.

My second-best early ornamental onion, the only long-term survivor among the large-headed kinds, is *Allium multibulbosum* (Zone 4; synonym *A. nigrum*). It has sturdy 4-foot stems topped with green-eyed white starry flowers packed into domes 4 inches across. The snag with this species, as with many large-headed ornamental onions, is that the foliage comes up early and by flowering time sprawls disheveled and rotting on the ground, so it calls for strategic placement behind something tall enough to hide the foliage without concealing the flowers.

Convallaria majalis

LILY-OF-THE-VALLEY

The wafted fragrance of lily-of-the-valley (*Convallaria majalis*; Zone 3) is the essence of spring. Few flowers more reward the picking and they scarcely need "arranging." Each stem is so firm and straight, each waxy bell so perfect, and the scent so sublime that only lavender is more in demand in soaps and perfumes. Lily-of-the-valley isn't really a bulb, but

grans). I did not plant this, it just appeared. Any onion with dozens of offsets like grains of wheat clustered at the base of the parent bulb is best consigned to the garbage, inside a plastic bag.

Allium triquetrum (Zone 5), too good to leave out, is not one of these. It does have a reputation for naturalizing in moist, summer-shaded places. To this I cannot testify, having only recently let a small clump loose in a spot where it is daily under my eye, and so I shall not forget to remove spent flowering stems before they set seed. This allium has, however, for several years been a superb container plant in a paved courtyard. I grow it in 10-inch-diameter plastic pots which, when the show is over, are hidden behind larger containers until it is time for them to take center stage again

bulb sellers are its main purveyors. So well known that it scarcely needs describing, it is so well loved that gardeners in warm winter regions have been known to douse it with ice cubes in an attempt to give it the cold it needs to bloom.

Such pampering is usually wasted effort with this all-or-nothing colonizer. Moist, acid soil in sun or light shade seems to suit it best, but either it likes your garden or it doesn't. If it does, don't mix it with less vigorous herbaceous plants. Resolve that as best you can—perhaps in a foundation planting, courtyard corner, or under shrubs. Mine has an eighth of an acre to itself under the trees behind the house, with freedom to roam until it reaches the brackish surrounding marsh. Here it seems entirely appropriate to the natural scene, among a litter of fallen leaves, pine needles and cones, and bits of broken branch. This setting is far removed from the general concept of a "natural garden," which usually means the integration of native plants into an orderly garden setting. Tidiness is not nature's aim and, yes, I do sometimes itch to take a hand. Years ago I bribed a youngster to pick up the pine cones at a dime a dozen, a rate that would have bankrupted me had she kept at it, but the short attention span of a 10-year-old made $5 the maximum paid out. Nowadays

Hippeastrum ×johnsonii

the cones are left where they fall. If this is among the lily-of-the-valley, they are soon engulfed.

Hippeastrum ×johnsonii

ST. JOSEPH'S LILY, AMARYLLIS

My preference for species and old hybrids, be it daffodils, gladiolus, or daylilies, is a recurring theme. Species and antique varieties have an elegance, and often a robustness, too often lost in their more glamorous newer counterparts. I do grow modern hybrid amaryllis, for their indoor Christmas bloom, afterward planting them out to take their chances. Some die the first winter, most survive for at least a few years. My namesake, the scarlet *Hippeastrum* 'Pamela', has put on a splendid show in the garden for 5 years now, the number of

Camassia leichtlinii 'Plena'

blooms steadily increased to a total of ten stems last year.

None of the large-flowered hybrids, though, has pleased me half as much as one known as St. Joseph's lily (*Hippeastrum ×johnsonii;* Zone 7), with a white stripe down each scarlet petal of the star-shaped flower. I first saw St. Joseph's lily on a 1987 visit to Baton Rouge, Louisiana, where it seemed to be growing in every garden. Noting my covetous glances, my host, architect Wayne Womack, sent me a bulb or two. It has bloomed faithfully every May since, proved adequately hardy, and multiplied to about thirty bulbs. From Roy Hay and Patrick M. Synge's *Dictionary of Garden Plants*, published in England in 1969, I learned that *H. ×johnsonii* is a hybrid of *H. reginae* and *H. vittatum* raised by a watchmaker named Johnson in 1799. How did it get to Louisiana? Did Mr. Johnson emigrate and bring this treasure with him? It is not now listed in the *RHS Plant Finder*. To forestall telephone calls asking for a source, I offer two suggestions: visit Baton Rouge, find a garden where it is plentiful, knock on the door, and beg, or order it from Louisiana Nursery, which also offers *H. ×johnsonii* 'Big Nellie', with larger flowers, and *H. ×johnsonii* 'Little Doug', with smaller flowers.

Camassia leichtlinii

The starry flowers on the inflorescence spires of most camassias open a few at a time from the bottom up. On the one hand, this sequence is less impressive than if all the flowers opened at the same time. On the other hand, with forty or more buds in each spire, the show goes on longer, usually a couple of weeks.

Camassia leichtlinii (Zone 5) is the most attractive species. A dozen bulbs make a substantial, shapely clump. The flowers, single or double, come in varying shades of blue or in what at first glance looks cream, but on closer inspection are seen to be pale ivory with hints of green and yellow. The form with most impact in my garden is *C. leichtlinii* 'Plena', with rosettes of creamy flowers opening more randomly and more at one time along the spire. These double blooms last longer than single ones, as usually is the case. 'Plena' makes the perfect echo companion behind the creamy foliage of *Sedum alboroseum* 'Mediovariegatum' (Zone 4).

Camassias aren't finicky plants. They need only moderately fertile soil that doesn't dry out completely. The flowers last longer if they are out of the direct path of the sun during the hottest hours of the day.

Gladiolus byzantinus (hardy gladiolus) behind *Fallopia japonica* 'Variegata'

Gladiolus byzantinus

HARDY GLADIOLUS

Bewailing what one cannot grow is a waste of time. There is always something else. In this case the "something else" is the gladiolus now considered a subspecies of *Gladiolus communis* but usually cataloged as *G. byzantinus* (Zone 5). Self-supporting at about 2 feet, it bears flowers that are dainty in size if far from dainty in color: brilliant magenta with a white stripe on the lower petals. Blue is a good companion color for this brilliant hue and, fortuitously, the gladiolus flowers at the same time as blue baptisias, amsonias, Siberian irises, and *Nepeta* 'Six Hills Giant'. Soon after the flowers of the gladiolus fade, the narrowly ribbonlike leaves die away, leaving an empty space. One large patch of hardy gladiolus in

Zantedeschia aethiopica 'Crowborough' (calla lily)

my garden is behind *Fallopia japonica* 'Variegata', a bushy shrublike perennial little more than 1 foot high when the gladiolus flowers, subsequently attaining 5–6 feet and hiding ground left bare by the dormant gladiolus.

For delicacy, seek out the white-flowered form of this gladiolus. Two decades ago the few corms I bought, now much multiplied, cost $1 for five. Never was money better spent. Sharing this lovely variety has proved easier said than done, for the corms have sunk 18 inches deep in the sandy soil. This is well below frost level and deeper than voles usually search for food, which may be the secret of the long-term survival of hardy gladiolus.

Triteleia

Triteleia laxa (Zone 6) was once known as *Brodiaea* (good words, these, for crossword puzzles, with their multiple adjacent vowels) and in some catalogs still is. It is in the first flight of reliable garden bulbs.

Triteleia ×*tubergenii* (Zone 6) is similar to *T. laxa*. Both have multiple starry flowers of an exceptionally brilliant blue on 15-inch-tall stems, opening in late spring and lasting about 2 weeks if the weather is hot, longer if it is cool. By flowering time the slender bright green leaves, present since early in the year, are flat on the ground and beginning to wither, so there is a gap when the flowers are over. This gap I fill with mealycup sage (*Salvia farinacea*), grown as an annual and put out when young. Placed in a triangle around the triteleias, the sages bush out and meet up over the resting bulbs.

Triteleia 'Queen Fabiola' (Zone 6), said to be superior to others of its kind, did not last for me or seem to be as bright a blue, perhaps because I put it in shade and moisture-retentive soil, while the other triteleias get a summer baking in sun and sand.

Zantedeschia aethiopica 'Crowborough'

CALLA LILY

Although calla lilies are not bulbs, the catalogs of bulb purveyors are the most likely source for them. After 25 years in my garden, the hardiness and adaptability of *Zantedeschia aethiopica* 'Crowborough' (Zone 7) is proven be-

yond doubt. It differs from the species only in its reputed extra hardiness. It sows around and I find it in such unexpected places as the deep shade under shrubs, where it is prosperous if flowerless. Its preference, in this region of relatively heavy rain, is for moist to wet soil, with sun for at least half the day; it then clumps up fast and needs dividing about every third year if bloom is not to diminish. Peak bloom is usually in May, along with Japanese primrose (*Primula japonica*; Zone 5), which is the best of the candelabra-type primroses for hot summer regions. There will be the odd white chalice on the calla lily off and on until frost.

Zantedeschia aethiopica 'Green Goddess', with the large green spathes so coveted by flower arrangers, is growing in a ditch where it benefits from septic tank run-off. Here it quickly builds up into hefty clumps of arrowhead-shaped leaves, which I have never yet observed with the moth-eaten look betokening

slugs. For contrast it has as neighbors the ferny leaves of *Thalictrum minus* 'Adiantifolium' and the slender blades of Louisiana irises and *Iris versicolor*.

If these and other arum lilies never flowered, their handsome foliage would still earn them a place, especially *Zantedeschia albomaculata*, with a rain-shower of white dots and dashes on its wavy, arrow-shaped leaves. This calla, the pink-flowered *Z. rehmannii*, and the yellow-flowered *Z. elliotiana* have survived for many years. They flower only once, for about 2 weeks in midspring.

Zantedeschia aethiopica has a rival in a new calla lily recently burst on the scene and erroneously distributed as *Z. aethiopica* 'Crowborough'. The leaves of the true 'Crowborough' are solid green. The imposter has leaves splashed with white, as if from a smattering of snow. Look for this under the name 'Whipped Cream'.

TREES

In choosing among the plethora of trees that flower in early spring, one inevitably makes the occasional poor choice. My mistakes arose mainly from too slow a recognition that trees grow faster and larger in the warm, moist climate of coastal Virginia than they do in England, and that heat fades flowers so quickly that bloom alone seldom justifies the space of such popular trees as crabapples. Which, then, would I still plant were I starting over? Because evaluations are usually comparative, an overview of some trees I grow (or not) will help to explain my preferences.

If one omits crabapples and cherries, both problem-prone, the majority of spring-blooming trees have white flowers (I wonder why?), so color plays little part in my assessments. The first white wave starts in late March or early April with two trees ubiquitous in local gardens and shopping malls. The purple-leaf plums (forms of *Prunus ceracifera*; Zone 5), with white or wan-pink flowers, and the Bradford pear (*Pyrus calleryana* 'Bradford'; Zone 5) seem able to sense and outwait the last frost, bursting into bloom just as the calendar announces spring. Thumbs down for purple-leaf plums, which attract innumerable pests, including borers and the Japanese beetles that

turn their leaves to netting. Bradford pears are well worth having, though susceptible to fireblight. They bear abundant white flowers, and their glossy leaves turn burgundy red in autumn. Neatly lollipop-shaped in youth, these trees grow rapidly and spread with age, becoming vulnerable to storm damage. I am tempted, though, by newer, narrower forms.

The shadbushes (*Amelanchier*; Zone 4) flower in April. Blink and you might miss them, for their white clouds of bloom last scarcely longer than a morning mist. Brevity of bloom might be forgiven if the leaves were less ordinary, if they turned the bright red I admired in cooler Toronto, or if I could anticipate a crop of the tasty "serviceberries" in autumn. None of these have been mine from *Amelanchier* 'Ballerina' (probably a hybrid of *A. laevis*), and it will make way for something else. Why put up with a mediocre plant if there are better ones?

By late April the wash of white in my garden includes three silverbells (*Halesia*). I tread warily around the nomenclature because taxonomic changes (with, as Michael Dirr points out in his *Manual of Woody Landscape Plants*, "pockets of resistance") have rearranged the names in a manner certain to cause confusion,

especially with *H. tetraptera* (formerly *H. carolina*) and *H. parviflora* (now most likely found as *H. carolina*). Read Dirr's book for the full story. Common names add to the confusion. Snowbells is the commonest popular name for *Styrax*, and silverbells the commonest popular name for *Halesia*, but both *Styrax*

Halesia diptera var. *magniflora* (silverbell)

and *Halesia* are sometimes called snowdrop-tree. They are in the same family, with similar pendulous white bell-shaped flowers.

Because the floral contribution of these flowers is so brief, one silverbell would really be enough, but which? I'd choose *Halesia diptera* var. *magniflora* (Zone 5) with flowers that have the ethereal loveliness of Swan Lake ballerinas. Swinging on 2-inch petioles, they are fewer but larger than those of other species. Tear-shaped buds become briefly bell-shaped as they open, then flare out into snowy, gossamer-textured skirts around prominent tufts of yellow-tipped stamens. In the wild this species favors moist sites, and that is what I gave it, in full sun. At first it had so tenuous a grip that after prolonged rain I found it listing badly, with roots on one side exposed. Pushed upright and staked, with extra soil over its roots and a few bricks for extra weight, it grew away without further ado. Other gardeners report a similar experience with this halesia, so it does seem that staking is advisable in its early years. My garden is not a windy one, and other young trees have seldom needed staking.

My second choice, *Halesia tetraptera* (Zone 4), flowers for a bit longer, the full length of its branches being hung with small clusters of white bells for up to 2 weeks, just as the tree is leafing out. The leaves turn yellow in autumn,

Styrax obassia (snowbell)

falling to reveal interesting winged fruits. The tree I planted 10 years ago now stands 15 feet high, broad at the base, narrowing further up.

Snowbells (*Styrax*) flower a week or so after the silverbells. They grow even more rapidly and recently, reluctantly, I had *Styrax japonicus* (Zone 5) cut down after 15 years. Innumerable seedlings were my main reason to gripe until the tree grew so large that only aucubas thrived in the deep shade beneath and annual pruning became onerous. I have two approaches to trees and large shrubs that have outgrown their space: cut them down and let them start over, or limb them up and let in light so that smaller shrubs can be grown underneath. Neither method suits the snowbell's widely arching habit, which, in the long run, made it a poor choice for my layered style of gardening. Its arching shape is best displayed as a specimen in a lawn, where the dainty white blossoms give a secondary display strewn over the grass. Having no such space to offer, I'm considering instead *Sinojackia rehderiana* (Zone 6), which is in the same family and almost identical to *Styrax japonicus* in flower and leaf, only smaller.

I still have three snowbells. The pale pink *Styrax japonicus* 'Pink Chimes' is probably good for another 5 years before it grows too large. *Styrax japonicus* 'Emerald Pagoda' (synonym 'Sohuksan') was a gift from the late J. C. Raulston, who collected it in Korea in 1985. It is a lovely thing, with larger, leathery, dark green leaves, and larger, fragrant flowers. Word was that its mature height would be about 20 feet. After 7 years it is apparent that it will attain that very soon unless pruned annually. It is more upright than the species. Where a large, fast-growing tree can be accommodated, this snowbell is a very good candidate.

Styrax obassia (Zone 5) is chunkier and takes up much less space. My 12-year-old plant is shaped like an elongated egg, 10 feet high with a girth of 7 feet at its widest point. Its short trunk is sinuous and striated. Unlike other snowbells, which bear their flowers in pendant clusters along the branches, this one has inflorescences with thirty or so flowers in long terminal wands that are later weighted down by tan-colored, acornlike seed capsules.

The flowers, opening in succession from base to tip, partly obscured by the leaves, continue for about 2 weeks. The leaves are almost round, 4 inches across, olive green above, and downy beneath. In full sun and sandy, humus-enriched soil, *S. obassia* tends to scorch in dry summers. I grade it B+, possibly an A in moister soil with light afternoon shade.

And so to the top contenders, those trees I would plant first were I starting over.

Cornus

DOGWOOD

In England, where the climate doesn't suit it, *Cornus florida* (Zone 5) is a mediocre performer at best. It was love at first sight when I saw it in the wild, and I still think it the most beautiful of all flowering trees. Of the many selections, some with pink flowers and some with variegated foliage, I consider the white-flowered species unsurpassed by any other form. Everything about it is pleasing: shape, autumn color, scarlet berries, the felted winter buds held up like pleading hands, and, of course, the snowy blossoms none the less pristine for their always blemished bract tips. Bloom tends to be prolonged when the showy part of a flower consists not of petals but of bracts, or of sepals as in hellebores, and *C. florida* remains a cloud of white for about 3 weeks.

Never has wind, snow, or an ice storm broken a branch of this sturdy tree. A big tree on the property when I came, it is now a veteran of some 50 years. It is growing in full sun just inside the front boundary fence, where much of its considerable girth overhangs the roadside ditch and verge. I treasure it, and it has first call on water during droughts—dogwoods suffer at parched or soggy soil extremes. The caveat emptor is that East Coast dogwoods have lately been afflicted with anthracnose, with dire predictions (not yet borne out) that they might go the way of chestnuts and elms. Knowing it to be a gamble, I would still make this dogwood my first choice among the larger flowering trees. As insurance I've planted *Cornus* 'Stellar Pink', one of the *C.* ×*rutgersensis* hybrids (*C. florida* × *C. kousa*) raised by Elwin Orton of Rutgers University in a breeding program aimed at pest and disease resistance. After 6 years it has yet to bloom.

Cornus kousa (Zone 4) is more adaptable than *C. florida*, tolerating more winter cold and blooming well in less sunny regions. My tree has been trouble-free except that it gets thirsty and the leaves scorch if the roots become dry during the heat of summer. It flowers, after leafing out, about 2 weeks later than *C. florida*, and I would always want both dogwoods if space could be found. The trunks of

Cornus kousa (Japanese dogwood)

old kousa dogwoods have attractively mottled bark, but I am still waiting to see it on a tree 18 feet high and wide that I bought from the old Tingle Nursery in Maryland (gone now) in 1975, before the container age got fully under way. When the well-branched, 6-foot specimen arrived in late winter, bare root and swaddled in straw, it took only an hour to plant and thrived from the start. My index card reminds me that the cost was $12 plus $2 for postage! Nowadays most trees and shrubs are grown in containers. Although this is convenient and extends the planting season, roots are pot-bound as often as not and I have grown accustomed to spending a messy hour washing out the bark or peat-based mix with a hose jet, then disentangling the congested roots, before the actual planting can begin.

The flowers of *Cornus kousa* vary greatly in shape and size. Take your pick from starry flowers with widely spaced bracts to the squarish flower of *C. kousa* 'Square Dance', one of several fine forms raised by Polly Hill on Martha's Vineyard. *Cornus kousa* 'Satomi' (synonym 'Rosabella') is a good pink-flowered selection, though not as brightly colored in hot regions as it is in cool ones. The strawberry-like fruits of *C. kousa*, which look tasty but aren't, also vary in size and number.

I don't have room for another big dog-wood, but a few years back I added *Cornus kousa* var. *angustata* with burnished evergreen leaves, reasoning that, at this stage of my life, this dogwood's considerable ultimate size will be someone else's problem. Smaller, narrower, leaves give this variety a distinguishing poise in summer, though they droop dismally in winter.

Variegated selections of *Cornus florida* and *C. kousa* cannot compete with *C. controversa* 'Variegata' (Zone 4), with white-edged leaves and tabulated form. Only recently has this dogwood become available, so I cannot yet attest to its long-term worth in hot regions. The similar but smaller *C. alternifolia* 'Variegata' (Zone 3) would be a better choice for small gardens.

Cercis

REDBUD

With species native to three continents, there's a redbud (*Cercis*) for most gardens. The European Judas tree (*C. siliquastrum*; Zone 7) was the one I knew in England, favored because it blooms where other species do not for lack of summer heat. Now, with summer heat all too prolonged, my choice lies between the Asian *C. chinensis* (Zone 6) and North America's wide-ranging *C. canadensis* (Zone 4), each with magenta pea-type flowers clinging so closely to the branches, and often the trunk, that they seem to have bled through the bark. These species are look-alikes except that *C. chinensis* is smaller and slower growing, often seen as a large shrub. One of the few named forms, *C. chinensis* 'Avondale', a selection made in New Zealand, blooms more profusely than the species in cool regions. In hot regions it would be hard to pack more flowers onto each branch than the species does.

Along a parkway near my home redbuds (*Cercis canadensis*) intermingle with dogwoods (*Cornus florida*) and loblolly pines (*Pinus taeda*), the green of the pines tempering the stridency of the redbud flowers. In those years when the bloom time of dogwoods coincides (about one year in two), traffic dawdles noticeably as drivers slow down to admire nature's combination of colors. In a garden's more complex or haphazard plantings, the redbud's typical magenta-purple color could strike a dissonant note. There are alternatives among the twenty or so named variants: deeper purples, paler pinks, a near-red ('Appalachia'), whites, purple foliage ('Forest Pansy'), white-splashed leaves ('Silver Cloud'), an occasional double, and a weeping form ('Covey').

Arresting though redbuds are for the 2 weeks they stay in bloom, consider also their foliage, bearing in mind that katsura-tree

(*Cercidiphyllum japonicum*; Zone 4) and *Disanthus cercidifolius* (Zone 5) have inconspicuous flowers and are extolled solely for their foliage, and that their names remark the similarity of their heart-shaped leaves to those of the redbuds. Yet only *Cercis canadensis* 'Forest Pansy', with claret-colored leaves, an international favorite and one of my chosen three, is selected by gardeners for its foliage.

Because their waxy, wavy edged leaves are exceptionally pretty, my other two chosen redbuds are selections of the Texas redbud, white-flowered *Cercis canadensis* var. *texensis* 'Texas White' and magenta-flowered *C. canadensis* var. *texensis* 'Oklahoma'. These are sometimes listed under *C. texensis* and occasionally as *C. reniformis*. Though ultimately 20 feet or more in height, Texas redbud is relatively more compact and slower growing than *C. canadensis*. Growing in light shade, in fertile soil neither squelchy nor dry, my redbuds have been pest-free except for an occasional infestation of tent caterpillar.

At its best *Cercis mexicana* (Zone 7; synonym *C. canadensis* var. *mexicana*) has the prettiest leaves of all the redbuds. They are about 2 inches across and almost round, with a lacquered shine and tightly waved edges. The species is variable, however, so see it before you buy it or ask some searching questions.

Cercis canadensis var. *texensis* 'Texas White'

My tree is still small, has not yet flowered, and I shall not mind if it never does.

Chionanthus

FRINGE TREE

By the end of April my two species of fringe tree, the North American *Chionanthus virginicus* (Zone 4) and the Asian *C. retusus* (Zone 5), are belatedly leafing out. Only *Clethra alnifolia* now remains leafless. If it had to be one fringe tree or the other, I'd keep the Asian species, which flowers a little earlier for a little longer. It is obviously content in full sun, sandy soil, and a raised bed that tends to get dry. (Another specimen, put in moist soil and light shade, grew lax and less floriferous.) Sprays of flowers with four slender petals turn it to white froth in May. Round-headed in

Chionanthus retusus (Chinese fringe tree)

shape, my 20-year-old tree is maintained by annual pruning at 15 feet high and rather more across at the top. This size is less space-consuming than the measurements suggest because the tree does not make basal suckers and is clear of branches to head height, permitting underplanting. Unlike the American fringe tree, the Asian species manages to be a single parent of big bunches of fruits resembling blueberries. Two forms of it are in circulation. One has longer leaves, while mine has round, shiny, and leathery leaves that look evergreen but aren't. The leaves are my only reason to give this tree a black mark. As stiff and tossable as Frisbees, and taking years to rot, they fall very late, and not all at once, creating a widespread mess needing repeated cleaning up.

In moister soil and a woodland-fringe setting, the soft leaves of American fringe tree (*Chionanthus virginicus*) rot quite rapidly, don't blow around, and can be left where they fall. The softly fragrant, greeny cream inflorescences of shredded flowers are held below leaves pricked up like rabbit ears. This species blooms for little more than a week. My two plants are berryless males. Males have flowers with longer petals, thus more substantial inflorescences; females are daintier. American fringe tree is multitrunked by nature. When the trunk of a 10-year-old tree was infected by canker, I cut it down to the ground. It regained its 10-foot height within 5 years.

Aesculus pavia

RED BUCKEYE

Just when it begins to seem that spring's white wedding has gone on long enough, red buckeye (*Aesculus pavia*; Zone 4) brings a welcome change. Inch-long calyces are the colorful part of the flowers: in bud they are shaped like half-inch crimson bananas, from which, like toothpaste squeezed from a tube, come four petals of ivory and yellow stained with pink, the lower two forming pouting lips under the long stamens. In light shade red buckeye has made a somewhat ungainly small tree, 10 feet high after 15 years. The 6-inch-long inflorescences, the individual flowers, and the lax branches seem confused about the direction they want to head in, and the palmate leaves bring to mind shoes in need of polishing. Nevertheless, this tree is worthy of a place in my garden for its color and moderate size. Later-blooming selections are available.

Magnolia

No plant I've grown has so repeatedly had its promise nipped in the bud as *Magnolia ×sou-langeana* (Zone 4), known locally as tulip tree.

Year after year it goes into winter laden with thousands of furry buds, like lambs heading for March's late-frost slaughterhouse. Frosted flowers become a squalid brown mush that takes weeks to dry up and fall. Knowing a plant's hardiness zone is not always enough: *M. ×soulangeana* performs splendidly considerably further north, where it isn't tempted into bloom by unseasonably warm weather.

Star magnolia (*Magnolia stellata*; Zone 5) does much better than tulip tree and gets nine marks out of ten for its moderate size, shapely form, tolerance for—indeed liking of—sandy, low fertility soil and hot sun, and its profusion of faintly fragrant starry flowers. It is my first magnolia to bloom, usually beginning in late March. Because the weather is still relatively cool at that time, star magnolia flowers for as much as a month. My tree is the pale pink *M. stellata* 'Pink Stardust', a rounded, twiggy 20 feet tall after as many years, multitrunked with silvery bark. The flowers don't all open at once, so if one batch gets frosted, as it usually does, there are more to come. The similar, white-flowered *M. kobus* (Zone 5) also gets a high mark. *Magnolia stellata* is bushier than most magnolias, with spreading lower branches that throw the ground beneath into deep shade in summer. My chosen underplanting is starflower (*Ipheion uniflorum*), with leaves

that appear in autumn and clothe the ground through winter. Grape hyacinth (*Muscari armeniacum*), which also has leaves through winter and blue flowers in early spring, would do as well.

It is at magnolia time that I most yearn for 20 acres and, of course, gardeners to match. There are so many covetable magnolias. Those with pink or yellow flowers are especially welcome among a surfeit of white-flowered trees. If only they didn't grow so large and flower so briefly—seldom much more than a week where April days are often hot. *Magnolia liliiflora* 'Nigra' (Zone 6) is of manageable size and the moonlight yellow chalices of *M.* 'Elizabeth' (Zone 5), which grows very big, very fast, bring a week of bliss, but a 2 percent flowering return on the year is poor interest on the space investment.

Magnolia virginiana var. *australis* (Zone 6) is evergreen. The white flowers are strongly fragrant and, though never plentiful, keep coming through summer. In the debit column come rapid leggy growth and brittle branches that are frequently storm damaged. The tree recovers quickly, however, when cut back and is indeed the better for it. This species merits a place in the garden but, space and climate permitting, cannot compare with *M. grandiflora* (Zone 7), a tree that has it all: prolonged if

spasmodic bloom from spring through autumn, intense fragrance, showy cone-shaped "infruitescences" (Mike Dirr's word I believe; thank you, Mike) dripping seeds like drops of scarlet wax suspended on slender white threads, and, in many selections, tan indumentum on the undersides of the highly polished evergreen leaves.

Accustomed in England to seeing *Magnolia grandiflora* trained against sheltered walls, I never thought to see the leftover 6-inch seedling I took pity on at a plant sale reach dimensions requiring an annual whacking back to restrain it at 30 feet high and wide. If I don't have this done, the electricity suppliers will—a fate worse than death for any tree with esthetic pretensions. Poles supporting an ever-expanding tangle of wires for electricity, telephone, and cable television are an unfortunate corollary to the luxury of our lives, and it was with the intention of concealing such a pole that this giant magnolia was planted where it is. I just did not expect it to reach the wires in my lifetime. When I say "whacking back," I mean just that. Pruning this magnolia does not call for either skill or finesse; it heals its wounds and replaces cut-off branches at remarkable speed.

LEFT *Magnolia stellata* 'Pink Stardust' (star magnolia)

Magnolia grandiflora 'Little Gem', planted later, would have been a better choice. Though by no means a dwarf, it is smaller in all its parts and starts flowering in babyhood. Bloom is spread over the season, a few flowers at a time, with the first one opening as early as late April after mild winters. Best in full sun, 'Little Gem' takes both dry soil and wet in its stride. I have only one, but were I starting over I'd plant it as a hedge along a sunny boundary, in place of the wax myrtle (*Myrica cerifera*; Zone 7), which is a good and easy evergreen hedging plant, but loose and leggy if not annually pruned or periodically cut down to the base.

Having cleared the decks a bit, I now present two flowering trees of early spring that have brought me delight for a quarter century.

Prunus 'Hally Jolivette'
FLOWERING CHERRY

The 1990s saw a gardening renaissance that is still gathering momentum. In an age of easy travel, quick communication, and sophisticated propagation techniques, new introductions hit the market with unprecedented speed. Plant collectors are scouring the world, breeders are deluging us with new things, keen-eyed gardeners making their own contributions, and plants grown without fanfare for genera-

tions are being rediscovered. Yet still some lovely things fall through the cracks, and one of these is *Prunus* 'Hally Jolivette' (Zone 5). Did it miss its moment because it came along when the world was preoccupied by war? A hybrid of *Prunus subhirtella* and *P.* ×*yedoensis* raised around 1940 by Karl Sax of the Arnold Arboretum in Jamaica Plain, Massachusetts, and named for his wife, *P.* 'Hally Jolivette' is smaller than either parent. It makes a large bush or small tree, rounded in shape and clothed to the ground in finely twiggy branches. Having teased with a sprinkling of flowers from autumn through winter, it becomes a blush-pink cloud of small, tutu-like blossoms for about a month at primrose time. Although now 15 feet high and more across, that has taken a quarter century in a region of rapid growth and this cherry will fit for many years into all but the smallest gardens. Cherries are not long-lived trees, and they are so often ravaged by borer that I had resolved to plant no more. I shall, nonetheless, plant *P.* 'Hally Jolivette' again when this one's days come to an end.

Xanthoceras sorbifolium
YELLOWHORN

Plants that bloom in March and the first days of April gamble on their performance not

being cruelly halted by frost. After Easter the risk is minimal. Many participants in spring's confirmation ceremony come appropriately clad in white. The most eagerly awaited is *Xanthoceras sorbifolium* (Zone 5).

How can a plant of such exceptional merit have been in limbo for more than a century, a Snow White awaiting the gardening world's awakening kiss? I can only guess that this lovely small tree did not lend itself to field production and so remained a sleeper until the era of container growing. Even so, growers have been slow off the mark. Yellowhorn is finally available from mail-order nurseries, but widespread popularity is dependent upon the wholesalers who supply garden centers.

Introduced from China in 1866, *Xanthoceras sorbifolium* has since gone largely unnoticed, even by avid collectors. The First Class Certificate given it by the Royal Horticultural Society in 1876 is usually based on cut specimens and xanthoceras has yet to be given the awards it deserves as an outstanding ornamental tree, better suited to gardens of moderate size than almost any other. P. J. Van Melle in *Shrubs and Trees for the Small Place*, published in 1943, reported it to be among the best small flowering trees: long-lived, adaptable to shade, capable of thriving in dry soil, and hardy in Zone 5. Hillier's *Manual of Trees*

Prunus 'Hally Jolivette' (flowering cherry)

Xanthoceras sorbifolium

and Shrubs indicates that it will grow in all types of fertile soil, including chalk formations. It has done well for the many friends to whom I have given seed or plants, including some in England.

"Yellowhorn," the English translation of xanthoceras, refers to yellow hornlike growths between the petals. Having mentioned that, compliments of *A Gardener's Dictionary of Plant Names* by A. W. Smith, I propose to forget it. Only common names with some obvious connotation are likely to be remembered; if the yellow horns are there, they are not apparent, and tongues that don't stumble over rhinoceros can cope with xanthoceras.

I first saw xanthoceras at the Barnes Foundation, Philadelphia, in June of 1970, shortly after my arrival in North America. Having never seen it before, I did not know enough to ask why a small tree I now know to be of fuller, though relatively upright form, there grew slimly perpendicular. I was not to see it again until 1977, when the late Bob Talley of the now defunct Gulfstream Nursery gave me a sucker from the one he'd grown for many years in sandy, acid soil similar to mine. I planted it in full sun, with, my file card reminds me, "a barrowful of peat, cow manure, bonemeal, potash, and superphosphate dug in." (Later plantings, in soil improved for years with compost, have had no such witches'-brew additions.) The 1-foot plant flowered the following April and has never failed to do so since, for as much as a month in cool springs, more often 2 to 3 weeks.

With no pruning other than removal of an occasional small dead branch, no further fertilizing, and only such water as the heavens provide (averaging 45 inches a year), the tree was only 8 feet tall two decades later. Eventually it began to look a bit gaunt, so some tentative pruning was done, which resulted in vigorous new canelike growth wherever it was cut, as well as new branches from the base. It therefore seems that rejuvenation is not difficult. The tree in my garden has never been damaged by snow or by the ice storms that wreak havoc on anything with brittle wood.

Though lacking fragrance, this small tree has so many admirable attributes. It takes up little space and can be underplanted. It blooms early, therefore longer than trees that delay until the weather gets hot, yet not so early as to play chicken with frost, and the flowers come before the tree leafs out, for maximum effect. The shiny, pinnate leaves resemble those of a mountain ash (*Sorbus*—hence the specific name) and in my experience have been completely free of disease, pest damage, or drought scorch. In bloom the tree gets a warm-white look from the dark red eyes of white flowers borne in dense upright or drooping panicles.

Suckers, sparsely produced, are one way of obtaining extra plants. Mature specimens of xanthoceras produce walnut-sized pods of pebblelike black seeds. Unless nursery-owning friends plead for these, I let them fall to the ground, where they germinate the following spring and grow quickly to knee height. Unable to let such a good thing go to waste, I waste time instead lifting and potting the young plants as gifts for visitors, whether they want one or not, for this charming little tree needs more advocates.

SHRUBS

Most shrubs are fairly easy to propagate from half-ripe spring cuttings, so propagation is mentioned only where this method is difficult or another method better.

Camellia

The sprinkling of flowers on spring camellias (Zone 7), starting as early as Christmas, becomes a torrent in late March and April. Unlikely though it is that chance seedlings will lead to fame and fortune, it costs nothing (except space) to keep them until they bloom, usually by their third year. I've come by several pretty ones this way, including my earliest to bloom, with single, salmon-pink cupped flowers. This plant cannot be bought, but to those who share my liking for simple form, I recommend the bell-shaped, crimson-petaled *Camellia japonica* 'Adeyaka'.

Dead brown blossoms clinging to the bush are one of the few camellia vexations. Blowsy, overlarge flowers, such as *Camellia japonica* 'Betty Sheffield', are the worst offenders. This phenomenon is partly weather related and varies from year to year. Most of my camellias cleave to their dead only when a hard frost brings flowers to an untimely end or they've been afflicted by petal blight. Midseason doubles such as *C. japonica* 'Debutante' are the most likely to get frosted, and late bloomers are the most susceptible to the petal blight prevalent during hot and humid weather. A camellia in a cool spot, against a north wall for instance, will bloom later than one in a sheltered, sunny place, so bloom can be advanced or retarded a bit by thoughtful positioning.

Camellia japonica and *C. ×williamsii* hybrids are fairly reliable in the warmer parts of Zone 7. In a quarter century I have experienced only one camellia-killing winter. Most gardeners then replaced plants killed down to ground level. For me, raised on waste-not-want-not, this went against the grain. Most of my plants grew back, and some were the better for nature's drastic pruning. It did, of course, leave gaps for a few years.

In my region camellias need no water beyond what falls from the skies. This self-sufficiency endears them to me during summer droughts, when my garden brings to mind nests of baby birds with pleading open beaks. Weary from dragging hoses, blinded by perspiration trickling down my brow, and shocked by the size of water bills, I sometimes look at a wilting plant and think, "All right then, die."

If I did cease watering, the camellias would survive.

Because white flowers are easily sullied by frost, snow, rain, or hot sun, I avoid white-flowered camellias at this unpredictable time of year. Hundreds of pink- or red-flowered selections must still be whittled down to what the garden can accommodate. It is perverse of me to love best the one that suffers most from winter freezes: *Camellia* 'Tiny Princess' (*C. japonica* 'Akebono' × *C. fraterna*) is romantic in its arching form, comparatively small, satin-finish leaves, and loose clusters of miniature blush-pink cupped flowers. Damage has been awful to behold after a couple of bad winters, but the shrub has soon recovered and regained its 5-foot height. If, perchance, one day it should be killed, I shall replace it.

The leaves of most *Camellia ×williamsii* hybrids (*C. japonica* × *C. saluenensis*) are less glossy than those of *C. japonica*, a welcome characteristic where skies are nearly always blue and light bounces around on mirrored surfaces. *Camellia ×williamsii* 'Donation', a British-bred international favorite with translucent silvery-pink petals, still sets the standard for this group. I grow instead the little-known 'Donation Variegated', also raised in

Britain. It is neither better nor worse for the few, scarcely visible, white blotches on its pink petals. The semi-double category of camellias includes everything from hose-in-hose (one flower within another) to a muddled mess of petals. The flowers of C. ×williamsii 'Donation' and 'Donation Variegated' have just enough extra petals to give them substance without obscuring form. I rank equally with these an Australian introduction, C. ×williamsii 'E. G. Waterhouse', a pink formal double of medium size that is later to flower than most, usually in early April. Yet were I forced to choose, all might give way to 'Freedom Bell',

Camellia ×*williamsii* 'E. G. Waterhouse' underplanted with *Lamium galeobdolon* 'Hermann's Pride'

Camellia 'Freedom Bell'

an American introduction by Nuccio's Nurseries. Although its parentage is unknown or unrevealed, it has the shuttlecock shape and translucent petal veining common among C. ×*williamsii* hybrids. Two rows of wavy petals form an outswung bell with a clapper of yellow stamens. The color is unusual, borderline between crimson and scarlet, a warm, bright hue that reminds me of red currants.

And so we come to the glossy-leaved *Camellia japonica* varieties that comprise the majority. Elegant face-powder pink 'Magnoliiflora' dates back to the end of the seventeenth century, under its Japanese name 'Hagoromo', according to Stirling Macoboy in *Color Dictionary of Camellias*, a book to drool over. Eight generations of appreciative eyes have admired just such a flower as I now gaze upon, and countless future generations may do the same. The formal double C. *japonica* 'Pink Perfection' (synonym 'Frau Minna Seidel') dates back more than 100 years as 'Usu Otome'. None outclass these old ones, but I have a penchant for American-raised miniatures come more lately on the scene, especially the exquisite blush-pink formal double 'Grace Albritton' and the dense and compact 'Fircone', with blood-red flowers that do resemble fir cones with opened scales when seen in profile. Rivaling 'Fircone' in color and outdoing it in

White-variegated *Camellia japonica* 'Governor Mouton' with white-flowered *Viburnum* ×*burkwoodii*

Daphne genkwa with *Buxus sempervirens* 'Elegantissima' at left and *Thujopsis dolobrata* 'Nana' in background

oriental red boldly splashed with white, echoing the white in the leaves of a nearby *Osmanthus heterophyllus* 'Variegatus' on one side and the white flowers on intertwined branches of *Viburnum ×burkwoodii* on the other (a tight planting my friend Elsa Bakalar calls "the school of stuff and cram"). That's the great thing about camellias: their flowers come in so many forms, colors, and sizes, from modest to voluptuous, that there's something to please everyone. And a mite of frustration that one cannot grow them all.

While camellias can be propagated by spring cuttings, air layering of young branches about 1 foot long brings quicker results and works particularly well in warm regions. Using a very sharp knife or a razor blade, make an upward slit in the stem between two nodes. Pack moist sphagnum moss in and around the sliced section and cover this tightly with polyethylene film (a plastic bag will do nicely) or aluminum foil, the object being to prevent the sphagnum moss from either drying out or becoming soggy from water trickling in. The branch will have been weakened by the cut and a supporting cane may be needed to prevent it snapping off. Check for rooting after 2 months and then at monthly intervals. When adequately rooted, sever the air layer, pot it up in a loose, peat-based mix,

quantity of bloom is midsized, semi-double *C. japonica* 'Glen 40'.

Whether it's camellias or hamburgers, I lack appetite for "whoppers" as a rule, yet there are always exceptions and *Camellia japonica* 'Fashionata' is one. The voluptuous coral-red flowers are described in the handbook of the American Camellia Society as a "large semi-double with curled and creped outer petals." Despite their size, the flowers do not droop and are spectacularly presented against a background of blue sky on a bush grown 12 feet high in 20 years. It is not, however, the most eye-catching of my midseason camellias. That claim can fairly be made by the swanky *C. japonica* 'Governor Mouton', vivid

water well, and keep it in the shade until it is well established in its container.

Daphne

As the scent of winter-blooming *Daphne odora* (Zone 7) becomes a memory for the year, two more daphnes start to bloom. These are growing under big oak trees, with bright light and a few hours of sun.

The deciduous *Daphne genkwa* (Zone 5), which in England suffers from lack of sun, likes Virginia's coastal plain, where it blooms on still leafless branches at Easter time. For its first couple of years the branchwork was so haphazard that I christened it "gawky genkwa," a useful crutch for remembering the name. As it developed and the branches thickened, the shrub became shapelier, though never dense. Conveying a sense of color is always difficult. Walking my garden in search of a familiar plant for comparison, I found it in the misty, light violet-blue of *Scabiosa columbaria* 'Butterfly Blue' which, if frequently divided, is seldom without a flower or two. The daphne's flowers are reminiscent of lilac, though not, alas, in fragrance, which is faint and elusive. If positioned out of hot sun, *D. genkwa* blooms for more than a month.

Daphne ×burkwoodii 'Carol Mackie' (Zone 4), with white-edged leaves, overlaps *D. genk-wa*, starting and finishing its bloom season 2 weeks later. The sweetly scented flowers open pale pink and fade to white. This daphne I have found easy to grow, remarkably drought resistant, and long-lived as daphnes go, say 15 years. Though it is by no means unappreciated in spring, I value it most for its neat shape and bright variegation in summer. So far, so good, with the exquisite *D. ×burkwoodii* 'Briggs Moonlight', which I've had 3 years. Only a thin rim of green edges the leaves of pale primrose yellow, and so scant a supply of chlorophyll does not auger well for longevity. If this plant lives it can be expected to grow a little slower than 'Carol Mackie', becoming about 2 feet high and wide in 5 years. *Daphne ×burkwoodii* cultivars keep some of their leaves, held in whorls shaped like starfish at the branch tips, through the average Zone 7 winter.

Berberis

EVERGREEN BARBERRY

In England my favorite barberry was orange-flowered *Berberis darwinii* from Chile, and its hybrid *B. ×stenophylla*. Chilean plants are ill adapted to temperature extremes, and there are new favorites now. *Berberis julianae* (Zone 6) is one of the spiniest members of a scratchy genus. I can cope with thorns provided they stay below eye level, which this dependable evergreen shrub can be made to do with an annual pruning. Left unchecked it soon exceeds 6 feet in height. In full sun it grows dense. My plant, in light shade for half the day, is gracefully loose in habit. The bright yellow, softly scented flowers, clustered in the leaf axils, start to open in late March or early April, combining pleasingly with the purple foliage of a neighboring *Loropetalum chinense* 'Rubrum' (warmer parts of Zone 7). In this protected location, the loropetalum's leaves have remained undamaged through seven winters, suggesting a mite more hardiness than the green-leaved species I have twice lost, but it is early days for this popular, ruby-petaled recent introduction. Easily propagated and fast growing, it would merit replanting should a colder-than-usual winter see its demise. It flowers less plentifully in light shade, but another specimen in full sun has twice defoliated.

Until they had to make way for a new well, a group of five plants of *Berberis ×gladwynensis* 'William Penn' (Zone 6; *B. verruculosa × B. gagnepainii*) made a pleasing small-scale ground cover for many years, with occasional dieback of a branch the only problem. An annual pruning kept them at an intermingled 2 feet. The bee-attracting golden-yellow flowers in April are fragrant, and the spiny leaves are burnished like well-polished leather, older

Prunus glandulosa 'Alba Plena' (dwarf flowering almond) with red camellias and *Acer griseum* in background

ones becoming bright red. 'William Penn' is definitely a shrub I shall replace, perhaps this time as a mounding 4-foot specimen.

Prunus glandulosa
DWARF FLOWERING ALMOND

Dwarf flowering almond (*Prunus glandulosa*; Zone 4) is a small deciduous shrub. *Prunus glandulosa* 'Sinensis' has pompoms of sugar-candy pink flowers along its wandlike stems, while those of the less common *P. glandulosa* 'Alba Plena' are bright white. Both flower for 2 or 3 weeks in early spring, and cut branches can be forced indoors much earlier. In my garden these two forms differ in habit: the white one is taller and more upright than the pink one. I've yet to see the species, with single flowers, nor do I know of any nursery selling it.

It isn't easy to kill this old-timer, but it does not prosper in soil overly rich, heavy, or moisture-retentive. Admiring, guiltily, the way it struggled on entangled with *Abelia ×grandiflora* in a hot, sandy part of my garden, I thought it deserved better and planted another group in pure compost. The new bushes straggled, developed mildew, and flowered little, while the old ones continued to prosper.

Invincible though dwarf almond is, if you would lift it from commonplace to commendable, prune it after the flowers fade. How this

Exochorda ×macrantha 'The Bride' (dwarf pearlbush) at right, with *Nandina domestica* at left, and in background *Lagerstroemia indica* and *Magnolia liliiflora*

Fothergilla gardenii with *Ajuga* 'Catlin's Giant' in background

is done and how often will vary with speed of growth, as well as preferred height and shape. I try to prune my pink ones every year, removing at ground level all dead, weak, straggling, or crowded branches and a few of the oldest. The other branches are then cut back by half. This treatment holds the plants at a height of about 3 feet. The taller, more upright white-flowered bushes are pruned less hard.

Exochorda ×macrantha 'The Bride'

DWARF PEARLBUSH

A painter I called in to redo ceilings complicated the discussion by asking which white I wanted among the dozen or so samples. With ceilings it does not matter to me, but in the garden it does. No color can more detract from another than a scintillating white next to one of lesser purity, and I grow no plant of a more crystalline white than dwarf pearlbush (*Exochorda ×macrantha* 'The Bride'; Zone 5). In early spring it becomes a snowy white waterfall of close-packed frilly flowers opening from chains of pearly buds and followed by appealing star-shaped seed capsules. Among other plants blooming at this time, candytuft (*Iberis sempervirens*), *Arabis procurrens*, *Phlox subulata* 'White Delight', and *Prunus glandulosa* 'Alba Plena' are bright whites that can hold their own. Other whites need to be distanced from dwarf pearlbush if they are not to suffer by comparison.

Dwarf pearlbush gets an honorable mention for its bridelike beauty notwithstanding the brevity of its bloom time—seldom much more than 2 weeks where early spring brings hot days—and its undistinguished, though not uncomely, appearance the rest of the year. Its thinly branched framework, sparsely clad in small gray-green leaves, is pruned when the flowers have faded, removing branches heading in wayward directions and trimming others back to keep it no more than 4 feet high and a bit more across.

Fothergilla

With fothergillas (Zone 5), placement is all-important. I got it right first time around with

Fothergilla 'Mt. Airy', believed to be a hybrid between *F. major* and *F. gardenii*. Five feet high after 10 years, it has the moist soil it needs and sufficient sun to develop bright autumn color, though all fothergillas are erratic about this and can't be relied upon to perform every year.

With *Fothergilla gardenii*, the smallest in size of bush and flower, the mistake I made was one of esthetics. The chaste white of a nearby *Prunus glandulosa* 'Alba Plena' makes the creamy fothergilla bottlebrushes look dingy by comparison. One or the other will have to be moved. Learning from this mistake, I gave *F. major*, which has the largest flowers, a background of lavender-flowered evergreen azaleas.

Around the time that fothergillas bloom we frequently get a hot and windy day or two, so the flowers seldom last much more than a week. The best fothergilla is therefore the one with the best foliage, the glaucous-leaved *Fothergilla gardenii* 'Blue Mist', a cultivar which put up with dryish shade under trees for several years, lacking autumn color but flowering well. Then came a rainless summer, and it languished in spite of frequent watering: water from hoses, no matter the source, is not as supporting of plant life as rain. Though the plant did not die, it did sound a warning bell, and I've started another to go in a part of the garden with less root competition.

Viburnum

Viburnum time usually starts in early April, sometimes March after a mild winter. This enormous genus has dozens of desirable species, though having too often failed as matchmaker, I've about given up on many of them grown primarily for their berries. They take up a lot of space when grouped or partnered, their sex lives remain a mystery to me, and berry display has been disappointing—with two exceptions, *Viburnum nudum* and *V. setigerum*.

Although it doesn't tug at the heartstrings as some others do, the most praiseworthy of the many viburnums I grow is *Viburnum ×pragense* (Zone 5), a refined version of one of its parents, *V. rhytidophyllum*. A sterling evergreen with glossy, spear-shaped, corrugated leaves, rough above and white-felted beneath, my 20-year-old bush has never been damaged by pest, disease, or the worst of winters. It attained a rounded 8 feet in as many years and has since been renewal pruned to keep it at that height. My only criticism is that the large, domed clusters of white flowers are unscented, a small quibble when measured against year-round good appearance.

The heart tuggers are, of course, the carnation-scented snowballs. I want them all, and have made a good stab at it, but don't recommend that others do the same. If we get a spell of hot, breezy weather when they are in bloom, as often happens, their flowers come and go in little more than a week. Given their undistinguished shape and foliage, the amount of time devoted to an annual pruning and the cost of hauling it away, I cannot make a good case for growing more than one or two of these, yet they do have individual merits. *Viburnum carlesii* (Zone 5) is medium sized and a neatly rounded shape, with foliage that sometimes turns deep red in autumn. *Viburnum carlesii* 'Compactum' is just that, compact, but it is marred by being grafted onto *V. lantana*, which means I must be ever watchful for suckers. *Viburnum ×burkwoodii* (Zone 5), my earliest snowball to flower, keeps all or some of its leaves most winters. Now that it is 15 feet high and as wide at the top, its branches are kept thinned at ground level to let in enough light for a carpet of snowdrops below. *Viburnum ×burkwoodii* 'Chenault' is somewhat slower growing. There's a downy look to the leaves of *V. ×juddii* (Zone 5), and the flowers are a powdery pink. This hybrid is said to be of sturdier constitution than *V. carlesii*, but all these snowball viburnums have been reliable for me in Virginia. *Viburnum ×carlcephalum* (Zone 5) is a rather graceless fragrant snowball, with fewer, though larger, clusters of white flowers from pink buds. It, too, is a

Viburnum plicatum 'Rosacea'

tis of moderate size. *Clematis florida* 'Sieboldii' (Zone 6) rambles through *Viburnum ×burkwoodii* 'Mohawk', and *C. texensis* 'Gravetye Beauty' (Zone 4) through *V. ×juddii*. These flower when viburnum bloom is done, extending the season of interest. Both the clematis die to the ground in winter.

The smallest and the whitest of my snowballs is the complex hybrid *Viburnum* 'Eskimo' (Zone 6; *V. ×carlcephalum* 'Cayuga' × *V. utile*), barely 4 feet high after 10 years. It loses a point or two because the fragrance of its parents somehow got lost in the hybridizing process. It blooms 1–2 weeks later than the fragrant snowballs.

The most stop-you-in-your-tracks snowball and a fine performer in southeastern gardens is *Viburnum macrocephalum* 'Sterile' (Zone 6), with huge scentless trusses crowded on branches sturdy enough to support them on a large rounded shrub. If you favor the peegee hydrangea, *Hydrangea paniculata* 'Grandiflora', you'll favor this viburnum, too. I pass.

Japanese snowballs, forms of *Viburnum plicatum* (Zone 5), aren't fragrant either, but their bright green, fan-pleated foliage gains them extra points. *Viburnum plicatum* 'Sterile', with white balls of bloom, is a first-rate large shrub. The most coveted snowball in my

garden is, however, *V. plicatum* 'Rosacea', with delicate pinkish apricot flower balls and bronze-tinted young leaves. Why a sell-on-sight shrub introduced, I understand, in 1953 should have been so rare puzzles me, unless, in failing to adapt itself to nursery schedules, it got a reputation for being hard to propagate. I have had 100 percent success with cuttings of half-ripe wood taken at flowering time, inserted in a peat moss and sand mix, and covered with a cloche or plastic bag, and I have had 100 percent failure with cuttings taken at any other time. Remaining elusive under the name 'Roseace', this snowball can be had as *V. plicatum* 'Kern's Pink'.

And so to the most garden-worthy group of the genus, the doublefile *Viburnum plicatum* var. *tomentosum*. With dogwoods (*Cornus florida*) at risk of disease, this species makes a good substitute, growing moderately fast into a dogwood-sized tree of tiered habit, laced with flowers in midspring and occasionally producing a spectacular display of bright red berries. My 10-foot-high doublefile viburnum provides just the right degree of shade for a carpet of hardy cyclamen on its west-facing side. If the species can't be found, and nowadays it is less common than named forms, *V. plicatum* 'Mariesii' comes close.

grafted plant, and suckers must be removed every year. I could spare it if it did not flower 2 weeks later than the others. The laurel wreath goes to *V. ×burkwoodii* 'Mohawk' for the combination of bright pink buds and white flowers in its early stages of bloom.

Branching is not dense on any of these viburnums, so they make good hosts for clema-

Shrubs and small trees growing under tall pines include hollies, azaleas, camellias, hydrangeas, *Viburnum plicatum* 'Fujisanensis', and *Enkianthus campanulatus*. The central pillar is *Hedera helix* 'Glacier' covering a dead tree. *Rosa banksiae* 'Lutea' (Lady Bankes rose) cascades down from a pine (far right).

Among the many named forms, all excellent in the right place, two call for a word of caution for southerners. *Viburnum plicatum* 'Pink Beauty', so exquisite in England, shows not the slightest trace of pink where the temperature soars high in spring. And *V. plicatum* 'Shasta', frequently touted for small gardens because it grows wider than high, is suitable only for large ones. At 15 years of age my plant is 10 feet high and 15 feet wide at the base. It responds in an ungainly way if branches are cut back, as do many plants in this group: the new shoots angle off in two directions. Sky room is less at a premium than ground space, and tall and thin, not short and fat, is what small gardens need, large gardens too if the aim is to squeeze in the maximum number of plants. First choice should then be *V. plicatum* 'Fujisanensis'. Though not a dwarf (my 10-year-old is 9 feet high), it grows in a vase shape with most of the width at the top. Flowers and leaves are proportionately smaller than those of the species, and branches and twigs are slimmer. Peak bloom is in spring, with a smattering through summer. *Viburnum plicatum* 'Nanum Semperflorens', 'Summer Snowflake', and 'Watanabe' (indistinguishable one from another) are a little larger than 'Fu-

LEFT *Viburnum plicatum* 'Watanabe' only 4 years old

jisanensis' but otherwise similar. These smaller doublefiles have a distinguishing waisted look, as if tightly corseted in the middle.

Wisteria sinensis

CHINESE WISTERIA

Sometimes plants decline to accommodate themselves to attempted classifications. *Wisteria floribunda* and *W. sinensis* (Zone 5) are cases in point. The direction in which they twine, supposedly one way of distinguishing between them, is not a reliable means of identification. Donald Wyman (*Shrubs and Vines for American Gardens*) has *W. sinensis* twining clockwise, *W. floribunda* the other way. Neil Odenwald and James Turner (*Southern Plants for Landscape Design*) agree. Graham Thomas (*Ornamental Shrubs, Climbers, and Bamboos*) reverses this. So does Michael Dirr (*Manual of Woody Landscape Plants*), who admits to finding the genus taxing. Wyman and Dirr both suggest that some plants placed in one species or the other may in fact be hybrids. Unwilling to rush in where angels fear to tread, I speak as I find.

My blue wisteria, here when my husband and I bought the property, appears to be the one seen leapfrogging over trees in America's southern states. My white wisteria differs only in color. The two twine counterclockwise, usually, though an occasional aberrant strand seems to get confused and go off in the wrong direction. The fragrant flowers come first, in chubby racemes about 1 foot long. Leaves follow close behind. Whatever its true identify, my white wisteria is one of the garden's stars, and well placed, alongside the drive, to receive homage at flowering time, when it excites three senses at the same time: sight, smell, and the sound of bees frantically gathering pollen as if there were no tomorrow.

These delights do not come without price. I have trained the white wisteria into a large shrub (the blue one also), now some 7 feet high and twice as much across. The basic structure was developed by eye, following, more or less, the process outlined in books on pruning. I wanted a low-branched shrub that wouldn't entail pruning from a ladder. The low-slung, wide-spreading form has another, unanticipated benefit. It is underplanted with *Narcissus* 'February Gold', which gets full sun through winter and early spring, when the wisteria is but a skeleton. The dying daffodil foliage is then mercifully concealed beneath the wisteria's leafy skirts.

But my wisteria wants to be a vine, and a rampant one at that. Like a cat, it won't take no for an answer and never gives up trying to extend its parameters. If I've been away for more than a week between May and September, the wisteria becomes a giant vegetable octopus, greeting me on my return with 6-foot-long waving tentacles. On a freestanding bush these are as apparent as whiskers on a face gone too long unshaven, and the process of removing them is much the same. In theory one cuts back to within two or three buds of the old wood, and now that I have turned over the pruning to my co-gardener, that it how it is done. When I was doing it, I couldn't see the wood for the leaves, so I merely cut off all vining stems wandering beyond the outline of the bush, leaving precise pruning for winter when I could see what I was doing. Either method works. From late spring into autumn tentacles must be cut off every couple of weeks. Suckers springing up as much as 10 feet away also have to be dug out occasionally or sprayed with Roundup (glyphosate). In April, when the plant is picture-perfect for 2 or 3 weeks, all this effort seems worth while. It gets full marks for beauty, unblemished foliage, interesting skeletal winter shape, and acceptance of poor soil, with deductions only for the time-consuming, though light and simple, maintenance.

I now hear one of the most-asked questions, and one to which no one has a certain answer: "Why doesn't my wisteria bloom?" The soil is too rich or over-fertilized. Winter

Wisteria sinensis 'Alba'

cold destroyed the buds or you cut them off. The plant is not getting enough sun. Or you have a nonflowering seedling. My wisteria, a sucker from a friend's floriferous plant, has bloomed from babyhood. Which are bloom buds and which are leaves is hard to tell in winter, so buying a plant already in bloom is advisable, when possible.

Evergreen Japanese Azaleas

That *Rhododendron* is both a scientific and a popular name confuses those unaware that every azalea belongs to the genus *Rhododendron*. I propose to use the names by which most gardeners know them.

In late April spring's pace accelerates and every garden is awash with the evergreen Japanese azaleas (Zones 6–7, varying with the cultivar) never called "rhododendron," though taxonomically that is what they are. Japanese azaleas prefer warm regions and, once past infancy, survive much abuse, though many succumb in their first year to overly deep planting or drying out of pot-bound roots not loosened from or washed clean of the peat or bark-based mixes in which they are usually grown. Labels on the two-for-$5 gallon pots in shopping malls read predictably: cerise 'Hinode-giri', pink hose-in-hose 'Coral Bells', orange-pink 'Fashion', and one of the best

whites, 'Delaware Valley White.' All these are excellent, but boringly few among possible hundreds, and too often planted in one-of-each groupings. The flowers of Japanese azaleas are so closely packed that they rival sheared chrysanthemums in solidity of color. Even pale colors have substantial impact, and it takes at least three plants of each color to prevent mixed groupings from looking spotty.

Size can be controlled by pruning, so unless true dwarfs are wanted, potential height does not matter a lot with Japanese azaleas. They can be sheared every year, though my preference is to let them rip until they become taller than I want, then saw them back to about 1 foot, which gives them a new lease of dense, bushy life. It takes a couple of years before they start to fill their space again, so only one grouping is hard pruned in a single year. Ground pine bark is mixed into the soil at planting time and a little leaf compost in sites likely to become dry. Ground pine bark or pine needles are used as mulch since azaleas dislike hardwood mulch. Evergreen azaleas are extremely drought resistant once well established and do not thrive in wet soils.

The design precept that open areas shape space and create restfulness need not apply only to enterable space such as lawns and courtyards. It can also apply to the visual

space of uniform plantings, as commonly achieved with ground covers such as ivy or pachysandra. If ground covers are interspersed with varied taller plants, the background uniformity remains a cohesive factor uniting the disparate elements. Heaths and heathers were a uniting feature in my English garden. In Virginia, where heathers don't do well enough to be worth the effort, two things in particular fill this role: sweeps of lily turf (*Liriope* and *Ophiopogon*) and groupings of evergreen azaleas.

Your color preferences may differ from mine. Consult Fred Galle's massive tome, *Azaleas*, product of a lifetime's dedication to his subject, for descriptions of many hundreds of azaleas and their suitability for different regions and purposes. My own nonexclusive preference is for singles over doubles, scarlets and apricots over pinks, and especially for the soft lavenders that blend so well into the general scene.

There are considerations other than the esthetic. Nature laid the curse of petal blight on Japanese azaleas. This fungus turns petals to a brown slime that remains glued to the leaves for months. Control consists of repeated, expensive sprayings from the time buds show color. Because petal blight is prompted by humid heat, early to midseason bloomers usu-

'Ben Morrison', an evergreen azalea

'Koromo Shikibu', an evergreen azalea

ally escape it, and so I concentrate on these plus a few later ones of proven blight resistance. Members of the Satsuki group, which flower in late May and June and include the popular Gumpos, are very prone to petal blight unless grown where no sun strikes them. This group also attracts rabbits, which can eat a sizeable plant down to a stump in a single night.

Light purplish-pink 'Dayspring' is always my earliest Japanese azalea, blooming along with *Prunus* 'Hally Jolivette' and English primroses (*Primula vulgaris*). Next comes 'Festive', with white flowers that have a few red stripes.

Then comes small-flowered 'Mizu-no-yam-abuki', with flowers of creamy lime touched with yellow. The flowers of 'Mizu-no-yam-abuki' and midseason 'Olga Niblett' are the nearest to yellow that Japanese azaleas have yet come.

Late April sees the first of my pastel purple Japanese azaleas, 'Mme. Butterfly', in bloom. It has white flowers faintly flushed with purple, a very delicate color. My plants have been cut back almost to ground level three times in

a quarter century after becoming head-high. Watch the spelling of this hybrid, for there is a 'Madame Butterfly' with deep purple flowers. Overlapping 'Mme. Butterfly' is an azalea that could not be mistaken for any other, the strap-petaled, pale purple, very fragrant 'Koromo Shikibu'. I have several of this color group, as I find pastel purple a very sympathetic color. 'Koromo Shikibu' attracts more favorable comment than any other and is the last I'd want to give up. It is readily available, but its

'Girard's Hot Shot', a red-flowered evergreen azalea, with *Forsythia* 'Gold Leaf', *Euonymus fortunei* 'Sparkle 'n' Gold' (climbing young dogwood), the yellow-flowered celandine poppy *Stylophorum diphyllum*, and in foreground *Sedum kamtschaticum*

Rhododendron 'Gigi'

brid evergreen azaleas (Zone 7). The large white flowers flushed purple and blotched with orchid pink are sweetly scented.

On the yellow-red side of the spectrum, my evergreen azalea season begins with 'Salmon Spray', a single-flowered soft salmon pink easily overwhelmed in the company of strong colors, therefore surrounded by the cream and green of variegated Solomon's seal (*Polygonatum odoratum* 'Variegatum'). Soon the Solomon's seal will be joined by the purple-flowered hardy orchid, *Bletilla striata*, so there is no color clash.

The azalea 'Ben Morrison' has broadly star-shaped single flowers of creamy terracotta flared with apricot, unevenly edged in white, its upper petals freckled with strawberry pink. All who see it want it. There is no such subtlety with neon-bright 'Girard's Hot Shot', a wavy-petaled scarlet with dark spotting. It is perfect for a hot color scheme where there is summer shade, along with *Acorus gramineus* 'Ogon', *Euonymus fortunei* 'Emerald 'n' Gold', and *Forsythia* 'Gold Leaf'. Another good scarlet, 'Stewartsonian', combines brilliantly with the young yellow foliage of a lemon balm, *Melissa officinalis* 'All Gold', which has such a cheerful color and is so refreshingly lemon scented that it is forgiven for being a pestilential self-sower.

pure white counterpart, 'Primitive Beauty', given to me by Fred Galle, is harder to track down. Next to 'Koromo Shikibu' I planted 'Winterthur', sold by Winterthur Gardens, Delaware, where it originated, and described by them as having "3-inch flowers of clear lavender, as close to blue as those of any azalea." In certain lights it does become a very lovely misty blue, a mismatch with 'Koromo Shikibu', neither alike enough to blend nor different enough to contrast. The divorce was not painful for them or me. One big asset of evergreen azaleas is that their compact, fibrous root balls make them easy to move without setback at almost any time except during summer's extreme heat. As these two fade 'George Lindley Taber' begins. It is one of the hardiest of the so-called Southern Indica hy-

Rhododendrons

What the popular name "rhododendron" immediately brings to mind is the group of bulky, large-leaved evergreen shrubs with massive trusses of bloom. These are often called hardy hybrids. "Hardy" means cold hardy; heat is another matter. Two of the progenitors of the numerous hybrids, *Rhododendron catawbiense* (Zone 4) and *R. maximum* (Zone 5), grow wild in the cool and misty mountains a 3-hour drive from my home. They are not well adapted to the hot and humid coastal plain, but some of the hybrids perform well provided drainage is impeccable and the soil not compacted. Planting high, with fine pine bark mixed into the soil and used as mulch, greatly increases chances of success. Compact bluish-red *R*. 'Gigi' (Zone 6) and crimson-pink 'Anna Rose Whitney' (Zone 6) are two of my best rhododendrons. In front of 'Anna Rose Whitney', *Rosa* 'Nearly Wild' opens its first flowers of dog-rose pink while the rhododendron is still in bloom. Roses and rhododendrons? An unexpected combination to these English eyes. All the *R. yakushimanum* hybrids I have tried have also performed well.

Also well adapted to heat are three smaller-leaved rhododendrons. Two are extremely popular, while the other is too-seldom seen. *Rhododendron* 'Mary Fleming' (Zone 6) is a

Rhododendron 'Mary Fleming' with *Hosta undulata* var. *albomarginata* in foreground

delightful, small-leaved, evergreen shrub with dense clusters of pale buff-yellow flowers with hints of pink, a color that glows without ever causing a rumpus, no matter what its companions. *Rhododendron carolinianum* (Zone 5; synonym *R. minus* var. *carolinianum*) is probably best known not as the species, but in the early blooming PJM hybrids raised at Weston Nurseries, Massachusetts, and famed for their tolerance of both heat and cold. The most widely available of these are *R.* 'P. J. M.' or 'P. J. Mezitt', with flowers of brilliant rosy purple (given added drama with an underplanting of early yellow daffodils), and the paler pink *R.* 'Olga Mezitt'. Both have dark green, glossy leaves that take on orange and reddish tints in winter.

An evergreen rhododendron unnecessarily rare in warm gardens is *Rhododendron chapmanii* (Zone 6; synonym *R. minus* var. *chapmanii*), an endangered species from Florida with glossy evergreen leaves and clusters of funnel-shaped flowers of medium clear pink. About 3 feet tall with branching becoming loose as it matures, it responds quickly with new growth if sprawling branches are cut back. I have found it easy to grow in humus-enriched sand with shade from afternoon sun, and very easy to propagate. Woodlanders Nursery, which was promoting native plants long

before it became fashionable to do so, and to whom I personally give thanks for many lovely things, is debarred by the Endangered Species Act from shipping its nursery-propagated plants of *R. chapmanii* out of state without obtaining cumbersome and costly permits. Buy this species if and where you get the chance, then propagate it and pass it on. Gardeners may be its best chance of survival.

Deciduous Azaleas

Notwithstanding that Exbury hybrid azaleas invariably die young in regions of tropical summers, their very gorgeousness has damaged the cause of less flamboyant, though often highly fragrant, deciduous azaleas. Now gardeners in Zones 6–9 can have both glamour and heat hardiness, thanks to the efforts of such plantsmen as Alabamans Eugene Aromi and Tom Dodd, who crossed the Exbury azaleas with heat-tolerant species to produce sturdy, upright hybrids with large, fragrant flower trusses and brilliant color. These hybrids ask only permeable, acid soil neither wet nor dry and light mulch. Finely ground pine bark is the ideal mulch and soil additive. To flower well, these hybrids need sun for at least half a day. They can tolerate full sun.

Yellow and orange flowers predominate in the Aromi hybrids, but each year sees a broadening of the range: 'Red Chameleon', with red flowers fading to rose, is one of the latest introductions. Dodd family hybrids include light pink 'Emma Sansom'. Many of these recent introductions derive their heat tolerance and fragrance from *Rhododendron austrinum* (Zone 6), a showy and easy species for hot regions, with large trusses of yellow or orange flowers. Several selections have been made: *R. austrinum* 'Millie Mac' is distinguished by the white edging to its yellow flowers.

Splendid as these large-trussed deciduous azaleas are, my first loves remain the smaller-flowered, fragrant, heat-tolerant species and their selected forms, and none more than the Choptank range. My first plants were grown from seed, the gift of Polly Hill, who found naturally occurring forms or hybrids of the stoloniferous *Rhododendron atlanticum* (Zone 6) near the Choptank River, Maryland. From this seed came stoloniferous plants with winsome pink and white flowers that lap me in fragrance in midspring. Undamaged by winter freeze or summer drought, they grew 4 feet high in about 5 years and have since been maintained at that height with occasional pruning. A later addition, 'Choptank Yellow', more densely bushy and not stoloniferous, has flowers of similarly delicate color, this time yellow and amber. A dozen or so others bear the Choptank name: whites, pinks, and yellows. Some of them are stoloniferous, others completely bushy.

The swamp azalea or swamp honeysuckle, *Rhododendron viscosum* (Zone 4), opens its fragrant white flowers between mid-June and late July. Until obliterated by housing developments and shopping malls, this species grew wild along wet ditches in my neighborhood. In my garden it thrives in sometimes-saturated soil and also where the soil is only moderately moist. It makes a large, mildly stoloniferous bush with small, glossy leaves. Named selections include pink-flowered 'Lollipop' and 'Pink Mist', and the creamy 'Lemon Drop', which is my last swamp azalea to bloom. Sandy soil and mulches of oak leaves, pine needles, or flaky pine bark meet the modest needs of these azaleas. They have no need for fertilizer.

Choptank hybrid of *Rhododendron atlanticum* grown from seed

Kerria japonica

April sees the first round orange-yellow double blooms open along the willowy, 7-foot-tall arching green stems of common kerria, *Kerria japonica* 'Pleniflora' (Zone 4). It peaks in early spring, but will not now be without bloom until late autumn, and its stems stay green through winter. Sometimes despised as plebeian, this kerria is, in my opinion, among the best shrubs. It is certainly the best of the kerrias in my region, where the others have only one flush of bloom in spring. Every year I resolve not to go away in April and May when my garden is at its peak, and every year I break that resolution, for other gardens are also at their best and they are a fount of new knowledge, plants, and ideas for ways of doing things. Some plants (peonies, for one) have come and gone while I am away, but I can count on the double-flowered kerria to keep on blooming. The color of 'Pleniflora' is similar to that of the highly touted daylily *Hemerocallis* 'Stella d'Oro', and the two make a good match. My own preferred color partners are *Narcissus* 'Ambergate' for spring and *Coreopsis integrifolia* with egg-yolk yellow flowers for autumn. The narcissus has petals of creamy yellow with a hint of apricot, and a shallow light orange cup. It isn't a stayer for

Kerria japonica 'Pleniflora' underplanted with *Narcissus* 'Ambergate'

me, and I top it up with new bulbs every few years.

Kerrias spread rapidly, and I devote half a day every autumn to cleaning the clumps of dead branches and cutting off roving roots. Neglect the annual control, and I come to regret it.

Kerria japonica 'Variegata' (Zone 4), a shorter bush with an often meager offering of bright yellow, somewhat scrunched up single flowers, and pretty white-edged leaves inclined to revert, is not nearly such a good shrub in hot regions as it is further north. It has suckered among azaleas to such an extent that it cannot be disentangled without making a clean sweep. Learning from this, I surrounded the green-leaved, yellow-flowered species with a native columbine, *Aquilegia canadensis* (Zone 3). The columbine self-sows so freely that any plants destroyed when working on the kerria can easily be spared.

Illicium

ANISE TREE

Gardeners on the East Coast of North America can forget about most plants from Chile or be prepared for disappointment. Either winter cold or summer heat will do them in, with few exceptions. So it was for me with *Drimys winteri*. Consolation came with the Asian *Il-*

licium anisatum, which has quite similar creamy, waxy-petaled flowers clustered in the axils of glossy, slightly wavy, oval leaves in April. A broadly conical 6 feet tall after 10 years, it is just hardy enough for sheltered sites in the warmer parts of Zone 7. In southeastern public gardens its name was for years misapplied to the suckering, yellow-flowered *I. parviflorum* (Zone 6), the hardiest species in the genus, but comparatively drab of leaf and flower.

Florida anise, *Illicium floridanum* (warmer parts of Zone 6), gets a black mark only for the way it sullies itself with dead leaves just as it starts to bloom. Many, if not most, evergreens shed leaves a few at a time, so inconspicuously that nongardeners often suppose evergreen leaves to be as permanent as plastic. Florida anise sheds about a fifth of its leaves at this one time, and that's not the worst of it. Before they fall, the leaves turn a diseased-looking, darkly spotted yellow. I want to shake them for so despoiling themselves, and shaking does, in fact, rid them of dead leaves faster. All else is praise. The flowers are burgundy-colored 2-inch spoked circles on 2-inch-long arched pedicels, grouped five or more at the branch tips, and followed by attractive, fleshy, star-shaped seed cases. The elliptic leaves are smooth but not glossy.

Wanting evergreens against a 6-foot fence on a shady boundary, I gathered up the numerous seedlings from under my solitary Florida anise and planted them in the moist, acid sand at 3-foot intervals. Here, with little sun, they flowered moderately at first, profusely in the upper half once they grew above the fence into the sun. Base in shade, head in sun seems to suit them, but not sun from head to toe. Pink- and white-flowered forms have been added. All are trouble-free save for removal of unwanted seedlings, which is not a big chore because most seedlings are clustered around the base of the parent, not scattered here and there.

Illicium mexicanum, which is marginally hardy in Zone 7, has slightly larger flowers of a lighter ruby red, with a twist in the petals that gives them a spidery look. The spear-shaped leaves are longer. *Illicium floridanum* and *I. mexicanum* bloom copiously in spring for about 3 weeks and sometimes spasmodically through summer and fall.

Though slightly less hardy than Florida anise, the Chinese *Illicium henryi* (Zone 7) gets the highest mark for shape and foliage. This shrub is a broadly conical (or narrowly pyramidal!) 10 feet after 15 years. Its lustrous leaves are smaller and darker than those of Florida anise, and they shed a few at a time

Illicium floridanum (anise tree)

without a tawdry period. Small groups of waxy, inch-wide, cupped flowers resembling semidouble water lilies open in early May. The inside color is a clear, bright pink, the outside greenish amber, and the overall effect approaches coral. Unfortunately, the flowers nod beneath the leaves on 2-inch petioles and could easily go unnoticed if a path does not run close by. This species would, nonetheless, be my first choice if I could have but one illicium. It produces fewer seedlings than the Florida anise, but an adequate number for most home gardeners.

Michelia figo

BANANA SHRUB

The flowers of banana shrub (*Michelia figo*; Zone 7) are not of a size or color to grab attention. Instead they do it with a beguiling scent that has nostrils twitching and faces rapt in a concentrated effort to track it down. The flowers resemble miniature magnolias, to

Michelia figo (banana shrub)

which family banana shrub belongs. Their color—chamois stained with ruby—brings to mind the cheddar and port wine cheese sold in little crocks for parties. The flowers start to burst from pointed, silkily pelted, cinnamon-tinted buds in late April. Their powerful fragrance is evocative of banana or acetone. Hundreds of blooms come in succession over a 2- to 3-week period.

Banana shrub is a handsome year-round ornamental shrub of dense, rounded habit, with exceptionally attractive lustrous, wavy leaves. My shrub is about 10 feet tall, after being killed almost to the ground once in its 20 years. It grows alongside a path, just where it ought to be for the tactile pleasure of the furry buds and for close inspection of winsome flowers that are not of a color or size to have visual impact from a distance. It obviously approves of the sandy, acid soil, somewhat enriched with years of mulch and fallen pine needles. The site is brightly lit and sunny for much of the day, with high overhead protection from the spreading boughs of pines.

Companion plants include camellias, such late-blooming deciduous azaleas as *Rhododendron prunifolium*, one of the few kalmias I've succeeded with, hellebores, corydalis, arums, ferns, *Arisaema sikokianum* (which comes and goes, as is its way), *Arisaema candi-*

dissimum (reliable, but so late to appear that it frightens all who grow it into supposing it lost), the quaint little mouse plant (*Arisarum proboscideum*), and bleeding heart (*Dicentra spectabilis*). The last two plants are sources of delight to visiting children. Part the leaves of mouse plant in early spring and there is the rump and long tail of the burrowing mouse. Pick a flower of the dicentra, ease the two sides of the heart apart, and you'll see how it got the name by which I know it, lady-in-the-bath.

Deutzia gracilis

Sometimes climate-related idiosyncrasies are obvious, but other times they are hard to understand. Damned by faint praise in English gardening books, which note its susceptibility to late spring frost, *Deutzia gracilis* (Zone 4), a small, dense, graceful shrub, performs consistently well in the more varied and extreme climates of much of North America, whether grown in full sun or slight shade. It must be that it needs sun and heat to ripen and harden the wood. May Day sees the start of bloom in coastal Virginia, continuing for 2 or 3 weeks. With an arching shape best displayed as a single bush, this shrub also lends itself to grouping. A light shearing when bloom is done keeps mine, in the garden now for two decades, below waist height and 6 feet across. The similar *D. crenata* 'Nikko' differs in habit. Branch tips root where they touch the ground, and 'Nikko' spreads slowly wider, staying low enough at 1 foot or so for *Oxalis rubra* 'Alba' to push its way through the outer branches and extend the flower season through summer into autumn.

When I spotted *Deutzia gracilis* 'Variegata' (synonym 'Marmorata') in a mail-order catalog, I had to have it. But it was hate at first sight when the plant leafed out, mottled with creamy white in a virused sort of way, and I made a mental note to hoick it out. Before I got around to doing this, it flowered so fetchingly that it got a stay of execution. In its hot place and gravelly soil (the gravel added to deter voles, which it does to some degree) it is very vigorous. Add the fact that the leaf is larger and unpleasantly raspy to the touch and I question whether this selection is correctly assigned to *D. gracilis*. The jury is still out on this one. Certainly there are many better deutzias.

Jasminum

JASMINE

In assessing the merit of a plant, vision is sometimes clouded by sentiment, and I've known Italian jasmine, *Jasminum humile* 'Revolutum', since my childhood in England, while *J. floridum* was new to me when I came

Deutzia gracilis

to live in Virginia. Both have emerged with flying colors from a 20-year trial. These jasmines are excellent, undemanding evergreen shrubs for sunny or lightly shaded sites, and amply hardy in the warmer parts of Zone 7. Occasional winter damage is not a serious defect when the shrubs recover so fast.

Because its flowers are scented and keep coming for twice as long, and because it is less of a challenge to prune, *Jasminum humile* 'Revolutum' (Zone 7) would be my first choice. It is the larger of the two shrubs, 6 feet high in as many years, with willowy arching green branches clad in pinnate, dark green, 4-inch-long leaves. In late spring, sometimes continuing into summer, the rounded bush is decked with slightly pendulous clusters of lightly scented, daffodil-yellow flowers of typical jas-

Jasminum humile 'Revolutum' with *Lagerstroemia fauriei* in background

mine shape, tubular and starry. Renewal pruning, removing a few of the oldest branches at the base when flowering is done, maintains this jasmine at its best.

The shorter *Jasminum floridum* (Zone 7) flowers a little later. In smaller gardens it could, with annual pruning, be grown as a shrub about 2 feet high and wide. If left to be what it wants to be, it resembles winter jasmine (*J. nudiflorum*) in its growth habit. For about 2 weeks in late May or June small clusters of scentless yellow flowers spangle tangled thickets of arching green stems clad in widely spaced, glossy, trifoliate leaves. I don't think there is a "right" way to prune this 2- to 4-foot shrub, and fortunately it doesn't need it for a good many years. When I finally tackled my plant, as soon as bloom was done, a combination of shearing and thinning left it looking mangled for a year. Next time I'll prune in late winter, sacrificing a season's bloom so that vigorous spring growth will more quickly restore its good looks.

Weigela florida

Weigelas bloom for such a short time in May that flowers alone are scarcely enough reason for growing them, hence the high regard everywhere for *Weigela florida* 'Variegata', as delectable as strawberries and cream when

Jasminum floridum

ivory leaf edges combine with its baby-pink flowers. In cool regions the leaf edging inclines to yellow. For those averse to pink with yellow there are alternatives. *Weigela florida* 'Suzanne' has flowers of similar pale pink, but the narrow edging to the leaf is consistently white. *Weigela praecox* 'Variegata' has a broader creamy edge to the leaf and flowers of deeper pink opening from crimson buds. *Weigela florida* 'Foliis Purpureus' (synonym 'Java Red') is a smaller, very compact plant with reddish-brown leaves and dusky pink flowers, and the bigger *W. florida* 'Alexandra' (synonym 'Roses and Wine') has dark burgundy leaves and bright pink flowers. All of them need sun for a good part of the day to be at their best. If you like the excitement of pink with yellow, *W. florida* 'Rubidor' with carmine flowers is less

Weigela florida 'Suzanne' with *Lagerstroemia* 'Natchez'

Sophora davidii

abashed about it than the paler-leafed *W. florida* 'Looymansii Aurea'. Both of these are likely to scorch in hot afternoon sun. All these selections of *W. florida* are hardy to Zone 7.

Sophora davidii

Although this shrub has been in my garden for only 3 years, it has been under my eye in a friend's colder garden for much longer than that, and there it has attracted repeated covetous requests for a source. There has not been one, but now there is, and so I can talk about it without causing frustration.

Belonging to the same family as caraganas, indigoferas, and crown vetch (*Coronilla varia*), *Sophora davidii* (Zone 6) shares with them such characteristics as pea-type flowers, pinnate leaves, and adaptability to poor, dry soil.

The 2-inch-long leaves, alternating along slender branches, are laddered with tiny leaflets slightly folded up to reveal silken undersides. There are small thorns at the base of the leaves, soft on young growth, never really fierce. The flowers, in April or May, plentiful where summers are hot, are a milky violet-blue, and the whole shrub has a bluish sheen. It has a similar charm to, and compensates for the absence of, yellow-flowered *Coronilla valentina* subsp. *glauca*, which is not hardy enough for my garden.

No shrub I grow except tamarix has accepted a place in poor, dry soil and hot sun with such equanimity. This site is, in fact, the best place for it. In shade or moist soil the slender branches ramble excessively, and the leaves lose much of their silken sheen. Although capable of attaining an airily open 6 feet or more, *Sophora davidii* produces new growth quickly from pruning cuts, and plants can be kept shorter and denser if one chooses.

Propagation is by seed or cuttings. My plants were grown from cuttings, which seemed to take forever to root. Cuttings potted on did not take kindly to the frame regime of frequent watering, rushing with obvious relief into rapid growth when put out in the garden.

Syringa

LILAC

Lilacs, it is widely reported, do not do well in hot-summer zones. True, the dooryard lilacs of cool regions (*Syringa vulgaris*) become mildewed and miserable in intense summer heat, but those described here rejoice in it. Their foliage usually remains unblemished by pest or disease, and their flowers scent the garden in the first half of May. Odd clusters of blossoms produced later in the season are really too few to be worth mentioning, though pleasant to pick and bring indoors. Cuttings taken in spring root quickly and grow fast, providing plants for testing in various locations. Lilacs

Syringa 'Miss Kim' (lilac)

are amazingly tolerant and drought resistant, and need no fertilizing. Humus-enriched soil and sun for most of the day are what suit them best. They put up with shade, even quite dry shade, but flowering is then scanty.

Syringa microphylla 'Superba' (Zone 4) and *S. meyeri* 'Palibin' (Zone 3) are good lilacs. The latter, the so-called dwarf Korean lilac, is far from being a dwarf: it becomes a wide-spreading thicket desirous of growing head high. Having planted it at the front of a bed, I must thwart its ambition with annual pruning. Both of these lilacs have small, neat leaves and pale lilac-pink flower trusses with deeper-colored buds. I grow *S.* ×*laciniata* (Zone 7) more for its finely cut leaves, laddered like those of polemoniums, than for its small clusters of flowers.

The very best lilac for hot regions is *Syringa*

'Miss Kim' (Zone 4), shuttled so often from one species to another that I'd rather not stick my neck out. It is a dense, sturdily branched medium-sized shrub. Buds are pale lilac purple, opening to a pale, almost silvery tint. The scent is reminiscent of the pinks (*Dianthus*) that bloom at the same time.

Enkianthus campanulatus

This veteran of almost 30 years, now 10 feet high and as much across, has never caused me a moment's concern. A shrub of subtle charm, *Enkianthus campanulatus* (Zone 5) is not eye-catching from afar, so I planted it alongside the drive, facing east with shade from behind. No shrub I know does a better job of displaying its flowers: the egg-shaped, egg-sized leaves grow in circlets on top of the branches, while pink-veined, cup-shaped, ivory flowers with pink scalloped rims swing below, averaging ten to a bunch and arranged at varying levels with each well spaced and distinct. The flowers last 2 to 3 weeks in May. I don't mind that the leaves do not turn red and yellow in autumn as they do in cooler regions. There is brilliant color all around me then, from red maple (*Acer rubrum*), sweet gum (*Liquidambar styraciflua*), tupelo (*Nyssa sylvatica*), tulip poplar (*Liriodendron tulipfera*), aronia, sumac (*Rhus copallina*), sassafras, and wild blueberries (*Vaccinium*). Because these grow wild within a mile or two of my home, I feel less need for autumn color in the garden than I did in England, where the amber of beech trees is about the best of nature's autumnal offerings.

Buddleia alternifolia 'Argentea'

Gray foliage is at a premium in hot and humid regions, because much of it mugs off in summer. Blessings, then, on *Buddleia alternifolia* 'Argentea' (Zone 5), which revels in the heat. It suckers in my sandy soil, so now there are three bushes where I planted one. I keep them pruned back to about 3 feet, cutting out flowered branches in June, with another cut-back later for any branches grown too lanky. The shrub still manages to bloom in May, wreathing with lavender flowers slim branches that arch over a carpet of golden oregano (*Origanum vulgare* 'Aureum'), a very successful partnership in a hot, sometimes dry, sunny place. Suckers have provided any extra plants I need.

Spiraea nipponica 'Snowmound'

Spiraeas fall into two main groups: those with white flowers and those with pink. The white ones bloom before the pink ones, with *Spiraea thunbergii* as early as late February and most of the others in May. *Spiraea* ×*vanhouttei* (Zone 3) is the archetype in cooler regions. In my area it grows too tall and wide too fast. Of the many white-flowered spiraeas I am growing or have grown, by far the best is the always-comely *S. nipponica* 'Snowmound' (Zone 4). Misled by its name I planted it near the front of a bed, then later had to move it further back. Snowy it is, but a mound it is not after the first few years, or not a small one, anyway. My 12-year-old, renewal pruned (oldest branches cut out at the base when bloom is done) these last 5 years, attains 5 feet by the next blossom time. Perhaps the name refers to the flowers, which do form small white mounds along twiggy branches dressed in neat little blue-green leaves. Full sun suits this shrub or a bit of afternoon shade. It suckers or layers (I haven't paid close attention) just enough to provide an extra plant or two each year.

Buddleia alternifolia 'Argentea' surrounded by *Origanum vulgare* 'Aureum' (golden oregano)

VINES

The ability to provide an appropriate means of support influences one's choice of vines. Is there a wall, fence, or tree for self-clinging kinds, or something around which twiners can wrap their tentacles and to which tendrils or leaf petioles can cling? Here and there around the garden I utilize such supports as house walls, a board fence, tree trunks, a telephone pole and stay, chicken wire on a post and rail fence, rebar tripods (which if not exactly picturesque are, in their rustiness, almost invisible), and shrubs for anything not so lush or vigorous as to throttle or smother them. Fishing line, which in my hot region lasts only one season, works well for annual or herbaceous twiners with very fine stems.

Many of my vines grow along what I call The Avenue, where 42 red cedars (*Juniperus virginiana*; Zone 4) limbed up to clean, 10-foot trunks, march along one boundary at 10-foot intervals. Every other trunk has been decapitated to let in more light. Once beheaded, red cedars don't grow out again, and the trunks last, if not forever, certainly a lot longer than I shall. Their rough, shreddy bark provides perfect support for such self-clingers as euonymus and climbing hydrangeas, and for such half-hearted clingers as *Trachelosper-mum asiaticum*. The beheaded trunks are a perfect place for ivies which, with no canopy to climb into, and sometimes smother, go to the top of their 10-foot support and then cascade gracefully down.

For twiners, tendril climbers, and some of those not equipped to cling at all (*Jasminum nudiflorum* and *Hedera helix* 'Erecta', for example), the red cedar trunks were at first encircled with 6-inch mesh concrete reinforcing wire. Besides being ugly, it was too wide a mesh for some vines. Deer fencing of stiff, black plastic 2-inch mesh has proved ideal. When cut from a roll 9 feet wide, the plastic mesh forms firm cylinders needing only a few staples to hold them in place around the trunks. As the trunks of growing trees increase in girth the plastic is easily snipped to prevent constriction. Two vines share some trunks: the tiny-leaved *Euonymus fortunei* 'Kewensis' (Zone 5) clings tightly to one trunk, while the white-flowered *Akebia quinata* 'Shirobana' (Zone 4), which flowers for all of 5 days but does have pretty foliage, laces the plastic mesh.

For a few thick-stemmed, nonclingers such as climbing roses and *Rubus rosifolius* 'Coronarius' I use black half-inch Adj-A-Tye, flat, slotted plastic chain-lock that comes in 100-foot coils. It also comes in a 1-inch heavy-duty width. Bands encircling a tree and prevented from slipping with a tack or two slot together at the ends in the same way as the plastic slotted ties that come with garbage bags. It takes only seconds to unslot and loosen these ties when old stems need cutting out or new ones tying in. Whoever invented this product deserves a medal.

Those who suppose that native plants are necessarily the best, or proper, choice for a garden lack practical experience. The very qualities that enable a plant to survive in the rough and tumble of the wild make some of them a menace when relieved of such competition. Though manageable in cooler regions and slowed a bit by heavy clay, the following natives of my region proved too rampageous, by seed, running roots, or both, in my sandy soil: trumpet vine (*Campsis radicans* and the hybrid 'Mme. Galen'; the Asian *C. grandiflora*, the loveliest of the genus, did not prove hardy); cross vine (*Bignonia capreolata*), an incubus I may never be rid of; *Wisteria frutescens*; Virginia creeper (*Parthenocissus virginiana*); and the local passion flower or maypops (*Passiflora incarnata*).

Natives aren't the only culprits, of course.

Every hardy passion flower I've tried has been invasive. I'm making one last attempt with white-flowered *Passiflora caerulea* 'Constance Eliott', incarcerated in a sunken plastic container thickly lined with newspapers to retain moisture and prevent escape through the drainage holes. This method has worked well with such other desirable but invasive plants as blue lyme grass (*Leymus arenarius*) and *Sasa veitchii*. I'm keeping a watchful eye on the herbaceous golden hop (*Humulus lupulus* 'Aureus'; Zone 5), being careful where I put *Lathyrus latifolius*, which is a mite too generous with its seedlings, though invaluable for the way it goes on flowering from early summer to winter, and struggling to be rid of sweet autumn clematis (*Clematis terniflora*; Zone 7), with seeds which, molelike, hit the ground burrowing and are down 2 feet before one notices, usually in the middle of a shrub or clump of perennials, where they can't be easily removed.

The following vines, more or less in order of bloom, have been my star performers.

Clematis armandii

This beautiful evergreen clematis is only just hardy in Zone 7 and a run of harsh winters killed the first one I planted. I estimate that I gain a zone of hardiness along The Avenue, where evergreen juniper branches give overhead protection, so that is where the next one went. After 5 years it formed a topknot on its decapitated tree, high overhead where I might have passed by its April blossoming had not its fragrance captured my attention. Unable now to go higher, *Clematis armandii* (Zone 7) is cascading down and will, I hope, be a white waterfall in a few more years. I shall think about pruning if, or when, it reaches and flows over the ground; meantime it needs none.

If I'm lucky, the bare lower sinews of my clematis will be clothed by one of two self-sowing, temporary vines: spurred butterfly pea (*Centrosema virginianum*) and mountain fringe (*Adlumia fungosa*). Both of these vines alight here off and on, though their preferences in the wild are of different orders: spurred butterfly pea usually chooses sun and sand, while mountain fringe opts for moist, leaf-littered soil in partial shade. *Centrosema virginianum* (Zone 6) is a small, finely wrought, local native with sprawling or climbing thread-fine stems, small trifoliate leaves, and masses of beautiful, oyster-shaped violet-blue flowers. It is so lightweight that it can climb a grass stem without causing it to collapse. This gem I never planted; it just came and stayed, changing its location by seed from time to time, never in excess. *Adlumia fungosa* is an elegant, biennial, lightweight vine that is always here and there around the garden, fending for itself. Related to bleeding heart (*Dicentra*), it is attractive not for its small, blush-pink, narrowly heart-shaped flowers, but for the delicacy of its thalictrum-like leaves that are widely spaced along threadlike vining stems. Capable of climbing 20 feet, *A. fungosa* more often tosses featherweight shawls of foliage over nearby shrubs. So minimal is its root and so light the grip of its leafy tendrils that one effortless pull removes an armful from anywhere it is not wanted.

Gelsemium sempervirens
CAROLINA JESSAMINE

To the sun-loving Carolina jessamine (*Gelsemium sempervirens*; Zone 7) I can give unstinted praise. Often seen spangling groves of the native bayberry, *Myrica cerifera* (Zone 7), with its bright yellow stars, its slender, twining stems prefer twigs to trunks and do not throttle small trees, as wisteria and Japanese honeysuckle (*Lonicera japonica*) do. Second only to *Clematis armandii* in coming into bloom, it continues from early April well into May. Seedlings are manageably few here at its northernmost outpost. Further south the double-flowered *G. sempervirens* 'Pride of August' might be a safer choice.

Gelsemium sempervirens (Carolina jessamine)

The twin stays of a telephone pole provide support for Carolina jessamine, the main stems twining up them, side stems curtaining down. To prevent this vigorous vine from reaching and tangling into the telephone and electric wires, I cut its main stems once a year, as high up as folding steps enable me to reach (there's nothing on which to lean a ladder). The double form, *Gelsemium sempervirens* 'Pride of Augusta', twines through the rabbit-proofing chicken wire to swathe a low post and rail boundary fence. With its height thus limited it cascades down, and stems trail out for as much as 12 feet in a season. The only maintenance called for is a couple of hours spent cutting off those trailing stems each autumn before they root into the ground.

Carolina jessamine blooms only once each year, so, pleased though I have been with it, the rarer *Gelsemium rankinii* (Zone 7), a more recent addition to my garden, is even better because it repeat blooms in autumn. In the wild it scrambles high up into the sun from a root-shaded place. My plants have not seemed to suffer from full sun.

Lonicera sempervirens

TRUMPET HONEYSUCKLE,
SCARLET HONEYSUCKLE

More years ago than I can now remember I took a cutting of scarlet honeysuckle (*Lonicera sempervirens*; Zone 4) from a plant growing wild in a nearby copse. Name notwithstanding (*sempervirens* is Latin for "evergreen"), this vine is not evergreen, though it may retain a few of its leaves in mild winters, and although I took it from a woods, it prefers sun for at least half the day. Shortly afterward I bought *L. sempervirens* 'Magnifica', with larger flowers and larger scarlet berries. Introduced half a century ago, this selection can still hold its own with the several more recent introductions. It and the species are twining vines that become semi-bushy when cut back to about 4 feet. Both grow on the same post and rail fence. One (with sun from the south blocked by bushes) flowers toward the north for the enjoyment of passers by, and the other toward the south as background for perennials in a hot color border. The main display comes in May, with a smattering of flowers through summer, along with scarlet berries. The splendid performance of these two honeysuckles encouraged me to add the light yellow *L. sempervirens* 'John Clayton', which originated in a local Virginia wood, and the orange-flowered hybrid *L.* ×*brownii* 'Dropmore Scarlet' (Zone 3; *L. sempervirens* × *L. hirsuta*) with orange flowers. There has been an occasional early-spring aphid infestation, but otherwise no problems. Lack of fragrance is my only criticism.

Lonicera ×*heckrottii*

GOLD FLAME HONEYSUCKLE

Provided its inapt name doesn't lead one to expect flowers of pyrotechnic color when the overall effect is pink, this honeysuckle will not disappoint. Whether *Lonicera* ×*heckrottii* (Zone 5) is fragrant is open to debate. I can detect no scent at all, but others say that they can. Frustrating its natural tendency to vine, I grow it as a mound at the front of a border. It is cut back almost to the base in early spring, then vining stems growing forward or sideways are repeatedly cut back, and those growing backward are tucked among the vigorous spreading branches of *Rosa* 'Carefree Delight' growing behind. The colors of the two plants, on the coral side of pink, are a nice match.

Lonicera ×*heckrottii* (gold flame honeysuckle) with vining stems kept cut back

Rubus rosifolius 'Coronarius'

CLIMBING RASPBERRY

Like climbing roses, climbing raspberry (*Rubus rosifolius* 'Coronarius'; Zone 7) makes long, vining stems that lack the means to support themselves. For years I grew it as a bush, lingering to admire it every spring, then spending a good deal of time removing youngsters sent far out on rhizomatous roots among the perennials sharing its bed, frequently getting my legs scratched when one found me before I found it. Finally, fed up with this vexation, I moved it to The Avenue, attaching it with Adj-A-Tye to one of the sunnier decapitated red cedar trunks, where, with a mulch path alongside, I spot the venturesome offspring while they are small. Big or small, they pull out easily, nicely rooted and ready for potting up. In this site my climbing raspberry has found its plant heaven. Old, dead stems are cut out during the post-bloom period and new ones fastened in. By flowering time in early May, it is an 8-foot pillar of green-eyed, white double flowers that could be mistaken (and often are) for a 'Mme. Hardy' rose, set off against dense, glossy green foliage. Nowhere have I seen it looking better.

Schizophragma hydrangeoides 'Moonlight'

CLIMBING HYDRANGEA

Of the five kinds of climbing hydrangea I grow, the most decorative is *Schizophragma hydrangeoides* 'Moonlight' (Zone 7). The other four, all good self-clinging vines, are *Hydrangea anomala* subsp. *petiolaris* (Zone 4), *Decumaria barbara* (Zone 5), *Schizophragma integrifolia* (Zone 6), and *S. hydrangeoides* 'Brookside Little Leaf' (Zone 7). Planted in 1988, 'Moonlight' has scaled a 30-foot red cedar and formed a dense, ground-covering pool around its bole. Having waited several years before blooming for the first time, it is now reliably generous. Each inflorescence consists of a plate of tiny sterile flowers with heart-shaped ivory bracts hung out like flags around the rim. In this it resembles the species; it is the leaves that distinguish 'Moonlight'. About 4 inches across, heart-shaped, and saw-edged, they are pewter gray with dark green veining, producing a silvery effect.

Like ivies, climbing hydrangeas prefer to head upward. If thwarted in this, they trail along the ground until they find something to climb. Had 'Moonlight' not had a tall tree to climb, it would have gone sideways instead, as

LEFT *Rubus rosifolius* 'Coronarius'

Schizophragma hydrangeoides 'Moonlight'

Parthenocissus tricuspidata 'Fenway' (a golden leaved Boston Ivy)

Hydrangea anomala subsp. *petiolaris* has done on the north-facing front house wall. Halted by pruning at the 5-foot window level, the hydrangea has completely covered the 36-foot width of the wall in its quarter century there.

Parthenocissus

Boston ivies (*Parthenocissus tricuspidata*; Zone 4) and their ilk clinging to wall, fence, or tree include the quaint, incised, and crinkled *Parthenocissus tricuspidata* 'Lowii', lime-green *P. tricuspidata* 'Fenway', which would be a brighter yellow in full sun if it didn't scorch, and the unusual Texan *P. heptaphylla* (Zone 7), with seven shiny leaflets. Best of the lot is *P. henryana* (Zone 7), with five sooty-green, silvery-veined leaflets. One cascades over a 6-foot topless juniper trunk; another

Parthenocissus henryana on a decapitated red cedar

mingles with *Hydrangea anomala* subsp. *petiolaris* on the front of the house. Sometimes the leaves turn dark crimson in autumn and sometimes they don't. Either way Boston ivies more than earn their places in the garden with comely foliage from April through October.

Trachelospermum

Twice I lost the evergreen Confederate jasmine (*Trachelospermum jasminoides*; Zone 7) in harsh winters. Then along came *T. jasminoides* 'Madison', said to be hardier, and so it has proved. I have it on the front fence, where, with light blocked by other plants in the border inside the fence, it flowers on the outside, notwithstanding that it faces north and gets scarcely a glimmer of sun. Encouraged by its performance, I have planted a variegated form on one of the trees down The Avenue, where it gets overhead protection.

The small-leafed *Trachelospermum asiaticum* (Zone 7) I grew for years as a ground cover, with nary a flower, learning at least that it is hardy before deciding that it lacks ornamental merit sufficient to justify the many hours spent preventing the vigorous, wiry stems from wandering off among the bushes. *Trachelospermum asiaticum* 'Variegatum' is, however, delicately pretty, along the lines of a variegated periwinkle (*Vinca minor*). At first I grew it on the ground. It is now slowly climbing a tree. Strapped at first against the trunk, it now has a tentative grip. How these trachelospermums manage in the wild puzzles me. Though I see them described as twining vines, I have yet to see the slightest indication of twining in any I have grown. The Confederate jasmine weaves its way through plastic deer fencing, but does not twine. *Trachelospermum asiaticum* 'Variegatum' has developed a few rudimentary aerial roots where it tucks its stems under platelets of bark on the tree trunk, again without the slightest sign of twining, not even around its own stems, as most twiners so readily do.

Clematis

Clematis armandii flowered in April. Most of my other clematis bloom in May and June. This genus has delighted and exasperated me in about equal measure. From an initial three plants (C. 'Ramona', C. 'Henryi', and C. *lanuginosa* 'Candida'; Zone 5), numerous seedlings have appeared, romping around among azaleas in unimproved, acid sand (forget the supposed marriage vows between clematis and lime), with an annual mulch applied by the falling needles of loblolly pines (*Pinus taeda*) overhead. As many more, planted in lovingly prepared beds of humus-rich soil, have languished or died. What matters most to clematis, I have concluded, is that water should regularly pass by without lingering. In a region where rain frequently comes as a deluge, I now amend the soil for clematis with bark fines (flakes of pine tree bark), Turface granules (calcined clay), or crushed oyster shell, rather than compost or peat moss.

Long ago I learned, in the garden of a great plantsman friend, the late John Treasure, how beguiling clematis can be growing through shrubs and ground covers and I grow most of mine this way. As well as suiting my laissez-faire style, this method has practical advantages: it resolves the dilemma of when and how to prune (I cut off in autumn or winter any stems straggling untidily out); it safeguards vulnerable basal stems from being kinked or snapped by clumsy feet; and it keeps to a minimum the need to train in young stems before they twist together in a tangled skein impossible to unravel without snapping them.

Because they do not get big enough to overwhelm their host shrub, I prefer clematis, both large-flowered and small, that either die to the ground in winter or can be cut hard back. *Clematis* 'Etoile Violette' finds ample support on the willowy stems of a Lady Bankes rose (*Rosa banksiae* 'Lutea'; Zone 7). One *C. texensis*

Clematis 'Etoile Violette' on the Lady Bankes rose, *Rosa banksiae* 'Lutea'

Clematis 'Blue Boy' with *Lagerstroemia fauriei* and *Chamaecyparis pisifera* 'Filifera Aurea' (goldthread cypress) in background

'Gravetye Beauty' (Zone 4), with crimson flowers the shape of a lily-flowered tulip, mingles with a honeysuckle on a rebar tripod; a second rambles through *Viburnum ×juddii*. Another tripod supports C. 'Blue Boy' (Zone 3), with plentiful, campanulate flowers of violet-blue. This C. *viticella* × C. *integrifolia* hybrid makes only an infrequent, half-hearted

effort to cling and has to be tied in at intervals between April and June, by which time it has attained 8 feet. Although raffia seems to be out of fashion nowadays, I still use it for fastening clematis to their supports: it is inconspicuous, has a certain amount of give in it, and single strands pull easily from the hank hanging on a nail in the shed. While this repeated tying in

may sound tedious, it is a less pressing task than dealing with plants that so quickly form a tangle, and much more quickly done, taking only a minute or two each time at weekly intervals, or thereabouts.

Clematis ×durandii (Zone 5; C. *integrifolia* × C. *×jackmanii*) inherited inability to climb from one parent and larger flowers from the other. It outdoes both in the intense violet-blue of 4- to 5-inch flowers with ribbed, wavy, and slightly reflexed sepals and is the only clematis I can count on to offer flowers, a few at a time, steadily through summer. Where winters are milder, old stems sometimes live over and, if not cut back, extend to 8 feet or more. In my garden this clematis dies to the ground in winter and the season's 4-foot stems sprawl pleasingly over a mound of curly leaved ivy, needing only a little early guidance to prevent them tangling together.

My biggest clematis triumph, or stroke of luck, is with *Clematis florida* 'Sieboldii' (Zone 6; synonym C. 'Sieboldiana'), which wends its way through *Viburnum ×burkwoodii* 'Mohawk'. Considered a miffy, somewhat tender clematis in England, in the 6 years I have had it, it has survived repeated drops to 15°F and occasional plunges to 0°F. Winter wet and lack of summer warmth rather than low temperature are apparently its undoing in England. It dies to the ground in winter and once dismayed me by wilting and dying in summer, only to make a quick comeback. In Virginia its bloom does not continue all summer, as it is said to do in England, but only for about a month. The purple, chrysanthemum-like center holds for a week or so after the fall of the outer ring of creamy white sepals.

Some years earlier a one-year old plant of *Clematis florida* 'Sieboldii' perished in its first winter. Many clematis are sold with insufficiently developed roots. The surviving plant came bare-root in March, well swaddled and moist, with roots extensive enough to need a 2-gallon container, which I filled three-quarters of the way with potting soil to which sand had been added. It was held in a cold frame for a year, then planted out following a method I often use in the struggle to ward off voles.

This method of planting takes a bit of practice, and the plant must be well established in the container. The hole is dug first, generously deep, keeping a pile of the excavated soil alongside. The container is then laid on its side at the edge of the hole and the bottom cut out with scissors. The rest of the container, with the plant, is eased into the hole with one hand

Clematis florida 'Sieboldii' (left) on *Viburnum ×burkwoodii* 'Mohawk', with *Tanacetum niveum* in foreground

while I push soil under it with the other hand to get the level right. I leave an inch or so of the rim above ground, fill in around the bottomless container with soil, and top off the container with gravel before watering thoroughly in and around it. For the first year water is poured directly into the container during dry spells, after which I assume that the roots have grown far enough down and out to get the benefit of water broadcast from sprinklers.

EARLY SPRING PERENNIALS

Bulbs and woodland flowers come first on the garden's agenda, then flowering trees and shrubs followed by sunbathing perennials. Not all plants fit the mold, however. Some perennials upstage the competition by flowering very early—in late March and April.

Trachystemon orientalis

Trachystemon orientalis (Zone 4) belongs to a family notable for bright blue flowers, the borages. Little grown and little known, if it is ever to be a commercial success this species needs a catchier name. A translation of the Greek name, "rough stamen," scarcely helps the plant's cause. I propose blue-shuttlecocks, descriptive of the galaxies of little flowers. Blue buds cuddled down near the ground can usually be seen by mid-March, rising on branched 18-inch stems to flower by Easter time. The heart-shaped leaves with scalloped rims start to appear at the same time, becoming large and raspingly rough. Spread, while easily controllable, is rapid enough for ground cover purposes. Were it a fussy plant or a competitor for attention in May's big display, it would just be an also-ran. Early bloom and ruggedness in dry shade boost its marks considerably. It needs no maintenance unless, for the sake of tidiness, dead stems are removed after flowering and dead leaves in late autumn.

Symphytum ibericum
COMFREY

Symphytum ibericum (Zone 4; synonym *S. grandiflorum*), another member of the borage family, is my ground cover of last resort for difficult dry shade. For once I embrace a name change, because its former name "grandiflorum" (large flowers) overstates the creamy, inch-long nodding tubes that start to open in late winter or early spring, continuing for close to 2 months. Though small, the flowers are very prettily packaged and, coming so early, there's time for a leisurely look instead of the passing glance they might get in the big spring rush. What at first seems a small knob of twenty or so little pink buds glistening with silky hairs is actually a crosier, reminiscent of snail shells or curled up cats, with many more buds hidden until it unfurls.

In the size and shape of its green leaves this comfrey resembles lungwort (*Pulmonaria*), also in the borage family, and in North America it circulated for years as *Pulmonaria lutea*. For me it has been evergreen. It spreads quite fast but is much easier to control than such ground covers as ivy, periwinkle, and pachysandra.

Symphytum ibericum 'Hidcote Pink' and 'Hidcote Blue', the pink and blue little more than a hint, are taller at 12 to 18 inches. *Symphytum ibericum* 'Goldsmith', with creamy edges to its leaves, has been a repeated disappointment, seeming to need moister, richer soil, and perhaps a cooler climate than I can offer.

Pulmonaria
LUNGWORT

Most lungworts (Zone 4) decorate their patch of earth for two-thirds of the year, first with flowers, then with foliage. It is easy to tell if you are pleasing them because then they seed around. They do so for me only in one place, a bed facing north with good soil and good light but little direct sun. *Omphalodes cappadocica* 'Starry Eyes' (Zone 6), another Easter flower, also flourishes only in this spot. Suited here also are *Ligularia tussilaginea*, *Ardisia japonica* (which can become invasive; Zone 7), *Dicentra eximia*, *Athyrium niponicum* 'Pictum',

Trachystemon orientalis

Carex phyllocephala 'Sparkler', milky white *Campanula poscharskyana* 'E. H. Frost' (Zone 3), epimediums, ferns, and *Begonia grandiflora*. Hostas, by their puniness, declared the site too dry.

Where several kinds of lungworts are gathered together many seedlings will be hybrids. Wise gardeners discard all but the best—a counsel of perfection to which I adhere too seldom. I will not name names because I like so many: leaves broad or narrow, green, pewter-spotted, or almost entirely silver; flowers white, pink, pale or deep blue, or pink and blue combined. Some lungworts have been selected for mildew-resistance, which is more a consideration in England or the Pacific Northwest than in the American Southeast, where mildew seldom occurs on lungworts.

Iberis sempervirens
EVERGREEN CANDYTUFT

"March," goes the old saying, "comes in like a lion and goes out like a lamb." In Virginia it does the opposite as often as not, coming in with shorts and T-shirt days, and going out with frost or ice storm. Candytuft (*Iberis sempervirens*; Zone 4) blooms anyway, often beginning before the snowdrops have gone. It is among my garden's oldest inhabitants and it is faultless. While many other plants have come and gone or become decrepit, candytuft seems likely to outlive me. Its weed-resistant evergreen foliage, long life, ease of propagation, and tolerance for poor soil and blazing sun endear it to the thrifty, the neat, and the novice, and its minimal need for the simplest kind of maintenance commends it to those who lack time, energy, or inclination for much gardening. My oldest patch cost nothing, having started life as cuttings from a friend's garden. Left untended most of the time, it drapes the edge of a slightly raised bed, where laxness doesn't matter. A handful or two of 10–10–10 fertilizer may be tossed its way once in a while,

Iberis sempervirens 'Snowflake' (evergreen candytuft) with blue-flowered *Veronica peduncularis* 'Georgia Blue'

but sun and well-drained soil seem to be the only essentials.

Good as this species is, newer forms are better. The old stalwart, sheared or not, offers only one crop of milky white flowers. Some newer forms bloom twice, sometimes three times, if sheared after each flush. Flowers may be brighter white or fuller in form, the foliage may be a fresher green, and there are sizes to suit both border and rock garden. Among those of border size, my best to date is *Iberis sempervirens* 'Snowflake'. Flowers like scattered flakes of snow are strewn over the spreading mounds sporadically through mild winters. 'Christmas Snow' is another name for this form, but don't expect a heavy fall for Yule, for that one must wait until early spring. As the year warms up, small snowballs of bloom, as close-packed yet distinctly round as apples in a barrel, jostle each other in patches of pure white, or so a cursory glance suggests. A closer look reveals slight speckling from green buds and yellow eyes. Wandering strands of *Veronica peduncularis* 'Georgia Blue' have intermingled with the candytuft in a combination that brings to mind ski slopes under blue skies. Early spring, before the weather gets really hot, is a good time to root cuttings in situ under jelly jars or transparent picnic cups, but there's much to be done at this time of year and early autumn will do as well.

Arabis procurrens

Candytuft (*Iberis sempervirens*) is the bright white color our grandmothers tried to achieve for linens by dipping a blue-bag into the rinse water. So is *Arabis procurrens* (Zone 4), the best of its genus by far for hot summer regions. By Easter its foam of small white flowers on slender 6-inch-long stems obscures the tiny bright green leaves plastered so densely against the ground that no earth shows. It wants soil neither sopping nor parched and prefers light shade, but rots if left buried under fallen leaves. Care consists of little more than shaving off the brown whiskery stems when the flowers have faded.

Strangely, the English *RHS Plant Finder* lists no source for *Arabis procurrens*, yet several for *A. procurrens* 'Variegata', for which I can find no source in North America. An exchange seems to be called for. *Arabis sturii* is similar to *A. procurrens*, but on a smaller scale, with fewer flowers on shorter stems.

Arabis procurrens makes an excellent ground cover over little bulbs and other plants. Up through the green carpet comes double bloodroot (*Sanguinaria canadensis* 'Plena'; Zone 3), which draws awed gasps from visitors who see it. Few do. Blooming for less than a week, and notwithstanding its attractive leaves, its claim to space is dependent upon sharing it with something else. *Mazus reptans* (Zone 3), prostrate and creeping, with flowers of white or lavender, is another first-rate counterpane for the bloodroot's bed and for *Arisaema candidissimum* (Zone 6), the charming, 1-foot high *Lathyrus vernus* (Zone 4), and such small, early bulbs as snowdrops. Stepping on the piquantly aromatic *Mentha requienii* (Zone 8) momentarily assuages the ennui of a sultry day, but I cannot claim long-term success and must replace it frequently.

My two best flat-growing creepers for bulb cover in sunnier places are *Linaria aequitriloba* (Zone 7; synonym *Cymbalaria aequitriloba*) here these past 20 years, and the less reliable *Pratia pedunculata* (milder parts of Zone 7), which has come and gone three times over the same time span.

Veronica peduncularis 'Georgia Blue'

This instant winner among newcomers was named for the former Soviet Georgia, where Roy Lancaster collected it. A shag carpet of wiry stems clad in tiny, evergreen leaves, *Veronica peduncularis* 'Georgia Blue' (Zone 6) sheets itself through the first weeks of spring with small flowers of as brilliant a blue as any gentian, and can one say more that that? This vigorous carpeter prefers full sun, but light shade is acceptable. Spread is dense and speedy, and propagation is fail-proof by means of cuttings, rooted layers, or simply slicing out sections with a sharp spade for transplanting elsewhere.

Lamium maculatum

SPOTTED DEAD-NETTLE

The dividing line between a useful ground cover and an invasive nuisance lies mainly in the ease with which excess can be removed. Spotted dead-nettle (*Lamium maculatum*;

Lamium maculatum (dead-nettle) at right with *Dentaria maxima* (toothwort) at left

Zone 4) is as easily pulled out as the related henbit (*Lamium amplexicaule*) that turns fields pink in early spring, and a great deal more ornamental, continuing to flower from late winter through most of spring and sometimes into summer in any shady or partially sunny site that doesn't become arid or waterlogged. The popular name is a poor one: the leaves are not spotted but have a clean white central stripe. One patch of the purple-flowered species makes an echo combination under *Daphne genkwa*, while Japanese painted fern (*Athyrium niponicum* 'Pictum') thrusts up through a carpet of pink-flowered *L. maculatum* 'Shell Pink' (synonym 'Roseum'), carpeting the ground around azaleas. These are the most reliable and long-lived of my dead-nettles, and the first to come into bloom.

Primula ×variabilis (cowslip primrose)

into silvery quilts that brighten the garden through winter. Of the gold-leaved forms, *L. maculatum* 'Aureum' has pink flowers, a combination I personally dislike, and white-flowered 'Beedham's White' is less robust, requiring shade and moderately moist soil.

Primula ×variabilis

COWSLIP PRIMROSE

For so long as memory brings glimpses of the English woods and hedgerows of my childhood, primroses will be for me the epitome of spring. There is a touch of sadness in this nostalgia. Half a century ago it was safe for me to wander alone in the lanes and woods several miles from home, returning with bunches of primroses, violets, or bluebells. How many parents dare grant that freedom to the children of today?

Given afternoon shade and provided I don't neglect to divide it every second year, the primrose of my childhood (*Primula vulgaris*; Zone 5), along with Barnhaven hybrids, does quite well in Virginia, though it definitely prefers cooler summers and heavier soils. The stoloniferous *P. kisoana* (Zone 5), with flowers of magenta, pink, or white, likes the same conditions as rhododendrons, and the cowslip (*P. veris*) and Japanese candelabra primrose (*P.*

There are umpteen named forms of deadnettle with silvery, gold, or variegated foliage. Most of them are fairly easy to grow in lightly shaded sites, though apt to die out periodically for no apparent reason. The oldest of the silver-leaved forms, *Lamium maculatum* 'Beacon Silver', frequently develops a purple mottling that disfigures the leaves. Grow instead 'Red Nancy' or my own 'Silver Surprise' (which arose as a sport on 'White Nancy'), both with similar lavender purple flowers. These two, along with such other silver-leaved forms as 'White Nancy' and delicate pink 'Pink Pewter', benefit from shearing in late summer, when they've begun to look sprawlingly thin and sorry for themselves. Then they thicken up

japonica; Zone 5) both thrive in a wettish, lightly shaded part of my garden, along with the astilbes that do well in this one spot and nowhere else.

But by far the most tolerant of heat and humidity, though I don't understand why given its origin, is the cowslip primrose or false-oxlip (*Primula ×variabilis*; Zone 5). This hybrid between the primrose and the cowslip is, say wildflower books, an English wildling found where primroses and cowslips grow together, yet I had to come to Virginia to see it, having never seen it in an English garden nor mentioned in an English gardening book. The friend who gave it to me a quarter century ago called it grandmother's primrose, so it must have been handed down through several generations. Each 1-foot stalk carries a dozen or more inch-wide, up-facing flowers of lemon yellow with a deeper yellow eye, well spaced on 2-inch petioles. Stalks, petioles, and calyces are fuzzy, and the whole plant has a downy look. This hybrid, like its parents, continues to flower for at least a month.

Primroses and cowslips were used in breeding the gaudy hybrids sold as polyanthus in garden centers and seed catalogs. Excellent though these are as colorful, short-lived bedding plants, they lack the charm of the hybrid nature created. Other graceful, rugged forms can occasionally be found. Most lack names. One with flowers of grayed purple-red was recently named 'Dale Henderson', honoring the Virginia gardener who has been so generous in passing it along, and it is now available from a mail-order nursery. At Montrose Gardens in Hillsborough, North Carolina, Nancy Goodwin raises hybrids with the charm of the wilding. These are sometimes available for purchase by those able to visit on the garden's open days.

Woodsy soil, moist in winter and spring, filtered or afternoon shade, and frequent division give a long lease of life to cowslip primroses. If they choose to retreat from summer heat and drought by going dormant, don't try to circumvent this by watering them; they can take care of themselves and will be back by spring.

Verbena

Whatever species (debatable, but I think *Verbena canadensis*) lays claim to *Verbena* 'Snow Flurry' (Zone 5) can be proud of its child. Its stamina, heat tolerance, extended bloom time, and year-round good looks when winter is not severe put it among the cream of perennials. On few days of the year is it without a flower or two, with the most abundant bloom coming in midspring and a pause sometimes coming in midsummer. It sows around, and most seedlings resemble the parent. Look closely and one sees that verbena flowers come in spikes, though utterly unlike the rodlike inflorescences of liatris and kniphofia. I counted twenty open florets in a single domed cluster, with close to a hundred unopened buds, ensuring a week of bloom, while new buds continue to develop down the 18-inch stems, complemented by small, bright green leaves with jagged edges.

Norman Beal has introduced some good selections of *Verbena canadensis*, including 15-inch pastel-lavender 'Lilac Time', and two lower, spreading forms—violet-blue 'Blue Mist' and lavender 'Greystone Daphne' (the scent reminiscent of daphnes). Where several plants are grown, seedlings and sports varying in color occur quite frequently. One of mine is pink; another a low and spreading white. I like them all so much that I have to be firm with myself about removing those that come up outside their designated quarters, as they readily do. The best time to do this is when I'm going round the garden with visitors, plastic bags in pocket, and can shove extras instantly into usually eager hands.

Verbena 'Snow Flurry' with *Yucca filamentosa* 'Variegata' at right

The only other verbenas that have been long-term hardy for me are the vigorous, trailing, violet-purple 'Homestead Purple' and the similar 'Ultraviolet'. These two put on a splendid show from spring through fall but are not usually evergreen and become a deplorably untidy repository for fallen leaves through winter. An electric hedge saw makes short work of cutting away the tangled mess, but I'm reluctant to do this before spring lest the shorn plants become more vulnerable to winter freezes.

Epimedium

April in southeastern North America is paradisal, sunny and comfortable, a welcome respite between heating and air conditioning, with no need yet to drag hoses around. Ground bare a month ago is now lush with the foliage of emerging perennials, and most shrubs and trees are leafing out, with crape myrtles (*Lagerstroemia*), fringe trees (*Chionanthus*), and clethras among the laggards. Like Eden, April has its serpents: in the shower, fingers smoothing flesh silky with soap detect the unevenness of the first tick of the season, aphids on a honeysuckle portend battles to come, clouds of pollen from the pines make the lives of the allergic miserable, and baby rabbits, not yet knowing what is or isn't good to eat, are sampling everything they can get at. Still, all in all it is one of the nicest months of the year and one of the busiest, with little time to accomplish all the cleaning up, pruning, placing new plants, and re-arranging old ones before it is too late. For epimediums it is already too late to use shears or hedge clippers to remove old wiry stems. This pruning must be accomplished by the middle of March. I always overlook a few, and then the old leaves must be cut out one by one with scissors if the flowers on their tender stalks are not to be injured.

Choosing epimediums (Zone 5 generally; evergreens top-killed below Zone 7) used to be easy, when so few were offered. Now there is a greatly expanded list from specialist growers. I'm barely acquainted with some of the newcomers to my garden, so I'll confine my comments to the tried and true, all pretty enough and easy enough to infuse enthusiasm for the genus, varying from vigorous spreaders to compact clumps.

Epimedium pinnatum subsp. *colchicum* and *E. ×perralchicum* 'Fröhnleiten' are so similar I would rather not be asked to identify them in any garden but my own. Evergreen and vigorously spreading, they have comparatively large, bright yellow flowers.

Epimedium ×versicolor 'Sulphureum', with smaller flowers of paler yellow, is another vigorous spreader. The leaves are winter-killed, as are those of *E. ×warleyense*, with flame-colored flowers on upright wiry stems. Compared with the latter, *E. ×cantabrigiense* is a drab thing.

Epimedium ×youngianum 'Niveum' is a dainty, white-flowered clump-former. *Epimedium grandiflorum* 'Rose Queen', 'White Queen', and medium-purple 'Lilafee' have larger flowers on slowly spreading clumps. All have dead or very shabby foliage by the end of winter.

Although epimediums put up with dry shade, "put up with" are the operative words; the plants do much better when given reasonably moist, humus-rich soil in a lightly shaded site. Whether the species is evergreen or deciduous, I cut off the old leaves to better display the flowers, the only difference being in the timing—so long as foliage remains decorative, it is left, once shabby, it is cut off.

Ajuga

BUGLEWEED, CARPET BUGLE

Blue flowers abound in early spring. As April progresses and ipheion fades, grape hyacinths and wood anemones linger, joined by *Ajuga reptans* (Zone 3) in sites where the soil stays moderately moist and there is respite from sun during some of the hottest hours. *Ajuga reptans* spreads by surface runners—ground troops—not the stealthy submarine warfare so much harder to control. Admittedly, it calls for patient hand weeding if it infiltrates a lawn. I don't have a lawn. I grow the blue-flowered species, along with white ones that appeared spontaneously, in a narrow north-facing bed between the house and the gravel drive, interplanted with mint for cooking (set a thief to catch a thief!). Car wheels keep both from spreading far, and the ajuga keeps the ground green when the mint is dormant in winter.

Ajuga reptans 'Catlin's Giant' has much larger, smoothly glossy bronze leaves and massive (for an ajuga) violet-blue spikes. Its tide of blue surges around trees and shrubs without bothering them in the least and if—I mean when—the flood threatens to submerge smaller outlying plants, the ajuga gives up its terrain so easily that an hour's work sees a barrow filled and control regained, a quicker and less fiddly job than removing the assorted weeds so quick to take up residence in any bare ground.

Ajuga reptans 'Purple Brocade' is a better dark-leaved choice for tighter quarters. I grew it for years before displaying it well. Low-growing plants with purple foliage do not show well against brown earth or mulch. Now it shines on the shady side of a bed topped with golden gravel, with some good rich soil dug into its hole. The rounded, frilly-edged, dark-burgundy leaves have a puckered surface resembling that of spinach leaves. It is as a foliage plant that 'Purple Brocade' excels, the typical blue flowers of spring being a bonus.

Long-term success has eluded me with pink-flowered forms and all those with variegated foliage. *Ajuga reptans* 'Burgundy Glow', replaced repeatedly, may stay for 3 or 4 years, and other variegated forms even less. With a

Phlox subulata 'Candy Stripe'

little effort I keep two tiny kinds of ajuga sized for the rock garden. Controversy and confusion surround their names, and while botanists debate to which species these two belong, gardeners and nurseries have dodged the issue by inventing the names 'Green Crispa' (alias 'Minicrisp Green' and 'Metallica Crispa') and 'Purple Crispa' (alias 'Minicrisp Purple' and 'Rubra Contorta'). Though identical in size, crinkled congested foliage, and the bright blue flowers that barely surmount the leaf pads, they are distinct in foliage color. The first is dark green with a strange metallic sheen, and the second purplish brown.

Phlox

Were it not that rabbits repeatedly shave them, the woodland phloxes, *Phlox divaricata* (Zone 3) and similar but shorter *P. stolonifera* (Zone 4) both of which appear from late April to late May, would rank high. As it is, I forego the drifts I'd like to have and scatter them in lightly shaded places in hopes that some will be overlooked. The hot-pepper spray that deters rabbits and deer must be reapplied after rain, which is costly in both time and money, so only a few special plants get this attention. One of them is *P. divaricata* 'Montrose Tricolor', Nancy Goodwin's find and gift, with blue flowers set off by foliage variegated in white with a touch of pink. Because it has never yet been rabbit-razed, *P. pulchra* (Zone 6) is a better bet for me. This thoroughly good plant is semi-evergreen in a site out of hot afternoon sun, where it grows through *Sedum lineare* 'Variegatum'.

Gardeners in hot and humid regions cannot aspire to thyme lawns, which rot out patchily in summer. They can, however, create small lawns of the sand phlox, *Phlox subulata* and its hybrids, which also make good ground cover on sunny banks and berms. A good many selections of sand phlox have come and gone in my garden, killed by kindness. They liked the sandy, acid soil through which water percolated quickly. Manure, compost, and mulch are anathema to them. They are not alone in this, achilleas and *Gaura lindheimeri* also have spurned mollycoddling and had to have sand dug back into their compost-enriched sites. Should I have left well enough alone? No. For every plant discouraged there are many I can now grow that I could not before.

Being sheared after it has flowered benefits sand phlox. Umpteen selections and hybrids can be had. Some of the best were introduced by the late Linc Foster and bear the name of his Connecticut garden, Millstream: 'Millstream Jupiter', a somewhat straggly grower, is the best blue, 'Millstream Laura' is a delicate blush pink, and 'Millstream Daphne' a bright reddish pink. The most popular sand phlox is probably the pink- and white-striped *Phlox subulata* 'Candy Stripe' (introduced in Tasmania as 'Tamanonagalei'). My most invincible is the pure white *P. subulata* 'White Delight', and my favorite is the small-flowered pale blue *P. subulata* 'Bluets'. Rising up through it is a clump of St. Bruno's lily (*Anthericum liliago*), a self-sustaining plant falling short of stardom only by reason of its rather brief bloom period. Spires of starry white flowers dance lightly on 2-foot wiry stems over a clump of slender, grassy leaves.

Lunaria annua 'Stella'

MONEY PLANT

One very lovely spring bloomer of three-season appeal is the biennial money plant (*Lu-*

Lunaria annua 'Stella'

Potentilla rupestris growing over *Yucca filamentosa* 'Variegata'

ahead, to about 1 foot apart. Some self-sowing plants take care of their own thinning by survival of the fittest. With money plant every seedling is fit, and the winter effect is diminished when the seedlings crowd each other. The leaves of young seedlings don't have the white margins, which develop during the summer.

Potentilla rupestris

This denizen of both North America and Europe is an undervalued perennial and is hardy to Zone 5. Over large basal rosettes of pinnate leaves, evergreen in mild winters, rise branched, knee-high stems bearing plentiful white flowers and a few smaller, strawberry-like leaves. Stems and leaves glisten with downy hairs. Flowering starts about mid-April and continues for a month. Flower stems then need cutting off and that is the limit of maintenance.

Corydalis

The twenty or so species of *Corydalis* with which I am familiar barely touch the fringes of this big genus. My biggest disappointment has been the beautiful blue-flowered *C. flexuosa* selections, none of them deigning to grace my hot garden for more than a year or two. The biggest menace came as *C. incisa*, a name I

naria annua). The species has green leaves and purple flowers, *L. annua* 'Alba' has green leaves and white flowers, and *L. annua* 'Variegata' has purple flowers and leaves with creamy edges. *Lunaria annua* 'Stella' is the loveliest, with snowy white flowers in late April and early May, silver dollar seed discs in autumn, and large, flat rosettes of leaves with creamy white edges through winter. It has little ornamental value in summer, but enough must be left to ripen seed and self-sow. Neglect, however, to remove most of the seed stems before the seed falls (flower arrangers are eager recipients) and a spell of spring thinning lies

cannot find in reference books. I greeted its pink flowers and finely cut foliage with excitement in the first year, then cussed for the next two years before I finally rid myself of this pernicious weed. From the in-betweens, two favorites have emerged: *C. ochroleuca* (Zone 6) and *C. cheilanthifolia* (Zone 6).

The flowers of *Corydalis ochroleuca* form dense racemes of white, open-mouthed tubes with yellow tongues and flecks of green on the upper lip. The overall effect is a blend-in-anywhere creamy white over lacy foliage resembling that of Venus maidenhair fern (*Adiantum capillus-veneris*). Though a short-lived perennial, disappearing in winter, it always reappears in spring from self-sown seedlings that shoehorn themselves in among other plants in lightly shaded places neither arid nor wet. It takes no effort to pull out plants that appear where they are not wanted.

Corydalis cheilanthifolia self-sows so densely that, in its own interests, it needs to be thinned. When in bloom in April, it is a showy species, more densely clumping than most, with spirelike bright yellow inflorescences over winter-green frondlike leaves. If it didn't flower I'd still grow it, for the same reason I grow ferns, and in similar places.

Corydalis ochroleuca with *Hosta* 'Golden Tiara' in background

LATE SPRING PERENNIALS

In early May it is easy to wear rose-colored spectacles. Bugs haven't made much headway yet, and the soil is still moist from winter rains. Vegetation is lush, and bare earth that earlier cried out for bulbs is now rapidly disappearing. Bulbs planted in pots the previous autumn have been tucked into some such spots, as I find this easier than making notes about where I want to put them, as well as ensuring that the bulbs are what they purport to be, which cannot be relied upon.

Perennials now come thick and fast. Every day something new blooms—peonies, pinks, columbines, salvias, and irises galore. *Dianthus* 'Bath's Pink', a proven success if regularly sheared, is joined now by 'Bath's White', and both these pinks are challenged by the denser-growing 'Mountain Mist', with pink flowers and intensely silvery foliage. Blue-flowered *Aquilegia alpina* and the scarlet-and-yellow-flowered *A. canadensis* have been my most reliable columbines, but the leaves of all columbines are disfigured by leaf miner. Among the salvias, *Salvia nemorosa* 'Blauhugel' and 'Mainacht' are my best. The prostrate, semi-evergreen *Sedum kamtschaticum* 'Weihenstephaner Gold' kicks off a succession of sedums. Its brief golden gleam in sunny places is rivaled in part shade by the yellow stars of green-and-gold (*Chrysogonum virginianum*) thickly scattered over a carpet of green leaves. Later it will probably get mildew. *Geranium sanguineum* is invincible and sows around. I grow several other geraniums, but none match their performance in cooler regions. I prefer to seek out plants that like the heat, a resolve constantly tested by such tempting introductions as *G. pratense* 'Midnight Reiter', with leaves of darkest bitter chocolate brown.

Bearded irises (Zone 4) are ravishingly lovely in May if deadheaded daily. Otherwise they are sordid, becoming even more sordid when the leaves begin to wither and rot. I can forgive this flaw only in a couple of rebloomers, especially the snowy, fragrant 'Immortality'. Many other irises flourish: *Iris verna* (Zone 5) in sun and sand, *I. cristata* (Zone 3) in light shade and leafy soil, and *I. pallida* (Zone 4) and Pacific coast hybrids (variable hardiness) in any sunny place where water doesn't linger. Spuria irises (Zone 5) thrive in compost-enriched sandy loam and sun, and *I. graminea* (Zone 5) in shade, preferably not dry. A host of moisture-lovers grow in heavy, wettish soil, including *I. pseudacorus* (Zone 5), which is loveliest in its white and pale yellow forms; *I. virginica* (Zone 7); Louisiana hybrids (Zone 6); and Japanese irises (*I. ensata*; Zone 5).

Two of the most enchanting flowers miss my top rating only by reason of brevity of bloom, undistinguished foliage, call for daily deadheading, and the need for frequent reduction of girth and, not quite the same thing, occasional division. Both prosper in a good, dark loam not allowed to become dry. The first, *Iris setosa* var. *nasuensis* (probably Zone 5), came to me from iris apostle Roy Davidson. An iris of demeanor befitting its royal blood, Roy thought it to be a sterile triploid, possibly a hybrid with *I. laevigata*, found by Emperor Hirohito on Mt. Nasu. The flowers are a deep cerulean blue, leaning minimally towards violet, on 3- to 4-foot stems that rise above slightly arching strap-shaped leaves. If the leaves are no great asset thereafter, neither are they the eyesore that those of bearded irises become. The other lovely iris is *I. sibirica* 'Butter and Sugar' (Zone 4), which marries the sturdiness of its species with creamy yellow flowers of such spellbinding gauzy loveliness that daily deadheading during its all too brief 2 weeks of bloom is a pleasure, not a chore.

While denying myself none of these perennials, I set greatest store by those that have given an outstanding long-term account of themselves in one way or another, without making taxing maintenance demands. Given moderately fertile soil, these are long-lived, undemanding perennials, seldom needing dividing or fertilizing, resistant to most pests and diseases, surviving dry spells without wilting or withering, and needing neither staking nor deadheading.

Iris tectorum

JAPANESE ROOF IRIS

Despite the fierce competition in this genus, my best iris these past two decades is the Japanese roof iris (*Iris tectorum*; Zone 5). In the French garden of the late Yul Brynner I saw it growing along the ridge of a thatched roof. It will not grow on roofs in the heat of coastal Virginia, but little else deters it. Though tolerant of poor soil and full sun, it rewards moderate fertility and a tad of shade with taller stems and up to a month of bloom, which is a long time for an iris. The flowers may be blue or white, the blue ones with varying degrees of purple tiger-striping. The white form is enchanting. The "standards" and "falls" of iris terminology ill describe the six crinkly edged "petals" which, when the flower is fully open, are all on the same plane. The size and shape

Iris sibirica 'Butter and Sugar' with ×*Cupressocyparis leylandii* 'Golconda' in background

Iris 'Aichi-no-kagayaki'

of large white teaspoons with short yellow handles (hafts), arranged in a well-spaced circle, they seem to float in space.

The variegated form, *Iris tectorum* 'Variegata', a shy bloomer, has a brief spring fling of luminous pale cream leaves, changing by June to indifferent streakiness and then to green. It is uncommon. The plant sold under this name by a major wholesaler and from there percolating into many retail nurseries is *I. japonica* 'Variegata', which is grown mainly for its boldly white-striped leaves. The variegated form has not been hardy for me, though the green-leaved species has not only survived this quar-

ter century but spread like wildfire by string-like runners just below the surface of the soil. Though *I. japonica* seldom offers more than a handful of flowers over its considerable expanse of low and arching, sword-shaped leaves, the flowers have a rare, orchidlike beauty. And so, while periodically weeding out barrow loads of plants, I leave a small patch, never quite accepting that there are plants, and this is one, of which one cannot have only a little. Within 2 years, it is back in force.

Iris 'Aichi-no-Kagayaki'

For 5 years *Iris* 'Aichi-no-Kagayaki' (Zone 5, possibly colder) has proved a lusty ornamental of great worth. A hybrid between the yellow flag (*I. pseudacorus*) and a Japanese iris (*I. ensata*), it got sturdy adaptability from one parent and beauty from the other, to which is added a quality all its own: chartreuse foliage. Immaculate leaves hold this color all season, but are at their most brilliant in spring. The June-borne flowers, of typical Japanese iris form, are pale yellow with brown markings. Though I'd rather have them blue, for better contrast with the leaves, they are lovely anyway. This hybrid does well in any moisture-retentive soil, clumps up fast, and is easily divided. *Hypericum androsaemum* 'Albury Purple' makes a good complement plant, its

mistily purple leaves contrasting without stealing the show.

Amsonia
BLUE STAR

The soft blue color of amsonias and the daintiness of their small starry flowers makes them the perfect foil for more voluptuous flowers of any color. *Amsonia tabernaemontana* could, for example, be paired with the soft pink, double-flowered *Paeonia* 'Sarah Bernhardt', or with the vibrant, bright red *P.* 'America'. Siberian irises (*Iris sibirica*) bloom at the same time and any blue- or white-flowered cultivar could be added to either of these pairings. Or how about complementary yellows and blues, with an amsonia and violet-blue *Iris sibirica* 'Dewful' against a background of such yellow-leaved shrubs as golden barberry (*Berberis thunbergii* 'Aurea') or yellow ninebark (*Physocarpus opulifolius* 'Dart's Gold')? Given the wide color range of peonies and Siberian irises, there are countless possible permutations with just these three kinds of perennials, and textural contrast of the leaves would endure long after the flowers were gone. Something brighter? Orange is the complementary color of blue, and orange geums (*Geum* ×*heldreichii*, Zone 5, is a good one for hot regions), which flower at the same time, shine out yet more brightly against blue amsonia. If you don't like yellow with pink, bear in mind that some amsonias make a second, late-season color contribution with yellow or amber autumn foliage.

Amsonias are adaptable plants, but a soil that does not long stay dry serves most of them best, and they welcome some afternoon protection from hot sun without visibly suffering for lack of it. Those with the slenderest leaves, such as *Amsonia ciliata* (Zone 7) and *A. hubrichtii* (Zone 5), tolerate dry sites best. If the taller amsonias and baptisias start to flop about, as they may in rich soils or rainy seasons, they soon resume their neat appearance if cut back by half, repeating this later if necessary. Though they bloom for only a few weeks, their foliage remains an asset until hard frost.

Though never common in gardens, two species have long been grown, the 3-foot North American *Amsonia tabernaemontana* (Zone 3) and the 18-inch Asian *A. orientalis* (Zone 5; synonym *Rhazya orientalis*), which is moderately stoloniferous, with flowers of a slightly brighter blue a bit later in the season. Try as I may, I have never flowered the latter, though friends nearby seem to have no problem. The leaves of *A. tabernaemontana* are spear-shaped, while those of *A. tabernaemon-*

Amsonia montana (dwarf blue star)

tana var. *salicifolia* are more willowy. They usually but not invariably turn banana yellow in autumn.

Dwarf blue star is one of the prettiest amsonias and the best one for small gardens. Found in catalogs under the names *Amsonia montana* or *A. tabernaemontana* var. *montana* (Zone 5), it has been grown in American gardens for at least four decades, but its origin is a mystery. Carried on 18-inch stems, its baby blue flowers are a trifle chubbier than those of other amsonias. So eager is the plant to get going in spring that the flowers thrust through the ground along with the foliage, broochlike clusters of blue-tinted buds in a circlet of spear-shaped leaves. One amsonia sent to me under the name *A. montana* grew taller at about 2 feet. The dwarf amsonia de-

Taller form of *Amsonia montana* with daisylike *Leucanthemum vulgare* 'May Queen' in center and *Stachys byzantina* 'Big Ears' (a large-leaved form of lamb's ears) at left

Amsonia hubrichtii seedling with purple-flowered bearded iris 'Lavish' and *Rubus cockburnianus* 'Golden Vale' in background scribed came from Garden in the Woods, Framingham, Massachusetts. Woodlanders Nursery sells cutting-grown plants true to this form.

A surge of interest in American native plants has led to the introduction of several other species, all rather new to gardens and with names often in flux. The 3- to 4-foot Arkansas amsonia (*Amsonia hubrichtii*; Zone 5) was named for Leslie Hubricht, but frequently is spelled *hubrectii*. It is the star among star flowers, less for its typical gray-blue flowers than for its sliver-fine foliage on sturdy upright stems. Always elegant, it is loveliest during its several weeks of autumnal honey gold. Keep a potted plant or two on hand as an instant gift for late-season visitors who eye it longingly. Otherwise, they must wait until spring because the plant's dense, woody roots, which defy division with spade or trowel, require an axe or mattock, and such brutal treatment is best carried out just before growth begins.

Some seedlings that came up under my big clumps of *Amsonia hubrichtii* have slightly wider leaves, though narrower than those of *A. tabernaemontana* var. *salicifolia*. *Amsonia ciliata* var. *texana*, a favorite of mine, is similar. *Amsonia ciliata* var. *tenuifolia* has extremely slender leaves on clumps of prostrate habit.

The 4-foot Louisiana blue star (*Amsonia ludoviciana*), handsome and highly rated for Zones 6–8, is another carefree, heat-tolerant species. The light blue flowers form more substantial panicles than do those of most amsonias, and the leaves, relatively broad, have a silvery sheen when young, remaining downy on their undersides.

The Asian *Amsonia elliptica* (Zone 4) is the most vigorous blue star I grow. It is a self-sower of such copious quantities of seed from bunches of long, slender pods that I am keeping an eye on it. Does it have potential for naturalizing, or will it be a threat to native species? So far the seedlings, thickly clustered around the parent clump, have not cropped up in other parts of the garden. This species is recommended where extreme vigor or tolerance of difficult conditions is wanted; otherwise *A. tabernaemontana* is the better plant.

These amsonias, along with *Amsonia illustris*, which resembles *A. tabernaemontana*, make a good beginning. I grow several others, all good garden plants. The slowest to get going, as might be expected of a miniature, is the slender-leaved, 18-inch *Amsonia jonesii* from Colorado and Utah. It has settled down in sandy, acid soil amended with crushed oyster shell (my slow-release alternative to lime) and with luck there'll be flowers in 2 or 3 years. Panayoti Kelaidis of Denver Botanic Gardens grows it in heavy loam on a steep bank and describes it as having "dazzling sapphire flowers on stems 8 to 12 inches long, forming a perfect mound of color from late April into June."

Baptisia
FALSE INDIGO, WILD INDIGO

Baptisias, or wild indigos, are native to the eastern half of North America, in habitats ranging from rich woods and prairies to dry pinelands and sunny sandbanks. Where their roots can delve deep, they are extremely drought tolerant. Gravel spread around them helps deter the voles that sometimes chew the roots. This genus has two handicaps: confused nomenclature and limited availability due to propagation problems. Division is tricky, and the success rate small with cuttings. Species can be grown from seed, which usually germinates fairly quickly if first put into very hot water and left to soak for 24 hours. Seedlings take 2 to 3 years to reach flowering size.

When propagation is mastered, and I doubt that it will take long with many plantspeople now taking on this challenge, expect an influx of baptisias in blue, purple, white, cream, yellow, bicolors, and the covetable silver-leaved *Baptisia arachnifera*. Height, habit, and texture also vary. Baptisias readily interbreed, and when two or more are grown close together spontaneous hybrids often occur. In *Contemporary Perennials*, by Roderick W. Cumming and Robert E. Lee, published in 1960 and still among the best books on perennials, there is mention of a strain called Old Orchard Hybrids, with a color range including tawny violet, buff, near yellow, blue, and intermediate combinations. These have long since disappeared, but new ones are now coming along. Two pretty ones appeared in my garden, guessed to be the progeny of *B. australis* and *B. lanceolata*, which are both growing nearby. One (named 'Serendipity') is creamy yellow with purple-flushed stems, the other ('Artistry') is a bicolor in cream and misty purple.

Baptisia australis and *B. alba* are the putative parents of *B.* 'Purple Smoke', a chance seedling of compact habit with flowers of dusty violet-blue. This cultivar was spotted by curator Rob Gardener at the North Carolina Botanical Garden and introduced by Niche Gardens. Another of Rob Gardener's introductions is pale yellow *B.* 'Carolina Moon'. Blue wild indigo (*Baptisia australis*; Zone 3) has been grown in English gardens for a quarter century, with lupinelike spires of blue pea-type flowers of somewhat variable blue and unblemished blue-green leaves on sturdy

Baptisia alba with *Miscanthus sinensis* 'Cabaret' in background

stems. It is the hardiest species, and the tallest at 4–5 feet. Where such a shrub-sized plant would be too bulky, there's a charming blue-flowered 18-inch miniature sold by nurseries as *B. minor* or *B. australis* var. *minor*, with lacily fine foliage and plump flower spikes. Plants sold at present are grown from seed and somewhat variable.

Some white-flowered species of *Baptisia* have the added attraction of dark stems. White-flowered baptisias have been so shuffled and reshuffled between the names *B. alba*, *B. lactea*, *B. leucantha*, *B. pendula* (the pods are pendulous, not the flowers), and *B. albescens* that nurseries can be forgiven for throwing in the towel and calling all the white ones *B. alba*. All white-flowered baptisias are worth growing, but they don't all have dark stems. What you see is what you get and buying a baptisia sight unseen can be a pig-in-a-poke, though all wild indigos are worth having. Expect a height of around 3 feet.

Baptisia sphaerocarpa (Zone 6; synonym *B. viridis*), *B. cinerea* (Zone 7), *B. lanceolata* (Zone 7), and *B. tinctoria* (Zone 6) have bright yellow flowers. Blooms of the first two come in

LEFT *Baptisia sphaerocarpa* with purple-flowered *Salvia* 'Wesuwe' in front and surrounded by *Viola tricolor*

spires on 3-foot-tall clumps. The vivid yellow flowers of *B. lanceolata* are spaced along dark, arching stems clad in narrow, dark green leaves. Clumps stand about 1 foot high and twice as wide. My plants have been in their present spot, on a slight slope, for 14 years. Wild indigo, *B. tinctoria* (Zone 6), a dye plant, is grown mainly for its foliage, which is the most lacy of any except *B. minor*. The yellow flowers are too small to make much of a show.

"Eucalyptus?" ask visitors, hazarding a guess about an unfamiliar plant with rounded gray-green leaves threaded on arching stems. *Baptisia perfoliata* (Zone 7) does look like eucalyptus and can be used as a substitute in dried arrangements. Foliage is its main attraction, but the small, solitary yellow flowers are presented in an amusing way. Centered on the circular leaves, they are followed by round seedpods that look like balls balanced on Ping-Pong bats. If grown in the sandy soil of low fertility it prefers, this baptisia produces a clump less than 2 feet high and rather more in width after 5 years.

A few other species are available, but finding them requires a diligent search of seed lists and nursery catalogs. Because they aren't tied to a production schedule, amateurs often succeed in propagating plants where professionals have failed, and a one-in-ten success rate

Baptisia perfoliata

(about what I've achieved so far with hybrids grown from cuttings), unprofitable for nurseries, is adequate for home gardeners. Hybrids won't come true from seed, but there's always the chance of getting a good new form worthy of naming. Clumps can be divided, but they build girth slowly and dislike disturbance, so there's a risk of loss.

Cuttings taken at flowering time root quickly. The problem lies in getting them to re-emerge after winter dormancy. Baptisia stems shear themselves neatly off at ground level after being blackened by frost. This characteristic makes cleanup easy, but is part of the propagation problem. Often there'll be living roots in apparently empty pots in spring, but no bud to initiate growth. Keeping plants growing in a warm greenhouse through winter

Bletilla striata (hardy orchid)

Bletilla striata 'Albovariegata'

improves the success rate. Drug companies justify high prices because of the cost of research, with much unrewarded effort along the way. Nurseries could often make the same claim.

Bletilla striata

HARDY ORCHID

Plaudits to the hardy orchid (*Bletilla striata*; Zone 6), one of the most admired perennials I grow. Half a day a year is more than enough for maintaining a patch several yards wide, light work involving little more than cutting off the wiry stalks when the flowers have faded

and the dead leaf stems in late autumn. One other small service pays dividends—watching the weather report in early spring and spreading a protective sheet over emerging shoots on nights when frost threatens. Only one lot of leaves is made each year, and if the tips get frost-nipped as they emerge, they'll remain truncated for the rest of the season.

This creeping terrestrial orchid grows from

crab-shaped, strung-together tubers that pile up on top of each other when clumps get congested. Crowding doesn't inhibit flowering, though it does reduce height. I've divided my oldest patch only twice in 20 years, replenishing the humus-content of the soil at the same time. Increase is faster, however, if they are frequently divided. If I'm passing by with a bucketful of balanced fertilizer I may toss a handful or two their way once in a while, and they are watered in times of combined heat and drought. They have done best for me in east-facing sites with morning sun and compost-improved soil that gets neither soggy nor dust dry.

Bletilla's leaves are lovely and of unusual shape and texture, striated, or finely pleated, sword-shaped but not sword-stiff, gently arching and soft enough to flutter when riffled by the slightest air movement. They start off light green, gradually darken, then turn coppery gold in autumn. If the plant never flowered I'd still want to grow it, but it does flower, unfailingly, for most of May, lingering into June. The winged flowers, with fringed and pleated lip, hover like butterflies on their wiry stems. The purple flowers of the species are radiant when set against the chartreuse leaves of *Hosta* 'Sum and Substance'. Variegated Solomon's seal (*Polygonatum odoratum* 'Variegatum') also makes an excellent companion plant

The purple-flowered species and white-flowered *Bletilla striata* 'Alba' are readily available. For sleuthlike gardeners willing to hunt them down there are several more. *Bletilla striata* 'Innocence' and *B. striata* 'Kuchibeni' have white flowers with a touch of lavender on the lip, and the one usually sold as *B. striata* 'Albostriata' has purple flowers and leaves narrowly edged in white. Many

Dicentra eximia 'Alba'

years ago I became the proud possessor of a white-flowered bletilla with white-edged leaves, included by mistake in a bulb shipment from Holland. So far as I can determine the name for this is *B. striata* 'Albovariegata', but the only source for this form lists it as *B. striata* var. *albostriata* (and the one with white-edged leaves and purple flowers as *B. striata* var. *variegata*) so buy by description rather than by name. The sweetly named *B. striata* 'First Kiss' differs from *B. striata* 'Albovariegata' only in having a tentative touch of pale purple on the lips of its white flowers.

Dicentra

BLEEDING HEART

Dicentra eximia (Zone 4) is native to the East Coast of North America, *D. formosa* (Zone 4)

Campanula garganica 'W. H. Paine' at base of *Acer palmatum* 'Sango kaku' (coral bark maple)

the-bath, *Dicentra spectabilis* (Zone 3), has made itself very much at home in my garden, sowing cheerfully around in lightly shaded places. I would not want to be without it, but the foliage soon becomes unkempt after its brief spring bloom and it is not therefore as worthy as the next two.

Dicentra eximia 'Alba' (synonym 'Snow-drift'), with gray-green foliage, is seldom without a flower from midspring to late autumn. The only attention it requires is to pull out surplus seedlings or pink ones that pop up among the white and tend to crowd them out. All these pull out easily when young. *Dicentra* 'Langtrees' (synonym 'Margery Fish') has glaucous foliage that stays pristine from spring to fall, and small white locket flowers, continuous though seldom profuse. Pink-flowered *D.* 'Stuart Boothman' has finely cut grayish leaves, sometimes purple-tinted, though less so in hot regions than in cool ones. Both these spreading kinds are at their best in lightly shaded sites.

Campanula garganica

By and large campanulas, or bellflowers, do not care for intense summer heat. Even that notorious spreader *Campanula poscharsky-ana*, unaccepting of hot sun, has taken 20 years to become wide-spreading ground cover

to the West Coast. The species to which selections and hybrids have in the past been attributed is sometimes questionable. No matter, bleeding hearts are all eminently garden-worthy. One difference between them is that *D. eximia*, an extravagant self-sower, stays in a clump, while *D. formosa* has densely running roots. *Dicentra eximia* is slightly taller at about 2 feet. All have white or pink flowers

and finely divided bright green or gray-green foliage that makes them good contrasting companion plants for hostas in the lightly shaded sites that suit them both.

Picking a few among so many good plants may be invidious. I do, nonetheless, have my favorites, primarily for their cool and pleasing appearance through summer's hot days. The much loved Asian bleeding heart or lady-in-under pines, and the charming milky white *C. poscharskyana* 'E. H. Frost' is a permanent resident only when cosseted with good soil. Yet over the same period, *C. garganica* (Zone 6), I think in the form 'W. H. Paine', with cause for complaint about its rooty place under *Acer palmatum* 'Sango kaku', has made not a single demand. Here, with the benison of summer shade, it peeks out from under the maple's skirts to flower for 2 or 3 weeks in May. Unmarred bright green foliage, short and dense, carpets the ground from early spring until the tail-end of the year, covering the dying foliage of snowdrops and later absorbing the fallen leaves of the maple. Maintenance has been zilch save for watering the plants during extended drought.

Leucanthemum and Lychnis

High on my list of also-rans come *Leucanthemum vulgare* (synonym *Chrysanthemum leucanthemum*) 'May Queen' and *Lychnis coronaria*. The somewhat pesky way these sow around brings with it the inestimable benefit of spare clumps of easily moveable plants, with good, long-lasting foliage for plugging into gaps.

Leucanthemum vulgare 'May Queen' (Zone 4) carries a succession of pristine white daisies on sturdy stems for many weeks. It and the later-blooming 'Becky' are the only two long-lived Shasta daisies where summers are hot and humid.

The gray foliage of *Lychnis coronaria* (Zone 4) helps keep the ground dressed for most of the year. White-flowered *L. coronaria* 'Alba' and delicate pink and white *L. coronaria* 'Oculata' (synonym 'Angel's Blush') take their place prettily in many color schemes. The magenta species gives a lift to beds of wishy-washy colors and combines gorgeously with the chartreuse bracts of a self-sowing, spring-blooming biennial or monocarpic British native, *Smyrnium perfoliatum*, which looks like a euphorbia but isn't even in the same family.

Nepeta

CATMINT

Under the broad umbrella of the name *Nepeta* ×*faassenii* (Zone 5) come several tip-top plants that thrive equally well in hot regions and cool ones, though the blue of the flowers is less intense where the temperature climbs high. Provided the soil is porous it makes no difference whether it is sand or richer loam, acid or alkaline. Gray-green leaves and flowers of blendable blue or soft white suit these plants to most color schemes. Heights vary, from the low and spreading, white-flowered 'Snowflake' (weakly, for me) through 15-inch 'Walker's Low' and larger-flowered, deeper blue 'Dropmore' to the one that tops my list, the 3-foot-tall hybrid 'Six Hills Giant', which starts to flower in May and peaks in June, when it is a classic companion for my favorite rose, *Rosa* 'Pink Pet'.

The ground occupied by the roots of *Nepeta* 'Six Hills Giant' is only a fraction of the space covered when plants are in full growth. Other things can therefore go in between the clumps, in my case the early magenta spires of *Gladiolus byzantinus*, continuing with lilies. Although lilies like my garden, rodents make them hard to keep. I continue to knock my head against this brick wall, covering the ground with gravel, planting in sunken containers, and using hot pepper sprays. The nepeta is my collaborator: three lily-protecting rings of chicken wire behind it are completely hidden when it is in full growth.

Sun and sandy or gravelly soil suit this catmint well, and it demands little attention save occasional reduction of clump size and an early autumn shearing to encourage fresh new growth. The only pest drawn to catmint is, of course, the cat, and *Nepeta* 'Six Hills Giant' is resilient enough to survive occasional scrabblings. Although cats are not noted for a ready response to obedience training, damage has been kept minimal by removing my mischievous, attention-demanding male, when I catch

Spigelia marilandica (Indian pink)

him at it, and depositing him firmly in a patch planted solely for his pleasure.

Although the flowering wands of *Nepeta* 'Six Hills Giant' may exceed 3 feet, they tend to lean a bit, reducing the overall height, so I have it close to the front of the border, with only the 1-foot, when in bloom, *Achillea millefolium* 'Oertel's Rose' (Zone 2) in front of it. Other achilleas come and go, most of them short-lived. Only *Achillea millefolium* does consistently well, and the compact, pink-flowered 'Oertel's Rose' is the best of its kind—aggressive but controllable in a hot, dry place.

Spigelia marilandica
INDIAN PINK

Indian pink (*Spigelia marilandica*; Zone 7) has been in my garden since way back when, refusing to die in spite of what I now know to be the cruel punishment of root-filled gloom. One such clump is still going strong, somewhat shrunken in size, hemmed in all round by plants with dense, shallow roots. Finally I got it right, in humus-enriched soil that stays moderately moist, with sun for at least a few hours. The more sun spigelia gets, the denser the plants and the more profuse the bloom. Three small plants put out in almost full sun 4 years ago, 9 inches apart, have made a yard-wide patch, with hundreds of flowering stems packed into a vivid sheet of color in late May and June and a smattering thereafter. Flowers last longer, however, in light shade.

It is worth making every effort to enable this native of southeastern North America to give of its best, for no other perennial remotely resembles the brilliant jesterlike perkiness of spigelia. Pairs of spear-shaped leaves are widely spaced along slender, firmly upright stems crowned with clustered scarlet buds shaped like Indian clubs. Fillets of yellow appear at the flower tip as it begins to open into an upfacing saffron-yellow star with the red of the tube showing through in the center.

Perennials with red flowers are a scarce commodity, and fewer still are those that flower in shade. Sites where hostas thrive also suit spigelia, and what an asset it is, contrasting in both color and form. The top ten hostas (and the top twenty for that matter) in the American Hosta Society's popularity polls are invariably those with blue, yellow, or variegated foliage. Scarlet never looks better than with green, its complementary color, and putting a clump of spigelia among green-leaved hostas might redress the balance in their favor. The combination is guaranteed to have photographers elbowing for space.

There are at least two forms of spigelia in cultivation, one about 15 inches high with leaves barely 2 inches long, and the other with leaves more than twice that size on 2-foot clumps. Spigelia can be propagated by seed, by careful division, or by stem cuttings taken just prior to flowering time. The success rate with cuttings is increased if plants are kept in growth, in a greenhouse or under lights, through their first winter. Seed has to be collected day by day, pinching off the tiny black balls that are the seed receptacles and putting them in a covered container before they explode and eject the seed.

Summer

FOLIAGE

Every year more plants grown solely for their flowers give way to those grown primarily for their foliage. There are so many good ones that limiting the list is difficult. Evergreens, discussed in the section on winter, remain important in summer, as do two dogwoods grown primarily for their winter bark, *Cornus alba* 'Elegantissima' and *C. stolonifera* 'Silver

LEFT *Canna* 'Pretoria' in center (more or less), with *Euonymus fortunei* 'Sparkle 'n' Gold' in front of it and dark-leaved, red-flowered *Dahlia* 'Bishop of Llandaff' to right. On the left bottom, with orange-yellow pompoms, is *Kerria japonica* 'Pleniflora' and on the left top is *Chamaecyparis pisifera* 'Filifera Aurea'. The yellow-flowered plant in the center of the photo is a selection of the blackberry lily (*Belamcanda chinensis*). On the right are the yellow daisies of *Rudbeckia fulgida*, with (not in bloom) *Chrysanthemum* 'Bronze Elegance' in front of it. Outside the fence is *Miscanthus sinensis* 'Zebrinus'. The leaves of *Cornus sanguinea* 'Winter Flame' can be seen top right.

and Gold', with variegated leaves. Ferns and grasses, present much of the growing season, and some all year, become increasingly important after peak spring color wanes in shaded places. Many flowering plants are valued also for their foliage: amsonias, baptisias, callas, *Daphne* ×*burkwoodii* 'Carol Mackie', dicentras, *Helleborus foetidus*, *Indigofera decora*, liriopes, and pulmonarias to name but a few. With its flowering completed and leaves grown to full size, *Pulmonaria* 'David Ward', with gray-green leaves edged in white, has a bold presence similar to that of a hosta.

Textural combinations captivate me: lacy *Baptisia minor* next to slim-bladed *Allium nutans*, both glaucous but opposites in texture; the bold silvery spears of *Pulmonaria* 'Excalibur' with ferny *Dicentra* 'Stuart Boothman' and the rounded purple leaves of *Heuchera* 'Montrose Ruby'; and Japanese painted fern

Baptisia minor with white-flowered *Allium nutans*

with the stiff round needles of *Juncus patens* 'Carmen's Grey'. Mental notes (too often forgotten) are made of combinations where some juggling is called for.

Seldom do I visit a gardening friend without returning home with a new acquisition. From the garden of designer Barbara Ashmun in Portland, Oregon, came *Cornus alba* 'Hedgerows Gold', with yellow-variegated leaves that

seemed to gleam more brightly than those of the time-tested *C. alba* 'Spaethii'. Would it shine as brightly in my hot garden as in Barbara's cooler one, and would it take summer sun without scorching? Yes, and yes. From David Culp in Pennsylvania came *Artemisia abrotanum* 'Silver'. Thus are a garden's occupants constantly updated.

As I write, the following foliage plants head

my list, which will, however, always be in flux. Some are grown for color, be it gray, gold, purplish, or variegated leaves, many for texture. It makes it more orderly if I group them accordingly, but first must come a genus that encompasses all these things save, at this time, purple foliage: hostas, the mainstay of shady gardens. Some of my other recommendations, sedums and barberries in particular, have candidates in more than one color category, but none in such great array as hostas.

HOSTAS

I am not a hosta collector, and having in the past been chided for putting too much emphasis on old, durable kinds, my starting point in this book will be the first ten names in the American Hosta Society's 1998 nationwide Popularity Poll, followed by my parenthetical evaluation of those hostas in my garden. Unless otherwise stated all my hostas are in light shade, without serious root competition from trees and shrubs. All are hardy to Zone 3.

Soon after I started growing hostas (Zone 3), there came a spring when not a single plant emerged. Voles had eaten the lot. Voles and slugs are major problems, and describing the varied efforts to control them, some highly inventive, would fill a book. Join the American Hosta Society and their outstanding journal will keep you up to date, and the many excellent color photographs will tempt you to buy more plants. My own trouble-shooting approach is threefold. As with every other plant, anything persistently unhealthy or unsightly is discarded. New hostas are grown in sunken containers until large enough to be divided and put, as insurance, in more than one place. Box turtles abound in my garden, their wizened visages, seen-it-all eyes, and calm acceptance of my presence reminding me of the family tortoise of my childhood. Their diet includes slugs. I am therefore chary about using slug pellet and seek instead the hostas least slug prone.

The Hosta Society honor roll reads: 'Sum and Substance' (slug-free, weatherproof except for hail, huge chartreuse leaves, dramatic and undemanding); 'Great Expectations' (bitter disappointment); 'Patriot' (superb); 'Paul's Glory' (not grown); 'Gold Standard' (so-so); 'Sagae' (perfection, my first choice); 'Blue Angel' (not grown—my vote among blues goes to 'Halcyon', No. 11 in the Popularity Poll); *Hosta montana* 'Aureomarginata' (splendid in its good years, sometimes disappointing for no obvious reason); 'Fragrant Bouquet' (not grown—my vote goes to 'So Sweet'); 'Krossa Regal' (a 10-year disappointment, getting a last chance in the best conditions I can offer).

Hosta 'Sagae' with white-striped blades of *Acorus gramineus* 'Variegatus' at top right, *Iris pseudacorus* at left, *Brunnera macrophylla* 'Langtrees' in front of the hosta, and in back a ground cover of *Myosotis scorpioides*

Hosta ventricosa 'Aureomarginata' with red-flowered *Primula japonica*, ferny-leaved *Thalictrum minus*, and water irises

None of these has weaned me away from some of the old hostas, which are inexpensive, often as attractive as newer forms, and frequently more reliable. For an utterly trouble-free naturalizer in less than ideal conditions *Hosta ventricosa* and some *H. fortunei* × *H. sieboldiana* hybrids grown from seed top my list, and *H. ventricosa* 'Aureomarginata' is my finest specimen. The tough old *H. undulata* var. *albomarginata* has survived total neglect for 20 years or more, unflawed if somewhat diminished in size, in sandy soil under pines with sun for part of the day. The old August lily, *H. plantaginea*, continues to stake its claim with an evening fragrance as yet unsurpassed by any hosta I have tried.

VARIEGATED LEAVES

Picking the "best" variegated plants from among the many I grow was difficult, and I changed my mind several times. It was with particular regret that I omitted plants with season-long pink variegation, but with one exception (*Berberis thunbergii* 'Rose Glow', included under purple foliage) none has done singularly well. The leaves of *Populus* ×*candicans* 'Aurora' remained determinedly green, and those of *Cornus florida* 'Welchii' and *Acer*

RIGHT *Acer palmatum* 'Butterfly'

negundo 'Flamingo' scorched. *Hypericum moserianum* 'Tricolor' was splendid for four years, but then was killed by a March ice storm after new leaves had emerged, so, ice storms being common in my region, it cannot be considered entirely reliable.

Acer palmatum 'Butterfly'

I wish I had planted more Japanese maples early on. They would have earned their place so much better than most of the ornamental trees planted for their flowers. Among the few I grow, the prettiest is *A. palmatum* 'Butterfly' (Zone 5). The lack of uniformity in its dainty leaves gives this maple a fluid, dancing grace. Each leaf is cut almost to the base into slender lobes with unevenly jagged edges. The color varies from gray-green with a narrow cream edge to wholly cream, with every possible intermediate permutation. Nor are the lobes alike in shape. A few are straight, most are sickle-shaped, and many swirl in varying directions. In early spring the cream parts of the leaf are partly tinted coral pink. After about 12 years my plant stands about 6 feet high and as much across at its widest points. Airily branched and of soft mien, it has never been pruned. Perhaps it should have been, but I am a cowardly pruner, intimidated by the thought that I might, with a misplaced cut, ruin the shape of a plant for years, if not for good. I tend therefore to follow advice I once was given about raising children: "have 'em and love 'em and leave 'em alone"—not always sound advice for either children or plants, but at present *A. palmatum* 'Butterfly' seems none the worse for it. It is growing in moving shade under high-branched trees.

Aralia elata 'Variegata'

There could scarcely be greater contrast between the daintiness of the maple and the imposing *Aralia elata* 'Variegata' (Zone 4), with huge, bipinnate leaves that look so much like branches that its out-of-season knobbly gauntness comes as quite a shock to the uninitiated. In my shrub's early days I would point out to winter visitors my "$160 stick." Its catalog price was justified by the necessity of grafting the plant and by the paucity of bud wood it produces for this purpose. Cost is not the only disadvantage of grafting; the favored rootstock is *A. spinosa*, a suckering North American species that got the name devil's walking-stick from the prickles on its branchlets. These prickles make wearing stout gloves advisable when removing suckers, which spring up far and wide. This trait is the only flaw I've encountered, and perhaps it could be avoided by planting the aralia in a large, sunken container.

The immense leaves can measure more than 4 feet long and 3 feet wide. They are flat and elegantly symmetrical, with pinnate leaflets in well-spaced opposite pairs. Some leaflets have a dark green and gray inner pattern, somewhat the shape of a red-oak leaf, set on a cream background. Most are predominantly green with an irregular narrow edging of creamy white. The overall effect is of a white variegation; only on close inspection is the white seen to be creamy. Large umbels of small white flowers are borne at the branch tips in summer, followed by masses of small black berries.

Aralia elata 'Variegata' is capable of growing quite quickly to 20 feet or more, but yet it does not take much effort, branches being comparatively few, to keep it pruned within the 8- to 10-foot range. Using loppers, cut to a bud pointing in the desired direction, watching out for the few scattered prickles on the branches.

Acanthopanax sieboldianus 'Variegatus'

FIVE-LEAF ARALIA

Just as this shrub was becoming better known, its name was changed to *Eleutherococcus sieboldianus* 'Variegatus' (Zone 4). Mail in your order and you won't have to get your mouth around this. All who see five-leaf aralia

Aralia elata 'Variegata'

Acanthopanax sieboldianus 'Variegatus'

central oakleaf silhouette in grayed green and pewter. In a part of my garden with no direct sun *Acanthopanax sieboldianus* 'Variegatus' vies with *Hosta* 'Patriot' as best brightener of shade. Companion plants include arisaemas, *Carex* 'Evergold', ferns, gingers (*Asarum*), epimediums, *Kirengeshoma*, voodoo-lily (*Sauromatum guttatum*), forgiven the stench of its flowers for the sake of its spectacularly large leaves on tall spotted stems, and a cute little violet with cyclamen-patterned leaves. The violet has for many years circulated among plantspeople as *Viola koreana* or *V. variegata* and can finally be bought as *V. koreana* 'Syletta'. This whole bed has an underplanting of *Anemone nemorosa*, which wanders in and out of other things, unharmed and unharming.

Fallopia japonica 'Variegata'
JAPANESE FLEECEFLOWER

When this shrublike perennial arrived as a gift it crossed my mind that what I earlier knew as *Polygonum cuspidatum* 'Variegatum' had been given a new identity under a plant protection program aimed at deflecting the wrath of gardeners struggling to be rid of a pernicious weed. Still, not to look a gift horse in the mouth and notwithstanding my dislike of spotty variegations, I reasoned that *Fallopia japonica* 'Variegata' (Zone 4) could not get the better

want it, and since my plantsman friend Gary Koller of the Arnold Arboretum in Massachusetts gave me a plant a dozen or so years ago, it has been passed on many times by means of rooted cutting or layered branch. Sized right for gardens of average size, it makes, with light annual pruning, a somewhat rounded shrub of 3–4 feet. The arching outer branches sometimes self-layer as they lie on

the ground, a process that can be helped by holding them down with a brick.

Few shrubs have leaves as beautiful. Five-lobed, about 5 inches across, and shaped like those of Virginia creeper (*Parthenocissus quinquefolia*), they are predominantly rich cream in color, and young leaves are often entirely cream. The green portion of mature leaves varies from a tiny trickle or blot to a

of me if I kept after it from the start. In a hot, dry site at the edge of the drive, under my eye, it has not tried. Under the stress of drought, the leaves, which start off mottled in cream and green, become mosaics of tan, crimson, cream, and green, and the height is limited to 4 feet. In moister soil it can attain 6 feet. Its spring tardiness leaves *Gladiolus byzantinus* behind it open to view while later concealing the dying foliage. In autumn it becomes fleecy with sprays of small white flowers. Commended for its valor in battling heat and drought, it should be viewed with suspicion under better conditions.

Symphoricarpos orbiculatus 'Follis Variegatis'

INDIAN CURRANT, CORALBERRY

Of the several coralberries I grow, *Symphoricarpos orbiculatus* 'Follis Variegatis' (Zone 2) is far and away the best. It has afternoon shade under a large oak, alongside and mingling with evergreen azaleas. Accustomed in the wild to similar conditions, it is bothered neither by root competition nor occasional dry spells, and it spreads just enough that pulling a few bits out to pot up for plant sales is adequate control.

This bright and dainty shrub is about 3 feet high with slender branchlets as straight and

Polygonatum odoratum 'Variegatum' (a variegated Solomon's seal)

firm as knitting needles held out horizontally in fanlike formation. Ranged symmetrically along them, in twinned pairs an inch apart, are flat, inch-long, matt-textured ovate leaves with bright green centers edged with creamy yellow. My plant has not yet produced the small bright pink berries that give it its common name. The narrow white leaf edging of *Symphoricarpos orbiculatus* 'Albovariegatus'

has less impact, but this selection has all the other good qualities and is a worthy, carefree shrub.

Polygonatum odoratum 'Variegatum'

VARIEGATED SOLOMON'S SEAL

If I cannot list my ten best plants with any degree of consistency, I can unhesitatingly name my best perennial for shade under all but the very worst conditions. It is the variegated Solomon's seal with a scientific name that has caused controversy as long as I have grown it. For the present it has come to rest as *Polygonatum odoratum* 'Variegatum', but in England this Solomon's seal is more likely to be listed as *P. falcatum* 'Variegatum'. *Polygonatum ×hybridum* 'Variegatum' (synonym 'Striatum') is a different plant of lesser appeal.

Polygonatum odoratum 'Variegatum' (Zone 4) gets top marks for its elegant arching form and lovely leaves, and also for its rugged ability to thrive where there is root competition from trees. It may be slow to settle in, but after a couple of years it extends its terrain quite rapidly by rhizomatous roots. Any surplus will be gratefully received by friends or nurseries: Solomon's seal cannot be propagated by cuttings and selected forms do not come true from seed, so there is pent up demand.

When the stout, pointed, lilac-tinted buds spear through the ground in spring, *Epimedium grandiflorum* is just starting to bloom and makes a pretty foreground planting for the 2-foot (3-foot in rich, moist soil) Solomon's seal. When the leaves of Solomon's seal first unfurl, their tips and edges are brushmarked with cream, later becoming whiter, but meantime nicely matched to the narrow ivory bells with frilly green edges swinging from the axils of the leaves for about 2 weeks before they wither neatly away.

From spring well into autumn the plants remain immaculate, their stems unbowed by storms and their leaves unmarred by pests, disease, or dry spells that scorch the leaves of many other plants. About the time that autumn cyclamen (*Cyclamen hederifolium*) comes into bloom and hosta leaves turn yellow, the leaves of Solomon's seal turn amber. As winter approaches the leaves are shed and soon afterward the stems sprawl on the ground, straw colored, and slow to decay, but self-severing at ground level and scooped up in minutes if their winter messiness is objected to.

Two closely related Asian plants, one variegated and one not, flourish (one too well) in similar shaded sites. Beware of *Disporum sessile* 'Variegatum' (Zone 4), with greenish white nodding bells and very pretty, narrow, white-striped leaves. I had to take Roundup (glyphosate) to this plant after it ran amok. I have it still, but corralled now in a sunken container. For those of hound-dog persistence, there's a substitute for this disporum in a white-striped North American merrybells of very similar appearance, *Uvularia sessilifolia* 'Variegata' (Zone 4). The latter increases slowly and remains scarce.

The disporum not to be missed is *Disporum uniflorum*, more often listed as *D. flavens*. In early spring pendant bells the color of lemon sorbet are suspended from the tips of 2- to 3-foot branched stems clad in deeply veined green oval leaves with a silken sheen on their undersides. I doubt that this plant could be any happier in its native Korea than it is in my coastal Virginia garden, where it clumps up much faster than it does on the West Coast or in Europe, without being the least invasive. Few plants are such a pleasure to divide: lift a clump and it shakes into single stems with fleshy white clawlike roots.

Asarum

WILD GINGER

It is ironic that North America's wild gingers should be clinging to the coattails of Asian species in a recent surge of interest in the genus. Only the deciduous *Asarum canadense* (Zone 3), an attractive and very cold hardy species, is included in most wildflower books. In warmer regions it is surpassed by a complexity of species native to southeastern North America, none better than *A. shuttleworthii* 'Callaway', a selection made by the late Fred Galle. Although this selection and the others I grow are evergreen in Zone 7, they look a bit weatherworn by winter's end and are at their best after making new leaves in spring. They are grown solely for their foliage, the flowers being typically little brown jugs tucked out of sight beneath the leaves.

My introduction to *Asarum shuttleworthii* 'Callaway' (Zone 5) came, while fresh off the boat from England, in the garden of the late Linc and Timmy Foster of Falls Village, Connecticut, mecca to rock gardeners for many years. "Cyclamen," I said confidently and was gently corrected. In size, shape, leathery texture, and silvery marbling on a dark green background, this asarum does bear close resemblance to a good form of *Cyclamen coum*. Unlike cyclamen, however, it is stoloniferous and forms dense patches quite quickly.

Other southeastern native gingers, all evergreen, that have done well include *Asarum virginicum* (Zone 5), with similar but larger leaves; *A. arifolium* (Zone 6), a clump former with a softer sheen to its arrow-shaped, pewter-gray patterned leaves; and *A. speciosum* (Zone 6), the gift of plantsman Gene Cline. The latter is distinguished by such spectacular (for a ginger) flowers that I got to wondering what advantage this display could be, hidden as the flowers are beneath the leaves. Can pollinating beetles really appreciate their intricacy and comparative showiness?

Local wooded slopes provided an object

Asarum shuttleworthii 'Callaway' (a wild ginger)

lesson in what these wild gingers like. Their main need is summer shade, even deep shade, and soil that does not lie wet. In the wild I see them in acid sand topped with a skim of duff from years of falling leaves and twigs. Garden soil does not need to be rich, though peat moss and leaf mold are helpful additions.

Non-natives doing well in my garden include *Asarum europaeum* (Zone 4), with high-ly polished bright green leaves (the only species in my garden to produce occasional seedlings); the Asian *A. splendens* (Zone 6); and a single clump of the West Coast *A. hartwegii* (Zone 6), planted in 1976 and lost to sight under other vegetation for 20 years before I rediscovered it, looking well though scarcely bigger than when I planted it. Its endurance was rewarded by a move, along with a hunk of the

Viola koreana (cyclamen-leaved violet)

patterning of the leaf. This cyclamen-leaved violet is persistent and increases modestly by seed from tiny, nearly invisible flowers, without ever becoming a nuisance, a rare quality in a violet.

While the "Did you notice . . . ?" that causes a garden tour group to retrace their steps has its own satisfactions, passing a plant by unnoticed suggests less than ideal placement. Such is the case with my *Viola koreana*. The color of the leaf is greenish gray, and the patterning very dark green, so the effect is on the purplish side. The light golden gravel in one section of my garden would set it off well: unfortunately the viola did not like it there. What it does like is the brown-surfaced woodsy places, where it does not show up well and stands a good chance of being over-run by Solomon's seals, ferns, and epimediums. I continue trying to present it better and have recently discovered that it can take a lot more sun than I had supposed.

Saxifraga stolonifera
STRAWBERRY GERANIUM

In England, London pride (*Saxifraga umbrosa*) was one of my shade staples. It does not adapt well to scorching summers and instead I grow the evergreen *S. stolonifera* (Zone 6),

dry soil laced with oak tree roots in which it had for so long eked out a living, to a shady spot alongside a path where it will not be overlooked. The success of these "foreigners" suggests the genus to be versatile, with my first choice, *A. shuttleworthii* 'Callaway', likely to succeed in many regions.

Viola koreana
CYCLAMEN-LEAVED VIOLET

If you like *Asarum shuttleworthii* 'Callaway', you will also like *Viola koreana* (Zone 4), which came to me many years ago as *V. variegata*. Except that it is herbaceous and the leaf lacks gloss, it is remarkably similar to the ginger in its low, dense habit and in the size, shape, and

which doesn't mind heat provided it is out of direct sun and does not become parched. For 1–2 weeks in spring it lightens shady corners with a cloud of small white dipterous flowers, each with two petals markedly longer than the others, like the dangling legs of a crane in flight. A single plant soon becomes a dense mat, by means of baby plantlets carried out into the world on threadlike stolons.

Rubbery leaves, circular and scalloped, and so flat they could be used as nonskid coasters have a network of silvery veining that brings to mind wetlands seen from an airplane, with rivers, estuaries, creeks, and threadlike inlets. In the glancing rays of the sun, leaf surfaces and edges glisten with a stubble of white whiskers that feel like Velcro when stroked. The pink underside is densely napped with short hairs.

There is contrast in shape and texture where the saxifrage circles the base of a gray-fronded fern, *Athyrium* 'Branford Beauty'. There could be color contrast as well with *Saxifraga stolonifera* 'Maroon Beauty', one of several selected forms hardy to Zone 6. Yellow-leaved *S. stolonifera* 'Aurea' and pink-tinted *S. stolonifera* 'Tricolor' are not reliably hardy in Zone 7.

Saxifraga stolonifera (strawberry geranium)

Lamium galeobdolon 'Hermann's Pride'

DEAD-NETTLE

Lamium galeobdolon 'Hermann's Pride' (Zone 4; synonym *Lamiastrum galeobdolon* 'Hermann's Pride') is just the ticket for deep shade and even tolerates dry shade. Unlike the stoloniferous *L. galeobdolon* 'Variegatum' (synonym 'Florentinum'), which should be avoided like the plague unless you have a woods you want to carpet, *L. galeobdolon* 'Hermann's Pride' increases its patch slowly. The yellow, dead-nettle flowers of spring are briefly pretty, but the 1-foot-tall plant is primarily grown for its jagged-edged, diamond-shaped leaves. The patterning of the leaf is unusual, with the

Lamium galeobdolon 'Hermann's Pride'

Sedum lineare 'Variegatum'

green-veined overlay pronounced against a background of silver-gray. It is as striking a variegation as any I had seen until the introduction of *Heliopsis* 'Loraine Sunshine', with a branched, dark green overlay on a background of light cream, these showy leaves accompanied by bright yellow, daisy-type flowers.

Sedum

Dozens of sedums earn their keep in my garden, with flowers, foliage, and a will to live so strong that they often survive being tossed on the compost heap. Moderately moist soil helps some of the less unconquerable survive torrid summers. I grow three first-rate kinds with variegated foliage.

Sedum lineare 'Variegatum' (Zone 7) makes a dense rug with a 6-inch pile of needlelike gray-green leaves narrowly edged in creamy white, its ghostlike pallor belied by its sturdy constitution. It just manages to be evergreen in Zone 7, dying back to little creamy nuggets

tight against the ground. Although broken pieces of the brittle stems have the capacity to root as they lie on the ground, this plant does not become a nuisance as some such sedums do, though I concede that it might in regions without winter cold to keep it in check. Most sites will do except full sun and deep or root-filled shade. I use this sedum alongside semi-shaded paths, doing absolutely nothing by way of maintenance save occasional removal of sections reverted to green.

Sedum alboroseum 'Mediovariegatum' (Zone 4) is on a much larger scale, with wavy, partially folded leaves of rich cream verging on yellow edged with bright green. It can be seen from afar, and it makes a first-rate punctuation plant along the front of a border, a constant presence as the flowers of other perennials come and go. Because the foliage combines the brightness of yellow with the blending ability of cream, there are few color schemes where it would be out of place. The blush pink flowers, late in the season, are incidental. Twelve to fifteen inches is ample height for this sedum. In my hot, moist region stems grow lankier if not cut back, something I do at intervals through summer, a stem here, a stem there, so it never gets the shorn look it would if all the stems were sheared off at one time. Occasional green reversions are removed and clumps reduced in size every couple of years. Cuttings root with ease, though they are seldom called for with division so easy and material so abundant. Although this sedum is not evergreen, its dormant time is minimal. It and the next sedum do best with sun for most of the day.

One of America's best plantsmen, Barry Yinger, introduced *Sedum* 'Frosty Morn' (Zone

Sedum alboroseum 'Mediovariegatum' with pink-flowered *Zantedeschia rehmannii* 'Superba' (calla lily)

4) from Japan just a few years back, and I now know few gardeners who are not growing it, attesting to the plant's charm and ease of propagation. The flowers of not-very-clean white (in hot regions) are of little account; the plant is grown for the uneven white margin around the gray-green oak-leaf outline center common to many variegated leaves. Much the same size as *S. alboroseum* 'Mediovariegatum'

and given the same cutting back, it has been a most welcome addition to my white border, where plants with variegated foliage take the place of the gray ones that rot in hot and humid climates.

YELLOW LEAVES

I am a pushover for plants with yellow leaves, so it is an act of great restraint to include so

Spiraea thunbergii 'Ogon'

few. This color is excluded from only two beds in my garden: one with a color theme of pinks and blues, the other a soft composition based on purple, gray, or white-variegated foliage and white or blue flowers, with occasional touches of pale yellow or apricot. Yellow foliage would be too dominant in either of these beds. The degree of yellow varies a great deal from one plant to another. Bright yellow-

greens, such as *Lysimachia nummularia* 'Aurea', work well with orange and scarlet, while violet or purple flowers are more pleasing with such greenish yellows as golden oregano.

High on my shrub list is *Spiraea thunbergii* 'Ogon' (Zone 4), the name under which I bought it, or 'Mellow Yellow', which is not appropriate because mellow it is not. I have praised it elsewhere for its very early bloom

and will not dwell on it now; I just want to be sure that it does not get overlooked. Likewise *Iris* 'Aichi-no-Kagayaki', included with the spring perennials, should not be overlooked here. And there are, of course, the several gold-leaved forms of *Spiraea japonica* (Zone 4).

Berberis thunbergii 'Bonanza Gold'

DWARF YELLOW JAPANESE BARBERRY
Berberis thunbergii 'Bonanza Gold' (Zone 4), a much smaller version of *B. thunbergii* 'Aurea', ties for first place with the above-named spiraea. This plant came so highly praised by Lake County Nursery in Ohio, which introduced it, that I was skeptical. In its 5 years in my garden it has justified every word and more. It is the bright yellow equivalent of *B. thunbergii* 'Crimson Pygmy', alike in its low, mounding shape and in its tolerance of summer heat. I have two plants, both in full sun. One is in the "moist but well-drained soil" so often prescribed that writers search their minds and dictionaries for other ways to say it, and the other is in a corner that sometimes becomes dry. They do equally well. The first of my plants forms part of the yellow punctuation along the front of a bed where colors are mainly creams and browns, with blues and purples as a secondary theme. Colors in the

other bed are mixed. Last year magenta-flowered *Petunia integrifolia* sowed itself nearby, a combination not the least subdued by the blazing summer sun. This yellow barberry would also be a splendid addition to hot color schemes embracing orange and scarlet.

Forsythia ×*intermedia* 'Gold Leaf'

Because my friend Gary Koller gave me this invaluable forsythia along with several other good things, I forgive him for also giving me *Houttuynia cordata*, one of the most invasive plants known to gardeners. In return I offered a purple-leaved poison ivy, which Gary declined. The forsythia gets a lot of sun in early spring, when it shines out brilliant yellow, underplanted with golden yellow celandines (*Ranunculus ficaria* 'Collarette'). Though somewhat less brilliant after the trees leaf out, throwing it into shade for most of the day, it still holds its color quite well. *Physocarpus opulifolius* 'Dart's Gold' (Zone 2), by comparison, also in summer shade and most brilliant as the buds burst open in spring, has turned to green by July.

Although I haven't tried it, I feel moderately sure that without the shade the leaves of the forsythia would scorch when temperatures climb so high that I can take a hot shower

Rubus cockburnianus 'Golden Vale'

from a hose left stretched out in the sun. This forsythia makes an arching mound about 5 feet high and as broad as one allows, the branches rooting where they touch the ground. Flowers are few. *Forsythia* ×*intermedia* 'Gold Leaf' is hardy to Zone 4.

Rubus cockburnianus 'Golden Vale'

When I planted *Rubus cockburnianus* 'Golden Vale' (Zone 6; synonym 'Wyevale Gold') in full sun, albeit with good, moist soil, I had my doubts. That, however, is where I needed the color, so that is where the plant went. It has triumphed. Slow and trailing through its first year, it then proceeded to form a 3-by-5-foot bush. The flattened, ferny sprays of leaves are a paler, more luminous yellow than they are in cooler regions, mostly unmarred, though a combination of heat and rain (or heat and sprinklers) may cause an occasional leaf to rot. In winter, when the leaves have gone, white-

Origanum vulgare 'Aureum' (golden oregano)

Among those that will put up with it I award second place to moss phlox (*Phlox subulata*) in its sundry selections and hybrids. My winner is golden oregano (*Origanum vulgare* 'Aureum'; Zone 5), not to be confused with golden marjoram (*Origanum onites* 'Aureum'), a less hardy plant distinguishable by its yellower, slightly crinkled leaves, which, alas, scorch in hot sun.

I prize golden oregano for its resistance to the many pests and diseases that plague plants in hot and humid climates, its tolerance of adversity, its dense, weed-suppressing growth, but most of all for its showy yet versatile chartreuse foliage through most of the year. Only when the temperature drops near 0°F does it go briefly dormant. It can be used in cooking, though the flavor is very mild.

Caring for golden oregano calls only for an occasional clipping of the plant. When and how often varies with soil, site, and climate. I have several yards of golden oregano bordering a path. It gets one clipping back to 3 inches in midsummer, frustrating its attempt to put up the flowering stems that spoil its neat appearance. Sometimes, if we've had enough rain to encourage vigorous growth, it needs a second clipping in autumn. Using hand shears, a clipping takes several hours. The hedge trimmer does it so effortlessly that it is easy to get

washed stems become prominent. That is the time to prune out dead stems, leaving only the handsome ones. Branches root at the tip when they touch the ground, often some distance away. Wanting a bush, not a thicket, I tip back any branches about to touch the soil. Flaws? 'Golden Vale' is thorny, though less so than most roses.

Origanum vulgare 'Aureum'
GOLDEN OREGANO

There are plenty of ground cover plants for shade if the soil can be kept moist. Golden creeping Charlie (*Lysimachia nummularia* 'Aurea') is one, though it leaves the ground bare in winter and sometimes rots out in summer heat. Far fewer tolerate full sun in regions where summer temperatures climb high.

carried away. Being shaved to the ground one year, during the heat of summer, was more than the oregano could stand and soon the ground was bare. It proved a temporary setback. By autumn the few patches that grew back were big enough to divide and plug into the threadbare areas. Another year saw it back from scatter rugs to close-carpeting, with another lesson learned. Green-leaved *Origanum vulgare* 'Compactum', equally good in hot, dryish places, stays dense and tight against the ground and needs no shearing.

Golden oregano has been in the same spot for many years, on the south-facing side of a large *Magnolia* ×*soulangeana*, unperturbed by the stressful combination of root competition and almost full sun. Companion plants with flowers in the purple or violet range, changed from time to time, have included bushlets of *Cuphea hyssopifolia* (an annual here), with neat little glossy green leaves and small purplish flowers, the trailing *Verbena* 'Ultraviolet' ('Homestead Purple' is similar), and the tall *V. bonariensis*. *Verbena rigida* was gotten rid of because it spread too fast and is scratchy to handle. Gray-leaved, lavender-flowered *Buddleia alternifolia* 'Argentea' is a fixture growing through the oregano.

PURPLE LEAVES

"Purple"-foliaged plants are a variable lot, ranging from the near-black *Ophiopogon planiscapus* 'Nigrescens' (Zone 6) through the light-reflecting strongly purplish *Perilla frutescens*, the baking-chocolate brown of *Eupatorium rugosum* 'Chocolate', the crimson-browns of many barberries and maples, the soft, unobtrusive color of *Lysimachia ciliata* 'Purpurea' (Zone 3), and the hazy grayed browns of *Rosa glauca* and many sedums. These colors are versatile, and their contribution as dramatic (with chartreuse) or calming (with gray, blue, and white, for instance) as one wishes. No wonder this color range has so many devotees that new introductions get an eager welcome. There has been quite a flurry of these of late, and being a fan myself I have tried most of them. Most penstemons are short-lived where summers are hot, but *Penstemon digitalis* sows around prodigiously in semi-shade. It was largely ignored until *P. digitalis* 'Husker Red' (Zone 3) took the country by storm. This cultivar, too, is excellent, though it should be propagated only by division since seedlings are variable in color and sometimes entirely green. *Anthriscus sylvestris* 'Ravenswing' eluded me for years, when seed failed to germinate (it must be fresh) and purchased plants arrived beyond resuscitation (it does

not ship well). I have it now, compliments of a friend, and we shall see. It is short-lived but self-sows where it is happy.

My experience with raising the purple-leaved form of *Cryptotaenia japonica* (Zone 5) was just the opposite. Every seed germinated and grew within 2 years into a clump 18 inches high and wide. And a handsome thing it is, with lustrous, mahogany-colored trifoliate leaves. It is adaptable, doing equally well in sun (where the color is brighter) or light shade, provided the soil is moist. Then began the weeding out of seedlings scattered surprisingly far away. Wanting to keep at least one clump, I pinched out the flowers each morning. Minute and palest lavender, they are the reverse of ornamental, giving the clumps a scurfy look. They do their job, however, all too well, and so this plant will have to go. A pity. It is a good plant only where (if anywhere?) seed is not set.

And what of the heucheras, now available in such bewildering profusion? They do not like to be wet. They do not like to be parched. And they do not like full sun, yet lose some of their color in shade. The flowers are more often a liability than an asset. The plants need frequent division, and in many years something or other chews the leaves into holes. In Virginia I have yet to stand in front of any

Berberis thunbergii 'Royal Burgundy' (a purple Japanese barberry)

Physocarpus opulifolius 'Diabolo'

Far from being devilish, this dusky shrub is a delight, demonstrating the same hardiness, vigor, adaptability, and freedom from problems as the rest of its sturdy species. Three-lobed, maplelike leaves of cooking-chocolate brown are highlighted with yellow-green new shoots and a few red older leaves. Happy in full sun or light shade, *Physocarpus opulifolius* 'Diabolo' (Zone 2) becomes a very large shrub if not pruned back each year, as mine will be. Its chartreuse-leaved counterpart has thrived on this treatment for a good many years.

Berberis thunbergii

JAPANESE BARBERRY

No new shrub is likely to impinge much on the popularity of Japanese barberries. *Berberis thunbergii* (Zone 4) is a garden cliche for the best of reasons: it is cold and heat hardy, healthy, and undemanding. Its popularity and its variability are reflected in more than forty selections, of which about half have purple foliage. For best color, they need sun for at least half the day. Their fine texture and constant color throughout the growing season make them excellent for hedging or as continuity plants spaced along a border.

Japanese barberries vary in size from the

heuchera and have well up that feeling of deep satisfaction that comes from a plant well grown or a grouping well composed. Until that happens, heucheras will remain on my mediocre list. *Heuchera* 'Montrose Ruby' (Zone 5), *H. americana* 'Garnet' (Zone 5), and the matt-leaved *H. villosa* 'Purpurea' (Zone 6) have been the easiest to accommodate. These purple heucheras are, however, top-notch plants for cooler regions. After giving a plant of *H.* 'Montrose Ruby' to my sister in England, I did not recognize it the following year—it was so much more handsome than mine.

Mindful of the maxim that when everyone is somebody, nobody is anybody, I tried to prune my list of purple plants. And could not. Those that follow are too good to omit.

compact *Berberis thunbergii* 'Bagatelle', little more than a mound one foot high after a good many years, through such columnar forms as *B. thunbergii* 'Helmond Pillar' to *B. thunbergii* var. *atropurpurea* at a rounded 6 feet or more if left unpruned. Nurseries often grow this last barberry from seed and the color then varies, so it is advisable to see the plant before you buy it. Having selected a suitable size, one can keep the plant that way with an annual pruning, combining shearing with the occasional removal of a few old branches. The scarlet, tear-shaped berries of winter extract a price in the weeding out of unwanted seedlings that are prickly even in babyhood.

I have never had berries on dwarf forms, of which, for decades, the most popular has been *Berberis thunbergii* 'Crimson Pygmy'. A group of five has needed, at a guess, less than an hour of maintenance for each of its 20 years, which makes it ungrateful of me to have lately switched my allegiance to *B. thunbergii* 'Royal Burgundy'. The leaves are a little smaller and most are purplish brown interspersed with redder young ones. The result is a brighter, almost two-tone look, overlaid with a misty sheen as if seen through gauze. Size and rate of growth are about the same as for 'Crimson Pygmy'.

A few of the purple barberries have bicolored leaves, with *Berberis thunbergii* 'Rose

Salix purpurea 'Gracilis'

Glow' the best known. Its earth-tone leaves are marbled with coral pink. I placed my plant as a background to a pink-flowered swamp milkweed (*Asclepias incarnata*; Zone 3) with the pink repeated again in the flowers of *Crinum* 'Hanibal's Dwarf' in front of the milkweed. The soil in this spot is light and well drained, with lots of compost dug into the planting holes of the milkweed and crinum to accommodate their preference for moisture-retentive soil. Barberries are not fussy provided the soil isn't squelchy.

Salix purpurea 'Gracilis'
DWARF PURPLE OSIER

A few plants are neither purple nor gray but somewhere in between. *Rosa glauca* (Zone 2; synonym *R. purpurea*) is one. This rose, sad

Eupatorium rugosum 'Chocolate' flowering in October, by which time the leaves are dark green. *Stachys byzantina* 'Big Ears' (lamb's ears) is in the foreground.

to say, has not liked my garden. Several of the taller sedums in this color range do well, and the same misty purple is there in the slender leaves and branches of the airily textured *Salix purpurea* 'Gracilis' (Zone 4; synonym 'Nana'). This shrub is a better choice for mixing with perennials in regions of rapid growth than the purple smokebush (*Cotinus coggygria*), which I had to cut back so hard and so often to prevent it becoming a large tree that it gave up the ghost. Although dwarf purple osier soon attains 6 feet, it is bushy, with multiple slender branches that can be sheared back to half that height. Any moderately moist soil seems to suit it, in sun or light shade. Spring cuttings are an easy means of propagation.

Eupatorium rugosum 'Chocolate'

One could not wish for a more rugged plant than this, nor one more densely held together. One at a time is enough in all but the largest beds and borders. In soil of moderate fertility, not over assiduously watered, plant height is around 2 feet and width a little more. The small leaves of tip growth are a lustrous deep purplish brown. Larger, older leaves are a lackluster dark green. Therefore it behooves one to trim back this plant from time to time to keep the young growth coming, which also serves to hold back the white flowers until early autumn. *Eupatorium rugosum* 'Chocolate' is hardy to Zone 4.

Sedum 'Bertram Anderson'

To my surprise, *Sedum* 'Bertram Anderson' (Zone 5) prefers moist soil, where it forms a pathside patch around two colocasias of tropical appearance. This low-growing sedum resembles the better known *S.* 'Ruby Glow', with identical ruby red flowers, a slightly more trailing habit, and smaller leaves of smoky purple. The leaves are not as dark as I have seen them in cooler regions, but considerably darker than those of the larger *S.* 'Vera Jameson' (Zone 4). For me 'Bertram Anderson' is a better doer, pleasing to the eye from spring well into fall and brilliant when in bloom for 1–2 weeks in midsummer. Like most sedums, it is easily propagated by division or cuttings.

Eucomis comosa 'Sparkling Burgundy'

Pineapple lily (*Eucomis comosa*) has had a thorough testing in the two decades I have had it, surviving our worst winters and my neglect in thin soil and sun. In late July the green-flowered, curiously crested inflorescences rise on stout stalks over the upright clumps of broad, shiny leaf straps. It is a good plant, especially in such dark-leaved selections as 'Sparkling Burgundy' (Zone 7). I have never seen this cultivar more stunningly displayed than where it speared up through a silvery mat of lamb's ears (*Stachys byzantina*) in Ellen Penick's Richmond, Virginia, garden.

The color of *Eucomis comosa* 'Sparkling Burgundy' and other dark-leaved forms is most dramatic in spring, becoming greener later in the season. My plant got royal treatment in compost-enriched soil. Division is not imperative for many years unless for propagation purposes. The flowers, too, are purple-tinted, nicely matching the dark-leaved colocasias behind them.

Colocasia esculenta

ELEPHANT-EARS

North America (and England as well, so far as cool summers permit) has embarked on a Victorian-era craze for tropical looking, tender bedding plants. I, meantime, as I plan for manageability of my 2 acres as long as possible into old age, am heading in the other direction and growing fewer plants that must be overwintered indoors. There are, of course, exceptions, including, at least for the time being, *Dahlia* 'Bishop of Llandaff' and two *Colocasia esculenta* cultivars, which often survive winter in the ground but not with certainty. In any case, the colocasias get off to a quicker start if a young, small section is separated off in autumn and kept growing under lights through winter.

Colocasia esculenta 'Black Magic' with *Eucomis comosa* (pineapple lily) in foreground and *Veronicastrum virginicum* (Culver's-root) in background

Oxalis regnellii 'Triangularis' at right, with silvery spotted *Pulmonaria longifolia* (lungwort) and *Athyrium niponicum* 'Pictum' (Japanese painted fern)

Colocasia esculenta 'Black Magic' (Zone 8) has broadly arrow-shaped leaves averaging 15 inches long and almost as much across, their color an exceptionally dark, matt, grayed purple. Carried on self-supporting 5-foot stalks, the leaves angle down for perfect presentation. Growth does not begin until the days get warm. Then it is rapid. A small plant from a quart pot makes a 3-foot clump by late summer. *Colocasia esculenta* 'Illustris' (Zone 8), taller at about 6 feet, has larger leaves of similar color, patterned with light green veins for dramatic contrast.

Elephant-ears want moist soil and do best in full sun. Neighbors for my plants are *Eucomis comosa*, white-spired *Veronicastrum virginicum*, tall *Thalictrum lucidum* (Zone 4) with fluffy, multistamened yellow flowers, *Zephyranthes grandiflora* (Zone 7), and, alongside the path in front of it, *Sedum* 'Bertram Anderson'. If you are wondering whether you could fit in such sizeable plants, keep in mind that the colocasias are friendly minglers: their running roots thread their way through such low growing plants as the sedum then loft the leaves up high, where they neither shut out light from the smaller plant nor smother it.

Oxalis regnellii 'Triangularis'

Having ricocheted for years between the names *Oxalis regnellii* 'Atropurpurea' and O. *regnellii* 'Triangularis' (Zone 7), by recent taxonomic decree this South American plant is now called O. *triangularis* subsp. *papilionacea* 'Atropurpurea'. Hmm. That should boost its popularity. Readily available and inexpensive, it is a fine plant indoors or in the garden, increasing rapidly without making a pest of itself as so many of its genus do. Although it has survived winter in my garden for many years, as also has the green-leaved species, as insurance I always wiggle off a section of the congested, rhizomatous 1-foot-high clumps for wintering under lights indoors. The triangular leaves are deep purple-black with royal purple centers. Wan flowers of palest lavender are of secondary importance. This oxalis likes moist soil, out of the sun, where Japanese painted fern (*Athyrium niponicum* 'Pictum') or silvery spotted pulmonarias make good companion plants. My friend Elisabeth Sheldon uses it in her hot color garden in New York State. It is not hardy there, and she grows it in pots so that it can more easily be moved indoors for the winter. In her book *The Flamboyant Garden* she recommends many plants with colored foliage for use in colder climates than mine.

Perilla frutescens 'Crispa'

It would be hard to be without *Perilla frutescens* 'Crispa', if only because this self-sowing annual is determined to stay. When the new crop comes up in May I reduce the seedlings to groups of three, transplanting them where appropriate. If all survive two more are removed later. One 3-by-2-foot bush to a spot is usually enough. The shimmering, saw-edged leaves of dark grape purple resemble curly cockscombs when young, becoming flatter and less fringed at maturity. If that is too fancy for your taste, grow *P. frutescens* 'Atropurpurea' with unfringed leaves instead. The flowers are not ornamental, and one plant produces more than enough seed, so I cut off the flowers from most of them if I get around to it, know-

Perilla frutescens 'Crispa', with yellow-leaved *Berberis thunbergii* 'Bonanza Gold' and yellow-leaved *Spiraea thunbergii* 'Ogon' in background

ing that if I don't I shall regret it come spring. Full sun or a few hours of shade suit it well, in any well-drained soil.

GRAY LEAVES

Many silvery gray plants have felted leaves, and fuzzy plants dislike the summer steambath of hot and humid regions. That most-loved of the fuzzies, lamb's ears (*Stachys byzantina*; Zone 4), has survived for many years when grown out of hot sun. *Stachys byzantina* 'Big Ears' is more tolerant than the species, but it often turns to mush in summer and so cannot be given more than seven marks out of ten. *Artemisia* 'Powis Castle' (Zone 6), the similar *A.* 'Huntington', and the several

Veronica incana

upon to provide a few seedlings. The flowers are fascinating: five curiously notched lemon-yellow petals seem to be whirling around an inch-wide hub consisting of thousands of sunny yellow stamens held out horizontally in a dense disc. My complaint about it is that browning dead flowers stay on the bush and, in a 2-acre garden, their daily removal is not a realistic undertaking. Small gardens are more easily kept manicured, and there this plant would earn its place, in sun or light shade.

The following gray-leaved plants have proved reliable and in the main long-lived.

Eucalyptus neglecta

OMEO GUM

Neglected indeed is *Eucalyptus neglecta* (Zone 7), the only survivor of winters that killed *E. gunnii*, *E. niphophila*, and a good many other gum trees. While this comparatively small gum cannot compete in beauty with the silver dollar foliage of the popular *E. cinerea*, it is a great deal hardier and must be given credit for that. Grown from seed from Canberra Botanical Garden, Australia, it has reached its quarter century. Twice it has been killed to the ground. Both times it recovered fast, and now it is a slender, double-trunked, blue-green spire 25 feet high, with camphor-scented leathery 5-inch leaves that are oblong on young trees, narrower

forms of *Senecio cineraria* can take full sun and do not rot; their flaw is a short life.

Glaucous blue-gray foliage holds up better than silvery gray, and two plants are worthy of mention despite their shortcomings. *Dianthus* 'Mountain Mist' is the best year-round dianthus I have yet come across. In spring it bears pink semidouble scented flowers on 1-foot upright stems. Then, for the rest of the year, it makes a dense, silvery mound, needing only a couple of light clippings by way of maintenance. I am hopeful that 'Mountain Mist' will prove one of few exceptions in a genus of usually short-lived plants.

The other plant is the semi-evergreen *Hypericum frondosum* (Zone 5), with really lovely narrow blue-green leaves. While not very long-lived, it grows fast and can be relied

on older ones. In the wild it is found in swampy ground; in the garden it does not seem fussy.

Veronica incana

The small spear-shaped silver gray leaves of *Veronica incana* (Zone 4; synonym *V. spicata* subsp. *incana*) are velvety to the touch and borne on short side branches from the lower few inches of a woody stem that extends in spring into 1-foot branched spires of violet-blue flowers. If, when spent, these stems are cut off flush with the ground, additional foliage develops and the plants form dense mats 2–3 inches high. My plants bask in baking sun along the front of a raised bed, in unchanged acid sand topped with a layer of gravel. In spring they mingle prettily with self-sowing *Dianthus deltoides*. They are divided and re-planted about every fourth year. Ideas from other gardens can often be carried out with different, more climate-amenable plants. The idea for this planting came from the Connecticut garden of writer Sydney Eddison, who uses lamb's ears as a silvery continuity band in front of a raised border. In her book *The Self-Taught Gardener* she writes: "Good edging plants and superior foliage are the secrets of an effective perennial border. Look to the leaves and the edges, and the rest of the garden will fall into place." Amen to that.

Santolina chamaecyparissus var. *nana* (lavender cotton)

Santolina chamaecyparissus

LAVENDER COTTON

Santolina chamaecyparissus (Zone 7) is an ever-gray shrub that tolerates heat and humidity better than most gray-foliaged plants, but it grows fast and soon sprawls if not frequently clipped. *Santolina chamaecyparissus* var. *nana* is more compact and needs less clipping. It lives at least 10 years if grown in low-fertility soil with a reasonable ration of sun (half a day will do), not overwatered, not planted where leaves or petals from taller plants fall on it and rot the foliage, and not clipped back into old wood. Little and often is the pruning technique, playing it by eye and weather, to no particular schedule, trimming off an inch or so in early spring, removing flowering stems when the myriad little balls of

Ballota pseudodictamnus with yellow-striped *Yucca* 'Color Guard'

leaf axils are eager to grow, and in no time at all ballota has renewed itself. Such cutting back, often repeated more than once, does prevent formation of the small white flowers that would otherwise be borne in whorls along the stems, but that is little loss. Never have I seen ballota looking more enchanting than in the garden of a friend who had placed it against a large rock lichened in gray and chartreuse to match the ballota's unusual coloring.

Ballota does well in well-drained soil in sun or light shade. Covering pots of cuttings with plastic has sometimes induced rot and I find it best to stand the pots in shade uncovered. The shrubby 2- to 3-foot *Phlomis fruticosa* (Zone 7), which belongs to the same family, has leaves of similar color and texture and tolerates summer humidity.

TEXTURE

Because poor foliage is not the smack in the eye of color clashes, foliage often gets short shrift when choosing and arranging plants. In regions where intense summer heat curtails bloom, gardeners are more likely to give preference to plants with foliage that remains attractive throughout the growing season. In shady sites, where few plants bloom in summer, groups of foliage plants can give quite as much pleasure as colorful sunny borders if

bright yellow bloom are done, and only nibbling at it thereafter. The requirements for the bright green *S. viridis* (synonym *S. rosmarinifolia* subsp. *rosmarinifolia*) are the same. This species, too, has done well. It makes a somewhat larger plant and has lemon-yellow flowers.

Ballota pseudodictamnus

Ballota pseudodictamnus (Zone 7) has amazed me. The whole plant is so cashmere soft that surely it must rot, yet it does not. Heart-shaped leaves in opposite pairs are spaced along chenille-textured stems. The older leaves are green flocked with gray, young ones a luminous silvery lime. The plant becomes bedraggled in heavy rain, and then it is cut back. Buds in the

thoughtfully composed for contrasts in shape and texture. The photo on page 145 shows an example of a grouping that remains attractive from spring through autumn, with continuing interest in winter from the evergreens.

Tamarix ramosissima 'Summer Glow'

To include this shrub with gray-foliaged plants would be stretching the point. Nonetheless, it does look gray in certain light, especially in the misty early morning. It was planted in 1986 in sandy soil and full sun. Since then the only care it has had is hard pruning in late winter or early spring, when one or two old branches are cut out at the base and others cut back to no more than 2 feet long. By June it has become an up-right 8 feet of finely feathery foliage, topped in early summer with plumes of equally airy pink flowers. *Tamarix ramosissima* 'Summer Glow' (Zone 3) is a shrub of consummate grace and wide adaptability, taking both heat and cold in its stride and asking so little in return.

Sambucus nigra 'Linearis'

CUTLEAF ELDER

In a region where shrubs grow so fast, I've learned to upsize descriptions. Thus dwarf equals midsized, medium equals large, and large means that mighty soon the shrub will be

Sambucus nigra 'Linearis' (cutleaf elder)

taller than me. The smaller versions of plants are therefore often the best choice. I discarded several of the larger elders as not worth the effort of constant pruning. Purple-leaved *Sambucus nigra* 'Guincho Purple', for instance, remained determinedly green, a not unusual manifestation in hot climates. I rushed to order *Sambucus racemosa* 'Tenuifolia' (Zone 5) when it finally turned up in a catalog, having always admired this look-alike for a mounding cut-

leaf Japanese maple. It is still on my wish list.

It took a couple of years for it to dawn on me that what I'd got instead was *Sambucus nigra* 'Linearis' (Zone 5), which at first appalled me by behaving like a would-be vine, in an untidy sprawl of sideways-growing branches. A lesson re-learned once again: prune, prune, and prune again, hard in winter with touch-ups thereafter whenever a branch becomes unduly long. By this means, this shrub is kept

Crinkled lacy leaf of *Tanacetum vulgare* var. *crispum* (fernleaf tansy)

about 2 feet high and 4–5 feet across, and I have become fond of it in its own right. The foliage cannot quite decide what it wants to be when it grows up. It starts off in congested, threadlike, swish-broom clusters of leaf midribs only. Older leaves look as if varying portions had been neatly chewed away, leaving tissue in strangely assorted configurations, sometimes on only one side of a leaf, sometimes frilled or wavy, grotesque, perhaps, but with a light and lacy overall appearance. This elder wants soil at least moderately moist and a sunscreen through the hottest hours. Assuming it performed as well, a reasonable ex-

pectation, I would still prefer *S. racemosa* 'Tenuifolia', but *S. nigra* 'Linearis' has grown on me. Besides, it makes a talking point. It is propagated by cuttings.

Tanacetum vulgare var. *crispum*

FERNLEAF TANSY

This tansy has been unduly maligned. For years I was frightened off by warnings about its invasiveness. While I cannot speak for the species, this variety, though spreading moderately fast, takes only occasional minutes to control. In return it offers bright green ferny foliage on a plant that does equally well with sun for the whole or half a day, in just about any freely draining soil. Pinching out the tips now and then limits the height of *Tanacetum vulgare* var. *crispum* (Zone 4) to 15 inches. My plant has never bloomed.

Saruma henryi

I am writing mainly about plants that have proved themselves over the long run. *Saruma henryi* is a recent introduction to American gardens, and I have had it for only 3 years. It was an instant winner and uncomplaining through two of the hottest, driest summers on record. Although not yet tested by a colder than average winter, being herbaceous it is un-

likely to be damaged where frost seldom penetrates the ground more than an inch or two.

"*Saruma*" is a rearrangement of the letters of "*Asarum*," a genus to which it is closely related. Its heart-shaped, fuzzy leaf is similar to that of *Asarum canadense*, only a little larger and on a rounded plant about 2 feet high. When shoots emerge, late enough in spring to make marking its spot advisable, they glisten with silky down. Almost as it bursts from the ground it is bearing the three-petaled lemon-yellow flowers, forming triangles an inch or so across, which will continue forming singly at the tips through summer, a few at a time, and pretty if not eye-catching. It is, though, mainly a beautiful foliage plant of unusual texture. My plant is neighbored by *A. virginicum* under a high-branched oak and backed by evergreen azaleas, where it gets only morning sun, along with epimediums, celandines (*Ranunculus ficaria*), *Hosta* 'Sum and Substance', the low, broad conifer *Thujopsis dolobrata* 'Nana', bletillas, toad lilies (*Tricyrtis*), and a few persistent strands of the periwinkle (*Vinca minor*) I mistakenly planted and am now struggling to eradicate as unmanageable. Saruma must set seed, for seedlings have appeared, but I have failed to find any. It can be increased by division or cuttings.

Saruma henryi at lower left, with conifer *Thujopsis dolobrata* 'Nana', *Photinia davidiana* 'Prostrata', *Buxus sempervirens* 'Elegantissima' (a dwarf boxwood) at center front, *Tricyrtis hirta* (toad lily) in right foreground, sword-leaved *Bletilla striata* (hardy orchid), and yellow-leaved *Hosta* 'Sum and Substance' at upper right

Saruma henryi in spring

Asparagus pseudoscaber 'Spitzenschleier'

In the same sort of hot, dryish site that suits sasanqua camellias, the fine-foliaged *Asparagus pseudoscaber* 'Spitzenschleier' (Zone 4; synonym *A. officinalis* 'Pseudoscaber') has spread slowly over its 15-year life into a 3-by-4-foot cloud of wiry stems with widely spaced, feathery branchlets of quarter-inch gray-green needles that turn yellow in autumn. A crop of bright red berries is reported by others but has been denied me. I do not know why, nor mind very much. This asparagus can be propagated by division.

Artemisia abrotanum

SOUTHERNWOOD, LAD'S LOVE

Having known lad's love (*Artemisia abrotanum*; Zone 5) all my gardening life, it was good to find out that it does as well in Virginia's hot summers as it did in England's cool ones. Clipped hard in late winter and lightly now and then thereafter, it makes a feathery, soft green, spreading mound about 18 inches high alongside a path, where I can pinch off a piece of the aromatic foliage as I pass by. If the plant is left to grow taller, the leaves tend to rot during hot, humid weather, leaving the stems bare. Once a year, between autumn and spring, sideways spread is curtailed. A new addition, *A. abrotanum* 'Silver', has come through two dry summers in good shape but remains to be tested by a wet season. It resembles the species except that the finely cut foliage is intensely silvery.

GRASSES AND FERNS

Taking a seasonal approach to this book posed several placement dilemmas. Where did grasses and ferns best fit, when most of them are ornamental from late spring through fall, and some in winter as well? The seed plumes of such grasses as *Miscanthus* and *Pennisetum* play a major ornamental role in my garden's autumn and winter appeal, and there are few more enchanting sights than the unfurling fronds of ferns in spring. The needs of grasses and ferns are very different. Excepting sedges and sweet flags, most grasses want sun, and tolerance of drought is one of their big assets. What they have in common is attractive long-lasting foliage, and it is through the summer doldrums that I, made listless by the unrelenting heat, appreciate this most.

GRASSES

Thanks largely to nurseryman Kurt Bluemel American gardeners can take their pick from a vast range of ornamental grasses and such other grasslike plants as reeds (grasslike plants with hollow stems, *Arundo*, for instance), rushes (*Juncus*), sedges (*Carex*), sweet flag (*Acorus*), and cat tails (*Typha*).

A quick flick through a current catalog shows sixty-three genera, twice as many spe-cies, and hundreds of named selections: grasses herbaceous or evergreen, for sun or shade, for soils acid or alkaline, dry or wet, even for salt marshes. There are dwarf grasses for rock gardens, vigorous grasses for ground cover or meadow, tall grasses for specimens or screening, and gracefully arching grasses. Blades may be green, gray, blue, yellow, red, brown, or variegated. The flowers may be in spikes, plumes, tassels, or hazy panicles.

Grasses, grasses, grasses. How ever do we choose? We talk to other gardeners. We visit public gardens or nurseries with display beds in our region. We attend lectures, read books, send for catalogs. And then we experiment, trying a few more each year that take our fancy. After a quarter century of doing all these things, I have sampled only a fraction of the available grasses, and some of my plants are in the early stages of evaluation. *Pennise-tum orientale* was a three-time failure. Then along came an exciting new cultivar, *P. orien-tale* 'Tall Tails', a splendid performer during the 3 years I have had it.

Presented here are a handful of the grasses that have performed well for many years. Among the very best are selected forms of the evergreen Japanese sweet flag (*Acorus gra-mineus*). These are invaluable for winter in-terest and are discussed in that section under "Broadleaf Evergreens and Conifers." Most grasses are readily propagated by division, which many of them need quite frequently. Early spring is the best time to do this.

Carex

SEDGE

The plant world has its tortoises, frustratingly slow to reach effective size; its hares, needing constant controlling; and its prima donnas, demanding coddling. If there's to be time to care for these in the relaxed, unhurried, and contemplative way that makes the work a pleasure, there must also be self-sufficient plants. Ratios will vary with such factors as the size of the garden and the age and energy of its caretaker. Suffice it to say that if garden-ing has become burdensome, some rebalanc-ing is needed.

Nothing in my garden has asked less of me than a dozen clumps of *Carex conica* 'Margin-ata' (Zone 5; synonyms 'Hino-kan-sugi', 'Snow-line'), a neat and graceful evergreen sedge with slender arching blades forming dense low domes. A pencil line of white edging each blade is insufficient for a bicolor look, but in-

Carex flagellifera in July with brown-flowered *Hemerocallis* 'Milk Chocolate', variegated-leaved *Kalimeris yomena* 'Aurea', and creamy leaved *Sedum alboroseum* 'Mediovariegatum' in background

stead gives to the clumps the softened silveriness of pewter. Neither pokily slow nor rapidly spreading, each clump, undivided for more than 10 years, now measures 18 inches across. *Ajuga* 'Burgundy Glow', which once wandered among them, gradually got squeezed out. Now the clumps touch each other and no weeds can intrude. There are flowers in spring, little creamy powder puffs rising slightly above the surface of the clump, pretty but of secondary importance.

Carex conica 'Marginata' is growing where the light is good but direct sun strikes for only a couple of hours a day, in root-free, compost-enriched sandy soil that stays moderately moist, never sopping, most of the year, and on the dry side for a few weeks in summer. The place is right and the sedge self-sustaining. No fertilizing is done, and no individual watering, though this sedge sometimes gets the benefit of water from sprinklers satisfying the needs of more demanding plants. The best of plants will fail when ill suited to the site, and clumps I tried in full blazing sun perished rapidly, while others in deep root-filled shade struggled on but looked too forlorn to be long tolerated.

This evergreen sedge does not respond favorably to shearing. If winter leaves it looking the worse for weather, I comb it lightly with a rake then allow it to recover in its own good time. It does not need dividing unless it outgrows its space, which is unlikely to be soon, in which case it is easily accomplished by the back-to-back forks method. For propagation purposes portions of the clump can be separated with a hand fork without lifting the clump.

Carex flagellifera (Zone 7) is one of the brown sedges often taken for dead. The very fine blades may be 2 feet or more in length, with an arching habit that leaves the clump little more than 1 foot high. Colorists wouldn't be without brown sedges such as this one and the more upright *C. buchananii* (Zone 7). In soil never soggy and seldom dry, it has gone undivided for its 7 years and now forms clumps nearly 3 feet wide. The color, always light brown, is deeper in full sun than in part shade, though this species seems to do equally well in both places. It is at its best in late spring and early summer when, far from looking dead, it glows with life and makes a perfect partner for the darker brown flowers of *Hemerocallis* 'Milk Chocolate'. I had never taken shears to it, but this year it got cut down in March by mistake. It was my fault—I had said, "Cut down the grasses." By May it was none the worse for the shearing. Still, a light combing usually suffices.

Two other evergreen sedges are more flamboyant but less accommodating, needing soil consistently moist and emerging from unusually cold winters alive but scathed. *Carex* 'Evergold' (Zone 7), which has had its species switched so often I refuse to commit myself, is best displayed in a slightly raised bed, where its long, arching blades don't get bedraggled trailing in the dirt. Boldly striped in creamy yellow, it is gay and cheerful without being raucous. As with *C. conica* 'Marginata', if it greets spring looking bedraggled, I have found it best to leave it to recover at its own pace.

The well-named *Carex phyllocephala* 'Sparkler' (Zone 7) bursts on the scene with whorls of lance-shaped, white-edged blades that look stiff and sharp enough to impale you but are, in fact, quite soft to the touch, an unusual texture guaranteed to draw covetous glances. It is worth the small effort to toss an armful of pine-straw around it to help it through cold snaps. Semi-evergreen, it will look disheveled by spring. I wait until strong new growth appears at the base before grooming it by removing stems with dead or browned blades. Scarcely noticeable bloom catkins result in small patches of seedlings, easily scratched out while small. Seedlings will not be variegated, but the one I let grow up is handsome nonetheless.

The score one awards a plant is based partly on how it compares with the competition. *Carex siderosticha* 'Variegata' (Zone 6) would get more marks, maybe a perfect score, in colder regions with fewer choices. It is a tough and handsome spreading sedge, with cream-striped blades comparatively short and broad, an excellent ground cover plant where the soil stays consistently moist, but herbaceousness counts against it when the competition is fierce. Another debit entry was the time it took to tidy away its dead leaves in autumn, leaves that do not yield to pulling and have to be cut off. So in the end, and not without regret, it ceded its place in moist shade to sweet flag (*Acorus*). In dry shade, where the sedge tends to shrivel, *Lamium galeobdolon* 'Hermann's Pride' performed better, and everywhere it is outranked by the variegated liriopes it rather resembles. The sedge went to a good home and should I move to a colder region I'll ask for a bit back.

Arundo donax 'Variegata'

GIANT REED

Going from one extreme of height to the other, the queen of my grasses is the striped giant reed (*Arundo donax* 'Variegata'; Zone 7). It has the proportions of a clump of sapling trees and one thicket is enough. Come summer, this most majestic of grasses hoists aloft glistening silky plumes to a height of 12 feet or more, yet it seldom topples: the broad leaf blades shrug off water from summer downpours that send many plants reeling.

Far from needing support, giant reed is itself support for such lightweight annual vines as the violet-blue butterfly pea (*Centrosema virginiana*), a morning-glory with small scarlet flowers (*Ipomoea coccinea*), or a clock-vine with white or yellow flowers (*Thunbergia alata*). Moonvine (*Ipomoea alba*) did prove a bit too much for it, bowing the stout canes down. Clematis was a tempting thought: imagine purple-flowered *Clematis ×jackmanii* among the arundo's white-striped leaves. But clematis stems are brittle and would probably be broken when the arundo clump is thinned, a task done with a mattock, calling less for skill than for what my father was wont to call brute force and (expletive deleted) ignorance. Fantasy must sometimes give way to common sense.

Arundo is (at present, anyway) placed in the Gramineae or grass family. Grasses, along with bulbs and a few other plants, are monocotyledons. Monocots lack the cambium layer that gives rise to roots and therefore, theoretically, cannot be increased by cuttings or layers. Arundo, however, does not live by the book. It can be rooted from cuttings and will layer itself if given half a chance. After thinning out some stems in midsummer I dumped these on what, in more orderly gardens, would be termed the compost pile but in mine is merely piled up plant debris left to rot down at its own speed. In this unlikely propagation bed, with no soil accessible, the arundo stems took root and grew.

Three years ago, in a soft-hearted (or softheaded) moment, when the colossal belowground buds dug out in the thinning process seemed to beg for a chance to live, I told them "sink or swim" and tossed them in the mud at the edge of the creek lapping the garden. Here, when the tide was in, they were submerged under 2 feet of salty water. Not one whit deterred, they crawled, they romped, they raced, and 3 years later they had to be removed before they overran the native wetland grasses. In the border, however, a biennial thinning keeps this arundo adequately in check. I have never found a seedling.

Variegated arundo is at its showiest in spring and early summer. Then the wide leaves, broadly striped in snowy white, enhance so many nearby flowers, whether they echo the white, like the pristine *Phlox* 'Miss Lingard', or contrast as do the bright pink pompons of tall double poppies. By midsummer the white in the leaves has turned to cream, a background that enhances the blue flowers of a chaste tree (*Vitex agnus-castus*).

Arundo donax 'Variegata' in June with *Consolida ambigua* (larkspur)

Where the growing season is long, arundo can be cut back hard in midsummer to keep it shorter and induce fresh white-striped leaves, but flower plumes are then sacrificed. The canes are usually winter-killed. They would live over in our mildest winters, but when the large leaves are shed the wind distributes them messily around the garden, necessitating a cleanup job I prefer to avoid by cutting them down before this happens.

Miscanthus sinensis

How many selections of miscanthus I grow and which ones varies from time to time. Some have been here for many years. Others have been discarded to make way for whatever new selection has taken my fancy from among the fifty or more cultivars of *Miscanthus sinensis* (Zone 5): white-plumed *M. sinensis* 'Graziella', as graceful as its name, is next on the waiting list.

When I planted it 20 years ago, 8-foot-tall *Miscanthus sinensis* 'Zebrinus' was the only yellow-banded miscanthus around. It clumps up fast, needs reducing every year, and thus was soon amply available to form a hedge in the ditch outside the front fence, where it screens the garden from the road for 9 months of the year. Shored up by the fence behind and other clumps on either side, the only place it

can topple is forward over the ditch onto the roadside verge, which actually seldom happens, though single clumps often do topple.

For most purposes there are now several better gold-banded selections. Porcupinegrass (*Miscanthus sinensis* 'Strictus') forms a stiffer, less stout, and somewhat shorter V-shaped clump. *Miscanthus sinensis* 'Puenktchen' has much narrower leaf blades, and in a genus of giants *M. sinensis* 'Hinjo', which tops out at about 4 feet, is an outstanding candidate for gardens of average size.

Where summer storms occur the blot on the otherwise unsullied escutcheon of most miscanthus is the way the outer stems splay out and smother surrounding plants. What to do? Stake them? Perish the thought! Grasses are supposed to be carefree plants. That is why, while others come and go, the 4- to 5-foot tall slender-bladed, white-striped *Miscanthus sinensis* 'Morning Light' is here to stay. The most elegant of them all, it and 'Hinjo' are the only two forms I have never had collapse.

Two 7- to 8-foot-tall, bold, broad-bladed, white-striped selections, *Miscanthus sinensis* 'Cabaret' and 'Cosmopolitan', splay out when the clumps get large. They are forgiven this tendency for the substance and permanence they bring as twin hubs among more ephemeral plants in a white border. White-variegated

plants are important components of white borders where a hot and humid climate precludes inclusion of most gray foliage because it is likely to rot.

Miscanthus is one of the joys of the off-season months, standing like straw-colored stooks of grain topped with scintillating plumes, so the clumps are not cut down until late winter. Not too late though. A careful eye is kept on them, and the job quickly done when the clumps come into growth; otherwise the new blades are decapitated. Stems are cut down quickly with an electric hedge saw, but not quite as quickly cleared away. Large clumps are then reduced in size by a third, using a mattock to hack out the surplus. Why is the mattock so seldom mentioned in articles on garden tools? My tools are minimal, but I could not manage without this one.

To keep clumps of miscanthus, or anything else for that matter, in precisely the same place, they would need to be reduced evenly all round, but that removes the youngest canes and leaves the congested middle that is a major cause of miscanthus collapse. With a little wriggle-room available, I hack away on the left one year, the right the next, after which it is time to lift the whole clump (a chore left to stronger arms and back than mine) and start afresh with a portion taken from young outer

Miscanthus sinensis 'Hinjo' in August with yellow-flowered *Rudbeckia triloba*

Panicum virgatum 'Heavy Metal' (foreground) in July with a Shasta daisy, *Leucanthemum* ×*superbum* 'Becky', and *Miscanthus sinensis* 'Cosmopolitan' in background

growth. Clumps of miscanthus are quite slow to attain their full height in spring, so such tall plants as hollyhocks, which flower early and make no summer contribution, are positioned behind them.

Panicum virgatum
SWITCH GRASS

Panicum virgatum (Zone 5) grows wild on the edge of the brackish marsh behind the house. *Panicum virgatum* 'Heavy Metal' is far superior for garden use, forming steel-gray pillars about 6 feet high, useful in my white border for its color, its firmly upright shape that does not intrude on the territory of neighboring plants, and its misty flowering sprays in summer. It grows densely and needs dividing only every third year. *Panicum virgatum* 'Prairie Sky' is bluer, looser, graceful in habit, and diaphanous in bloom. With sun for half the day it became unkempt in its second year. It will get another chance to shape up in full sun. If it does not, out, for there are always plants in waiting in my nursery beds.

Pennisetum
FOUNTAIN GRASS

Coming further down the size scale, the fountain grasses are among my staples. *Pennisetum alopecuroides* (Zone 6), 3–4 feet when in bloom, makes just the right companion for *Sedum* 'Autumn Joy', with the pink-flecked leaves of *Berberis thunbergii* 'Rose Glow' behind. Blue asters, and chrysanthemums in white and pale apricot are additional components in a carefree sunny corner never lacking interest from late spring well into winter. When I pull into the drive in autumn and winter what immediately catches my eye is the glistening backlit seed plumes of five 2- to 3-foot plants of *Pennisetum alopecuroides* 'Hameln' grouped at the front of a bed, where they hide the winter skeleton of *Rosa* 'Carefree Delight'. That these fountain grasses need dividing is made manifest when new blades cannot push their way up through the congested dead tuffets. For me this is every third year, when I lift the clumps while new growth is young, pull off and replant small living outer sections (bunching them when they come off as single rooted stems), and discard the rest.

Few sights have brought me more joy than the bitter-chocolate brown foxtail flowers of *Pennisetum alopecuroides* 'Moudry' dew-coated and scintillating in the early morning sun. And few tasks have been more exasperating than trying to disentangle zillions of its seedlings from among nearby clumps of Siberian iris, unless it be the similar task with wild oats (*Chasmanthium latifolium*). 'Mou-

Sasa veitchii in January

dry' had to go, but it should be high on the list in regions where it is less fecund. Pretty pink-plumed *P. setaceum* is an enviable tender species for frost-free regions, or as an annual. So also is the tall *P. setaceum* 'Rubrum', with broad burgundy leaves and reddish inflorescences. Even when swaddled in Remay (a protective landscape fabric) inside a frame I've lost these plants when the temperature drops to our average winter low of 15°F. I could

grow them in pots and bring them indoors for the winter, but already I have to pick my way to the washing machine through pots of dahlias and other nonhardies wintering in the laundry lobby.

Sasa veitchii

Bamboos, of which *Sasa veitchii* (Zone 7) is one, are a varied lot, but all can be described by one of three "un-" words: unobtainable, unaffordable, or uncontrollable. Make that four! One bamboo I've coveted all my gardening years, *Chusquea culeou*, is ungrowable (insufficiently hardy) in my region. Bamboos are often planted as screens along boundaries, frequently arousing animosity from the unwilling recipients of their largesse on the other side of the fence. Be wary of any inexpensive bamboo; those few that stay in their clump are costly.

Resisting two that tempt me, gold-striped *Pleioblastus auricomus* (synonym *Arundinaria viridistriata*) and white-striped *Pleioblastus variegatus* (synonym *Arundinaria variegata*), both rampant runners unless corseted in concrete, I've succumbed to only one bamboo, *Sasa veitchii*. Though said to reach 3 feet or more, my plant is not much more than 2 feet tall. The leaves, with the somewhat starry shape of spread-out chubby fingers held horizontally, have the fascinating characteristic of becoming variegated, or seemingly so, in winter, when the leaf edges bleach out white. "Slow spreading" says the American Horticultural Society *Encyclopedia of Garden Plants*, which had its birth in England. Ha-ha. One year after the quart pot plant went into place in dry shade, it had spread 1 foot in each direction. It is now incarcerated in a large sunken plastic container lined with a thick layer of newspaper to prevent the roots from making a getaway through the drainage holes. An inch or two of the rim is exposed to prevent the plant's escape at surface level, an inexpensive way of controlling stoloniferous plants.

Leymus arenarius
LYME GRASS

Leymus arenarius (Zone 4; synonym *Elymus arenarius*), too, is in a sunken container, where it has been for 5 years with no sign of escape. Soon it will have to be extracted, thinned, and replanted, for it cannot be expected to live forever deprived of the opportunity to make new shoots. So far, so good. Given the tendency of so many gray plants to rot, the glaucous, silver-blue gleam of this one is a welcome addition to my border of pinks and blues. Cut to the ground in late winter, it attains a height of 2–3 feet by midspring. Thus restrained, it gets my top rating among the glaucous silvery grasses for humid regions.

The similar, lovelier plant I acquired as *Agropyron pubiflorum*, now *Elymus magellanicus*, proved intolerant of hot and humid summers. So did the blue oat grass, *Helictotrichon sempervirens*. There is a promising alternative in *Schizachyrium scoparium* 'The Blues' (Zone 3), a selected form of bluestem grass and a got-to-have when I saw it in a friend's garden. 'The Blues' makes a dense, silver blue clump of slender blades, rising to 3 feet when it bears its narrow plumes in late summer. Blue-gray *Festuca* 'Sea Urchin' (Zone 4) makes dense evergreen tuffets 6 inches high (a foot high when in flower), rejoicing in sun and sand. My only gripe is that this fescue, like most of its kind, needs to be divided every third year, just as the clumps are meeting up, resulting in an always-gappy look.

Juncus patens 'Carmen's Grey'
RUSH

This rush, introduced by Ed Carmen of Carmen's Nursery, California, has proven easy and evergreen in any moderately moist to wet soil in sun or light shade. It makes a dense clump of flexible steel-gray 2- to 3-foot knitting needles angled slightly out. Forget about the flowers, which form a single brownish warty protuberance from the side of the stem. I saw immediately that *Juncus patens* 'Carmen's Grey' (Zone 5) would be the perfect textural contrast for the Japanese painted fern

RIGHT *Stipa tenuissima* (feather grass) in May with pale pink *Dianthus* 'Mountain Mist', deep pink *Dianthus deltoides*, blue *Salvia* 'Blue Mound', and *Veronica incana* running as a ribbon along the front edge, and yellow-flowered *Potentilla recta* var. *sulphurea* at center bottom.

(*Athyrium niponicum* 'Pictum') and put it in front of a group of three. Subsequently, I moved it behind and then decided I liked it better where it was in the first place but with a slight change in the composition of the group. As an architectural plant the rush is best seen in its entirety. The ferns will be reduced to two, side by side a little apart, with the rush in front in the middle. Although it is by no means essential, pulling or cutting out dead stems in spring or early summer is time well spent in keeping this rush pristine.

Stipa tenuissima
FEATHER GRASS
Although short-lived and treated as an annual, this most ethereal of grasses takes little time to manage and vacates its space so briefly that there is no consciousness of gaps. When, by the end of winter, one-year-old plants look disheveled and brown, they are lifted out: "pulled" suggests effort not required, so lightly do they rest on the ground. Scattered around are baby tufts, just a comfortable amount, not to excess. Lifted and put into place these tufts grow in what seems no time at all, perhaps a month, to billowing 18-inch blonde tresses, wafting mesmerically back and forth in scarcely detectable movements of air. Sun, light soil, and dry weather suit feather grass

best, but when rain or sprinklers bring about a wet dog look, blades as fine as baby hair dry quickly in sun or breeze. Hair grass would be a more suitable common name than feather grass. *Stipa tenuissima* is hardy to Zone 7.

FERNS
A fern-infatuated friend complains that many of us name all the other plants in a grouping, then homogenize her favorites by adding "and ferns." Ferns aren't always easy to tell apart, but that's a poor excuse for those of us who wouldn't think of lumping together as "daisies" such different plants as chrysanthemums, asters, and rudbeckias. Their attractiveness is far from being limited to the summer months, but it is when the days are hot that I most appreciate their cool, calm presence.

If I were awarding medals to the ferns I grow, I'd give the gold to Japanese painted fern (*Athyrium niponicum* 'Pictum'). Three ferns would tie for the silver: ghost fern (*Athyrium* 'Branford Beauty'), tassel fern (*Polystichum polyblepharum*), and Chinese lace-fern (*Selaginella braunii*), which isn't a fern but looks like one. Running neck-and-neck for the bronze would be autumn fern (*Dryopteris erythrosora*), Japanese holly fern (*Cyrtomium falcatum*), the confusingly named variegated holly fern (*Arachniodes simplicior* var. *varie-*

gata), southern maiden fern or river fern, which came to me as sun fern (*Thelypteris kunthii*), and Japanese climbing fern (*Lygodium japonicum*).

Adiantum ×mairisii
One of two honorable mentions, *Adiantum ×mairisii* (Zone 7) has veil-like cascades of little tear-shaped leaves. Some consider it a hardier form of the southern maidenhair (*A. capillus-veneris*), and it likes the same moist and shady conditions. Himalayan maidenhair (*A. venustum*) is similar. Why omit the northern maidenhair (*A. pedatum*)? Sour grapes! It has made clear its preference for cooler, moister conditions than what I can provide. The second honorable mention is the 6-inch-high evergreen, sun-loving hairy lip fern, *Cheilanthes lanosa* (Zone 5). It is content and trouble-free in the gravelly soil of a raised bed with sun for half the day.

Athyrium niponicum 'Pictum'
JAPANESE PAINTED FERN
Many ferns are look-alikes, but in a family of plants predominantly green, the burgundy-ribbed and purple-feathered gray fronds of Japanese painted fern (*Athyrium niponicum* 'Pictum'; Zone 4) are unmistakable. The delicate appearance of this exquisite fern belies its

hardiness and ease of cultivation in any acid, moisture-retentive soil where there's shade from hot afternoon sun. Where winters are mild, evergreen ferns are apt to be preferred, but the herbaceousness of Japanese painted fern can be turned to advantage. Some of my plants were planted over snowdrops, so there's no bare ground when the bulbs have gone to rest. A primrose yellow celandine (*Ranunculus ficaria* 'Citrina') also manages to push up and flower through the fern's dense fibrous roots before the fronds emerge.

Gray goes with everything so, posing no color quandaries, painted fern affords countless opportunities for winsome combinations: in spring with primroses, hardy orchids (*Bletilla striata*), pulmonarias, and double bloodroot (*Sanguinaria canadensis*), and in autumn with *Begonia grandis* in white or pink, or toad lilies (*Tricyrtis*). The gray fronds are a perfect foil for the purple foliage of *Oxalis regnellii* 'Atropurpurea', for purple-leaved heucheras such as 'Montrose Ruby' and 'Pewter Veil', or for a purple cutleaf maple. For contrasting texture there are hostas galore, hellebores, pachysandra, shade-tolerant woodrushes (*Luzula*), and such other grassy leaved plants as sedge (*Carex*), sweet flag (*Acorus*), and liriope.

Yet the simplest settings are often the best, and today I've been lingering over a single

Athyrium niponicum 'Pictum' (Japanese painted fern) with silver-veined *Saxifraga stolonifera* (strawberry geranium) and creeping *Mazus reptans* 'Alba'

clump of painted fern amidst the short, dark blades of a dwarf form of mondo grass (*Ophiopogon japonicus*). The fern sowed itself in there and, to my amazement, not only survives but flourishes among the dense tufts of the mondo grass, where I'd never have dreamed of planting it. Standing in front of it and admiring its temerity, I remembered a scene in a friend's garden, where, with no other plants in sight, the delicacy of the fern was emphasized by adjacent rounded boulders.

Few ferns are more bountiful, and numerous variations have been selected from its self-sown progeny, including a crested form. A few seedlings in any batch may have green fronds, but most will be gray, be it silver, dove, pewter,

Athyrium 'Branford Beauty' (ghost fern) surrounded by *Lamium maculatum* 'White Nancy'

by alternating in a row the Japanese painted fern and the red-stemmed form of lady fern. One of the resulting hybrids has been named *Athyrium* 'Branford Beauty' (Zone 4). It increases quite fast, divides and transplants without any problems, and is now available from both wholesale and retail nurseries.

Gray can be combined with gray provided there is contrast in size, form, texture, or shade of gray. All these contrasts are achieved when ash gray ghost fern rises out of a carpet of silvery leaved cultivars of *Lamium maculatum*, choosing a flower color from among purple ('Beacon Silver'), soft pink ('Pink Pewter'), or white ('White Nancy').

Polystichum polyblepharum
TASSEL FERN

Tassel fern (*Polystichum polyblepharum*; Zone 5) makes knee-high 2-foot clumps of slightly arching evergreen fronds that look as if they've just been waxed, while new fronds seem to be wearing brown furry overcoats. It enjoys the same lightly shaded location as *Arum italicum* 'Pictum', hellebores, mouse-plant (*Arisarum proboscideum*), *Arisaema sikokianum*, and *Corydalis ochroleuca*, alongside a path under high branched pines. It increases slowly and seldom needs dividing. Several other polystichums also perform well.

ash, or steel, with differing proportions of dark feathering down the center of the fronds. Size may differ, too. *Athyrium niponicum* 'Samurai Sword' is a named clone selected for its burgundy ribbing.

Athyrium 'Branford Beauty'
GHOST FERN

"Ghost fern" sounds appropriately ethereal and mysterious for a group of ferns the subject of much conjecture. Also called giant painted ferns, they have the height, habit, and frond dissection of the lady fern (*Athyrium filix-femina*) but the fronds are silvery gray. It is very beautiful, and it tolerates drier shade than the painted fern. More than one clone exists, and where some of them came from remains a mystery but I can tell you the origin of mine. Dr. Nickolas Nickou in Connecticut encouraged nature to create something new

Polystichum polyblepharum (tassel fern) in August with *Helleborus orientalis* and red berry spikes of *Arum italicum* 'Pictum'

Selaginella braunii (Chinese lace-fern)

Selaginella braunii

CHINESE LACE-FERN

The bright green fronds of Chinese lace-fern (*Selaginella braunii*; Zone 5) remind me of the doilies, weighted with jet beads, my grandmother crocheted for covering the milk jug to keep flies out. Evergreen to about 20°F, this fern survives much colder weather, but the wiry-stemmed top growth is then killed. Though stoloniferous, the plant spreads quite slowly, and slicing off chunks from the outer edges about every third year suffices to prevent it overrunning a neighboring bletilla. *Heuchera americana* 'Dale's Strain' adds further textural variety, its white-netted leaves so much easier to place than the purple heucheras that disappear visually against brown earth. Another neighbor is maroon-flowered *Helleborus abchasicus*, which self-sows in such abundance and grows at such a pace that, notwithstanding the vigor of the lace-fern, I would put my money on the hellebore in a territorial fight.

Thelypteris kunthii

RIVER FERN

Nothing is safe in the path of the 4-foot *Thelypteris kunthii* (Zone 7) if it is planted in moist, fertile soil. What my plant has is filtered

Thelypteris kunthii (river fern) in late November, with seedling form of *Arum italicum* 'Pictum' and *Camellia sasanqua* 'Jean May'

survives in the midst of *Thelypteris kunthii*, adding winter interest, though I cannot say it looks exactly delighted with its lot.

Dryopteris erythrosora

AUTUMN FERN

Though evergreen, the 2- to 3-foot V-shaped autumn fern (*Dryopteris erythrosora*; Zone 5) frequently looks unkempt by spring, which may be a good thing because it prompts me to cut off the old fronds, thus making way for the new ones of soft satiny bronze, a color echoed by a brick-red primrose growing at the base of the fern. *Dryopteris erythrosora* 'Prolifica' has daintier fronds, with narrow, slightly curly segments.

Cyrtomium falcatum

HOLLY FERN

For contrast with bushy, small-leaved Japanese azaleas, I know of nothing better than the broad, 2- to 3-foot fronds of Japanese holly fern. Pinnate, leathery, and with a mirrorlike gloss, they look more like the leaves of mahonia than of holly. The frond segments are toothed and in some selections coarsely fringed, crested, or tridentlike. The bold, arching clumps are unfazed by high summer temperatures if given a modicum of shade and a humus-enriched soil. Low temperatures are

sun and low-fertility soil infiltrated by the dense roots of red cedar (*Juniperus virginiana*). And there, unfazed by adversity, it grows fresh, green, and lacy with nary a scorched frond from late spring until hard frost, vigorous but controllable in the company of such shrubs as *Hydrangea macrophylla* and evergreen azaleas. How could one not appreciate

such an accommodating plant? Sometimes called sun fern, it will grow in full sun but to me looks out of place there. (If one wants a ferny look in sun then sweet fern [*Comptonia peregrina*; Zone 4] is the thing. This small mildly suckering, deciduous shrub is native to eastern North America, where it grows in dry and sunny places.) *Arum italicum* 'Pictum'

Coppery new fronds of *Dryopteris erythrosora* (autumn fern) in April with brick-red *Primula vulgaris* hybrid at bottom left, *Aquilegia canadensis* at top left, and blue *Brunnera macrophylla* in background

Cyrtomium falcatum (holly fern) with the evergreen azalea 'Fashion'

less to its liking and, although it has survived occasional plunges to zero, its survival cannot be counted on below 15°F. *Saxifraga stolonifera* romps under and around one group, its airy white flowers playing a lightening role similar to gypsophila in a flower arrangement. *Cyrtomium fortunei* (Zone 7) is hardier than *C. falcatum*, but a poor thing by comparison,

with dull green fronds that usually die away in winter.

Arachniodes simplicior var. variegata

VARIEGATED HOLLY FERN

As if this desirable fern was not handicapped enough by its unwieldy botanical name, dubbing it variegated holly fern has caused it to be confused with the cyrtomiums. The name in no way lessens this plant's sales appeal at garden centers and nurseries. Once you see *Arachniodes simplicior* var. *variegata* (Zone 6), it will be in your shopping cart. If the fronds were solid green this pinnate-leaved fern with a satiny sheen would be garden-worthy: the addition of bright yellow stripes makes it unique among available, hardy ferns. It is not the most adaptable of ferns, and during my 6-year stewardship I've been less concerned with presentation than with finding a site to suit it. The best site has proved to be almost total shade in moist but not wet soil. Morning sun has proved acceptable in another spot, where a late-blooming, purple-flowered

LEFT *Lygodium japonicum* (Japanese climbing fern) with a red clematis, climbing on *Jasminum nudiflorum* and fishing line

ornamental onion, *Allium thunbergii* 'Ozawa's Variety', provides striking color contrast in late summer and early autumn.

Lygodium japonicum

JAPANESE CLIMBING FERN

Japanese climbing fern (*Lygodium japonicum*; Zone 7) has just the right degree of adaptability in my garden, where I have found only a handful of seedlings during its 10-year sojourn. In the North, it isn't hardy; in the Deep South it is a pest. The parent plant, happy but poorly presented, rambles through an evergreen azalea, a green-on-green fine-textured duo that renders the fern almost unnoticeable. After several attempts I found a better place on a corner of a small wellhouse, where the thread-fine "stems" (actually an extended midrib) and lacily dissected fronds of this herbaceous species reach a height of 6 feet by midsummer, supported invisibly by nylon filament fishing line thumbtacked into place.

The challenge now is to do as well by the Hartford fern (*Lygodium palmatum*; Zone 3), an uncompromising, evergreen native species challenging to cultivate. It has thrived in my garden for 20 years, in acid, sandy soil kept moist by seepage from the septic tank drainfield, but to say that it is poorly presented is an understatement. It is in a shady east-facing niche at the base of a fothergilla, where even the most observant eyes usually fail to spot it. There it supports itself as best it can on a 1-foot-high piece of encircling wire mesh made blessedly inconspicuous by rust. It is not that I haven't tried. There has never been a seedling, but every year or two I manage a small division, plant it lovingly in a likely spot, and envisage the showpiece it will become. It has balked at my every effort. I dream on and continue trying, meanwhile, blessed it seems by beginner's luck, adopting a "have-it, love-it, and leave-it-alone" approach to the parent plant.

If your appetite for ferns has been whetted, read *Ferns for American Gardens*, by John Mickel, the most practical book on ferns that I have encountered.

EARLY SUMMER FLOWERS

Will summer be wet, or will it be dry? It could be either, so only those plants that can accommodate themselves to both drought and heavy rain would be long-term survivors without my intervention. *Stokesia laevis* is one such plant, omitted from my winner's list only because it flowers for less than a month and needs daily deadheading. Joining the ranks of low-growing stokesias with blue or white flowers are two recent introductions: *S. laevis* 'Mary Gregory', with flowers of creamy yellow, and *S. laevis* 'Omega Skyrocket', with blue flowers atop upright 3-foot stems. I can and do supplement such water as nature provides, but I cannot stave off summer storms, so I must forego plants intolerant of heavy rain combined with intense heat. The most missed of these are such ornamental forms of culinary sage as *Salvia officinalis* 'Icterina', 'Purpurascens', and 'Tricolor'. Three years is the longest I have kept any of these. Under a regime of rain or sprinkler-applied water many plants grow lank and lush, calling for a lot of cutting back. *Lobelia cardinalis* does well in part of the garden where the soil is heavy and moist and distant trees cast light shade during the hottest hours, but here they grow twice as tall as the 3-foot height I was accustomed to in England.

Often they then fall over, so nowadays I cut them back in late spring, trading the elegance of single spires for self-supporting bushiness.

JUNE

No matter what the calendar says, June is summer in southeastern North America. As I write, on the first day of June, the air conditioner, set to come on at 75°F, kicked in at 8 A.M. The temperature invariably climbs into the nineties on at least some days in June, aggravated many years by lack of rain. Still, with luck there will be some pleasant days before the endurance test of July and August.

Spiraea japonica

Summer's routine is to go out early, to attend to essential maintenance, see what is to be seen, and perhaps take a few photographs. What greets me in June is an appalling color clash from the fluffy, purplish pink, yarrow-like inflorescences of *Spiraea japonica* 'Goldflame' (synonym *S.* ×*bumalda* 'Goldflame') in jarring juxtaposition with its own olive-green leaves and the few last lingering orange flowers of *Geum* ×*heldreichii*. Matters can only get worse, because orange butterfly weed (*Asclepias tuberosa*) is getting ready to bloom. I hasten to cut off the offending spiraea flowers and later shall do so again, for these pink-flowered spiraeas are cut-and-come-again shrubs, flowering a second time, and sometimes a third if cut back, in a bloom season extending from late spring through summer.

Disparagement notwithstanding, goldflame spiraea is high on my list of desirable shrubs. Not only do I want it, I want it where it is, in a hot color bed. No other shrub compares with its newly emerged leaves of bronze, amber, and soft orange (there's pink as well if one looks close, but it is not apparent), perfect with the scarlet and yellow columbines and tulips blooming at the same time. It was earlier removed from a bed with a color scheme of pinks and blues, for I have found that hot colors can absorb a bit of pink more readily than pinks can absorb orange.

Although no other compares for spring foliage, there are numerous yellow-leaved selections of *Spiraea japonica* (Zone 4) with flowers of a less harsh pink. Many of these can still be found under *S.* ×*bumalda*, a defunct distinction that never was apparent. The foliage of *S. japonica* 'Goldmound' has summer leaves of brighter yellow than 'Goldflame', touched with bronze and orange in autumn. Keep it sheared to match its name (it grows taller and looser if left unpruned) and there'll be no flowers. *Spiraea japonica* 'Golden Princess' is similar but taller. The newer *S. japonica* 'Candle Light' has leaves of buttery yellow, objectionable with its flowers only to those with a total aversion to pink and yellow combinations. In that case, turn to those with green leaves.

Green-leaved selections of *Spiraea japonica* lack sufficient thrust to hold the spotlight as the yellow-leaved selections do. Conversely, they lend themselves much better to grouping, merging into a single evenly shaped mass. Because it offers the bonus of leaves with fringed edges, along with the familiar purplish pink flowers, my first choice among this group is *Spiraea japonica* 'Crispa' (sold for years as *S. dolichica*). Several plants grouped at the front of a bed are kept about waist high. Further back, a larger group of *S. japonica* 'Shibori' (synonym 'Shirobana') is allowed to grow a little taller. Catalogs show it with crimson, pink, and white flower clusters mixed on the same bush. My plants have mostly pale pink flowers, with occasional crimson clusters, and one member of the group is totally white. Although the name *S. japonica* 'Little Princess' suggests dwarfness, this selection exceeds 3 feet quite soon if left unpruned. *Spiraea japonica* 'Alpina' is smaller, less than knee-high after

Coppery young leaves of *Spiraea japonica* 'Goldflame' with orange *Geum ×heldreichii*

many years. For rock gardens and raised beds there is *S. japonica* 'Bullata', a congested miniature with dark pink flowers and small, dark leaves with the texture of savoy cabbage.

Few plants are more carefree than this group of spiraeas, taking in their stride just about anything save sodden soil and deep shade, though at their best in moderately fertile, moderately moist soil with sun for most of the day.

If sheared as the blooms fade, the plants go on to bloom again. In winter I cut them back to control size, at the same time removing some of the oldest branches from congested bushes. That's the total maintenance except for routine renewal of mulch, which in this hot region disappears with almost the speed of melting snow. Although they are commonplace, I would no more oust these undemanding spiraeas than

Spiraea japonica 'Crispa'

part with well-worn clothes, for the same can be said of both: they are comfortable and need not be worried about.

Indigofera decora

In dryish shade or semi-shade, where ivy, periwinkle (*Vinca minor*), or lily turf (*Ophiopogon japonicus*) might otherwise hold sway, *Indigofera decora* (Zone 6; synonym *I. incar-*

LEFT *Spiraea japonica* 'Goldflame', with tulip 'Queen of Sheba', *Aquilegia canadensis*, *Lagerstroemia fauriei*, *Photinia ×fraseri*, and *Abelia ×grandiflora* 'Francis Mason'

nata) makes a change of pace if evergreenness is not a requirement. Where summers are cool, it can be grown in full sun. It is puzzling that such a good and easy plant should remain so uncommon. Adaptable, and hardy to Zone 5, it needs no care except cutting off dead stems in winter, for the sake of tidiness, and occasionally curtailing its spread.

I first saw this indigo more than two decades ago, in the gardens of two plant connoisseurs: the late Harold Epstein of Larchmont, New York, who was growing the species with phlox-purple flowers, and the late Betty Miller of Seattle, Washington, who grew the white-flowered *Indigofera decora* 'Alba'. Reference books refer to blush pink forms, but I have yet to see them. *Indigofera kirilowii*, a slightly taller plant with flowers of wild peach pink, is common under the live oaks of old southern plantations. I discarded it as overly invasive, though now I wish I had it back to try in a sunken container.

Indigofera decora looks like a miniature wisteria, with pea-type flowers and laddered, pinnate leaves on semi-upright, wiry stems. I grow the species as a frill around the skirts of evergreen azaleas, where it dies to the ground in winter and starts anew in spring, remaining little more than 1 foot high while creeping steadily sideways. The white one, however,

Indigofera decora 'Alba' climbing into the late-blooming evergreen azalea 'Fourth of July'

has crept far back under a late-blooming azalea called 'Fourth of July' and, with its protection, does not die back to ground level. It rambles vinelike through the azalea to a height of 4 feet, where it softens the purplish pink of the azalea flowers with its lacy foliage.

Lilium

LILY

"June brings tulips, lilies, roses . . . ." In coastal Virginia the tulips are done, if not done-for by voles, and like as not lilies have met the same fate, or been breakfasted on by rabbits. Oh, the lilies, the lovely lilies. I've more than once come close to tears on finding an erstwhile stand lying prostrate on the ground. Instead I seek revenge with poison pellets or head off for another truckload of gravel to spread around vulnerable plants. The pity of it is that lilies like it here, and there could be breathtaking sweeps.

This saga of woe notwithstanding, there are

Lilium canadense with ground cover *Polygonatum odoratum* 'Variegatum' and *Acer griseum*

a few long-surviving groups that have managed modest increase. One, with white trumpets of *Lilium longiflorum* type, was probably a potted Easter lily, afterward put out in the sandy soil by the previous owners. And there it has flourished for well over three decades, on the east-facing side of what is now a large, pine-sprinkled island bed encircled by the gravel drive. Further along I planted three bulbs of *L. canadense* (Zone 5) some 15 years ago. Now there are fifteen stems, some sufficiently far away that they must have come from seed. A single clump of an up-facing, dark spotted, yellow hybrid—'Destiny', perhaps—has also been in this spot for 10 years or more. Voles, which prefer to stay below ground, cannot tunnel through the hardpacked gravel of the drive and it may be the position of the lilies rather than their type that has preserved their lives, though this doesn't explain why rabbits, with no such inhibitions, have left them alone. These lilies all flower the last half of June.

The Philippine lily (*Lilium formosanum*; Zone 6) is the most reliable lily. "A weed," said the donor, a hybridizer who wants nothing trespassing on the turf of his daylilies, and "potentially invasive by seed" warns a southern nursery. It does have wildling willfulness in its eagerness to grow almost anywhere except in those places I so carefully prepare for it, a characteristic that may be the clue to its survival. Voles, drawn immediately to fluffy, newly prepared soil, work it thoroughly once they begin. By scattering itself around, one here, two there, three somewhere else, with no disturbance of the surface of the soil, this lily is less likely to be found, and given that it flowers in one year from seed, its chances of staying ahead of its predators are good. In the donor's garden it grew in full sun; in mine it usually seems to choose light shade, where, in August, it opens several faintly fragrant, white, trumpet-shaped flowers atop firmly upright, 6-foot stems clad in long, slender leaves. Regal lily (*L. regale*), so easy to grow in England, lasted only 2 years in my Virginia garden. The Philippine lily is much more than second best, and could one really have too much of such a lovely thing? Not yet, anyway.

Lilium formosanum with *Miscanthus sinensis* 'Cabaret' in background

Rosa

ROSE

Long before gardeners became apologetic about using chemical sprays, I had concluded that this was not my idea of fun. Living now in bug paradise, I do resort to chemicals occasionally, but not routinely. And that philosophy, as rosarians readily admit, precludes growing such roses as the showbench hybrid teas. Plenty remain, for many old heritage roses are disease-resistant, and breeders have done a sterling job of raising carefree new ones. Because the hardiness of roses varies considerably, local groups of the American Rose Society are the best sources of information on regional adaptability.

I have no rose beds as such. My roses are mixed with other plants, hence my preference for shrub roses over those beautiful in bloom but the antithesis in form. They get water during drought, occasional top dressings of fresh soil mixed with manure, and a scattering of slow-release fertilizer if their appearance suggests a need for it. In my region most roses bloom abundantly in late May and early June, produce a smattering of flowers through summer, and then put on another good show when

Rosa 'Nearly Wild' with crimson-pink *Rhododendron* 'Anna Rose Whitney'

Rosa 'Carefree Delight'

the weather cools in autumn. Between times overly long stems are headed back and dead flower clusters cut off.

Rosa 'Nearly Wild' blooms in late spring, then again in autumn. In their simplicity the single white-eyed pink flowers remind me of England's hedgerow dog-rose (*R. canina*). *Rosa* 'Carefree Wonder', with semi-double flowers of a bright, clear pink on an upright bush follows the same bloom pattern, joined in early summer by the mothlike flowers and willowy leaves of *Gaura lindheimeri* 'Siskiyou Pink', and in autumn by the single crimson daisies of a Korean chrysanthemum. All the

Carefree range of roses live up to their name, needing little but pruning to keep them prosperous. *Rosa* 'Carefree Delight', which goes on blooming through summer, is almost rambling in its vigor, and allowed to stay that way until late winter, when branches are cut back to about 1 foot. The cup-shaped single flowers are apricot-tinted in bud, opening to white-eyed wild-rose pink.

Semi-double *Rosa* 'Meidiland Scarlet' is such a vigorously spreading rose that I grow it in a sunken container to keep it in check. Few roses have leaves of brighter, glossier green, and the scarlet flowers are seldom missing from late spring through autumn. Until recently I had *R.* 'Red Cascade', a miniature climber or trailer, growing in a barrel in front of 'Meidiland Scarlet'. They had to be separated because one was scarlet and the other crimson—colors best kept apart.

I grow the old chestnut-rose (*Rosa roxburghii*) for its ferny foliage and for its burrlike buds, not for the double flowers, which are sparingly borne, form a nest in which Japanese beetles can elude me, and ball up when wet. It makes a very large bush. *Rosa* 'Petite Pink' has foliage even more fernily fine, which is its main claim to a place in my garden, for it blooms only once, for 1–2 weeks in early June. Later interest comes from clematis rambling through it.

Rosa 'Red Cascade' with *Vinca major* 'Variegata'

Rosa 'The Fairy'

Before May is out the old, low-growing polyantha rose 'The Fairy' starts a display that, if sprays of spent flowers are cut off, will not cease until hard frost. Could there be a better rose than this, with its glossy leaves and sprays of inch-wide, semi-double, baby pink, frilly flowers opening from diminutive buds? Lack of fragrance is the only criticism I can level at a robust rose competing for my affection only with the next two.

Rosa 'Graham Thomas', one of the English roses bred for a combination of old rose charm and modern rose recurrent bloom, merits all the accolades heaped on it. The color of the large, cupped, double flowers is hard to pinpoint, falling somewhere between amber, apricot, and deep yellow. They are fragrant, too. Only be aware that the size given for England seems a joke once one has seen what this and most other English roses can do in a hot-

ter, wetter climate. *Rosa* 'Graham Thomas' could, in fact, be trained as a vine, so long do its stems become. When stems reach 6 feet, I cut them back. My plant is adjacent to a path and necessarily so because Japanese beetles are drawn to this rose more than any other. Fortunately the beetles have passed their flying stage by late July, while the rose will go on flowering as late as November. Meantime they must be dealt with and I do this by tapping them, frequently in copulating pairs or clusters, into a bucket of soapy water, turning to my advantage their escape mechanism of dropping straight down rather than attempting flight.

My number one rose is *Rosa* 'Pink Pet', which comes in both bush and climbing form. According to the *Combined Rose List*, Beverly Dobson and Peter Schneider's invaluable annual source guide, this is a China rose introduced in 1928. It seems to have been overlooked ever since by writers about roses, so I will sing the praises of a rose demure in form, foliage, and flower, while exuberant in its abundance of bloom. After being pruned quite hard just as it is breaking into growth, it becomes about 3 feet high and 4 feet across by the beginning of June. Smallish, unpolished leaves of a soft gray-green are the background for multiple sprays of petite crimson buds

Rosa 'Pink Pet'

Rosa 'Graham Thomas' with *Ilex cornuta* 'O'Spring'

opening on small pink flowers of old-fashioned double form. Remove the sprays of spent flowers and more soon follow. Planted in 1986, my 'Pink Pet' has remained uncomplaining in the poorest conditions of any rose in my garden, in full sun and sandy soil improved only slightly with compost. Its immediate companions include *Achillea millefolium* 'Oertel's Rose' (a compact form), *Nepeta* 'Six Hills Giant', *Lespedeza thunbergii* 'Pink Fountain', *Tamarix ramosissima* 'Summer Glow' and, in summer, the annuals *Petunia integrifolia* and *Ipomoea batatas* 'Tricolor'.

Itea virginica

VIRGINIA SWEETSPIRE

As we move into June the long and dramatic display from spring azaleas is coming to a close, though a few are still to come, including the intensely fragrant *Rhododendron viscosum*. Satisfaction with its moist, sunny spot is evident in the glossy healthiness of its small leaves and the steady outward spread of its

modestly suckering roots, which, until I took a hand, were being infiltrated by *Itea virginica* in a civil war (both are locally native) the azalea seemed fated to lose.

Common sense dictates that I give up trying to grow the evergreen *Itea ilicifolia* after three failed attempts: it wants cool summers and mild winters, while what is on offer is certain sizzling summer and treacherous, change-

Itea virginica 'Sarah Eve' (Virginia sweetspire)

able winters. So I settle for *I. virginica* (Zone 5), complaining only about the need to keep it in check. While peeling back its root thongs works for a few years, this practice removes the young and healthy growth, leaving the center to progress to senescence. Eventually I had to dig the whole lot out and replant a group of the younger sections. While not as arduous or time-consuming as might be supposed (muddy, though) provided the soil is free of roots from other trees or shrubs, the job was hampered by the need to salvage bulbs of a white starflower planted among the suckering stems. Although the name sweetspire suggests upright inflorescences, the inflorescences are, in fact, long pendulous tails, creamy in the species, and in *I. virginica* 'Henry's Garnet', a selection noted for its good autumn color, the leaves garnet when frontlit, coppery-orange when the light shines through from behind.

Sweetspire's companions in the wild might include *Clethra alnifolia*, *Rhododendron viscosum*, *Gordonia lasianthus* (Zone 7), the swamp cypress (*Taxodium distichum*; Zone 6), and *Zenobia pulverulenta*. By happenstance I have all these except swamp cypress in the same moist part of my garden, along with such other North American species as Louisiana irises, ostrich fern, and *Filipendula rubra*. *Zenobia pulverulenta* (Zone 6) in its best forms is an immaculately lovely small, arching shrub clad in silver and white. The young wood is silvery, the spear-shaped leaves blue-green above and silvery beneath, the flowers snowy quarter-inch cups with fluted rims, nicely spaced in loose clusters of twenty or so. Its beauty merits star billing and I give it somewhat less not because I lost it once (from failure to water during drought), but because I seldom see it in other gardens, American or English, which suggests that it may be a tad selective about where it will and will not thrive. Acid, sandy soil bulked up with years of added mulch (oak leaves, mainly) and kept consistently damp, with shade during the midday hours, is the recipe here.

Non-natives in this same moist site include white and creamy forms of the yellow flag (*Iris pseudacorus*), Japanese irises, callas (*Zantedeschia aethiopica*), astilbes, *Primula japonica*, hostas, and a carpet of the water-loving forget-me-not (*Myosotis scorpioides*; Zone 5), almost constantly in bloom from May to autumn, surrounding a large dawn redwood (*Metasequoia glyptostroboides*; Zone 5). Dawn redwood is a swamp cypress look-alike. When looking at one or the other away from home, I use the first three letters of the name as a memory jog: *met*, for leaves that meet in pairs. In swamp cypress they alternate.

Although sweetspire prefers moist soil, it will settle for less. I have *Itea virginica* 'Sarah Eve', a pink-budded selection with smaller leaves, growing where it gets some competition from the roots of other trees and does sometimes get dry. Here, with a sheltering canopy overhead, it has been partly evergreen through mild winters, at the cost of autumn color. Although smaller than the species or 'Henry's Garnet', it is still a vigorous spreader and has to be prevented from infiltrating its background of evergreen azaleas. Sweetspire's suckering stems provide a ready and immediate source of new plants. It can also be grown from cuttings.

EARLY JULY

With peak bloom from shrubs over and self-sown summer annuals only now getting under way, there would be a blossom lull in early July were it not for two key groups, hydrangeas and daylilies. In my early gardening days the three most popular plants for the English rockery all began with an *A*: arabis, aubrieta, and alyssum. Curiously, the four darlings of the present era all begin with an *H*: hellebores, hostas, hemerocallis, and hydrangeas. Three of these are stars in the summer garden.

Hydrangea quercifolia
OAKLEAF HYDRANGEA

The oakleaf hydrangea (*Hydrangea quercifolia*; Zone 5) is the first of my hydrangeas to bloom, usually beginning early in June. The flowers remain ornamental, dead or alive, through to winter. The leaves are quite variable in size and shape; some vaguely resemble those of the English oak (*Quercus robur*), while others are closer to those of the sycamore-maple (*Acer pseudoplatanus*), certainly in size, at up to 1 foot and sometimes more in length and width. This hydrangea is native to southeastern North America, and the name must puzzle many residents of the region, surrounded as they are by dozens of native oaks with leaves very different from this plant. In any event, the leaves are handsome, and they often turn a deep ruby red approaching black in autumn, sometimes tinged with orange and amber. This coloration seems to be the luck of the draw, varying with the plant, its position in the garden, and the season's weather. Oakleaf hydrangea inflorescences look like giant inverted ice cream cones, 1 foot or more in length, vanilla ice cream in most cases. Under the showy, bractlike sterile florets are thousands of tiny fertile florets packed into little fuzzy tuffets and it is from these that the faint fragrance emanates.

Hydrangea quercifolia 'Snowflake' (oakleaf hydrangea)

There are many named selections of oakleaf hydrangea, often with little to distinguish them, though size may be a factor to consider. *Hydrangea quercifolia* 'Harmony' (strange choice of name!) was quickly discarded: its massive heads of double flowers are so heavy that they trail down dismally. In tight quarters *H. quercifolia* 'Peewee', with smaller, daintier flower trusses, would fit the bill. Although it did not turn out to be the dwarf shrub I expected, annual pruning, done during late autumn and winter, keeps it compact.

In my opinion the best of this very good bunch is *Hydrangea quercifolia* 'Snowflake', with what appear to be flat, semi-double flowers an inch or more across, with three or four rows of overlapping oval sepals, ivory flushed lime green at first, becoming white, surrounding a tiny green eye. In fact this eye contains many embryo sepals, which enlarge in succession until the flower in profile resembles an opened fir cone. Gradually the inflorescence, upright or level at first, becomes pendant under the weight. Slowly the sepals turn pinkish, then coppery, with faded inflorescences no less ornamental than fresh ones. Only in winter do they hang so broken-necked and crumblingly bedraggled that they beg to be removed. In this respect they fall short of the standard set by *H. arborescens*, which holds its dead heads attractively through to spring.

I grow oakleaf hydrangeas in almost full shade, where they still manage a fair number of flowers, in afternoon shade and sometimes dry soil, where bushes originally grown from seed attained 5 feet in as many years and have since been kept pruned to that, and in a moist and sunny place, where they soon attained 7 feet, blooming from the start in prodigious quantity. They definitely prefer moist soil and sun, though I get the impression they'd grow about anywhere. They sucker, layer, and self-sow mildly, certainly not enough to cause a problem. As they age, a further attractive feature develops: coffee-with-cream-colored flaking bark that catches the eye when frontlit by the sun.

Hydrangea macrophylla and *Hydrangea serrata*

Close on the heels of the oakleaf hydrangea come *Hydrangea macrophylla* and *H. serrata* (both Zone 7, with some forms Zone 6). The only surprising thing about their present popularity in southeastern North America is that it took so long. The answer to the casual gardener's prayer, hydrangeas do well in acid or alkaline soils, provided it is moderately moist. In hot regions they need afternoon shade if they are not to wilt dismally. Their leaves appear to secrete something distasteful to pests: occasional small holes indicate that they have been sampled, yet I've never seen them noticeably disfigured, an appreciated attribute in a region where pests proliferate.

The flowers of these two species come in two very different forms. *Hydrangea serrata* and some forms of *H. macrophylla* have "lacecap" flowers. The term, coined by Michael Haworth-Booth in his book *The Hydrangeas*, evocatively describes inflorescences made up of a shallow central dome or plate of tiny fertile florets, with an outer ring of ornamental sterile florets of varying size and number. The "mophead," or hortensia, forms of *H. macrophylla* are the familiar florists' hydrangeas, with a great many sterile florets tightly packed into large balls. Mopheads have such visual

impact that they stand out from afar. Some of the daintier *H. serrata* lacecaps should be nearer a path.

Hydrangea selections and hybrids are legion. I grow a couple of dozen varieties and covet a lot more. Many are illustrated in Corinne Mallet's *Hydrangeas*, and the majority can now be obtained from one source or another in North America and Europe. Flower color varies not only with the variety and the soil (blue hydrangeas often turn pink in alkaline soil), but is often inconsistent from year to year in the same garden. The colors I describe are those most often present in my garden. Although my soil is basically an acid sand, considerable quantities of such humus-forming materials as leaf mold, compost, sawdust, manure, and sewage compost have been added, and topsoil is sometimes trucked in.

My choice of mopheads is influenced by such individual characteristics as the compact size of 'Miss Belgium' (the most intense violet-blue of any I grow) and deep pink 'Pia'; the black stems of the vigorous, pale pink 'Nigra', and the consistent deep pink of midsized 'Glowing Embers'. Zone 7 is probably the limit of reliable hardiness for one of my favorites, 'Ayesha' (synonym 'Silver Slipper'). The leaves are exceptionally bright green and glossy, and the flowers unique in their curled-in, lilaclike

Hydrangea macrophylla 'Ayesha'

petals. In alkaline soil 'Ayesha' is usually lilac pink, but in my acid soil usually blue. In my experience, acid soils pose few limitations that can't be overcome by improving the humus content. I am skeptical about the importance of pH and seldom tamper with it, but I make an exception with 'Ayesha', which I insist be blue only because it is next to lemon-yellow *Hemerocallis* 'Hyperion', their bloom times coincide, and I prefer yellow and blue to yellow and pink. When 'Ayesha' tries to be pink, as it did after getting a top dressing of sewage compost, sulfur is dusted around it to return it to blue.

An unidentified mophead form of *Hydrangea macrophylla* with palmlike, white-variegated *Carex phyllocephala* 'Sparkler' in front, round-leaved, variegated *Ligularia tussilaginea* 'Argentea', the gray-green, ferny foliage of *Dicentra eximia* 'Alba', spotted leaves of a pulmonaria, and a few white flowers of *Hydrangea serrata* 'Amagi Amacha'

Only *Hydrangea* 'Preziosa' (*H. macrophylla* × *H. serrata*) has been a color disappointment, not because it is not lovely in powder blue or blush pink, only that I want the unique clear, bright pink I knew in England, akin to that of *Aster* 'Alma Pötschke' and *Rosa* 'Betty Prior'. I might yet give it a dressing of lime to see if that makes a difference. From its *H. macrophylla* parent 'Preziosa' got mophead inflorescences, with *H. serrata* influence shown in their smaller size.

While I've yet to see a hydrangea I did not like and I value the mopheads for their impact, with every inflorescence a bouquet, the lacecaps appeal to me most. Lacecap forms of *Hydrangea macrophylla* combine the grace and elegance of *H. serrata* with much of the size and impact of the mopheads, as well as their vigor. The three I have long grown are all tall, vigorous plants. *Hydrangea macrophylla* 'Blue Wave' is just that—a wave of blue. It layers very readily and an initial three plants now form a long drift. *Hydrangea macrophylla* 'Lanarth White' gets individual presentation befitting its purity, the rings of snowy four-sepaled florets surrounding the blue central plates rendered brighter by the single, small blue floret that forms their eye.

Desirable as these and others are, for long-term ornament none holds a candle to *Hy-*

Hydrangea macrophylla 'Mariesii Variega'

drangea macrophylla 'Mariesii Variegata', long available in southeastern North America though still uncommon in England. Each inflorescence is a diadem of white sterile florets rimming a blue center. It does not flower freely every year, but the white-edged leaves are pristine and striking for more than half the year. With or without flowers, no deciduous shrub better earns its place in my garden, and I was quick to add *H. macrophylla* 'Brilliant Beacon', a 1999 introduction by a local nursery, where it arose as a sport on *H. macrophylla* 'Mariesii Variegata'. 'Brilliant Beacon' has a leaf edge of creamy yellow instead of white. Both hydrangeas are superior in stamina and beauty to the somewhat miffy *H. macrophylla* 'Quadricolor', which has leaves variegated in a rather scrambled mix of green, cream, and yellow.

Hydrangea serrata 'Grayswood'

Members of the *Hydrangea serrata* group have the practical advantage of being generally less bulky, therefore generating smaller piles of pruned branches to be hauled away. Among the most finely wrought is *H. serrata* 'Beni-gaku'. Its small, flat plate of minute fertile florets is hidden under a dense fuzz of blue stamens. The sterile florets, thinly spaced round the perimeter, are white fading to blush,

with a touch of deeper pink as they fade; some have four deckle-edged sepals, but most have a triangle of three. With sun for about half the day, bloom time is little more than 2 weeks, which is very brief for a hydrangea.

The small *Hydrangea serrata* 'Amagi Amacha', which looks frail but is really quite robust, fits nicely into a corner of the garden devoted to plants with white flowers or white-

variegated foliage, where, with no direct sun, it flowers for several weeks, starting in late June. Its companions include *Ligularia tussilaginea* 'Argentea', *Pulmonaria* 'Mrs. Kittle', *Euonymus fortunei* 'Silver Princess', *Carex phyllocephala* 'Sparkler', *Dicentra eximia* 'Alba', and *Begonia grandis* 'Alba'.

A low and spreading shape is the attraction with *Hydrangea serrata* 'Blue Billow' which, however, has refuted its name and blooms in a deep lilac-pink. The flowers exactly match the scattered flowers of *Lamium maculatum* growing next to it still in bloom after a 3-month performance, a match not of my making, just serendipity. To *H. serrata* 'Grayswood', though, I gave a lot of thought, not this time to match-making but rather to the avoidance of competition, and so it is staged against a fence, with only the green leaves of earlier blooming shrubs on either side and green ivy at its feet. It earns such showcasing with waxy-textured 6- to 8-inch blooms as pretty when faded as they are when fresh. The center is a tapestry of creamy green buds and blue-stamened, lilac-pink fertile florets, tiny but distinct, encircled by numerous four-petaled sterile florets resembling miniature dogwood (*Cornus florida*) flowers. As these sterile florets fade, they arch down on slender pedicels, revealing an underside dotted and flushed with crimson pink. This hydrangea is my first choice in its group.

Stated heights for hydrangeas are invariably exceeded in such regions of rapid growth as mine. Having paid attention to whether plants are small, medium, or tall (the best that can be said as a guide to size), I control height by pruning. Otherwise small plants soon outgrow their space, while larger ones reach tree size within a few years, becoming vulnerable to storm damage, sprawling over and smothering their neighbors, or lofting the flowers out of sight on the tops of their branches. Most of my hydrangeas are pruned annually to keep them little taller than 6 feet.

By way of comfort to reluctant pruners, in southeastern North America (I cannot speak for all other regions) hydrangeas are hard to kill and no matter how much of a hash-up is made of pruning, they will survive and offer another chance to get it right. When, from pressure of work, I had neglected to prune my extensive spread of *Hydrangea macrophylla* 'Blue Wave' for 3 years, I eyed the 10-foot-high mass despairingly, then finally, lacking time to do it the slow and thoughtful way, cut the whole lot down to the ground. Only one year of bloom was lost, and within 2 years the plants were 6 feet high again. The wood is soft and easily cut, though it may take loppers to cut out old branches, with occasional recourse to a pruning saw.

So, how and when does one prune *Hydrangea macrophylla* and *H. serrata*? I had to let go of Mother England's hand and find out for myself. One's own garden is always the best lesson book, and the plants are the teachers if one pays attention. To begin with, if a hard late frost, mercifully rare where I now garden, occurs when buds have burst into tender new growth, there will be few, if any flowers that year no matter what the pruning method. In England the oldest stems are cut to the ground in winter and that is that. This practice is sound as far as it goes, but it does not go far enough in my region. "My region"—that's the crunch. In the varied climates of North America one size seldom fits all and much must be determined on a regional basis. *Hydrangea macrophylla* and *H. serrata* seldom bloom (I have seen the odd bloom or two) on a branch that is new from ground level to tip. To say, however, that they "bloom on old wood," can be misleading. They bloom on new wood growing from old.

During winter I prune out old branches which, being thick, gnarled, and grayish, are easily recognized. I then cut the other branches back to maintain the desired height—some at my leisure during winter, and others in a last-minute rush when bursting buds, in late March or early April, remind me it is time to get the job completed. Cut branches extend at the tip by as much as 4 feet during the next 2 to 3 months, with slightly less growth on side branches. By about mid-June inflorescences have formed at the tips of this new growth, on the main branches and usually also on the two pairs of side branches below.

My only dissatisfaction with this group of hydrangeas is that they flower so early, in late June and July, when we need more flowers for the dog days of August. Experiments aimed at delaying or extending bloom have so far been inconclusive, due mostly to weather vagaries, but with results also varying from one kind of hydrangea to another.

Propagation could scarcely be quicker or simpler. Six-inch cuttings of green, half-ripe stems (firm enough not to wilt, while not yet brown and woody) inserted in a soil-less mix, or a mixture of peat moss and sand, covered with a plastic bag and placed in the shade root within a few weeks. With hydrangeas, and any plant with leaves more than an inch in length, I cut off the tip half of the leaves of cuttings. Not knowing what winter will bring, I usually leave the young plants in a frame until the following spring. They flower within 2 years of taking the cuttings.

Hydrangea arborescens

Hydrangea arborescens 'Annabelle' (Zone 4) presents no pruning problems. Having remained ornamental since the previous June, it is routinely cut to the ground in early spring. This pruning slows the plant in its tracks, with bloom commencing a trifle later than that of its oakleaf hydrangea compatriot. Though I'm more a fan of Audrey Hepburn than of Dolly Parton, in this case I prefer the white domes of *H. arborescens* 'Annabelle' to the small white lacecaps of the species. Much depends on the setting. I have 'Annabelle' in the shade of a large magnolia, at one end of a perennial bed. In a woodsier setting I'd use the species. In any event, I have them both, and more, because 'Annabelle', it seems, is not entirely stable. Among the thicket that has developed over the years have appeared, by seed, sport, or stoloniferous root, three other forms: a simple, species-type lacecap, a mophead resembling *H. arborescens* 'Grandiflora', and *H. arborescens* subsp. *radiata*. The main ornamental quality of the latter is the intensely silvery undersides of the leaves, a quality wasted on my flat, non-windy garden, where the leaf undersides are not seen. It would be displayed to better advantage atop a bank, viewed from below, or where wind might flutter its leaves and cause it to flash its underwear. Don't hold these changes

of character against 'Annabelle'; unwanted metamorphs are easily cut off or dug out.

The inflorescences of 'Annabelle' are pleasing from infancy into death, progressing from green to white to green again, and finally, still holding their shape and substance, to the brown of winter. In spite of the size of the inflorescences, branches do not bend under the weight, as they do with the somewhat smaller inflorescences of *Hydrangea arborescens* 'Grandiflora'. The annual cutting down, and water during severe drought, are the only attentions 'Annabelle' gets, and it would get by without either.

Hemerocallis

DAYLILY

Of all the perennials I grow, daylilies (Zone 3) are the most fun to play with, also the most time consuming. The fun part first. Daylilies are so diverse in size, shape, color, and pattern that putting them all together in daylily borders wastes opportunities for combinations that emphasize each daylily's individuality. The grand, yew-backed borders of estate gardens look gorgeous even without much thought to the combinations within them. Smaller gardens need the more thoughtful composition of vignettes, and no plant offers more opportunities for this than the daylily, nor a greater

feeling of accomplishment when one pulls off a fetching combination, matching a purple eye-ring with a purple barberry for instance. I had not cared for the color of the much-vaunted *Hemerocallis* 'Stella d'Oro' until I got it together with the creamy yellow and apricoty orange spires of *Kniphofia* 'Shining Scepter'.

And now the other side of the story. Much has been written about the flowers of these undisputed stars of hot, summer gardens, while seldom mentioning another attribute—the way their foliage greens up the ground at daffodil time, in neat, unblemished clumps. These early leaves are starting to die by flowering time, making way for new ones already pushing through. The post-bloom shabby period can be forestalled if yellowing, dying leaves are removed daily, along with spent flowers and scapes with no remaining buds. Because this task is time consuming, I have learned not to bite off more than I can chew, nor put daylilies needing these daily attentions way back in a border, where getting at them means trampling on other things. When I have been remiss in these daily attentions, the whole clump is cut to the ground after flowering is complete, an approach perhaps suitable only for those in regions of rapid growth. Provided they are watered during drought, these

Hydrangea arborescens 'Annabelle' in center right, with yellow-leaved *Ilex crenata* 'Yellow Helleri' at bottom right, *Phlox paniculata* 'Norah Leigh' at bottom center, *Monarda* 'Blue Stocking' at center left, blue spikes of *Vitex agnus-castus* and white *Hydrangea arborescens* subsp. *radiata* in background, and in the foreground *Salvia* 'Purple Rain' at left and *Tanacetum vulgare* var. *crispum* at right

Hemerocallis 'Joan Senior' with *Ilex crenata* 'Yellow Helleri' (Japanese holly) in background

to visit a specialist grower and see how the whole plant looks. I view with distaste many squat, recent hybrids with flowers of a size disproportionate to their height. My breeder friends say that this is what most customers want, much the same response that I got when complaining to the manager of a bookstore I used to patronize about the wailing din passing for music that afflicted my ears. Perceived esthetics apart, there is a practical advantage to less fleshy flowers: they soon shrivel and drop.

I like *Hemerocallis* 'Moon Traveller', an early bloomer, for the elegance of its 3-foot scapes of lemon-yellow flowers. For foliage contrast and flowering succession it is grouped with *Baptisia* 'Purple Smoke', done flowering now, a calla lily (*Zantedeschia* 'Rubylite Rose') with upright, sword-shaped leaves and flowers yet to come, mounding *Osmanthus heterophyllus* 'Goshiki', and false-willow (*Baccharis angustifolia*), with glossy, bright green, leaf slivers. False-willow is periodically cut back to keep it knee-high and fairly dense. 'Moon Traveller' flowers only once, so if it had to be one or the other I'd keep the shorter 'Happy Returns', with slightly frilly flowers of a more crystalline lemon yellow, sized for the front of the border and valued for its recurring bloom.

I doubt that any daylily will ever please me more than 'Corky', with funnel-shaped flow-

daylilies are back in lush growth in 2 or 3 weeks. Though most do not flower again, their foliage remains an asset well into autumn.

To avoid scattering them around I'm including all the daylilies here, although, with appropriate choice of varieties, bloom extends from spring to late summer. Late June and July is their peak, however, and with flower color waning after the spring rush, the time when they are most appreciated. My two earliest daylilies, *Hemerocallis dumortieri* and *H. minor*, came and went early in May. Come late June, the season is in full swing and the daily valeting begins.

One cannot assess a daylily from a catalog picture, which usually shows only a close-up of the flower, giving no sense of proportion and frequently distorting the color. It is far better

ers of ripe-lemon yellow, bronze-brushed on the outside, presented on dark, wiry stems. The flowers shrivel neatly enough that the deadheading isn't essential. Likewise with the similar, warmer yellow 'Golden Chimes' and the brilliant coppery orange 'Stafford'. By contrast with the elfin charm of these daylilies, 'Joan Senior' carries her stout scapes of crisp, creamy white flowers with stateliness. She is a lady and demands a ladies' maid (me!), for she cannot be left wearing yesterday's soiled gown without loss of dignity. The creamy petals shade to lime at the throat, so while Joan looks gorgeous just about anywhere, she is breathtakingly staged against a large mound of a lime green Japanese holly, *Ilex crenata* 'Yellow Helleri', further accessorized with *Hedera helix* 'Lemon Swirl' at her feet. The wavy leaves of this pretty ivy vary from cream through lime to dark green. These evergreen companion plants yield the limelight for the 3 weeks or so the daylily holds court, then take the stage for the rest of the year.

I enjoy such oddities as the brown *Hemerocallis* 'Milk Chocolate', which follows a Louisiana iris called 'Buff Dancer' in echo partnership with a brown-bladed sedge, *Carex flagellifera*, and accompanied by the creamily variegated leaves (by far the best thing about it) of *Kalimeris yomena* 'Aurea', which will bear its asterlike flowers of insipid lavender much later in the year.

Once a daylily is in the garden other combinations often suggest themselves. Darrel Apps's *Hemerocallis* 'College Try' is a nicely proportioned plant with a good bud count and 4-inch flowers of glowing cherry red. It pleases me with the clear pink flowers of *Rosa* 'Carefree Wonder' and *Gaura lindheimeri* 'Siskiyou Pink', but I can also see how well it would complement a drift of midpink *Astilbe* 'Cattleya' in another bed. Moves can, if one wishes, be carried out immediately when inspiration strikes, because daylilies move well at flowering time if well watered in.

Four daylilies bloom late in the season on very tall scapes. All have flowers that shrivel fairly neatly, though the plants still look better if deadheaded. First to bloom, usually in late July, is 5-foot 'Statuesque', with 4-inch warm yellow flowers. Then comes 'Boutonniere', with narrow leaves and rounded 3-inch flowers of buff and pale apricot on slender 4-foot scapes, and finally, sometimes as late as September, more often August, 'Autumn Minaret', the tallest daylily I have seen, with 5-inch somewhat spidery flowers the color of cooked corn lightly flushed plum red atop slender but self-supporting 7-foot scapes. Its bloom time overlaps that of 'Autumn Prince', which has

Hemerocallis 'Autumn Minaret'

lemon-yellow flowers shaped like a champagne flute.

Erythrina herbacea (eastern coral-bean)

Erythrina herbacea

EASTERN CORAL-BEAN,
CARDINAL-SPEAR

Climate debars me from growing such spire-like perennials as delphiniums, lupines, and the stately red *Lobelia tupa* so admired in mild English gardens. Conversely, my English friends envy me the vivid spires of *Erythrina herbacea* (Zone 7), not yet known in England, though it probably could be grown wherever *E. crista-galli* (too tender for me) thrives.

Eastern coral-bean calls for patience. My specimen, planted in 1976 and now a dense clump 2–3 feet wide, took 5 years to bear its first flowers. Since then it has gone from strength to strength: this year I counted 54 self-supporting spires, in staggered heights from 2 to 5 feet. Bloom peak lasts about 2 weeks in early to mid July, with fewer spikes for another week or so on either side.

Glowingly bright flowers start off as small pink-tipped fans along stout stems, developing into whorls of 2-inch scimitars that open, beaklike, at the mouth only briefly before they fall. The color, cardinal red on my color chart, lies borderline between crimson and scarlet. One big improvement over many spikelike inflorescences is that the spires never have dead flowers. The lower flowers drop while still looking fresh, to lie in a pool of color around the base of the clump. The pendant pods, in small groups, resemble no others I know. Each sealing-wax-red bean is separated from the next by a constricted section of the pod.

If it did not bloom this coral-bean would still be worth having for the distinctive foliage that appears when bloom is halfway through. Three deltoid-shaped leaflets, waxy to the touch, make up a triangular leaf as flat as an herbarium specimen. Small prickles at the leaf bases are benign, neither scratching nor embedding themselves in fingers. While the clump in bloom is compact and upright, the fully developed leaf stems, 4 feet or more long, arch out wide and low, presenting a challenge as to how best to fill this considerable ground space during the coral-bean's dormancy. If early daffodils are an unimaginative choice, I have yet to find anything better.

The habitat of eastern coral-bean is the coastal plain from North Carolina southward, usually in the sandy soil of pineland fringes. Only in very favorable microclimates is it likely to survive in regions colder than Zone 7. My plant is growing on a bank where sun reaches it in the morning but not in the afternoon. No pest or disease has yet bothered it, and it has needed neither fertilizer nor water beyond what nature provides. An occasional self-sown seedling appears. When top growth

Gladiolus ×*gandavensis* (a hybrid gladiolus)

has been killed by frost I cut the trailing stems about halfway back, leaving the rest as protection for the woody base until late February. New growth seldom appears until well into May. The species is usually propagated by seed and the rarer pink- and white-flowered forms from cuttings of young stems just beginning to firm up. These cuttings root within a few weeks.

Gladiolus ×gandavensis

Wistful longings for *Gladiolus tristis*, pale yellow and scented, and too fragile for Zone 7, recurred every time I saw it, until solace came with the equally lovely, hardier G. ×*gandavensis* 'Boone' (possibly Zone 6, but little tested). Richard Bir, author of *Showy Native Woody Plants*, found the hybrid in the yard of an abandoned old house near Boone, North Car-

olina, and gave a few bulbs to Allen Bush of Holbrook Farm and Nursery (now closed), who gave it to me. I, in turn, have passed it along to English friends. Thus do good plants get dispersed.

How this gladiolus got to Boone remains a mystery. A brief listing in the *Index of Garden Plants* by Mark Griffiths states that *Gladiolus* ×*gandavensis* is a group of hybrids between two South African species, G. *dalenii* and G. *cardinalis*. Might there, somewhere, be other color forms awaiting rediscovery? This one would be hard to improve upon. About 2 feet high, with flowers that start off pale creamy yellow, fading to apricot, it multiplies quite rapidly and is heading for great popularity in warm regions. For me this gladiolus usually starts to flower in June, continuing through July and sometimes into August.

Abelia ×grandiflora 'Sherwood'

eral years, by which time the twiggy branches are so entangled that finding and cutting out the oldest ones would take hours. Instead the whole mass is cut down to a rather naked 1 foot before being selectively thinned. Recovery is rapid and the shrub all the better for what seems to be harsh treatment.

The introduction of two new compact, mounding selections, 'Confetti' and 'Sunrise', infused excitement into a taken-for-granted species. My three bushes of *Abelia* 'Confetti', each 18 inches high and 3 feet across, grouped in a triangle, are beginning to merge, which works well as year-round ornamental ground cover yet in a way is a pity. 'Confetti' is such a pretty little shrub that I want also to stage it as a specimen, perhaps in a container. The name, suggestive of polka-dot patterning, is misleading. Each tiny leaf, smaller than those of the type and more congested, is edged with white, and young leaves at branch tips are tinted pink. *Abelia* 'Sunrise' has a creamy yellow leaf edge.

Like most variegated plants, these two produce occasional green reversions that should be removed; however, the first spring after planting 'Confetti' I came close to digging it out in disappointment when new growth emerged entirely green. This stage was temporary; the variegation reappeared as leaves ma-

calyx that remains colorful when the flower falls.

The original *Abelia ×grandiflora* hybrid (*A. chinensis × A. uniflora*) is a medium- to large-sized shrub that remains dense and shapely to a height of around 6 feet, at which size it makes a splendid hedging plant for full sun. If let grow to greater height it becomes thinner and arching. A boundary hedge is kept at about 5 feet with winter pruning, removing one or two of the oldest stems and cutting others back to about 3 feet. Vigorous *A. ×grandiflora* 'Francis Mason', brilliant chartreuse in spring becoming mostly green later, is pruned the same way to keep it at 3–4 feet.

Abelia ×grandiflora 'Sherwood' is shorter and denser but still very vigorous. An early spring shearing keeps it under 3 feet for sev-

tured. Abelias are easily propagated by spring cuttings or separation of layered branches.

Vitex agnus-castus

CHASTE TREE

I have seen chaste tree (*Vitex agnus-castus*; Zone 7) grow as tall as 20 feet, but it is a mistake to let it do so. When kept at no more than half that height, the flowers are nearer eye level and the branches accessible for the fairly severe summer pruning that results in a second crop of bloom after the first big show in July. A sturdy shrub or small tree, chaste tree has stiff, straight branches that are seldom bowed or broken during storms, and its seven-fingered, hand-shaped, glossy leaves attract neither pest nor disease. The branched spires of violet-blue flowers in encircling clusters at regular intervals along main and side branches show particularly well against the cornlike (sweetcorn), creamy giant reed, *Arundo donax* 'Variegata'.

Chaste tree is tough enough to be grown in city highway center strips. It thrives in most soils except wet ones and calls for supplemental watering only in the severest drought. Because dead flowers don't cleave to it, I rate it higher than *Buddleia* 'Lochinch', a substantial shrub with gray-green leaves and lavender-blue flowers that would be my alternative for hot, full sun sites where vitex is not sufficiently hardy.

Lagerstroemia indica

CRAPE MYRTLE

Most gardens in my neighborhood consist mainly of lawn with a couple of flowering trees. More often than not those trees will be a dogwood (*Cornus florida*) and a crape myrtle (*Lagerstroemia indica*; Zone 7 as a tree, but root hardy in Zone 6), the latter commonly a vibrant (well, all right, raucous) watermelon pink. Gaudiness, eschewed where the light is gentler, becomes welcome with bright blue skies and brilliant sun. There was such a crape myrtle on the property when I came and it is there still. Now a large tree, it is high branched over multiple, handsome, snakily barked smooth trunks, carpeted around in late autumn with crimson and scarlet fallen leaves small enough that they do not bother plants below and need not be swept up. I have added other crape myrtles, including *Lagerstroemia fauriei*, grown not for its flowers but for its bark and so included with plants of winter interest.

Most crape myrtles have attractive bark. The two I value most for flower, however, are kept as multibranched large shrubs. Naturally smaller than most, these two are pruned in late winter to limit their height to 7 feet. Both are in a large, sunny mixed bed, where their first burst of bloom usually comes in early August, with another full flowering after a short pause. *Lagerstroemia indica* 'Victor', as near to true red as crape myrtles come, looks splendid against the creamy background of *Arundo donax* 'Variegata' looming over it. The frilly flowers of *L. indica* 'Prairie Lace' are the same clear pink as *Aster* 'Alma Pötschke', edged with sparkling white. The foliage of both these crape myrtles emerges coppery, with young tip growth retaining this color. With those two autumn color is occasionally brilliant, sometimes yellow, and often lacking. Mildew is an often-reported problem of crape myrtles. Neither this nor any other problem has so far affected any of those I grow.

Fully hardy in Zone 7, crape myrtles become die-back shrubs at their Zone 6 hardiness limit. Sun and heat are what they like, and they seldom bloom where summers are cool. With such a rich selection of crape myrtles available I do not want more of the same, but propagation experiments made out of curiosity found spring cuttings of soft wood to root within a few weeks and to grow on well.

Viburnum nudum

I mentioned earlier my failure to decipher the sex life of viburnums and consequent absence

A red-flowered crape myrtle, *Lagerstroemia indica* 'Victor', with creamy *Arundo donax* 'Variegata'

Viburnum nudum var. *angustifolium*

of berries. One of the exceptions, the narrow-leafed possumhaw, *Viburnum nudum* var. *angustifolium* (Zone 5), makes up for all the rest. For years my sole representative of the species, with no other within miles, has never failed to bear trusses of berries that remind me of some of the rowans (*Sorbus*) with which I have had no success in Virginia. They are borne at the tips of willowy branches clad in narrowly spear-shaped smooth but not glossy 3-inch-long leaves, following short-lived white flowers that are not this shrub's best feature. With occasional renewal pruning over its 20 years, it rises up among evergreen azaleas in a good

deal of shade to a thinly branched 8 feet. More sun and pruning back of branches would keep it more compact. In mid to late August the berries gradually turn from green to rosy pink, holding that color for about 2 weeks, then gradually changing to white, blueberry blue, and finally black, with all colors briefly present simultaneously.

Having admired it for years at Winterthur in Delaware, I recently added *Viburnum nudum* 'Winterthur' (Zone 5), keeping my fingers crossed that it will berry as reliably. Should it not, it will still be well worth having for its exceptionally attractive dark green, egg-shaped, quilted, and highly polished leaves. Both these viburnums root quickly from spring cuttings.

Lespedeza thunbergii

Lespedeza thunbergii (Zone 5) is a shrub, but in Zone 7 it behaves like an herbaceous plant, restarting from ground level in spring. That is a very good thing because if the plant began where it left off, its proportions would soon be formidable. *Lespedeza thunbergii* 'Pink Fountain', an apt name for a seedling selected at Montrose Gardens in Hillsborough, North Carolina, is my first choice among the several available selections. Slender branches shoot upward at first, then arch out and down. In

late summer or early autumn small pea-type flowers turn the bush to a shimmering silvery pink. So numerous are the flowers, born in little bunches at the base of neat, silkily textured trifoliate leaves that are evenly spaced along willowy stems, that they smother small plants on which they fall. Their color—medium lilac purple on the RHS color chart—is bright enough to catch the eye but softer than the magenta of the species.

Usually maturing at about 5 feet high, 'Pink Fountain' got off to an early start these past 2 years, following mild winters, growing taller than usual and showing its intention of flowering in late June. With permission denied, by means of the pruning shears, cutting off about 18 inches, it went on to regain its shapeliness and bloom at the designated time in early August, along with *Aster* 'Alma Potschke', which had followed the lespedeza's jump-the-gun lead and was given the same treatment.

With weeping plants more than most, presentation is important. It took me three tries to get it right. My 'Pink Fountain', moved as a 4-year-old, is now placed to perfection, sun-baked all day long at the tip of a peninsula bed approached from the south and fully open to east and west. It is well pleased with sandy soil of minimal fertility, a common characteristic of pea family (Leguminosae) plants. It had

Cestrum parqui (willow-leafed jessamine) at center, with yellow-spotted *Ligularia tussilaginea* 'Aureoma-culata' at bottom left, yellow-edged leaves of *Daphne odora* 'Aureomarginata' at bottom right, and faded heads of *Hydrangea macrophylla* at top left

Cestrum parqui

WILLOW-LEAFED JESSAMINE

Although I have grown willow-leafed jessamine (*Cestrum parqui*; Zone 7) in Virginia for only 5 years, and it is considered marginally hardy in England, it is such a fine plant and fills its space so rapidly that I would certainly buy it again should a worse-than-usual winter kill it. Because in Zone 7 it is killed to the ground in winter, its summer height is constant at a rounded 6–8 feet. Its spread, however, is indefinite if layered branches are not removed each year. My plant is in moderately moist soil, facing the morning sun and also getting some sun from the south. Companion plants include *Hydrangea macrophylla*, *Fatsia japonica*, *Daphne odora* 'Aureomarginata', *Ligularia tussilaginea* 'Aureomaculata', and *Sedum lineare* 'Variegatum'.

Between early summer and frost this jessamine produces innumerable large trusses of jasminelike, tubular and starry flowers of a luminous greenish yellow at the tips of supple branches clad in lustrous, dark green willowy leaves. The flowers drop neatly, no deadheading is called for, and the bush looks always fresh and clean. There is no fragrance by day, and do I imagine the faintest touch in the air at night? It is elusive. I cannot be sure, and when I put my nose close to the flowers, I catch only

Woody-based and deep-rooted (therefore drought resistant), they are not easy to lift and divide, but this job may never need to be tackled. Size can be curtailed by hacking pieces off with a mattock—also a rough and ready means of propagation. Where summers are hot and autumns warm and sunny, tiny pods containing a single seed ripen around Thanksgiving, but cuttings must be used to be sure of getting a plant identical to a named selection. Among seedling surprises recently named and introduced are *L. thunbergii* 'Edo Shibori', with bicolored white and purple flowers, and purple-flowered *L. thunbergii* 'Variegata', with spring foliage mottled and streaked with creamy white, later becoming green.

a rank smell from the leaves. The flowers are pretty, anyway, in the beam of the flashlight.

Hydrangea paniculata

The last wave of hydrangeas comes from *Hydrangea paniculata* (Zone 3). Actually, with appropriate choice among the many selections of this species, one or another could be in bloom from spring to autumn, with *H. paniculata* 'Praecox' kicking off and tardy *H. paniculata* 'Tardiva' bringing up the rear. Put off for years by the obese inflorescences of the commonest selection, the peegee hydrangea (*H. paniculata* 'Grandiflora'), I was later won over by *H. paniculata* 'Tardiva', now grown these many years with no maintenance other than pruning.

The 8-inch (or thereabouts) inflorescences resemble snowy mountain peaks, white throughout save for a faint flush of creamy green on tightly clustered young buds. There are just sufficient four-petaled, sterile florets among the small, fertile ones to make the inflorescence showy while remaining lightweight and upright. A site in full sun is acceptable, but the flowers last longer with afternoon shade. *Hydrangea paniculata* 'Tardiva' grows rapidly to small tree size and one has two pruning options. It can be trained as a tree by removing lower branches, so that other plants can be

Hydrangea paniculata 'Tardiva' underplanted with *Anemone tomentosa* 'Robustissima'

grown right up to its base, or it can be pruned hard back before new growth starts in spring to keep it bushy, though far from small. In my region it blooms between mid and late summer, coinciding with bloom on an extensive underplanting of the Japanese anemone currently known as *Anemone tomentosa* 'Robustissima' (synonym *A. vitifolia* 'Robustissima'), the most rampageous of its kind.

I have only recently begun to add other selections not readily available until now. They vary in size of bush, in size, laciness, or solidity of the inflorescence, and to some degree in color: all are basically white, some flushed with pink or purple, especially as they fade. The loveliest so far is *Hydrangea paniculata* 'Brussels Lace', with 2-inch sterile florets spaced over chaste, 1-foot panicles.

These shrubs need rather minimal maintenance and are pest-free. Adaptable to sun or light shade and most moderately fertile soils, they flower freely in both hot regions and cool ones, and are extremely cold hardy. They are pruned after flowering and propagated by spring cuttings or by separation of layered branches. Descriptions of other selections can be found in Michael Dirr's *Manual of Woody Landscape Plants* and in Hillier's *Manual of Trees and Shrubs*.

PERENNIALS & BULBS

Of the many perennials I grow, I can count on few to bloom all summer. Three of those described, *Phlox paniculata*, *Kalimeris pinnatifida*, and *Coreopsis verticillata*, stay open all day. *Gaura lindheimeri* begins afresh each morning and takes a break on hot afternoons. The others included here flower for a month or less, but remain presentable when not in bloom.

Phlox paniculata

I surprise myself by including *Phlox paniculata* (Zone 4). It sows around, it needs annual thinning and curtailing, spent inflorescences need cutting off, and it is mildew prone. What it offers, though, is a big range of colors, a light fragrance, a long bloom season, and stems that stay upright without staking, righting themselves fairly quickly if bashed down by storms. And phloxes have oomph: where gaura and astermoea are a whisper, phlox's bouffant heads of bloom are a hurrah. This shout becomes a scream, however, if ill-assorted colors are mixed together, especially if 'Orange Perfection' (not, anyway, among the best phloxes) is included among a predominance of pinks and purples. With the quieter green companionship of earlier or later flowering plants, phloxes hold the color fort through summer's harrowing heat.

Provided the soil is reasonably moist, phloxes have no objection to hot sun. If the flowers wilt a bit in the tropical heat of afternoon, they recover in the evening. They average 4 feet tall, with some a bit taller and a few little more than 18 inches. Of the many I've tried only *P. paniculata* 'Starfire', a brilliant crimson red, has so far declined to do more than cling to life, although several others have been cast out as exceptionally mildew-prone.

White-flowered *Phlox paniculata* 'David' was introduced as a mildew-resistant selection, and so it has proved to be (mildew resistant, mark you, not mildew-proof, there's been a touch now and then, usually towards the end of the season). *Phlox paniculata* 'Fujiyama' (synonym 'Mount Fuji') has long been the standard by which other white phloxes are judged. So how do they compare? At 5 feet 'Fujiyama' is a little taller than 'David'. Put them together and it becomes apparent that 'David' is whiter: skimmed milk compared with homogenized. 'David' has smaller, though still generous-sized clusters of flowers, and the individual flowers are thinner in texture, less full and rounded in form, and slightly smaller than those of 'Fujiyama'. 'David' is dainty, 'Fujiyama' voluptuous. Both are refreshing sights on hot summer days.

Phlox paniculata 'Bright Eyes' is my favor-

Alongside path, front to back: *Calamintha nepeta*, white petunias, white-variegated leaves of *Sedum* 'Frosty Morn', white flowers of *Gladiolus callianthus* 'Murieliae', little white double daisies of *Kalimeris pinnatifida*. Center: *Phlox paniculata* 'Norah Leigh' (variegated foliage), 'David', and 'Fujiyama'. Back: purplish *Monarda* 'Blue Stocking', white daisies of *Leucanthemum ×superbum* 'Becky', cloudy gray *Panicum virgatum* 'Heavy Metal'. Far back: *Miscanthus sinensis* 'Cosmopolitan' at right and *M. sinensis* 'Cabaret' at left.

Kalimeris pinnatifida, better known as *Astermoea mongolica*

more stems each spring than is good for them. Removing thin, weak stems, along with a few of the stouter ones, makes the clump less vulnerable to mildew and stems less likely to be toppled by rain. Root cuttings are a common means of commercial propagation. Division yields more than enough plants for home gardeners.

Gaura lindheimeri

"Tolerant of poor soils," I read. I'd say demanding of it. Sun and sand make *Gaura lindheimeri* (Zone 5) happy, and my best plant is a seedling that came up in the hard-packed gravel of the drive, where it tops out at around 3 feet. If it grows taller than this it may need cutting back to prevent it from sprawling. White flowers with the grace of butterflies dance over its wiry stems, a delicacy ruined, in my opinion, by the gold-edged leaves of *G. lindheimeri* 'Corrie's Gold'. *Gaura lindheimeri* 'Siskiyou Pink' is, however, a splendid addition, with bright pink flowers and a reddish flush to the leaves, though I have found it inclined to sprawl. White-flowered *G. lindheimeri* 'Whirling Butterflies' is somewhat shorter than the type and apparently sterile, and *G. lindheimeri* 'Dauphine' gets a multicolored look from flowers that fade from white through blush to clear bright pink.

ite pink-flowered phlox and 'Franz Schubert' the prettiest pastel purple. Both have been mildew-free most years. The reputedly temperamental 'Norah Leigh' (also being sold as 'Darwin's Choice' and 'Darwin's Joyce') usually flourishes, with an occasional off year when it seems to lack the strength to get going in spring. At such times I lift it, divide it, and give it a change of soil and scene in a nursery bed before returning it to soil replenished with compost. There is more ivory than green in many of its spear-shaped leaves, a clean, bright variegation that stands out. Its pastel lilac flowers have a purplish eye nicely picked up by *Monarda* 'Blue Stocking' (which is not, by any stretch of imagination, blue) in the background.

After their first year or two, phloxes put up

Established clumps of gaura would rather not be moved, though moving them can be done with care and a sharp spade. Seedlings move quite easily, and additional plants can be raised from cuttings taken in spring before growth hardens off.

Kalimeris pinnatifida

Kalimeris pinnatifida (Zone 6; synonym *Astermoea mongolica*) resembles a refined feverfew (*Tanacetum parthenium*, itself a good plant, short-lived but self-sowing), with leaves more finely cut, thinner stems, and smaller double white daisy flowers borne without pause from early summer to hard frost. Spread is rapid yet not invasive, and the clumps go for years before signaling a need for division with bare patches among the thickets of wiry stems. At this point it can either be lifted and divided into small clumps, or thinned by pulling older stems out from the middle of the clumps. It forms the front tier in part of my white bed, with *Phlox paniculata* 'Fujiyama' behind and *Miscanthus sinensis* 'Cabaret' behind the phlox. Full sun or light shade suits it, and most soils. Propagation is easy by division. Divisions sent to friends in cooler regions have twice shown a strange tendency to produce single flowers, which they never have done in my garden, nor have I ever found a seedling.

Coreopsis verticillata (threadleaf coreopsis)

Coreopsis verticillata

THREADLEAF COREOPSIS

With so much in its favor, threadleaf corcopsis (*Coreopsis verticillata*; Zone 3) has to be forgiven a degree of invasiveness if it is ignored. It takes no more than a couple of hours a year to keep it in check. This low-maintenance plant is supremely well adapted to heat, dry soil, and drought. In the wild it tends to favor woodland clearings. In the garden it can take full sun. No perennial has prettier foliage, filament fine and bright green from early spring through autumn, or more bright and cheerful flowers through the hot months. The species grows about 18 inches high and *C. verticillata* 'Zagreb' little more than 1 foot. *Coreopsis verticillata* 'Golden Shower', about 2 feet, is somewhat slower to spread and less accepting

Euphorbia corollata

of poor, dry soil. I am refereeing a contest between it and the autumn-blooming, stoloniferous *C. integrifolia*. Neither has yet declared victory.

If only *Coreopsis verticillata* came in other colors! I need its foliage and fortitude in so many places, but there are limits to where strong yellow can be fitted in. The pale lemon-yellow C. 'Moonbeam', perfect in color, form, and texture, spurns my fawning efforts and is little more than an annual. Although frequently listed as a cultivar of *C. verticillata*, this relationship is doubtful.

Euphorbia corollata

Most euphorbias I have grown have been short-lived. *Euphorbia corollata* (not to be confused with the weedy *E. corallioides*), which looks more like a gypsophila than a euphorbia, is one exception. Walking the garden on a July afternoon so hot that nobody in their right mind would choose to be out of doors and most plants were visibly cringing, I and my visitors passed such dejected plants as wilting phlox, collapsed *Phlomis russeliana* (its last chance), and rotting lamb's ears (*Stachys byzantina*). And there, as we rounded a bend, was *Euphorbia corollata* (Zone 5) as fresh as a bride in a white broderie-anglais gown.

Stems up to 3 feet long and a trifle lax are so lightly clad in small blue-green leaves, and their thinly branched upper part so airily strewn with confetti-sized flowers that they do no damage to the neighboring plants on which they lean. Full sun will do nicely, though a few scattered seedlings also crop up in lightly shaded places. These I transplant to where I want them or pot up while they are small. Although seed is an obvious means of increase, the nurseryman from whom my first plants came propagated it by keeping his parent plant in a large sunken container, periodically lifting it and potting up pieces that had escaped through the drainage holes, which suggests that root cuttings might also work.

Veronicastrum virginicum
CULVER'S-ROOT
Culver's-root (*Veronicastrum virginicum*; Zone 5), named for an obscure doctor said to

have used it for some now-forgotten medicinal purpose, looked equally fresh on a sweltering July day. By mid-June, when the rodlike stems with spaced whorls of spear-shaped leaves have attained a height of 5 feet, I cut them back by half. From the cuts come five new stems (one from each leaf axil), which grow another 18 inches by mid-July, terminating in one or more wands up to 1 foot long, made fuzzy by long stamens protruding from small flowers that are most often white, occasionally pale pink. If cut back as described, the tall stems do not need staking. The clumps increase quite fast and thinning or division provides ample new plants for home gardeners. This species can also be increased by seed or cuttings.

In monochromatic color schemes it is important to have contrast in shape and form. *Euphorbia corollata* and *Veronicastrum virginicum* make a yin and yang of form perfect for the white garden. Although the former is usually found in dryish, open places and the latter in moister soils, both do well in reasonably deep, porous soil of average moisture retention.

Sedum

The sturdy, clumping sedums embraced within *Sedum maximum*, *S. spectabile*, *S. telephium*, and various hybrids of uncertain parentage are good plants one and all. All are hardy to Zone 4. (The latest botanical name for these species is *Hylotelephium*, but most gardeners know them as *Sedum*.) One common name is live-forever, and certainly only the most purple-thumbed can kill these plants. In hot regions, however, they thrive best in a moisture-retentive soil. Some are included with foliage plants. Picking out but two for their flowers is not to cast aspersions on the rest, only that one must draw the line somewhere among so many good ones. Doing this is easier on paper than in the garden for who, after all, could resist a sedum called 'Gooseberry Fool', my very favorite dessert, a concoction of sieved gooseberries and cream?

New gardeners could do no better than to start with *Sedum* 'Autumn Joy', top ranker among perennials. Although herbaceous, it is an almost year-round presence in warm regions. Nubbins of new growth push through the ground while the sere old stems still stand and can be used as handles for pulling small rooted divisions out. Vigorous mounds of fleshy gray-green leaves on sturdy stems follow, then green-budded inflorescences, then the plates of pale pink flowers, crowded with bees and butterflies, then the rusty rose of faded flowers, and finally the brown of winter, while still firmly erect. If stems are splayed out at flowering time the clump needs dividing, which can be done at almost any time.

Sedum 'Autumn Joy' poses only one dilemma for color coordinators. Where to put it? The pale pink of its flowers does not fit well in hot color schemes, nor the terracotta of fading flowers among pinks. Grasses, blue flowers, and gray foliage make good companion plants. *Sedum telephium* 'Matrona' poses no such problem. Its dusky pink flowers on upright 2-foot stems, enhanced by the purplish flush on its glaucous leaves, harmonize with all the assorted pinks, blues, lavenders, and creamy or lemon yellows. The similar *S.* 'Joyce Henderson' is more inclined to flop.

In England these sedums are October bloomers. In southeastern North America, it is more likely to be August. Only in seasons both hot and wet do they need cutting back in midsummer to prevent them from sprawling. Increasing rapidly while remaining tightly clumping, easy to divide or move, and seldom pest attacked or messy, they are as near to perfection as any perennial comes.

Canna

I hope that my trial separation from most of my canna collection will be temporary, for few, if any, alternatives offer the same self-sup-

Canna 'Panache'

porting size, texture, foliage color, and non-stop bloom from early summer to hard frost. Alas, after displaying a clean sheet for years, my cannas blotted their copybook with severe infestations of canna leaf roller, a common problem in southeastern North America. The moth lays its eggs in the tubular unfurled leaves, then glues them together. When the tiny caterpillars emerge and feed, the canna leaves become ragged and brown, ruining the appearance of these majestic plants. Cannas (Zone 7) like hot climates and the number of species and selections I grew had been steadily climbing. It has now been brought home to me that I should grow only as many plants as I can monitor.

In an attempt to rid myself of this pest by depriving the moths of a place to lay their eggs, most of my cannas were lifted, plastic-bagged, and consigned to the garbage dump. One piece of tuberous root saved from each was thoroughly washed, potted in a soil-less mix, and sunk in a nursery bed under my eye. Only the two cannas least affected were left in the ground, with all foliage, surface litter, and mulch removed. The two could scarcely be more different. At one extreme is the bold, brash *Canna* 'Pretoria' (synonyms 'Striata', 'Bengal Tiger'), gorgeously, unabashedly gaudy, with striped chartreuse leaves and orange flowers and, at the other, *C. glauca*, with slender glaucous leaves and dainty, lemon-yellow flowers. Its delicate appearance belies its behavior: it alone of my cannas spreads at such alarming speed that it has now for several years been confined in a large, sunken container. Or somewhat confined, for it escaped through the drainage holes and came up in cracks between the paving stones of an adjacent path. The canna I shall miss most is the lovely 'Panache', with amber and apricot flowers of trim proportions perfectly set off by gray-green leaves.

Many gaps left by the cannas have been filled with ginger-lilies (*Hedychium*) of similar size and rate of increase. Splendid, healthy plants for several years now, they flower in late summer and autumn and many of them are fragrant. They still await the test of a really severe winter.

Allium tuberosum

GARLIC CHIVES

From midspring onward the slender, hollow leaves of garlic chives (*Allium tuberosum*; Zone 5) form fresh-looking, dark green, 1-foot clumps. In late August they bloom on 2-foot stalks, and a fleet of butterflies finds them almost instantly. So numerous are the flattish umbels that they form an almost unbroken sheet of lacy white for 2 or 3 weeks. As the umbels fade, green seed capsules form, pretty still, but they must be cut off before the black seeds form. I wear disposable surgical gloves to avoid reeking hands. So seriously do I take this task that if I am to be away long enough for seed to be set before my return, I cut garlic chives down in full bloom before I leave, knowing that failure to do so will mean weeding out young onions for years to come.

Zephyranthes candida

RAIN LILY

A wise friend once advised me not to claim hardiness for a plant in a particular locale until it had survived for a quarter century. *Zephyranthes candida* (Zone 7) recently crossed that finishing line, having survived many weather excesses along the way.

A soaking rain prompts this South American species to burst into bloom with a suddenness that always surprises—one day no noticeable buds, the next a white sea of bloom. Someone, observing this tendency for flowers to follow rain, gave to the genus the name "rain lilies." Another name is zephyr lilies. Scattered flowers follow showers from midsummer on, opening from crocuslike buds into up-facing, starry, six-petaled chalices a couple of inches across, one to each bright green stalk. Peak bloom comes between late summer and midautumn, and lasts for about a month, during which there are hundreds of flowers, bright white against the dark green, glossy, rushlike leaves. Spent flowers shrivel neatly, and the flower stalks and leaves are so

Allium tuberosum (garlic chives) with tiger swallowtail butterfly

similar in color and length that they merge almost indistinguishably, so this self-sufficient plant needs neither deadheading nor deadstalking to keep it tidy.

My plants set surprisingly little seed; the profusion of bloom in a yard-wide expanse yielded only five propeller-shaped pods, each of the three stubby sections containing a single round black seed. This stinginess is puzzling, because in other species growing nearby, tightly packed capsules of flaky seeds follow each flower. No matter. Bulb increase is prodigious, making possible experimental plantings in several parts of the garden: in sun, in light to heavy shade, in soils from wet to dry, sandy or dark and rich, with and without fertilizer. Only in shady, root-filled soil under trees did plants finally disappear, after struggling on,

Zephyranthes candida (rain lily), with fernlike yellow-leaved *Rubus cockburnianus* 'Golden Vale'

on arching stems of *Lespedeza thunbergii* 'White Fountain' weeping down behind. I planned this combination, and the reality has matched the dream. I can claim no credit for another appealing combination; it was my garden's gift to me. The zephyr lilies are alongside a path, and behind them I planted a white-stemmed blackberry with ferny yellow leaves, *Rubus cockburnianus* 'Golden Vale'. Though later a mounding bush, during its first 2 years it branches trailed over the ground. A couple of wandering stems mingled with the rain lilies, drawing attention, by repetition of color, to the yellow anthers of the flowers and the whitewashed stems of the blackberry.

Zephyranthes candida is the hardiest rain lily and the easiest to grow. It is readily available and inexpensive. The lovely spring-flowering North American atamasco lily (*Z. atamasca*; Zone 7) is, by contrast, scarce, expensive, and at risk of extinction, lost less to collectors, too often the whipping boys, than to housing developments, roads, and shopping malls. It likes swampy ground with spring sunshine and summer shade.

Another zephyr lily that increases rapidly is the pink-flowered *Zephyranthes grandiflora*. For me it comes and goes, surviving some winters and killed in others. *Zephyranthes reginae* 'Valles Yellow', a delicate, creamy yellow,

flowerless, for several years. What suits them best is moist, compost-enriched soil in full sun. Fertilizer is not needed. Clumps can go for years without attention but benefit from division every other year. The bulbs are not far down, the roots relinquish their hold quite willingly, and the leaves do not wilt, so thinning the clumps is quickly and easily done, using a trowel to lift small bundles of congested bulbs in spring or autumn. If these clusters are replanted without further division, and watered in, they suffer no setback at all.

The size, neatness, and evergreen foliage of *Zephyranthes candida* make it suitable for the front of beds and borders. One large drift grows around and between three clumps of white-variegated yucca (*Yucca filamentosa* 'Variegata'), with the white pea-type flowers

has the largest and most plentiful flowers of the yellow zephyr lilies I've tried. The bulbs are quick to increase, but this species is as yet a novice in my garden and "very promising" is all that I can say. Likewise with 'Labuffarosea' (species uncertain), white or a delicate pink, said by Yucca Do Nursery, from whence it came, to grow and flower well in deep shade, though mine is in sun and moist soil. Mid to late summer is the flowering time for these three. Their narrowly straplike leaves, less glossy than those of *Z. candida*, die away in winter.

Liriope muscari

Someone (if they read this, my apologies for not giving credit where credit is due) coined the word "liriopogon" for the genera *Liriope* and *Ophiopogon* because they look so much alike. Though often indistinguishable, they differ in one big way: liriopes have spikes of ornamental flowers raised up on stiff stems, while the flowers of ophiopogon are usually carried in smaller, looser clusters, partly hidden among the foliage. Only when dividing a patch of *O. japonicus* did I spot the brilliant blue berries that followed the flowers I'd never noticed.

Although I dispensed with the repetitive chore of mowing grass, mine is not a low-maintenance garden. Trees and shrubs provide abundant shelter and nesting sites for birds, with food near at hand from worms, grubs, insects, seeds, and berries. The birds are a delight, but from the seeds they daily excrete come such weeds as smilax, pokeweed, and poison ivy. Loblolly pines provide shade for plants and me, but tidying up around them is an unremitting task: pollen, cones, needles, and a litter of broken twigs and branches after ice storms, snow, wind, or heavy rain. Liriopogons come to the rescue with clumps too dense for weeds to penetrate, while their "comb-able" foliage and firm grip on the ground makes tidying them with a rake a quick and rewarding task. Large sweeps of liriope add a restful look to the garden, and the minimal care they require frees time to devote to more demanding plants.

If the price was high and there was a waiting list, the long-suffering lilyturf, *Liriope muscari* (Zone 6) might more often be used to optimum effect instead of being relegated to the role of workhorse in shady places, along with ivy, periwinkle, and pachysandra. A plant with such an impressive résumé deserves better of us. It is evergreen. It is neat. It forms noninvasive clumps. It greets temperatures of 15°F or 100°F with equanimity, and if it does get winter-battered, it soon refurbishes itself after a spring shearing. It needs no staking, no watering save in prolonged drought, no fertilizing, and infrequent division. It flowers during the late summer dearth, in blendable lavenders, violets, and white, and picked flowers last a long time. The only routine chore called for is removal of dead flowers for the sake of tidiness. Some gardeners make a practice of shaving lilyturf close to the ground in late winter, and plants do look delightfully fresh and springlike after the new leaves fill in. It isn't essential and I used not to do it, but nowadays I tidy into a close crop the punk hairstyle brought about during winter by browsing rabbits, a job quickly and effortlessly accomplished with an electric pruning saw. If it tears the leaves, the saw needs sharpening.

Words from an old song applicable to liriope are teasing my mind, something like "If what you ask is nothing, that's what you'll get." Because liriope will put up with poor soil, deep shade, drought, and root competition, that is often what it gets, but better conditions reap dividends. Deep soil that doesn't get dry is ideal, and a site with bright light and morning or filtered sun. Some selections can take full, hot sun, especially the variegated kinds. So why is this near-perfect plant seldom considered for a place in the border, as edging, punctuation, or small drifts that contribute spiky form among such other late-season

Liriope muscari 'Monroe White' between house and drive

bloomers as physostegia, goldenrod, and the plethora of aster and boltonia daisies?

Twenty forms of *Liriope muscari* can be bought from a single mail-order nursery, many more if one searches around, yet the millions of liriopes grown are mostly limited to three kinds: *L. muscari* 'Big Blue', a good commercial name but the flowers are not blue—they are pale purple; *L. muscari* 'Variegata', monotonous in its ubiquity but one of the best forms; and the similar 'Silvery Sunproof', another misleading name because the leaves are creamy, not silvery, and the flowers are the typical liriope purple. If one wants to be different, there is a variegated liriope with white flowers, though, truth to tell, white flowers go less well with the cream-striped leaves than the purple spikes of 'Variegata'. There are, however, better selections than 'Big Blue' in 'Majestic' and 'Royal Purple', with fatter spikes of richer color. The flowers of 'Majestic' are somewhat crested, but the best of the crested kinds is 'Christmas Tree', named for the shape of its pinkish lavender flower clusters. The leaves of two other cockscomb kinds, 'John Burch' and 'Gold Banded', sometimes show slight marginal variegation but are as often solid green. The most elegant liriope I know is 'Lilac Beauty', with long, slender spikes of light lavender opening late in the season.

For reasons not always definable, there's usually a favorite child, and in the large liriope family mine is *Liriope muscari* 'Monroe White', a bright, clean white set off wonderfully well by the arching clumps of dark green leaves. One thinks of white gardens as always being sunny, but they are achievable in shade if variegated foliage is included. I have 'Monroe White' in a shady bed that gets barely an hour's sun each day, along with *Ligularia tussilaginea* 'Argentea', *Carex phyllocephala* 'Sparkler', gray-fronded Japanese painted fern, white-flowered bleeding hearts, *Campanula poscharskyana* 'E. H. Frost', and a variegated form of the low, creeping *Ardisia japonica*, all underplanted with an evergreen mat of white-flowered *Arabis procurrens. Daphne ×burkwoodii* 'Carol Mackie' grew there for several years until, by mistake, I left sprinklers running for 2 days and drowned it.

A liriope for a different color scheme is *Liriope muscari* 'Pee Dee Ingot', with leaves of chartreuse-green in shade and brilliant chartreuse-yellow where it gets a few hours of sun. With the sweet flags *Acorus gramineus* 'Ogon' and *A. gramineus* 'Minimus Aureus' this liriope gives continuity at the sunnier end of a moist and shady border, joined by the scarlet of 'Hot Shot' azaleas in spring, impatiens in summer and autumn, and, in winter, red-

Liriope muscari 'Pee Dee Ingot'

berried branches of 'Sparkleberry' (*I. verticillata* hybrid) holly overhead.

Finally, two look-alikes and a warning. *Liriope spicata* (Zone 4) is a useful plant for controlling erosion in places where it can be allowed to spread without being a nuisance. *Liriope spicata* 'Silver Dragon' (relegated to the far side of a roadside ditch outside the front fence) is an alluring form with blades striped in bright white, but it is equally aggressive and the leaves frequently revert to solid green. If you live in the warmer zones, resist the temptation to buy 'Silver Dragon' and seek instead the similar *Ophiopogon jaburan* 'Vittatus' (Zone 7), which can be trusted to brighten a shady border without making a bid for the whole garden.

Ophiopogon japonicus

Short, dense, fine-bladed mondo grass (*Ophiopogon japonicus*; Zone 6) is a no-mow alternative to grass where it doesn't get frequent foot traffic and isn't exposed to hot sun. Grass, though, is a lighter green than surrounding vegetation, while mondo grass is darker. Where one of my mulch paths splits to pass on either side of a large oak tree, *O. japonicus* 'Compactus' (synonym 'Nanus'), half the height of the species at 6 inches, makes a dark lozenge shape at the base, space-defining and weed-suppressing. If the paths were paved it would be confined; in mulch it spreads slowly out and needs tidying back to shape every other year. *Ophiopogon japonicus* 'Kyoto Dwarf' is shorter still, only an inch or two, and as dense as the pile of a Wilton carpet, perfect for creating patterns between paving. *Ophiopogon japonicus* 'Aritaki' (synonym 'Kigimafukidama') has very slender white-striped blades and would be a winner except that it is often winter damaged and occasionally killed, and it frequently reverts to green. *Ophiopogon japonicus* 'Torafu' is a strange little thing with slender blades randomly banded in yellow. This oddity needs to be displayed as such, perhaps in pebbles or gravel against a rock in Japanese-style gardens. Rabbits are drawn to this cultivar like moths to a candle flame, not, unfortunately, with the same dire consequences.

Among ophiopogons with broader blades, more like lilyturf, I give ten marks out of ten to one introduced from Korea by Barry Yinger in 1974 and occasionally sold as *Ophiopogon japonicus* 'Little Tabby'. If 'Kyoto Dwarf' is a Wilton carpet, 'Little Tabby' is a shag rug, altogether softer and less formal. The cream-striped blades arch randomly, weaving together in a 6-inch pile with a wavy, misty look when compared with the upright stance and brighter striping of *Liriope muscari* 'Variegata'. In my garden 'Little Tabby' shows up well against dark, bark mulch paths and is particularly beautiful in a pathside patch in front of azaleas with pale purple flowers, along with *Sedum lineare* 'Variegatum', another cream-variegated plant of hazy effect. 'Little Tabby' spreads with satisfying but non-invasive speed and seems willing to grow anywhere short of the extremes of bog or desert.

My only complaint about black mondo grass (*Ophiopogon planiscapus* 'Nigrescens'; Zone 6) is that in light soil it wanders thinly. I have squeezed it into a corner where two paved paths meet to force more density. One friend did the opposite, letting it roam and interplanting it with the little gold-leaved *Hosta* 'Kabitan'. The near-black blades of this mondo grass need contrasting color to set them off, subtly with the gray or buff of rocks, paving, gravel, or other plants, or in can't-be-missed combinations with chartreuse foliage such as golden Scotch moss (*Sagina subulata* 'Aurea') or golden creeping Charlie (*Lysimachia nummularia* 'Aurea').

Begonia grandis

HARDY BEGONIA

Some gardeners in southeastern North America spurn the hardy begonia (*Begonia grandis*; Zone 6) as weedy, which is to say it takes care of itself and, by means of small bulbils in the leaf axils, increases steadily in quantity. Not here and there yards apart, however, but in small colonies, pullable in minutes if they become too plentiful. Hardy begonia is not without its foes. Slugs find the leaves attractive, and a fungus occasionally causes rotting spots, not often enough, or severe enough, for me to bother with preventive measures. It is otherwise an easy-going plant, content with any reasonably moist soil out of the afternoon sun.

The large, dark green, angel-wing leaves are handsome from midspring on, filling in as Virginia bluebells (*Mertensia virginica*) goes dormant. One of the hardy begonia's most appealing features is the spider-web network of ruby red arteries and veins prominent against

Backlit leaves of pink-flowered *Begonia grandis* (hardy begonia)

Begonia grandis 'Alba' (white-flowered hardy begonia)

the grayish undersides of the leaves. In shady spots where the sun comes in from the back or side for an hour or two, the leaf is rendered translucent and the veining prominent. The species has flowers of candy pink, beginning in early August and continuing for several weeks. Leaves of many white-flowered plants lack the touch of red present in the leaves of their pink-flowered counterparts, a characteristic that makes it possible to separate the pinks and whites from mixed batches of seedlings. The red veining of white-flowered *Begonia grandis* 'Alba' is, however, just as prominent as in the species.

By the time *Begonia grandis* finishes blooming I can bid goodbye to summer, without re-gret, and welcome the long and sunny autumn. Gardening will be more pleasure than penance for the next 2 months or more, a blessed pause between cooling the house and heating it. Soon, now, I shall wake in the night and reach for a thin blanket, one of life's small pleasures.

ANNUALS

Plenty of annuals and tender perennials glory in long, sunny days, high temperatures, and warm nights. Many self-sow to become permanent residents, and it is on these that I mainly rely. There were failures until I grasped that most are best sown, initially, in autumn. Winter-hardy annuals such as love-in-a-mist (*Nigella damascena*) germinate in autumn, become sturdy plants by spring, and flower early. If sown in spring they have insufficient time to reach blooming size before high temperatures set in. Autumn-sown annuals that are not winter hardy do not germinate until they gauge it safe to do so in spring.

Once established many annuals and biennials self-sow with a prodigality that crowds out other plants if they are not hard-heartedly culled by the handful into spaced clumps early on, then further thinned as they develop. These include larkspur (*Consolida ambigua*), love-in-a-mist, cleome, poppies, honesty (*Lunaria annua*), and impatiens.

Although nursery-grown summer annuals such as impatiens are on sale a month or more before my self-sowers appear, I am content to wait. There is ample color from shrubs in spring, and self-sown seedlings are less needy during dry spells. They emerge in their own good time and then, through summer days of such enervating, steamy heat that even the cats, so quick to annex the warmest spots, lie torpid in the shade, those annuals energized by warm days and nights carry the garden color torch through to winter with Olympian stamina.

Before honing in on some of the best of the self-sowing summer bloomers, there are a few others too good to overlook that I buy or replant each year.

Salvia farinacea
MEALYCUP SAGE

Mealycup sage (hideous name for a beautiful flower) is a tender perennial that does not survive the average Zone 7 winter. It has never self-sown for me, so I buy bushy, blooming plants in early June, choosing such compact, 18-inch selections as deep blue 'Victoria', or seemingly bicolor 'Strata'. All white-flowered selections I have seen have been drab, but 'Strata' is lovely, the blue flowers emerging from silvery calyces for a blue and white effect. In any reasonably good soil, in full sun or a few hours of shade, watered only during protracted drought, these undemanding plants will bloom non-stop until hard frost.

Ipomoea batatas
SWEET POTATO

The three splendid color forms of sweet potato are foliage plants. If they flower, I have never noticed. My favorite is *Ipomoea batatas* 'Tricolor', with leaves of pink, white, and green. Grown as summer ground cover at the front of a bed, it makes vigorous, vining stems that trail over the ground or clamber up into nearby *Rosa* 'Pink Pet'. *Ipomoea batatas* 'Blackie' has leaves of dark purple-brown, and

An ornamental sweet potato vine, *Ipomoea batatas* 'Tricolor', with magenta-flowered *Petunia integrifolia*

I. batatas 'Margarita' is bright chartreuse. They are all at their best trailing from raised beds or containers. They are not winter hardy and do not self-sow, but the tubers can be lifted and stored, or eaten if you wish.

Lablab purpureus

HYACINTH BEAN

Where there is space for a vigorous annual vine, *Lablab purpureus* (synonym *Dolichos lablab*) is one of the best, as much for the large, glossy, purple pods as for the purple flowers. It needs a stout support. I use a tripod formed of 10-foot lengths of rebar rammed well into the ground in triangular formation and tied together at the tips. Hyacinth bean usually does self-sow but not always, so to be on the safe side I collect a few seeds in autumn to be put straight into the ground, after an overnight soaking, when the risk of frost has passed. Large plastic containers with the bottoms cut out guard them against the young rabbits that are numerous when the hyacinth beans are small and succulent. Hyacinth bean starts to flower in midsummer and continues until frost.

SELF-SOWERS

Several self-sowers share a gold medal for the long show they put on—impatiens in moist soil and shade, and the others in sunbaked

Lablab purpureus (hyacinth bean)

sites. They cost nothing after their first year, contribute color from midsummer to frost, and require no deadheading or other maintenance at a time when gardeners, made languorous by heat, are ill-disposed to play nursemaid to plants. All germinate in spring.

Petunia

It is neither a boast nor an apology when I say that I have never grown the bedding petunias bred for stumpy habit and outsized flowers. Snobbish, perhaps, but we are all entitled to our peccadillos so long as we don't force our opinions down other people's throats. The petunias I grow have a less artificial look and wilt less, if at all, in the heat.

Petunias cross so readily that unraveling the parentage of modern hybrids is a challenge

Petunia integrifolia with yellow-leaved *Berberis thunbergii* 'Bonanza Gold' and *Stipa tenuissima*

that defeated me. I am guessing that it is *Petunia axillaris*, or an early hybrid strain, that graces many a garden in southeastern North America, having survived for generations under conditions of benign neglect, sometimes over-wintering, otherwise coming back in spring from self-sown seed. Be wary if offered "wild petunia," which could be either this plant or *Ruellia caroliniensis*, a pretty but weedy southeastern native perennial.

On days when I feel as if I were enveloped in a warm, wet blanket, smothering for lack of air, there grows the petunia, fresh, fragrant, and cool-looking in white. And so it will continue week after week, recovering quickly if left bedraggled by a thunderstorm. The flowers are about 2 inches across, the height a loosely bushy 15 inches if cut back when stems grow lax. Pale lavender is the commonest color among a range of purplish pinks. Plants root quickly from summer cuttings and by gradual reselection I have a pure white strain that self-sows true if kept segregated.

This petunia of wildling grace has a rival now in *Petunia integrifolia*, which lacks the fragrance but shares the other good traits and adds others of its own in the neat size of its flowers and a vigorous, trailing habit perfect for slopes, raised beds, and containers. The flamboyant magenta-crimson flowers are so

White and pink forms of *Catharanthus roseus* (annual periwinkle)

profusely borne that they form a lava flow of color in full sun and light soil. In richer soil the stems can be kept cut back or left to climb into taller plants. A white-flowered selection I bought did not self-sow, but seedlings with flowers of intermediate size and color are appearing where this pink and white ones were grown close together. *Petunia integrifolia* is

killed by hard frost, returning from self-sown seed in late spring.

Catharanthus roseus
ANNUAL PERIWINKLE

Annual periwinkle (*Catharanthus roseus*) is a tender perennial usually grown as an annual. It is available in pure white, white with a red

Zinnia angustifolia with *Ilex crenata* 'Golden Gem'

drive, there 9 inches high, a little taller in deeper soil. *Zinnia angustifolia* 'Tropical Snow' neither wilts nor melts in the heat. Holding its gray-green linear leaves firmly out, it tips each branch of its slender stems with an orange-eyed up-facing daisy that is ivory with a hint of green, fading out to white. A golden yellow central stripe makes the orange-flowered species neon bright, a glowing addition to a hot color bed. These small zinnias seem impervious to the mildew that sometimes plagues the bigger *Z. elegans*.

Salvia coccinea

Typically red, *Salvia coccinea* also comes in pale pink, apricot, bicolors, and white. Firmly upright, branched plants begin growth in June, soon reach 6 feet, begin to bloom early in July, and keep it up until hard frost. During intense summer heat the flowers are spent by noon, so the dewy early morning is the best time to visit them. Bees will already be at work, and the cross-pollination they effect may result in a few misplaced colors and sometimes new ones. After heat abates in early autumn, the flowers last all day.

Between thinning the seedlings in early summer and cutting plants down in late autumn, nothing need be done except occasional removal of unwanted colors and any salvia

eye, and various shades of pink, including the luscious red-eyed 'Apricot Delight', not truly apricot but near enough to be tolerable against red brick walls. White forms, originally in a raised bed, have sown into the gravel of the drive, where they make chunky 1-foot bushes, mostly true to color and bringing the freshness of spring to summer with sparklingly bright flowers set off to perfection against glossy,

bright green leaves. In rich, moist soil, or in shade, annual periwinkle grows lanky and less floriferous. The flowers stay open at night, white beacons in the dark.

Zinnia angustifolia

This small-flowered zinnia comes back faithfully year after year in its raised, sunny bed, and it, too, has sown into the gravel of the

seedlings crowding permanent occupants of the bed. Scarlet flowers are kept well away from a crimson crape myrtle, only whites and pale pinks are permitted in the white border, and pink flowers are yanked from a border of hot colors. In one part of the garden the seedlings remain a random mix, and it is here that new colors most often occur. Desirable new colors can be increased by cuttings.

Euphorbia heterophylla

PAINTED LEAF, ANNUAL POINSETTIA

Want a poinsettia for the summer and autumn garden? *Euphorbia heterophylla* is it. And while I'm on the subject, don't toss out that Christmas poinsettia after the color is gone. It makes an excellent foliage plant for the garden between frosts, remaining unmarred and needing little water.

Painted leaf is an annual American wildflower with a native range, according to William Carey Grimm (*Recognizing Flowering Wild Plants*) embracing Virginia, Indiana, Minnesota, South Dakota, south to Florida and Texas, usually in moist, sandy soil in open woods and waste places. I only once bought and sowed the seed; the plant has since taken care of itself, seedlings appearing faithfully in spring. It attains a branched 3 feet by late July, with attractive fiddle-shaped (pandurate) 4-

Salvia coccinea 'Sea Shell'

inch leaves. It then resembles a miniature scarlet poinsettia. Because the color comes not from the unshowy little flowers but from bracts and the petal-shaped lower portion of inner leaves, it remains colorful until frost. Although seedlings manage well enough on their own, I usually thin them before pinching out the remainder to make them bushier. Seedlings may need protection from young rabbits, which ignore the plants once they grow taller and branch out.

Ipomopsis rubra

STANDING CYPRESS

Scarlet flowers and spirelike shape are at a premium. The biennial *Ipomopsis rubra* contributes both, along with the unusual texture of closely placed fennel-fine bright green

Ipomopsis rubra (standing cypress)

leaves all along its slender, unbranched 6-foot spires. It blooms in July and August. Commonly scarlet-flowered, it also comes in an amber yellow strain. Full sun and deep sandy soil that retains moisture during drought are its preference. After an initial sowing of seed 2 years in a row, it has returned each year without any effort on my part except for leaving patches of seedlings undisturbed when reworking the bed or shifting perennials around. Seedlings do not move well except when very small, so I leave them where they choose to be. They grow into such slender columns that they do not impinge on other plants.

Portulaca oleracea hybrids

ORNAMENTAL PURSLANE

There are differing opinions about the merits or otherwise of color-coordinated gardens. I have my own unyielding opinion: a garden should be whatever you want it to be, limited only by such circumstances as size, climate, and time available to manage it. For me, high summer brings two different needs: for the green quietude of ferns and other plants of the shade, and for brilliant color in those sunny sections not always under my eye but rather tucked away where they can be visited when I need the sort of color shot delivered by my perennials border of analogous hot colors.

Perennials, however, are demanding plants, calling for attentions I am not always willing to give when perspiration trickles.

Portulaca oleracea lets me relax on a shaded bench and absorb my fill of brilliant mixed color. This place is ideal for a morning coffee break. Tea break is too late, because most of the flowers are single and close soon after lunch, neatly, with no need for deadheading. Double forms stay open all day, but I've found only one, a nameless clear yellow bought in a hanging basket from the supermarket.

Glimpsed under the head-high branches of the great spruce (*Picea abies*) that separates my sand lawn and its surrounding borders from the rest of the garden, the portulacas invite me in with a gorgeous cacophony of color that almost obliterates the bright green succulent foliage. The flowers measure an inch or two across, sometimes a bit more in the Yubi range, a group of hybrids now available at garden centers and in a few mail-order catalogs. Most are a solid color, but a few are bicolors. About every hue but blue and true red is found in these showy hybrids of the humble, weedy purslane: delicate blush, brilliant purple, sunrise orange, apricot, salmon, yellows cool, clear, warm, or amber, all co-mingling without the jarring clashes that might re-

Portulaca oleracea hybrids

sult were they not united by uniformity of shape and size. Only white (used elsewhere) is sometimes removed. White is such a dominant color that it can bring a spotty look to otherwise cohesive plantings.

Each year sees some new colors appear. Increasing them could not be easier, for this portulaca has a characteristic, unique in my experience, that makes it my most valued annual. Break off a fleshy stem, insert it in the ground, water it in and, without further ado, it becomes in a few weeks a dense, weed-suppressing mat smothered with flowers. Each lush mat emanates from a single, slender root, so pulling plants up when frost turns the tops to mush takes little time or effort. In autumn, when nights become cool, the flood of bloom slows to a trickle, and with the coming of frost the flowers are done. But, like Phoenix from the ashes, they will be back, from seed, next year.

The double form sets no seed, so in autumn, while days are still warm, 5-inch-long fleshy strands of this plant and a few favorite colors are inserted an inch or two deep in pots of a soil-less mix. The uncovered pots stay in an open frame until frost threatens. Then they are covered with plastic bags, held in place with rubber bands, and put under lights indoors. The plants stay there through winter, untouched except for occasional removal of any dropped leaves. In spring they go back in the frame to harden off for 1–2 weeks, then back into the garden, and the cycle starts anew, with plants grown from cuttings getting a month's start on the self-sown seedlings that later pop up in great numbers.

Seed is miniscule and quickly shed but easily collected nonetheless. Seed capsules resembling tiny blue-green acorns follow the flowers at the tips of the stems. I have yet to spot one of these beginning to open; they are either firmly closed or seed has already been shed. No matter. Pinch out tips with seed capsules, put them in an open container, shallowly or they will rot, and stand this in a light, dry place. Give it a shake now and then, and remove the fleshy bits after the seed is shed. Sow the seed in early spring, where you want the plants to grow. Portulacas will not start into growth until the days get warm. Because plants grow quickly from cuttings inserted in the ground, there is no better annual for plugging into bare spots, over dormant bulbs for instance. One year I grew them along the edges of the gravel drive, but they are most spectacular in my sand lawn, which I should explain.

A quarter century ago I became a no-mow gardener. If mowers started at first pull, and if my efforts resulted in the neat, close-cropped green sward of my English lawn, mowing would be a tolerable, even pleasurable job. Where lawns look little better than mown fields, and the prevalence of ticks and chiggers makes it inadvisable to sit or lie on them, I begrudge what they demand of time, energy, and money.

I did want to retain as open space the roughly oval, border-surrounded center of a secluded "room" behind a giant spruce (*Picea abies*), and thus began experiments to find a no-mow alternative to grass. It had to grow in full sun, look neat all year, and stand up to foot and occasional wheelbarrow traffic. What the next 5 years taught me is a deep respect for the tolerance of lawn grasses. Thyme grew sparse and rotted out in patches, chamomile likewise. *Phlox subulata* needed frequent dividing and replanting, clover refused to recognize limits and invaded surrounding beds, and dwarf mondo grass (*Ophiopogon japonicus*), which does the job splendidly in shade, scorched in the hot sun. Eventually I admitted defeat and covered the surface with sand, thereby creating Virginia's biggest kitty litter box until the sand was topped with gravel. Here the portulacas grow, and this part of my garden has brought more moments of unalloyed summer bliss than any other.

Those who wage war against wild purslane, and who does not, might well be reluctant to introduce the ornamental form. In many years of growing the hybrids, I have never found them a nuisance. They are quite the opposite, in fact, making mats so dense that they keep out other weeds.

Impatiens

A scarlet-flowered selection of busy Lizzie (*Impatiens walleriana*) bought years ago self-sows about 95 percent true to color when flowering begins in June. I pull out the few pink seedlings that appear. The plants spread out low and wide, intermingling with chartreuse-foliaged plants in a lightly shaded bed where the soil is dark and humus-rich from years of added mulch. Impatiens survives light frost, and bloom sometimes continues beyond Christmas.

Of late I have also been delighted with the charm and all-season performance of the Sea Shells range of impatiens, in pink, apricot, and creamy yellow. These hybrids make 18-inch-high bushes. They are not frost hardy. Although the plants do not self-sow, cuttings root in soil or in water with the same ease as *Impatiens walleriana*, growing big enough to plant out so rapidly that there is no need to buy more than one plant of each color form.

Impatiens walleriana in a courtyard trough

BEAUTIES OF THE NIGHT

On languorous, high summer days the garden's needs are met by making an early start, thwarting nature's intent to create a jungle by pulling weeds and cutting back plants before the most vigorous smother the less robust. Then I retreat to the air conditioned house until, at dusk, the outdoors beckons again. Now, with darkness concealing the garden's imperfections, there is for a while the nirvana of total absorption in what is lovely. During daylight hours only half the mind is on beauty; the other half is fidgeting to tidy something up. At night I am not pulling chickweed or making mental lists of pressing tasks, just looking. One must plan for it, though. Not only does darkness lower a veil on such distractions as the wild smilax infiltrating a shrub, the tangled stems of a clematis, and the aphids on a rose; it also shrouds most color, repainting the scene in black and white. Pink annual periwinkles (*Catharanthus roseus*) have become invisible, while *C. roseus* 'Blanche', the best pure white, shows ghostlike in the dark.

At the opera I like to watch the audience arrive. Among the beads and bangles and fashion's latest styles and colors, what strikes me afresh every time is the elegance and drama of simple black and white. This effect, impossible to achieve in the garden by day, is the color world after dark.

Pardanthopsis dichotoma
VESPER IRIS

White is the dominant color of the night, followed by pale, lucent lemon, but my vesper iris (*Pardanthopsis dichotoma*; Zone 7) marches to its own drum in lavender, a recessive color even by day, let alone at night. Yet this color contributes to the daintiness of faintly fragrant flowers raised on wiry stems over fans of gray-green leaves. Tongues of white on the purple-spotted falls of the flowers obviously suffice to guide insects to the flowers because they do get pollinated, presumably by the flies that hover around them at dusk. A white-flowered form of vesper iris is said to exist, but I have failed to find it.

Vesper iris is reportedly short-lived, but I've had mine for years. It must like the acid, sandy soil. Nurseries seldom sell it, but it appears on the seed lists of the Hardy Plant Society and North American Rock Garden Society, which is reason enough to join them. Seed is easy to raise, and there'll be sufficient plants to try in different places. My vesper irises flowered in considerable shade, but were moved to a sunnier spot when the 3-foot plants signaled this need by leaning towards the light. The flowers are larger than those of the day-blooming, orange-flowered blackberry lily (*Belamcanda chinensis*), but the plants are similar in habit and with the same neat way of twisting dead flowers into tight spirals. The two have been crossed and the color range broadened in a group of day-blooming plants known as ×*Pardancanda norrisii*.

Mirabilis jalapa
FOUR-O'CLOCK

My four-o'clocks (*Mirabilis jalapa*; Zone 7 as a perennial) can't tell the time—they don't open till twilight. They then usually work a 12-hour shift, closing when sun-warmed. The English name is marvel of Peru, marking the plant's origin. Considered tender, it has been perennial for me, surviving winter freezes, spring floods, and summer droughts for a decade, and scattering progeny plentifully nearby. It likes to sink its tuberous roots deep and fares less well in shallow or root-filled soil. The bushy plants, their unblemished bright green foliage smothered with fragrant flowers like miniature petunias, commonly yellow or magenta, are undeniably attractive. Still I felt

White forms of *Mirabilis jalapa* (four-o'clock)

Oenothera glazioviana (an annual evening primrose)

lukewarm toward four-o'clocks until I grew the exquisite white-flowered form. Seed exchanges have this one, too. At night it lights the way for pollinating moths lured by its siren song of sweetness. Most four-o'clocks grow 2–3 feet high, but a new one is on offer that sounds intoxicating: *Mirabilis* 'Champagne' (synonym 'Baywatch'), with pale yellow flowers on stems said to attain 9 feet. Where four-o'clocks don't survive winter, the tuberous roots can be lifted and stored like dahlias.

Oenothera glazioviana

At dusk an evening primrose prepares to perform. By daylight it seems such a commonplace thing to prize, weedy even, but after a day in the air conditioned house or car, to go into the dark of a balmy night and watch pointed buds start to quiver, then, in quick succession, burst open and spread their petals into luminous yellow bowls—these are enchanted moments, and that's the magic of *Oenothera glazioviana*. Go out before break-

Ipomoea alba (moonvine)

for several weeks will celebrate the night with champagne-glass-shaped, narrow-petaled, lemon-yellow flowers. Having partied all night, the flowers, still fresh in the morning, go to rest in the afternoon. White-striped *Acorus gramineus* 'Variegatus' lining this path offers guidance similar to white lines on a dark road. The white-edged leaves of *Hosta* 'Patriot' also stand out, but it is the August lily, *H. plantaginea* and the double-flowered *H. plantaginea* 'Aphrodite' that I grow for the fragrance of their large (for a hosta) night-blooming white flowers.

Ipomoea alba
MOONVINE

The big white chalices of the moonvine (*Ipomoea alba*) draw me next. Their intense perfume draws the hawkmoths too, arriving eerily on silent wings for nocturnal nuptials with flowers as fresh and flawless as a bridal dress, and as briefly worn. By dawn the flowers are crumpled and spent. The hawkmoths sip nectar on the wing, hovering like hummingbirds, never settling. I try to hold them in the flashlight beam to get a closer look, but they evade it and dart away. Where do they come from, and where do they go? I never see them resting by day in the garden. Perhaps,

fast and you may catch the last of the flowers, but what bewitches is watching them pop open and gleam out in the dark of the night, beacons for the flying insects that will pollinate them and assure a crop of seedlings. The crop will be big if most of the dead flowers, hanging like dishrags, aren't cut off, but don't take them all, untidy though they look; this species is a biennial and a few flowers must be left for regeneration. *Oenothera glazioviana* makes a big, bushy plant, and I've watched 27 flowers open within 15 minutes, leaving clusters of many more pointed buds for the next day's show.

I follow my nose to a daylily, *Hemerocallis citrina* (Zone 4; synonym *H. vespertina*), that

after all, I don't want to know. The mystery is part of the magic.

Moonvine needs a strong support. Having reached the top of a 9-foot wigwam of iron rods, this vigorous twining vine scrambled through a clump of giant reed (*Arundo donax* 'Variegata') and mingled with the red flowers of a nearby crape myrtle (*Lagerstroemia indica* 'Victor')—all in a matter of months. Seed, first soaked for several days, is sown in February under lights. The seedlings are hardened off in a frame and planted out after the last frost date. Moonvine is not hardy, and fresh seed is collected before the first frost to continue the cycle. Seed can just be tucked into the ground after it warms up, but flowering then starts later.

Datura innoxia

Datura innoxia (Zone 9 as a perennial) is the queen of the nightbloomers. Its buff-tipped pale lavender buds, furled like umbrellas, open to white chalices as much as 9 inches across, with a honey and lemon redolence tempting one to taste. Don't! All parts of the plant are poisonous, so don't grow it if toddlers share the garden, and warn older children not to touch. The flowers stay open long enough in the morning for photographs by natural light. Low, rather sprawling bushes of

Datura innoxia with lilac-flowered *Calamintha nepeta*

handsome gray-green leaves bear many spiny seed cases, and sufficient seedlings appear late in spring to replace the parent plant if it has been winter-killed.

Gardenia jasminoides

The scent of *Gardenia jasminoides* (Zone 8, but selected forms in Zone 7) wafts towards me, too cloying for indoors, but delicious hanging on the night air. I waited many years for this plant and spent many dollars on gardenias soon winter-killed, meantime overlooking what was right under my nose a few gardens away. Planted by a keen gardener some 40 years ago and neglected by his successors for the last three decades, it lives on, many

Gardenia jasminoides

Nicotiana

TOBACCO

The starry white flowers of two tobacco plants, *Nicotiana alata* (Zone 8) and the taller, 6-foot *N. sylvestris* (Zone 8) flower the whole 24 hours, though the scent is intense only at night. *Nicotiana alata* often looks a bit bedraggled by day, so does the daintier 18-inch *N. suaveolens*, an annual I hesitate to recommend because much seed offered is not the right thing. *Nicotiana sylvestris*, which prefers moist soil and a bit of shade in hot regions, sometimes survives winter, but sometimes does not. It is my first choice among tobacco plants. Some years plant lice disfigure it, and it always self-sows so copiously that weeding out the surplus takes several hours each spring. Walk by the plant at night and these defects are forgiven.

times killed back in bad winters, only to spring back to life come spring. I helped myself to cuttings, which rooted quickly, and now I have it, too. A typical gardenia, with the same double flowers as those sold by florists in pots, it has proved hardier. I cannot say why this should be so, only confirm that there are gardenias that will survive occasional spells of 0°F.

Gardenias flower by day as well as night. So do magnolias. White and fragrant, again the familiar pairing of characteristics. The flowers of *Magnolia grandiflora*, a giant now, and the smaller but fast-growing *M. virginiana* come a few at a time from midsummer into autumn. More might be overwhelming, so powerfully are they perfumed.

A garden at night is mysterious and calming, the darkness lit only by pale flowers and firefly Tinkerbells, another world within the more familiar one of daylight. Those whose work allows them only evenings at home might want to expand my menu of night-blooming flowers. Peter Loewer's book *The Evening Garden* describes many more.

Autumn and Winter

AUTUMN FLOWERS AND BERRIES

Autumn more than compensates for the miseries of summer. Local motorways bordered with red maple (*Acer rubrum*), sweet gum (*Liquidambar styraciflua*), tulip poplar (*Liriodendron tulipfera*), sassafras, and sumac (*Rhus copallina*) are a pleasure to drive along. Because foliage color is abundant all around, there has been no urge to seek it for the garden, though it comes as a bonus, some years, from witch hazels, fothergillas, *Itea*, and oakleaf hydrangeas. The warm amber of coral bark maple can always be counted on, and, briefly, the bright yellow leaves of *Hamamelis virginiana*, falling all at once to reveal branches laden with bright yellow flowers. Colored foliage falsely signals the end of the gardening year when really autumn brings a new beginning and much else is going on.

Dahlia 'Bishop of Llandaff'

When I first saw scarlet-flowered *Dahlia* 'Bishop of Llandaff' (Zone 8) about 40 years ago, I had to have it. I still do. There are many more dahlias now with purple leaves, but in no other I have seen are the leaves as finely cut. 'Bishop of Llandaff' is not hardy in Zone 7, so it lives in a large plastic container, which is plunged to the rim in my hot color border early in spring, there to remain until frost blackens the foliage, when the container is lifted for wintering indoors. It does not need light during dormancy and any cool, frost-free storage place will do. In March it is watered and moved into full light. In April it is given a

LEFT The garden in winter, with the trunks of *Lagerstroemia* 'Natchez' in the foreground and the bright red berries of *Ilex* 'Sparkleberry' in the background. Other plants include amsonias with brown or yellow foliage, dwarf evergreen conifers, *Miscanthus sinensis* 'Hinjo', and *Viburnum plicatum* 'Mariesii'.

Dahlia 'Bishop of Llandaff' with orange-flowered *Lantana camara* 'Miss Huff' and yellow-foliaged *Euonymus fortunei* 'Sparkle 'n' Gold'

sprinkling of slow-release fertilizer and put back in the garden. I am, with few exceptions, a no-stake gardener, so in June the tall stems are cut back to 1 foot. Foliage is the main summer attraction. The flowers are at their best when the weather cools in autumn, by which time the plants will again have attained 3 feet.

Euonymus americanus
HEARTS-A-BUSTIN
Some call *Euonymus americanus* (Zone 6), which is scarcely known in England, strawberry-bush or wahoo. Locally, where it grows wild, hearts-a-bustin is the vernacular name. Accustomed to squeezing its way up through woodland undergrowth, it does the same in my garden, rising well up over evergreen azaleas, green-stemmed, small-leaved and so inconspicuous most of the season that I forget it is there. Until autumn. Then, with shining scarlet seeds dripping from crimson capsules, it becomes a showpiece. This sight is a big reward for perhaps an annual hour of maintenance, spent removing surplus seedlings scattered around the plant's base.

Chrysanthemum
My father had a fondness for chrysanthemums, and so do I, but his plants and mine have little in common except the distinctive chrysanthemum smell. Dad's were the jumbo kind bred for the showbench, grown in pots, staked, fertilized, and disbudded to achieve one perfect exhibition bloom on each plant. My first loves are the late-flowering mums that revel in hot summers and more or less take care of themselves.

In the rearrangement of a genus admittedly overstuffed with dissimilar plants, chrysanthemums ceased to be *Chrysanthemum* (Zone 5) and became *Dendranthema*. This reclassification caused such a brouhaha that they were returned to the familiar name and are once again called *Chrysanthemum*. Some nurseries have not yet caught up, so look under both names.

Although split off from such erstwhile members of the genus as Shasta daisies, painted daisies, and feverfew, chrysanthemums remain a large and varied group, many of them bedding plants but with a nucleus of undemanding, soundly perennial plants. There are two main kinds—those of somewhat lax habit with 2- to 3-inch, mostly single flowers, blooming in early autumn, and the bushy button ones that are among the last flowers of the season. Both groups have attractive foliage from spring to hard frost. Spittle bug has been the only pest to bother my plants, and that only twice in many years.

A mum called 'Apricot', 'Single Apricot', or 'Sheffield' is the heartwinner of the first group, an exquisite pale salmon fading to flesh pink. The color is lovely but needs placing with care. Blue and gray are safe companions, if a bit mundane. I've liked it best in a threesome with fountain grass (*Pennisetum alopecuroides*) and the rusty dead heads of *Sedum* 'Autumn Joy', and with blush and coral bicolor forms of *Salvia coccinea* such as 'Coral Reef'. A mistake I made was putting 'Apricot' in front of a blue-pink sasanqua camellia that bloomed at the same time. It has been replaced with *Chrysanthemum* 'Pink Sheffield', a cooler pink containing no yellow. 'Sheffield' is sometimes sold as 'Pink Sheffield', so check descriptions before

Euonymus americanus (hearts-a-bustin)

you buy, or play it safe with 'Innocence', which is white fading to pale pink, or the light pink 'Venus'.

Button mums start to bloom when the weather cools in midautumn, then keep it up for several weeks. Full sun is best, but they perform well where there's shade for no more than half a day. Don't indulge them with rich, moist soil or they'll get leggy. In moderately fertile, sandy soil they grow so dense and bushy that weeds can't find a toehold. They don't need dividing, but they spread fast, densely, and need curtailing every few years to maintain proportions. Alternatively, grow them as weed-resistant ground cover where they can spread at will, which is what one big patch of pink *Chrysanthemum* 'Mei Kyo' has been doing for 20 years in my garden, some-

Chrysanthemum 'Apricot' with rusty dead heads of *Sedum* 'Autumn Joy' and *Pennisetum alopecuroides* (fountain grass)

Chrysanthemum 'Innocence' (pale pink) and 'Mei Kyo' (bright pink, sporting to a different form) with blue 'Fanny's Aster'

Chrysanthemum 'Nantyderry Sunshine'

The lemon-yellow *Chrysanthemum* 'Nantyderry Sunshine' arose as a sport on 'Bronze Elegance' in the Welsh garden of Mrs. Glynne Clay. Lemon and chocolate make a delectable combination, and I have used as companions for this button mum both *Eupatorium rugosum* 'Chocolate' and the larger *Physocarpus opulifolius* 'Diabolo'.

Ceratostigma willmottianum
CHINESE PLUMBAGO

Early autumn brings some of the most brilliant blue of the year in a shrubby blue plumbago, *Ceratostigma willmottianum* (Zone 7), a loosely bushy 2-foot shrub with dark, wiry stems, neat little diamond-shaped leaves that redden before falling, and flowers resembling small periwinkles. Bloom doesn't come in a deluge but in daily sprinklings for several weeks, starting in late August. This plumbago is a have-it, love-it, and leave-it-alone kind of plant that doesn't benefit from feeding or watering. Seedlings spring up in the most unlikely places, evincing a preference for poor, dry soil. Several have put themselves under the outer skirts of a big spruce, spreading out over a narrow path to brush my legs as I pass by. Because the leaves and stems are bristly, this feels like being stroked with sandpaper. The winter-killed stems are left for protection until new

what corralled by the driveway on the front, sunny side, big trees (*Cornus florida* and *Magnolia stellata*) to left and right, and several sturdy bushes of *Spiraea japonica* 'Shibori' behind. *Chrysanthemum* 'Anastasia' is similar to 'Mei Kyo'.

These button mums are given to sporting branches with flowers of a different color (mine have produced two promising sports),

adding a touch of excitement to growing them. *Chrysanthemum* 'Bronze Elegance', which began life as a sport on 'Mei Kyo', is a beautiful coppery color, warm enough to hold its own in scarlet, orange, and yellow schemes, yet not overwhelming in echo combinations with salmons and apricots such as *Canna* 'Panache' and the butterfly ginger-lily *Hedychium coccineum* 'Aurantiacum'.

growth commences in early spring. Zone 7 is about the hardiness limit for Chinese plumbago, and another semi-woody species, *C. griffithii*, has not been a stayer for me. Gardeners in colder regions can get the same brilliant blue from low-growing *C. plumbaginoides*, which for me blooms a bit earlier. Because it breaks dormancy late, the latter makes a good ground cover over early crocuses.

Aster

Gardeners in cool summer regions would probably give their vote to *Aster ×frikartii* (Zone 6) as the best aster. Where summers are very hot, it is not reliable. As an alternative, though I won't pretend that it flowers for as long, I suggest *A. spectabilis* (Zone 5), which makes a spreading mat of glossy, almost evergreen leaves, topped for a few weeks in late summer by violet-blue flowers on 15-inch stems.

By and large I've found Michaelmas-daisies, the popular name in Britain for autumn-flowering *Aster* species and cultivars, including *A. novae-angliae*, *A. novi-belgii*, and sundry complex hybrids, more trouble than they are worth, but because they fill a late summer gap between the daylilies and the chrysanthemums, I do cleave to two selections of the New England aster, *A. novae-angliae*: violet-blue 'Hella Lacy', selected by journalist Allen Lacy and

Ceratostigma willmottianum (Chinese plumbago)

named for his wife, and the somewhat shorter bright pink 'Alma Pötschke' (synonym 'Andenken an Alma Pötschke'). Both need dividing every other year, and I must either clip them back, sometimes twice during summer, or stake them. For once, I stake, and 'Hella Lacy' rises to a billowing 4 feet behind *Spiraea japonica* 'Crispa', which conceals the supporting metal link stakes. Part of this plant's appeal is the way its flowers attract hordes of butterflies and honeybees, along with praying mantises, which, alas, dine on good and bad bugs with equal appetite. *Aster* 'Alma Pötschke', near the front of a bed, is sheared to limit its height to about 2 feet and to retard bloom to coincide, in an echo combination, with the bicolored cerise and white flowers of the crape myrtle *Lagerstroemia indica* 'Prairie Lace'.

Aster spectabilis

There are plenty of heat-tolerant asters: *Aster lateriflorus* (Zone 4), with its nebula of wee maroon-eyed starry flowers (especially dark-leaved *A. lateriflorus* 'Prince'), waxy-leaved *A. laevis* 'Bluebird' and the taller, black-stemmed *A. laevis* 'Calliope' (Zone 4), for sun and white-flowered, dark-stemmed *A. divaricatus* (Zone 4) for shade—to name just a few. Where sunny autumn days are assured, a few asters stand head and shoulders above the rest—literally in the case of *A. tataricus* (Zone 3), the great size of its basal leaves and its rapid spread reminding me of comfrey. *Aster tataricus* is not for the small border, but for me it is quite manageable in a sunny bay hedged in to back and sides by stalwart shrubs *Hydrangea arborescens* 'Annabelle' and a little-known but worthy tall wild blueberry, *Vaccinium elliot-tii*, with small leaves and small edible berries. The aster can hold its own in this robust company. Its 7-foot stems of large lavender blue daisies need no support. If this aster is too big, try the 5-foot *A. tataricus* 'Jindai'.

The climbing aster, *Aster carolinianus* (Zone 6), blooms all through October. The flowers are shallow bowls of rather ragged pale lavender rays. Individually they'd win no beauty prizes, but what they lack in quality they make up for in quantity, with thousands upon thousands packed into a far-flung shawl of foliage-obliterating bloom.

What makes this species unique among asters is its ability to climb, though it lacks any obvious means of doing so. It has no tendrils or curling leaf petioles like grapes or clematis, no rootlike holdfasts or adhesive discs like ivy and Virginia creeper, no twining stems like wisteria or honeysuckle, not even the thorns that help some climbing roses hitch themselves to twigs and branches. It can be fastened to a trellis, lathhouse, arbor, or fence, but in the wild it supports itself on trees and bushes, clambering to heights of up to 12 feet. The way it does so is fascinating. Slender woody stems, limber when young, becoming stiff with age, grow up and out. At about 2-inch intervals stiff, 1-foot-long side branches grow out horizontally, each in a different direction.

Climbing *Aster carolinianus* with ferny foliaged *Rosa roxburghii* and a yellow-leaved hickory (*Carya*) tree

Once a few of these have lodged themselves across a twig or branch, the aster has its scaffolding in place to support other stems. If the searching stems find no means of support, they loll and interlace, piling up branch over branch, much as one might stack sticks for a fire, becoming an intricately interwoven, self-supporting mass.

Climbing aster grows wild in coastal plain swamps of southeastern North America, indicating a preference for moist, acidic soil, sun, heat, and a long growing season. Where the plant is suited, its vigor is impressive and sometimes destructive. A smokebush (*Cotinus coggygria*) was the chosen host for my climbing aster. The first year it lolled through a low crotch, the second year it spilled down from a 5-foot height to pool on the ground like a bridal train, and in the third year the smokebush collapsed under its weight. The skeletal remains, with branches stubbed back, sufficed to support the aster for another year, by which time its own branches had formed a sturdy framework. Now it is trying to smother a neighboring *Rosa roxburghii*. If I grew the rose only for its flowers, I'd let this happen (they are pretty when newly opened but quickly brown and ball, and they attract Japanese beetles), but the ferny foliage is charming and stays unblemished, so the aster's

takeover bid must be discouraged. Pruning, which took me half a day with secateurs, now takes half an hour with an electric hedge clipper, a birthday gift from my husband, who finally accepts that I'd rather have a load of manure than a diamond ring. The saw, a full-sized commercial model, also makes short work of cutting down woody-stemmed perennials. If eyes or mind are allowed to wander it might also lop off something unintended, like a finger or two! The natural tendency to gather up stems to be sheared with the free hand has to be resisted. A lightweight, battery-operated hedge clipper proved inadequate even for such finely twiggy shrubs as abelias.

The climbing aster also walks. Some of the lower branches arch down and take root, by which means the aster extends its terrain several feet in a season. These rooted branches provide all the extra plants home gardeners are likely to want. If I had a sunny chain-link fence, I'd put more of this bounty to use in an experimental flowering "fedge," a word coined in England for a hedge-fence combination. What a sight that would be!

Good as these plants are, where Halloween does not mark the end of the growing season, the cream of the aster crop is a group usually attributed to the species *Aster oblongifolius* (Zone 5). These are asters you can plant and

leave more or less alone until they outgrow their space. All bloom for several weeks in October and November. The first of mine to open is 'Raydon's Favorite', and the last, late in November, is 'Miss Bessie', which has the smallest flowers on the tallest plant and is quite invasive in good soil. In between come 'October Skies' (the shortest), 'Our Latest One', and 'Fanny's Aster'. They are alike in their small, unmarred leaves, and their healthy longevity. Charles and Martha Oliver of the Primrose Path nursery, who found and introduced 'October Skies', advise: "It wants full sun and is highly tolerant of drought and poor soil, where it will have the best growth habit." I concur, and this advice applies to the others as well. Each is a billow of blue for a month or more, not a pure blue but getting close. Height varies with variety, soil, and available moisture, from 18 inches to 4 feet. 'Fanny's Aster', for example, exceeds 3 feet in a wet year, if allowed. It then sprawls, so I shear it back in summer to keep it half that height. Cutting dead stems down in winter is the only other maintenance needed.

Manettia cordifolia
FIRECRACKER VINE

I know that I am not alone in coveting the scarlet-flowered climbing nasturtium, *Tropae-*

olum speciosum. I grew it in England, and that I do not grow it in Virginia is not for want of trying. It took me years to accept that it is neither cold hardy nor heat tolerant in this region. Instead I have firecracker vine (*Manettia cordifolia*; Zone 7), an herbaceous perennial hailing from South America and accustomed to hot days and warm nights. It starts to produce its scarlet flowers in late summer, reaching a peak in autumn. Though small, the flowers, shaped a bit like goldfish, are numerous, vivacious, and accompanied by small, lustrous, spear-shaped leaves.

My appetite for plants gobbles up every available hour, and shortage of time is sometimes apparent in failure to display a plant to best advantage. Firecracker vine has graced my garden for a quarter century, making the best of things as it rambles over the ground, climbs the chicken wire on a fence inadequately high, and gets rather lost among the tangled stems of *Kerria japonica*. It deserves better of me and of those who design and sell vine supports. What it needs is a tall trellis panel strung with vertical wires for the slender twining stems to climb. It would then, like clematis, need early attention to getting the stems on track and preventing them from climbing each other.

Acid sand of low fertility, sometimes dry,

Manettia cordifolia (firecracker vine)

has suited it well enough. Slight root suckering provides all the additional plants I need. One such division recently planted in richer soil is growing much more luxuriantly, which may or may not turn out to be a good thing.

Dicentra scandens

CLIMBING BLEEDING HEART

Having flowered from July on, *Dicentra scandens* (Zone 6) reaches its peak in late summer and early autumn. It hitches itself up to a height of 10 feet or more by tendrils that tip short side-growths of delicate leaves at 3- to 4-inch intervals along zigzag succulent herbaceous stems. Nodding axillary clusters of about a dozen green-tipped buds open into yellow hearts dangling like charms on a bracelet. The fishing-line fine tendrils hook themselves onto the cylinder of deer-fence plastic mesh encircling a tree trunk, with some

Dicentra scandens (climbing bleeding heart)

stems wandering off to drape nearby shrubs. Bright light with only a few hours of direct sun seem to suit this climbing bleeding heart very well in soil that does not get dry.

Coreopsis integrifolia

Gardeners owe a vote of thanks to Bob Mc-Cartney and Robert and Julia Mackintosh of Woodlanders Nursery, who were evaluating and introducing southeastern native plants long before "going native" became politically correct. Many fine plants now widely disseminated originated with them, including the cheery, autumn-flowering *Coreopsis integrifolia* (Zone 7), a Florida native. I predict this star-shaped and star-bright plant will attain star status once it becomes better known. I have a patch of it in front of *Kerria japonica* 'Pleniflora', which still bears a smattering of flowers at this late season in a color that nicely matches the dark-eyed, egg-yolk yellow flowers of the coreopsis. Frost nips the coreopsis in the bud, but where the weather stays sunny and warm beyond the autumnal equinox, 6 weeks of steady bloom can be expected. Meantime the coreopsis fills its space with upright stems clad in neat, dark green leaves with a waxy sheen. Thonglike white stolons run out far and fast, but are easy to peel back when they go too far.

Ligularia tussilaginea

While asters and chrysanthemums are flowering in sun, *Ligularia tussilaginea* (Zone 7; synonym *Farfugium japonicum*) is brightening the shade. Praise is often heaped on two other ligularias, *L. dentata* 'Desdemona' and the look-alike 'Othello', but their large, darkly polished rounded leaves lose their appeal when chewed by the slugs that flourish in the same damp soil favored by these plants. Their leaves have purple undersides, and the flowers are orange daisies, a color combination that thrills the artistic but appalls many gardeners. *Ligularia dentata* cultivars are winter dormant and very cold hardy, but signal their dislike of heat by drooping dismally, even in moist soil.

Where it is hardy, *Ligularia tussilaginea* is a better bet for hot summer regions. In late autumn its sturdy, branching 2-foot stems bear quantities of bright lemon-yellow daisies, an easier color than orange to fit into the scheme of things, and its shining, leathery leaves seem unattractive to slugs and other chewing pests. It is evergreen to about 20°F and survives occasional plunges to 0°F provided frost does not penetrate deeply into the ground. I throw an armful of pine-straw over my plants when the temperature seems likely to drop well below freezing, removing it when the weather warms up, an on-again-off-again process

Coreopsis integrifolia, where *Narcissus* 'Ambergate' was in spring

through winters with frequent temperature swings. Otherwise these plants get no special attention. Where insufficiently hardy, this species makes a handsome container plant for those with a conservatory, greenhouse, or bright frost-free garage where it could be overwintered. Like other ligularias, it prefers soil that doesn't get dry and shade for a few hours from hot afternoon sun, but the leathery leaves are much less inclined to droop from heat or dryness than those of other ligularias.

The popular name, leopard-plant, is appropriate only for *Ligularia tussilaginea* 'Aureomaculata'. Yellow coin-spotting on the leaves makes this selection much sought after by flower arrangers, and it is the easiest form to find. It brings a sun-dappled look to shady places, where its large leaves could contrast

Ligularia tussilaginea 'Argentea' with flowers removed to better show off the foliage

its clumps of glossy leaves strikingly variegated in white. *Ligularia tussilaginea* 'Crispata', also grown for its foliage, has a cuddlesome look, with ruffled leaves crimped and tan-felted at the rim. These two look best grown as single specimens. Terra Nova Nurseries (wholesale only) celebrated the year 2000 with the introduction of *L. tussilaginea* 'Crested Leopard', which combines the crisply crinkled edges of 'Crispata' with the yellow spotting of *L. tussilaginea* 'Aureomaculata'. I'm ambivalent about the only other form I've seen, *L. tussilaginea* 'Intaglio', an oddity with thick, raised veins on the surface of the leaves.

Salvia leucantha
MEXICAN BUSH SAGE

Salvia leucantha (Zone 7), growing side by side with a relatively compact purple-fruited beautyberry, *Callicarpa dichotoma*, marries the season of flowers to the season of berries in echoing violet-purples. This duo once was a threesome with a 1-foot, purple-flowered, autumn-blooming ornamental onion, *Allium thunbergii* 'Ozawa's Variety'. Came a drought year and the onion made clear its preference for quarters cooler and moister than this hot spot.

The salvia's fuzzy white open-mouthed flowers are extruded from densely packed purple calyces in 15-inch wands stretching to-

with a gold-striped sedge such as *Carex dolichostachya* 'Kaga Nishiki' (Zone 5; synonym 'Gold Fountains') or *Carex muskingumensis* 'Oehme' (Zone 5). The flowers, which stay fresh for weeks, echo the coin-spotting. Behind such a grouping I have *Cestrum parqui* with greenish yellow flowers.

It takes a bit of sleuthing to find other forms of *Ligularia tussilaginea*. The species itself is the hardest to track down, which is puzzling considering that it can be grown from seed. Its plain green leaves set off the flowers better than the fancier selection, and if I could have only one ligularia, the species would be my choice. It would be hard, though, to part with *L. tussilaginea* 'Argentea', such a beautiful foliage plant that I often cut off the flowers, which detract from the pristine symmetry of

Salvia leucantha (Mexican bush sage) in late November, against yellow autumn foliage of *Hydrangea anomala* subsp. *petiolaris* on north-facing house wall

wards the sun over head-high, wide-spreading bushes of willowy leaves with white-napped undersides. Flower and calyx contrast is lost in a form with purple flowers, but that selection works well with an underplanting of chartreuse foliage for contrast, say *Ilex crenata* 'Golden Gem' or golden feverfew (*Tanacetum parthenium* 'Aureum').

If frost holds off until after Thanksgiving, as it often does, *Salvia leucantha* racks up 10 weeks of bloom, reigning over its sunny corner as the leaves of coral bark maple (*Acer palmatum* 'Sango kaku') turn amber and gradually fall, autumn crocuses come and quickly go, and a witch hazel (*Hamamelis virginiana*) strips overnight to reveal the yellow flowers previously secreted beneath the leaves. The salvia stems are always winter-killed, but my plant, in the same spot for 20 years, has always come back strongly in spring. It is vulnerable to freezing until its roots have taken firm hold in the soil, so spring is the best planting time. An inch or two of mulch applied at the end of the year helps it through the winter.

Allium thunbergii 'Ozawa's Variety'

When its partnership with *Salvia leucantha* was dissolved, *Allium thunbergii* 'Ozawa's Variety' (Zone 5) settled down in a bed where it gets shade during the hottest hours. One clump is in front of *Arachniodes simplicior* 'Variegata', where the onion's violet-purple flowers contrast with the yellow stripe in the fern's fronds. This little onion is a charmer, modest in size and vivid in color, with linear leaves 1 foot or longer, triangular in section, of a dark, glossy green that looks good throughout its long growing season. One of the few references I found rates this species as hardy only to Zone 8. Do not believe it. My plants, hardy for 20 years in Zone 7, came from a friend in Zone 5. Clumps are easily pulled apart and benefit from this treatment when they begin to look crowded.

Lantana trifolia

This self-sowing annual is one of autumn's most striking plants. It is late to appear and does not attain its full, free-blooming 3-foot bushiness until August. From the axils of spear-shaped leaves on stiff, bristly stems come domes of lavender flowers held upright on 3- or 4-inch stalks, becoming tassels of berries similar in size and violet-purple color to those of callicarpas. Flowers and berries continue in unison until frost, by which time fallen berries will have secured next year's succession in more or less the same place. I suggest this as a bushier, shorter alternative to *Verbena bonar-*

Allium thunbergii 'Ozawa's Variety' with yellow-striped *Arachniodes simplicior* var. *variegata* (variegated holly fern)

iensis, which also does well in this same sunny, sandy location.

Hibiscus syriacus 'Puritan'
ROSE-OF-SHARON

In Virginia *Hibiscus syriacus* is called rose-of-Sharon, which in England means *Hypericum calycinum*. In England this sun-loving Asian shrub cannot be counted on to bloom every year. In Virginia it blooms reliably, copiously, and long, starting in late summer and continuing through autumn. The abundance of seed set by this species was a cause of complaint until such sterile hybrids as white 'Diane' and maroon-eyed 'Helene', both singles, were introduced. Yet all the time the best of the lot was biding its time, unhonored and unsung save for the few who cherished it in old gardens. This seems an appropriate place to say that America owes much to its black community for so often giving asylum to plants discarded as commonplace. This rediscovered hibiscus now has a new name, *H. syriacus* 'Puritan' (Zone 5). Its pure white, double flowers come in succession from midsummer to frost. Spent flowers drop quite quickly from the bush, leaving it pristine.

In hot regions *Hibiscus syriacus* grows so fast that unpruned bushes come to resemble gnarled old apple trees, with lichened trunks and branches. If this is not the goal, hard pruning in winter or early spring is advisable, limiting plant height to about 6 feet, with a dense and fairly upright habit. If, by autumn, some branches have become long and lax, I prune them back. *Hibiscus syriacus* is not fussy about soil, provided it does not get sodden. Full sun or a few hours of shade suit it equally

Hibiscus syriacus 'Puritan' with *Miscanthus sinensis* 'Morning Light' and pink-flowered *Lagerstroemia indica* 'Prairie Lace'

well. Though this species of hibiscus is reportedly prone to sundry pests and diseases, I have so far encountered none.

Six-inch-long cuttings taken in spring, before the wood has hardened, root readily. This double form sets no seeds.

Osmanthus heterophyllus

HOLLY-LEAVED OSMANTHUS

Spring in such mild climates as England, Vancouver, and California finds the enviable *Osmanthus delavayi* in perfumed bloom. I've lost it once and doubt its hardiness in Zone 7, but don't let me deter you from trying if you can find it. Plants are constantly surprising me.

The autumn-blooming holly-leaved osmanthus (*Osmanthus heterophyllus*; Zone 6; synonym *O. ilicifolius*) is where gardeners in hot regions with long, warm autumns have the edge. It looks like an English holly, and many homeowners, having picked up an unlabelled plant outside the grocery store for a dollar or two, think that's what they are growing. Osmanthus leaves are in opposite pairs; in hollies they alternate. The lustrous leaves of osmanthus are not as highly polished as those of English hollies, which is in their favor where relentless sun dances dazzlingly from reflective surfaces. Never dressed to kill, this osmanthus is the tailored suit or little black dress of shrubs

and appropriately perfumed with a non-cloying scent. Why are so many fragrant flowers tiny and white? A rhetorical question, but do write to me if you know. This osmanthus crowds so many small flowers onto its branches that a multitrunked old specimen becomes a white cloud from late October until frost.

As with hollies, some leaves of osmanthus are spiny while others are smooth-edged, with the spiny ones predominating on the lower parts of the bush. I once supposed that prickliness was a deterrent to browsing animals, but osmanthus, hollies, and barberries are among the first plants to be ravaged by the rabbits that infest my garden. My two cats solved that problem for many years, but now they are geriatric, so young shrubs must be encircled with chicken wire until sufficiently mature and tough-wooded to be less appealing. My sympathies, once with Peter Rabbit, are now entirely with Mr. McGregor.

Apart from rabbits and squishy soil, holly-leaved osmanthus seems invincible, preferring full sun but tolerating light shade and surviving even the hacking inflicted on so many potentially tall evergreens mistakenly used in foundation plantings. Specimens left unpruned will eventually become small, wide-spreading trees, but it takes little effort to maintain them at or below head height. They are among the

best low-maintenance hedging shrubs, needing trimming only once every couple of years to control height and maintain density. The species is good enough for the purpose, but the very dense *Osmanthus heterophyllus* 'Gulftide' is even better. Other desirable forms include the slow-growing *O. heterophyllus* 'Rotundifolius', with spineless leaves, and three variegated forms described later. *Osmanthus heterophyllus* is one parent of *O. ×fortunei*, which is a larger version of that parent and of similar hardiness. The sweet fragrance that visitors to the charming town gardens of Charleston, South Carolina, remark on is likely to emanate from the other parent of *O. ×fortunei*, namely, *O. fragrans*, which in Charleston flowers from late autumn to spring. *Osmanthus fragrans* is not quite hardy enough for Zone 7.

Fatsia japonica

FALSE ARALIA

Between mid-November and mid-December *Fatsia japonica* (Zone 7) drew me back repeatedly, not just to stand there awestruck, but to seize a photo opportunity that doesn't come every year. In its flowering years fatsia is among the most eye-catching of evergreen shrubs. Dozens of tiny starry flowers with prominent stamens form fuzzy, evenly spaced

Fatsia japonica (false aralia)

ivory balls, sixty or more on each of several branched pyramidal inflorescences held above leathery hand-shaped leaves. The fuzziness is lost when the florets fall, but the shape remains, with potential for blue-black berries realized when winter is moderately mild. Its hybrid with ivy, ×*Fatshedera lizei*, blooms a bit earlier and more often sets berries.

In its off years fatsia is still of exceptional architectural quality and year-round good looks, perfect for a shady courtyard, yet not so exotic as to be out of place in a woodsy setting. Fatsia doesn't like wet soil nor does it appreciate full exposure to sun in hot regions. It isn't otherwise fussy. If it gets gangly or outgrows its space, it can be cut hard back. My plant, given to me many years ago as "dwarf fatsia" (possibly the cultivar 'Moseri'), took many years to reach 5 feet in height. Suckers provide occasional extra plants. Fatsia can also be propagated by cuttings and seed.

Camellia sasanqua

Unperturbed by summer drought and oblivious to imminent frost, sasanqua camellias (Zone 7, but a few selections Zone 6) turn late autumn into spring with copious bloom. My only criticism is the plethora of selections with pale pink flowers. As the coldest months approach I feel a need akin to that expressed in Dylan Thomas's "Do not go gentle into that good night." Of the dozen or so sasanquas I grow, the two that most rage against the coming of winter are 'Yuletide', a round, flat single of almost pure red, and cerise 'Kanjiro', a color similar to *Aster* 'Alma Pötschke'. 'Shishi Gashira' and 'Bonanza' are also bright reddish pinks.

If the weather permits, which in Zone 7 it seldom does, 'Yuletide' greets the festive season like a Christmas tree strung with red lights, but it isn't among the hardiest and takes a drubbing in colder-than-average winters. Sasanquas respond well to hard pruning when winter damaged and often regenerate from the roots when killed to ground level—if one has the patience to wait 2 or 3 years—but the clean cut of death is sometimes preferable to the festering sore of winter-battered bushes.

'Kanjiro' is frequently sold as 'Hiryu', which I've never seen but covet on the strength of its picture in Stirling Macoboy's *Color Dictionary of Camellias*, a book guaranteed to send all who can grow these camellias on a search for their own preferred colors and forms. Don't misunderstand me. I like pale pink, especially the gentle shell pink 'Jean May' and single-flowered 'Yae Arare', with blush-pink reflexed petals edged with a brighter pink. My top award goes to 'Showa No Sakae', with frilly semi-double flowers of a soft but by no means wishy-washy pink. This long-term survivor, now 10 feet high, starts early and stays in bloom longer than any other camellia I grow. Fresh flowers open each day in seemingly endless succession, mingling with the heart-shaped petals of shattered flowers sprinkled like falling tears along arching sprays of glossy leaves.

Camellia sasanqua 'Kanjiro'

get too close. So it was a special delight, while photographing 'Snow Flurry' on 1 November, to find honeybees working the flowers with typical conscientious concentration, unharassed by the bigger, bullying bees that ceased work more than a month ago. 'Snow Flurry' took the place of the popular sasanqua camellia 'Mine No Yuki' (synonym 'White Doves'), which has similar white double flowers. It is cold hardy in Zone 7, but frost usually destroys the flowers. The shaggy blossoms of 'Snow Flurry' shatter when lightly frosted, strewing still-white petals prettily on the ground.

Clifford Parks of Camellia Forest Nursery has also bred and selected camellias for hardiness. White 'Survivor' and pink 'Twilight Glow', both singles, are two such introductions. The nursery stresses the importance of placement, which can make the difference between delight and disappointment. Heat leaking through house walls and windows creates a warmer microclimate for nearby plants—a consoling thought when the heating bills come in! Shelter from wind is important, and large paving slabs placed over the camellia roots help prevent the ground from freezing. Overhead shade in winter helps but may reduce the amount of bloom.

Apart from occasional winter losses I've

Until recently Zone 7 was the limit of winter hardiness for sasanqua camellias. Thanks to William Ackerman at the U.S. National Arboretum in Washington, D.C., this limit has been pushed to Zone 6 with hybrids between *Camellia sasanqua* and the hardier *C. oleifera* such as 'Winter's Charm', 'Winter's Dream',

'Winter's Interlude', and 'Winter's Star'. These four are all soft pinks.

My first choice of the Ackerman hybrids is 'Snow Flurry', which starts early and goes on to hard frost. Honeybees have been sadly few of late, their place usurped by a bigger, darker, less friendly bee that issues a warning buzz if I

had only two problems with sasanqua camellias, one esthetic, the other cultural. They bloom at berrying time, and I'm averse to pink with orange. One selection 'Navajo' somehow came to be planted next to a pyracantha also called 'Navajo'—twins, but far from heavenly. Thus the second problem. I move plants all the time, including shrubs as large as I can lift, drag, or somehow maneuver, usually without mishap, but once past babyhood sasanqua camellias don't take kindly to being moved, and nor does pyracantha. If I have doubts about the chosen spot, I now sink sasanquas in containers for a year or two before planting them.

In a mild southeastern winter a few sasanqua flowers will bloom beyond the turn of the year, overlapping with *Camellia japonica* and *C. ×williamsii*, which commence their long season when snowdrops and hellebores bloom, reaching their peak in the first weeks of spring.

Camellia sasanqua 'Showa No Sakae'

TRANSITION TO WINTER

If winter were longer I might be motivated to do such indoor chores as removing cobwebs from ceiling corners and dusting the tops of books, but in coastal Virginia the seasons overlap with scarcely a pause, many years none, between the last flowers of autumn and the first of spring. The degree of summer heat advances or retards bloom times, which consequently vary from year to year. Such inconsistencies led to a debate with myself about whether such flowers as *Iris unguicularis* and *Mahonia ×media* hybrids were autumn or winter bloomers. I concluded that they bridge the gap. *Cyclamen hederifolium* is, indubitably, an autumn bloomer, but the leaves, present through winter, are equally important. This and the remaining plants included in this section I call my "summer escapees," because they escape the heat of summer by retreating into dormancy, re-emerging in autumn to adorn the garden through winter.

Iris unguicularis

WINTER IRIS

"Winter," says the calendar. "Spring," shouts the weather, sometimes treacherously as it zaps with frost flowers it yesterday lured into bloom. Plants that give their all in one dramatic burst of bloom would lose such a toss of the coin more years than not. *Iris unguicularis* (Zone 7) behaves cautiously, adopting a few-at-a-time approach through the most risky weeks. Late autumn is the time to prepare a fit setting for the flowers by removing shabby old leaves. They are too tough and leathery to be pulled out, so I choose a warm day and settle down on a kneeling pad to do the job in a leisurely way, cutting them out with scissors one leaf at a time.

Seldom will more than a week go by between November and March without a bloom or two on winter iris, usually just a handful at a time, occasionally as many as fifty on an apron-sized patch. Each year I marvel anew that such a frail looking flower should be so resilient. Incipient buds, low among the leaves shoot up overnight, opening so rapidly when sun-warmed or brought into the house that the patient observer can watch a live performance of what is more often captured on a timed-release camera. The camera, however, cannot record the delicate, violetlike fragrance of the flowers. Watching a bud open during a meal ensures a topic of conversation. Simply pick a bud in the morning, while tightly furled, then put it in a vase and keep it in the fridge until dinner time.

The several forms of winter iris vary in color from pale lilac to deep violet-blue or white. The leaves vary as well, from low, arching, and narrowly grassy to wider and more upright. I have loved and lost two white-flowered forms, which seem to be less hardy or more pernickety. *Iris unguicularis* 'Walter Butt' has been the most persistent and free-flowering, and I think the loveliest. I got a start of it many years ago from Joe Witt in Seattle, gone now but living on in his gifts to other gardeners. But take what you can get, all forms sell out fast; one or another can be found in catalogs each year, but seldom the same form or catalog 2 years in a row.

In England I followed the standard advice and planted winter iris against a south-facing wall, mixing mortar rubble into the soil to meet the plant's purported need for lime. Few flowers rewarded the effort. In my Virginia garden winter iris thrives, unblessed by lime, in acid, sandy soil somewhat improved with compost, and mulched with gravel to deter voles. There it shares a slightly raised bed in a sunny corner with sasanqua camellias, *Eucalyptus neglecta* (proven the hardiest eucalypt), platycodons, yuccas, and *Salvia leucantha*. A tall-trunked, ivy-clad loblolly pine among them sops up a lot of water, but all these are drought-tolerant plants that need occasional watering only in rainless summers. This hot site is unattractive to slugs, which in my English garden sometimes lurked among the leaves and nipped off emerging buds.

Mahonia

By late November leatherleaf mahonias (Zone 7) are yellow with bud at the start of a flowering season that will last 3 months or more. *Mahonia japonica* and *M. bealei* (synonym *M. japonica* 'Bealei') are the archetypes. *Mahonia bealei* is cold hardy to 0°F and heat hardy at over 100°F, it is almost as tolerant as aucubas of deep shade and root competition. If uncertain about hardiness in your garden, let this tough mahonia be the canary down the mineshaft. If it doesn't survive, neither will any of the others here described. (The smaller Oregon-grape [*Mahonia aquifolium*] is hardier to cold but ill-adapted to extreme heat.)

Where the climate is a half zone more benign, the spotlight shifts to *Mahonia ×media* hybrids, which have *M. japonica* or *M. bealei*

Iris unguicularis 'Walter Butt' (Algerian iris)

as one parent. The other parent, *M. lomariifolia*, has herringbone-shaped leaves with up to nineteen pairs of narrow leaflets. It is an elegant shrub, but considerably less hardy than its hybrid offspring, which grow steadily in number: 'Charity', 'Lionel Fortescue', and 'Underway' from England, and 'Winter Sun' from Ireland are some of the hybrids available in North America.

My long-time favorite is an American introduction, *Mahonia* 'Arthur Menzies' (*M. bealei × M. lomariifolia*). When (three times in 18 years) ice storms or unusually low temperatures have scorched its leaves, it has outgrown the damage by midsummer. It is usually my first mahonia to bloom, often before Thanksgiving. Flowers that would fade fast in the heat of summer can be counted on to last 6

Mahonia 'Arthur Menzies'

weeks at this cool time of year, undamaged by light frost and even emerging unscathed when a coating of ice melted away. Upright racemes of bright lemon-yellow bells rise well above stout shoulder-high bushes with ruffs of large shiny, spiny, pinnate leaves. Unlike such modest cold-weather flowers as wintersweet and winter honeysuckle, whose allure lies mainly in their fragrance, the yellow flowers of mahonias stand out in landscapes stripped of summer leafiness. Notwithstanding its lack of pronounced fragrance and the rather skimpy spikes of smallish berries, I rank 'Arthur Menzies' among my top ten plants. 'Lionel Fortescue', with flowers of a slightly warmer yellow, follows hot on its heels.

As the flowers of *Mahonia* 'Arthur Menzies' and 'Lionel Fortescue' fade, *M. japonica* is just breaking into bloom. The long strings of primrose yellow bells are prevented from being pendulous by the dense whorls of lustrous pinnate leaves that support them in radiating starfish shape. Common in England but hard to find in North America, this species has the most pervasive scent of any mahonia I have grown.

Mahonia bealei is the last to bloom. Its closely strung, delicately scented little bells of light lemon yellow are clustered in stubby upright spikes that lengthen and arch when fully open. Bloom time overlaps that of early witch hazels (*Hamamelis ×intermedia*), with coppery 'Jelena' a good companion for color contrast. That the pendulous bunches of grape-like blue-black berries that follow the mahonia flowers are relished by birds is evident from the many seedlings that appear under trees and bushes in distant parts of the garden. This mahonia, long common in gardens of southeastern North America, has not always had good press. "Clumsy" and "gaunt" are among the unflattering adjectives applied to it. Nonsense. With minimal reasoned pruning it lends itself to whatever form one chooses. In bare-stemmed sculptural form (three to five stems is about right) it is the perfect candidate for that shady corner found against many L-shaped houses, with space beneath for such shade plants as hellebores and hostas. Pruned for bushiness its chunky presence would improve many plantings of small-leaved evergreen azaleas.

If left unpruned indefinitely, leatherleaf mahonias become leggy. That this is commonly their fate is understandable: there is no twiggy growth to nibble at with secateurs. Cuts must be few but bold—more like lopping off an arm than trimming fingernails. There are no obvious buds along the chunky stems, never mind the outward-pointing ones we are taught to look for. Yet, unlikely as it seems, new growth soon sprouts from the yellow-sapped stubs left by the lopping, and there's a good chance the amputated pieces will root if the lower leaves are removed and the stem inserted in peaty compost, covered with transparent plastic and kept moist and shaded.

Through the long sojourn in my garden of several leatherleaf mahonias, time spent on pruning, mulching, and the infrequent strewing of a handful of fertilizer can scarcely have totaled half a day. They have no shabby season and have yet to be disfigured by pest or disease. They can't be blamed for delivering an occasional scratch when I've been foolish enough to prune them, or pick out dead leaves from the oak tree overhead, while bare-armed and gloveless.

RETURN OF THE SUMMER ESCAPEES

Some "summer escapees" also bridge autumn and winter. Many plants brave hot summer but wait until autumn to bloom. Others have a different approach, retreating into summer dormancy. Most, like tulips and daffodils, stay sensibly tucked up under their earth blanket until the weather warms in spring. Harder to understand, but very welcome, are the intrepid few that re-emerge in autumn and grace the garden through winter, most with foliage and a few with flowers.

Cyclamen hederifolium

IVY-LEAVED CYCLAMEN

The first of my summer escapees to return from its retreat is ivy-leaved cyclamen (*Cyclamen hederifolium*; Zone 5). Why, when asked to recommend plants for dry shade, do I seldom think to mention this? I reel off the standard cast of tough ground covers: ivy, pachysandra, periwinkle, *Lamiastrum*, *Symphytum ibericum*, and, if all else fails, mulch on which to stand containers of impatiens. Inexpensive, surefire plants (the two usually go together), preferably evergreen, are usually what is wanted, but not always. Anyway, one should try to light new fires, not merely add sticks to those already burning strongly. This cyclamen is as tough as it is dainty and could often be grown in ground left bare or given over to such plants of last resort as variegated goutweed (*Aegopodium podagraria* 'Variegata').

Once a passion for cyclamen is ignited there are several species to feed the flame, but this species is the easiest to obtain and grow, and the hardiest (Zone 5). Patience is needed (or a lot of money) to achieve a large stand, but then it is yours for life. I've grown cyclamen in England and North America for 40 years and never known them anything but healthy. They have even (touch wood!) escaped that scourge of my present garden, the vole, and rabbits don't seem to find the foliage palatable.

What will kill cyclamen? Soggy soil, certainly, and the tubers may not survive being planted upside down, which probably happens often because the bottom is smooth and rounded with no vestige of roots, while the top is knobbly. Too diminutive to pose a threat to any other plant, they can themselves be overrun by such rapidly spreading shade plants as sweet woodruff (*Galium odoratum*). When planted shallowly, as they should be, young, small tubers are sometimes dislodged by squirrels or birds. Chicken wire under a thin layer of mulch prevents this happening. Plastic netting lasts longer, but after two of us spent an hour untangling a 4-foot blacksnake found hopelessly enmeshed and waiting quietly to die (it lived), I gave up using it. Many years ago I stopped using string mesh fishing net after entangling birds and hedgehogs. I have never found chicken wire harmful to wildlife.

The ideal site for ivy-leaved cyclamen is under deep-rooting deciduous trees or large shrubs with small to medium-sized leaves, where there's winter sun, some summer shade, and an annual mulch of fallen leaves. If the ground slopes, so much the better. If the tubers start to show above the surface, add a thin layer of leaf mold, sandy or loamy soil, compost, or finely ground bark. Where heavy rain leaches nutrients from the soil, a scattering of a general fertilizer every couple of years will do no harm.

My biggest patch is under a large double-file viburnum (*Viburnum plicatum* var. *tomentosum*), which in turn grows under a massive small-leaved water oak (*Quercus nigra*). The first pink or white flowers appear in September, looking so dainty and fragile that they kindle the mood of tenderness expressed by Vita Sackville-West's description of their "little leveret ears flung back." By mid-October there are thousands of blooms, continuing through November. The leaves that follow and carpet the ground through winter are among the loveliest I know; most of them are exquisitely patterned in silver and green. Occasionally one with plain green leaves will appear, or a nearly solid silver. Seedlings don't always resemble their parent, but there'll be no ugly ducklings.

Cyclamen coum, another easy-to-grow species, is mixed in with these. With the ivy-leaved cyclamen flowers come first and then leaves, but *C. coum* does the opposite: leaves come first and then flowers at snowdrop time. Come late spring the leaves of both cyclamen

Cyclamen hederifolium (ivy-leaved cyclamen)

die neatly away. No cleanup is needed. The plants do not need watering during their summer dormancy, and the occasional handful or two of slow-release fertilizer strewn over them is more a gesture of gratitude than a response to need.

Happy ivy-leaved cyclamen self-sow copiously. When the flower fades the stalk coils down like a spring and the round seed pod develops close to the ground, opening to deposit the seed on top of the mother tuber, where the strong will crowd out the weak unless you intervene. Each seedling consists of a single leaf, 1–2 inches of threadlike stalk, and a tiny pearly tuber. The seedlings appear in tight clusters, and I use a teaspoon handle to loosen little bunches and wiggle them gently out for planting elsewhere. "Like a monkey searching another for fleas," remarked a friend, coming upon me crouched down and poking among the leaves of my best forms in search of seedlings. I could save myself time by collecting and scattering seed before it is spilled out, but this calls for fine timing. Seedlings start to flower in 2 to 3 years.

The first cyclamen I planted, 40 years ago in my English garden, cost 4 pence each (old pennies, 240 of them to the pound, which translated to less than a nickel) for tubers the size of small saucers. They'd been collected in the wild, a practice now condemned but still going on. Nursery-grown tubers are shipped in pots, making it easy to tell which side goes up. They'll be small and not inexpensive, but they'll usually flower the next year.

Each year I grow a few selected forms from seed obtained from commercial sources or plant societies. Seed germinates best in the dark, and if not freshly collected it benefits from being put in lukewarm water and soaked for 24 hours. I raise my seedlings in margarine containers with holes drilled in the bottom. These are two-thirds filled with soil-less compost, the seed spaced out and covered with a fine layer of vermiculite or fine grit, the lids put on, and the containers stacked by a window on the kitchen counter. The containers don't need watering, take little space, and need checking only once a week to see if the seed has germinated. The seedlings are then hardened off in a shaded, frost-free frame, where they stay for a year to gain size before being planted out.

Arum italicum 'Pictum'

CUCKOO PINT, LORDS-AND-LADIES
Just when most plants are going dormant, up pop the arrow-shaped leaves of *Arum italicum* 'Pictum' (Zone 6), in which name lie a couple of traps. First, don't confuse it with *A. pictum*, which is a different species. Second, see the plant before you buy it, because the name harbors more than one selection of a variable species. In the prettiest forms the leaves are attenuated triangles with overlapping basal lobes and undulating edges, checkered in green and silvery gray and edged with a ribbonlike dark green band. If you can track them down, the vegetatively propagated *A. italicum* 'White Winter' and the dwarf *A. italicum* 'Tiny' are such forms. *Arum italicum* 'Marmoratum' has larger leaves less conspicuously patterned. Arum leaves last a long time in water, and these fancy forms are much sought by flower arrangers, so there's pin money potential in selling them to florists.

These names are an early chapter in a developing story that began for me with gifts from two plantsman friends. From Bill Baker in England came a form resembling *Arum italicum* 'White Winter', and from Seattle's John Jerry Flintoff an arum he thought might be a hybrid between *A. italicum* 'Marmoratum' and *A. maculatum*. Similar plants can now be bought from at least one mail-order nursery. Over the years intermediate forms have cropped up around my garden, differing in leaf shape and size and with greater or lesser proportions of silvery gray in the patterning. One is almost entirely silver. Start with the best form of *A. italicum* 'Pictum' you can find, add a few hybrids, and pollinating midges will do for you what they have done for me. Most of my seedlings appear among leaf litter under deciduous trees and shrubs, a place that suits them well where summers are hot.

Spring sees the appearance of a creamy flower-bearing spadix within a parchment-colored hooded spathe of silken texture. The spathe quickly withers and the leaves die away soon afterwards, leaving the spadix to ripen into a rod of scarlet berries by late summer. These rods are showy even in isolation and are spectacular when complemented by green ferns or hellebores, or rising over such carpeting plants as periwinkle (*Vinca minor*), *Mazus reptans*, creeping Charlie (*Lysimachia nummularia*), partridge berry (*Mitchella repens*), and small-leaved ivies such as *Hedera helix* 'Spetchley'. In England, where the arum can take full sun, I admired a dignity-and-impudence echo in color and form from scarlet spires of a head-high torch-lily (*Kniphofia*) towering over chunky stalks of arum berries.

Arums don't like wet soil. Dry soil and deep shade will not harm them during dormancy, but they need moisture and light while they are in leaf. They make pretty underplantings for deciduous trees and shrubs but fruit more freely if exposed to spring and summer sun for

Arum italicum 'Pictum', a form that cropped up in my garden, seen here in April but present from late October through spring. *Corydalis cheilanthifolia* is in the background.

at least part of the day. They need dividing only when the clumps get so overcrowded that leaves diminish in size. The easiest time to do this is just as new growth emerges through the ground in autumn. Arums survive temperatures well below 0°F, the leaves going up and down with the mercury, lying limply on the ground through freezes and rising again on warmer days.

Dentaria
TOOTHWORT

Dentaria comes from the word *dens* (a tooth), alluding to the toothlike scales on the roots of

Daphne jezoensis in January

much alike, with *D. maxima* merely a bit bigger than *D. diphylla*. By early summer they appear to have vacated their space, but in fact they continue to fill it, just below the surface of the ground, with rhizomes so densely interwoven that weed roots cannot penetrate them.

In autumn, after rain, the handsome trifoliate leaves appear, glossy with toothed edges. At this stage they form a ground cover only a few inches high, as close-packed and weather-proof as pachysandra. Come spring more leaves are raised on 1-foot stems tipped with loose clusters of dainty four-petaled white flowers. When the trees leaf out they depart for their summer siesta. I have grown them under dogwoods, viburnums, hydrangeas, and a large fig tree, and have concluded that there are few places they won't grow provided the ground is moist in winter and spring.

Daphne jezoensis

In the 10 years I've had it (yes, the same bush) *Daphne jezoensis* (Zone 6; synonym *D. kamtschatica* var. *jezoensis*) has alarmed, surprised, and then delighted me. Summer dormancy is uncommon in shrubs, and daphnes are notoriously capricious and short-lived. When this one shed its leaves the first summer, I mourned it, but fortunately didn't pull it out.

this early flowering herb that led to the supposition that it might be good for toothache (*A Gardener's Dictionary of Plant Names* by A. W. Smith). Hence, its common name is logically "toothwort" in a nice pairing of botanical and folk names. Not any more. Now we must call these herbs *Cardamine*, which is bittercress, cuckoo flower, or lady's-smock. Vexing.

Under whatever name, *Dentaria diphylla* and *D. maxima* (both Zone 5) are undervalued plants. Weeds under trees and shrubs often escape detection until after leaf fall, by which time they have become well established. I've taken preventive action in several places with underplantings of these two attractive and serviceable summer-dormant toothworts. They are

When, in December, it leafed out again—leaves slender, bright green, and fragile looking—I took this for the plant's dying gasp; but no, this is its natural schedule, and bright yellow flowers followed. Bloom time usually starts during the "January thaw," a few days of high temperatures that briefly detach winter's grip.

That the flowers of this small, twiggy daphne have only the faintest scent is my one criticism. Now 3 feet high and about the same across, this shrub has required nothing of me since I planted it under the high shade of limbed up red cedars (*Juniperus virginiana*). Seedlings appear in modest numbers. None of my other daphnes produce them. One plant lives content in the summer shade of an oak, another where it gets sun for most of the day. The common denominator of these assorted sites is perfect drainage; wet soil is the surest way to kill a daphne.

WINTER BERRIES

Although there will be flowers off and on through the year's coldest months, the winter garden relies more on beauty of bark and berry, and on colorful evergreen foliage present all year but more prominent when summer's lushness has been stripped away. Some shrubs berry reliably every winter. Others, such as purple barberries (*Berberis thunbergii* 'Atropurpurea') and viburnums, are unpredictable.

Callicarpa dichotoma
BEAUTYBERRY

Beautyberries jump the gun, sometimes ripening their berries as early as September. By Christmas only a few shriveled clusters remain. Although the hardiness zone of my Virginia garden is similar to that of my previous garden near London, England, the hot summers change the performance of many plants. This change is decidedly for the better with the beautyberries, which unfailingly set copious quantities of berries the color of the bitter-tasting gentian violet my mother would paint on fingernails to discourage nail biting.

The only beautyberry to crop reliably where summers are cool is *Callicarpa bodinieri*, usually the selection 'Profusion', a tall Chinese shrub with lilac-purple berries. Conventional wisdom has it that several callicarpas should be grouped together to ensure fruit set. Heat has more to do with it, and only one plant is needed where the wood gets a thorough summer ripening. None I've tried has failed to bear copious quantities of berries unless grown in the shade. Even the locally native *C. americana*, usually found on woodland fringes, berries best in sun.

My first choice, *Callicarpa dichotoma* (Zone 5), is the most compact and graceful callicarpa, and probably the hardiest. Its spear-shaped leaves are smaller and neater than those of the

Berberis thunbergii var. *atropurpurea* (purple barberry) after an ice storm

others, held out in ladderlike close-runged pairs along stems that arch to the ground and drip with comparatively small but brilliantly colored berries. It bears fruit on wood of the current season's growth, so the best display is on shrubs pruned back to about 1 foot between berry time and the start of growth the next spring. This pruning holds the shrubs at a height of about 4 feet in the soil of moderate fertility that adequately meets their needs. A white-fruited form being sold in North America, *C. dichotoma* 'Albifructus', grows much taller and may be misidentified. Because its berries brown quite quickly, this variety is less appealing than the species.

Danaë racemosa

ALEXANDRIAN LAUREL,
POET'S LAUREL

By late January the peak berry display on Alexandrian laurel (*Danaë racemosa*) has passed, but small clusters can still be seen at the tips of side branches ornamented with pixie-ear leaves (cladodes, if one wants to be technical). All parts of this elegant evergreen are curvaceous and lustrous green: the arching willowy main branches, wiry side branches, and tapering leaves. *Danaë* is one of the compensations for gardening where summers are stickily hot, for it takes to heat and humidity like a duck to

water and would be commonplace were it more readily available from nurseries.

Finding the perfect spot for this elegant shrublike plant can be tricky if there is to be a bountiful display of fruits resembling small cherries, with glistening light-orange flesh over a single round seed-pit. The display peaks in autumn and continues into winter. It is usually recommended that Alexandrian laurel be grown in shade, and indeed it prospers even in deep shade without a single ray of sun. But plants from bird-excreted seed growing cheerfully away in unpropitious places taught me that this beautiful evergreen plant is more adaptable than usually supposed. If sunbaked all day long, the foliage becomes tarnished, but fruit is abundant only when danaë is given a reasonable ration of sun. The fruits are a nice bonus, but barrenness would not lessen my esteem for a graceful shrub that is easy to care for and never unkempt. The flowers are so inconspicuous that after growing Alexandrian laurel for more than two decades I have yet to notice them.

In the junglelike climate of southeastern North America Alexandrian laurel grows much faster than it does where summers are cool. In well-drained soil expect a bush 3 feet high and wide in about 5 years. It is then the sort of plant that gardeners fantasize about,

Callicarpa dichotoma (beautyberry)

making no further tip growth and thus stable in height. *Danaë* is in the lily family, as also is asparagus, and the relationship is apparent when new stems squeeze their way up through

Danaë racemosa (Alexandrian laurel)

the old ones in spring. At this time a proportion of the old stems should be pruned out to make way for the new, cutting the old off at ground level. On older, congested bushes all the old stems could be removed. Henceforth the initial investment will yield an annual cash crop of cut foliage: branches last almost forever in water and are much in demand by florists.

Plants in the lily family can't be grown from cuttings, and while self-sown seed germinates readily, seed collected and stored does not. Clumps don't spread fast enough for division to be a practical means of large-scale propagation, so this sought-after plant always commands a high price. It is worth every penny.

Butcher's broom (*Ruscus aculeatus*) is a closely related, chunkier, 1- to 2-foot ever-green shrub with small, spine-tipped leaves unpleasant to handle and said to have been used for scrubbing butcher's blocks. The species is dioecious (male and female flowers on separate plants), but *R. aculeatus* 'Wheeler's Variety' is self-fruiting, though not in my experience very generously so. The bright red berries are poised on the leaf and seem at imminent risk of rolling off. An interesting, if gardener-unfriendly plant, butcher's broom has one big asset: it tolerates dry shade.

Aronia arbutifolia
CHOKEBERRY

Chokeberry (*Aronia arbutifolia*; Zone 4) is another autumn berry-bearer. The scarlet fruits are at first disguised by the fiery color of the leaves, which perform a duet with the beet-red leaves of a neighboring oakleaf hydrangea. My chokeberry began life as a seedling from berries collected by the roadside, where it grew in a ditch. It prefers moist soil, but does not visibly complain about the drier place advisedly accorded it. Beware misguided proselytizing by some with admirable ideals but little gardening knowledge—native plants can be every bit as invasive as any other. Some make better garden plants where they are *not* native, and thicket-formers such as chokeberry, Virginia sweetspire (*Itea virginica*), and the delightful, easy, still uncommon Alabama snow-wreath (*Neviusia alabamensis*) are more controllable where they have to struggle a bit. In any case, they should be kept away from less robust plants that they might overrun. There is no risk of this with celandine poppy (*Stylophorum diphyllum*), which has naturalized among the stoloniferous roots of the aronia and must itself be weeded out when it spreads too far afield.

Nandina domestica

HEAVENLY BAMBOO

An early settler in the region I now call home described it in less than glowing terms, listing bugs, mosquitoes, hornets, ticks, thunder and lightning, excessive heat, and excessive cold among its "irregularities." I'd extend the list to include a varying, unguessable ratio of drought and gully-washing storms, summer humidity rivaling that of a Turkish bath, frequent autumn and winter days when a bathing suit would be adequate attire, then an overnight plummet to temperatures well below freezing. There are funguses that rot roots, and voles and weevils that eat them. There are rabbits, ants, crickets, slugs, molds and mildews, scale, spider mites, Japanese beetles, tent caterpillars, bagworm, and a large assortment of other chewing and sucking pests.

Berries of *Aronia arbutifolia* (chokeberry) and red-black leaves of *Hydrangea quercifolia* (oakleaf hydrangea)

Few of these bother nandinas, which are as long-lived and adaptable as their close relatives the barberries, averse only to water-logged soil. Winter cold is their main limitation; they are damaged at 10°F and may die to the ground if the temperature stays long below 0°F. If the ground freezes only shallowly, they recover quickly in spring and often look the better for nature's drastic pruning.

On a day cold enough to put a skim of ice over ponds and puddles, nandinas strike a cheerful note with scarlet berries hanging in huge trusses well clear of the elegant leaves, a sight that has visiting English friends agape. Summer inflorescences of small white flowers upright at branch tips become pendulous under the weight of the berries, which have little appeal to birds and remain well into spring.

Nandina domestica berries

When the berries fall, they germinate quickly, carpeting the ground with seedlings around the base of the bushes. Although yellow-fruited forms appear in catalogs under several names, all I've seen have looked alike: a pale greenish yellow, less dramatic than the typical scarlet but in better accord with the pink camellias that bloom through the same season.

It was dismaying to find nandina included on a broadly based list of invasive plants to be avoided. Given the varied soils and climates of North America, invasiveness needs to be defined regionally. Nandina isn't hardy north of Zone 6, and it seldom bears berries where summers are cool. In any event, there are no woods or fields for nandina to despoil within miles of my garden and I've yet to see it popping up in the parking lots of the endless string of shopping centers, half of them abandoned, built during the last 20 years.

With or without berries, nandinas earn their place in my garden with a fine-textured airy grace reminiscent of bamboos or royal fern (*Osmunda regalis*). If grown in sun the leaves of most nandinas turn crimson and orange in winter and some, *Nandina domestica* 'Moyer's Red' for one, don't depend on cold for their color. Finely wrought though nandina is, it is well able to defend its turf against such rapidly spreading plants as *Alstroemeria psittacina* (synonym *A. pulchella*), a plant I struggled hard to get established and now strive even harder to keep in check. Placement is, as so often, a matter of compromise. Winter foliage color is better and berry set heavier in sun, but there's more damage in bad winters and sometimes defoliation. A sheltered, lightly shaded spot could make all the difference in regions of marginal hardiness.

Left unpruned nandinas may attain 8 feet or more, with an attractive naked-stemmed lankiness. Annual removal in spring of the tallest stems keeps them half that height or less. An alternative, painstaking pruning method, taught me by the late Fred Heutte, director of Norfolk Botanical Gardens in Virginia, avoids the barelegged look. When old, lower leaves die, they do not drop smoothly from the stem but leave a stub or cuticle that seems to inhibit growth of the dormant bud tucked into the leaf axil. Stripping these off in early spring allows the buds to grow and keeps the bushes leafy to ground level.

There is only one species of *Nandina* (Zone 6) but many selected forms that vary in hardiness, size, leaf shape, and foliage color. Nandina makes an excellent informal hedge for the back of a hot color border. *Nandina domestica* 'Gulf Stream', a compact selection, is suitable if the height of the hedge is to be restricted to no more than 4 feet, while such larger forms as *N. domestica* 'Umpqua Warrior' are suitable for a taller hedge. Low-growing *N. domestica* 'Harbor Dwarf' is rhizomatous, needing only removal of an occasional strongly upward-growing branch to maintain it as a dense, weed-resistant ground cover. It does bear berries, but less abundantly than the species, and not when young.

Dwarf, compact forms include *Nandina domestica* 'Nana Purpurea', a dense, chunky berryless mound of distinctive character, with broad, cupped, sometimes contorted leaves that turn brilliant red in winter if grown in acid, sandy soil of low to moderate fertility. *Nandina domestica* 'Firepower' is a similar size, with narrower leaves that lack the contortions. *Nandina domestica* 'San Gabriel' is the textural opposite; its filamented leaves give the plant a wraithlike look. For rock gardens, trough gardens, or bonsai dishes there are such tiny forms as *N. domestica* 'Tama Shishi', a 6-inch bun, or the slightly larger, nearly leafless *N. domestica* 'Senbazura' with its wire-netting look. These selections are but a sampling of some forty available forms.

Ilex opaca
AMERICAN HOLLY

American holly (*Ilex opaca*; Zone 5) is part of the native vegetation where I live, and some large specimens are scattered around my 2 acres. Dull-leaved, they are not the ornamental equal of several other species and, refuting the myth that native plants are more pest resistant than the foreign born, leaf miners riddle their leaves while leaving the other hollies alone. But they are well adapted to the soil and climate, tough, and a port of call for cedar waxwings, so they stay. They were supplemented fairly recently with *I. opaca* 'Steward's Silver Crown' and 'Christmas Snow', which, with leaves irregularly edged in cream and very large red berries, promise to be handsome specimens when they've put on a bit of height. A male and female pair of the "blue hollies" (referring to a blue cast over the foliage, not to the berries), *I. ×meserveae* (*I. aquifolium* × *I. rugosa*), bred for hardiness, have been content for many years in a shaded spot, but don't compare with specimens I've seen in cooler regions. Many other holly species and hybrids remain as yet untried, but few are likely to oust from my favor the following long-term successes.

Ilex 'Sparkleberry'

After a decade of berryless years the deciduous and dioecious *Ilex* 'Sparkleberry' (Zone 3; *I. verticillata* × *I. serrata*) is finally creating fire-engine excitement from November through winter with a flamboyant display of scarlet berries that dominates a mostly muted landscape and gains additional drama viewed against a goldthread cypress (*Chamaecyparis pisifera* 'Filifera Aurea'). Its intended pollinator, *Ilex* 'Apollo', another hybrid, failed to live up to his godlike reputation. Was I expecting a boy to do a man's job—he was just a stripling when planted—or is the father *Ilex* 'Raritan Chief', planted more recently? Can plants be DNA-tested to establish parenthood? If I knew for sure which of them I have to thank I would remove the surplus male. (My supposed 'Raritan Chief' has started to bear berries, so it seems that 'Apollo' is the pollen parent for 'Sparkleberry'.)

Birds show little interest in this holly. Early in March a flock of cedar waxwings sweeps through. Companionable birds, never squabblesome, they chatter quietly together as they strip and eat the small berries of the red cedars (*Juniperus virginiana*) with concentrated speed. Those of the indigenous *Ilex opaca* are then sampled before the birds swoop off in unison, as quickly as they came, leaving untouched the conspicuous scarlet beacon of 'Sparkleberry'. All its berries drop at once towards the end of March.

Ilex cornuta 'Burfordii'
BURFORD HOLLY

Many gardeners, me included, are unwilling to give space to a pair of shrubs when only one of the pair is ornamental. All praise then to *Ilex cornuta* 'Burfordii' (Zone 7), which defies the dioecious mores of the holly clan and bears

Ilex 'Sparkleberry' berries, dead heads of *Hydrangea arborescens* 'Annabelle', flowering plumes of white-striped *Miscanthus sinensis* 'Cosmopolitan', and *Magnolia* ×*soulangeana* in foreground

The same *Ilex* 'Sparkleberry' seen from another angle, with *Chamaecyparis pisifera* 'Filifera Aurea' (goldthread cypress) at right

Ilex cornuta 'Burfordii' (Burford holly)

large scarlet berries in profusion without benefit of a partner. And tough! I once watched a neighbor hitch a tractor to a 6-foot bush, drag it out of the ground and across the lawn, dump it in a shallow hole and scrape the soil half-heartedly around it. It thrives there still. Seen in countless suburban gardens, where it is too often pruned into balls, it becomes a beautiful multitrunked small tree of pendulous habit if allowed to grow unchecked.

Burford holly is common because, in hot summer regions, it is all one could ask of a shrub. Besides, it can be bought for next-to-nothing at grocery stores and mass merchandise outlets. The glossy leaves are an unusual shape, more rectangular than round, cupped down, and usually smooth-edged except for a short spine at the tip. There'll be more berries in full sun, but this holly also does well in shade. Only when it signals distress with yellowing leaves is fertilizer needed. Waterlogging also yellows the leaves, so check first that the soil isn't soggy.

Southeasterners can grow so many good hollies that we are spoilt for choice, but unless disease sets in, as it frequently does when something becomes overplanted (*Photinia ×fraseri*, for example), Burford holly will remain hard to beat. It makes an excellent and inexpensive screen or hedge. If it grows too tall it can be cut down almost to the ground and will quickly bush out again. Because light bouncing from the highly polished leaves can be distracting, my holly hedging preference would be *Ilex* 'Nellie R. Stevens' (*I. aquifolium × I. cornuta*), a hybrid with darker, less waxy leaves.

Ilex cornuta 'Dwarf Burford' has smaller leaves and fewer, smaller berries of a darker red, partly hidden among the dense leaves. Relatively compact for many years, it eventually makes a very tall, dense, and rounded shrub. If it outgrows its position it makes a quick recovery when hard pruned.

Gardeners too often get stuck in a rut, and professional designers, with greater need for predictability, even more often. Growing untested plants is a gamble, but why not a different version of the tried and true? A yellow-fruited version of Burford holly, *Ilex cornuta* 'D'Or', remains uncommon, which is a pity because a plant as good as 'Burfordii' becomes mundane from overuse and yellow berries would lift it out of the ordinary. When I raise my voice at garden centers I'm told that they don't stock 'D'Or' because when they did nobody bought it: holly berries, it seems, like tomatoes, are supposed to be red. I think the nurseries should try again—gardeners are much more venturesome today than they were 10 years ago.

So many plants, so little space. What shall I include? What shall I leave out? All gardeners know the dilemma, and many will be wondering why I've omitted the following flamboyant berry-bearers.

Only one deciduous tree I know can rival the berry display of *Ilex* 'Sparkleberry' and that is a hawthorn, *Crataegus viridis* 'Winter King'. I resist it only because, as a child, my husband almost lost an eye and suffered permanent damage from a hawthorn scratch. For those not scratch-averse, 'Winter King' or the Washington thorn, *C. phaenopyrum*, would be a good choice if space cannot be spared for a berryless mate for winterberry hollies.

For the same reason I do not plant hawthorns in my garden, I took out several pyracanthas inherited from a previous owner, then later planted *Pyracantha* 'Navajo', a hybrid from the U.S. National Arboretum's breeding program that met its goal of disease resistance. This pyracantha is naturally compact and mounding, and an annual pruning just before new growth begins limits its height to about 3 feet, well out of eye range, without forfeiting its abundant crop of bright orange berries.

Chinaberry (*Melia azederach*), with handsome bipinnate leaves that hide the small panicles of lilac flowers, grows cheerfully in waste-places and around old homeplaces throughout southeastern North America, unperturbed by summer drought or deluge. Many times I've pulled in by the roadside to sit and admire the yellow, beadlike fruits displayed against blue sky, but this tree's prevalence counsels caution about introducing it to gardens in the hot and humid regions where it thrives, perhaps, too well.

WINTER BARK

In an average year January is the month with the least to offer, but no matter how severe the winter, attractive bark, colored or otherwise, can prevent the winter garden from seeming barren. There are ample trees to choose from, with something for every region and climate: white or creamy barked birches; green-striped maples; python-patterned eucalypts; cinnamon-skinned stewartias, arbutus, and *Luma apiculata*; yellow-barked ash (*Fraxinus excelsior* 'Jaspidea'); and reddish brown, highly polished *Prunus serrula*, to name but a few. These trees, for reasons of space, soil, site, or climate, I must forego, but such beauties as crape myrtles (*Lagerstroemia*) and coral bark maple (*Acer palmatum* 'Sango kaku') more than compensate.

A large shrub or small tree I miss is the hardy orange (*Poncirus trifoliatus*; Zone 7) that I grew for many years. I miss its white, orange-blossom flowers in spring, its glossy leaves, its crop of little oranges in autumn, and, most of all, its silvery, antlerlike, winter skeleton. As I grew clumsier with age, the shrub's vicious spines became too much of a risk. Magazine articles periodically recommend planting hardy orange close to house windows as a means of burglar-proofing the house, but this is not a good idea, for who will clean the windows? Hardy orange is much more likely to bite the hand that feeds it, so to speak, than it is to ward off burglars. It adapts to sun or light shade and to most well-drained soils, and I found it drought tolerant and pest-free. It has a lot to offer. Just be careful where you put it.

Another plant I mourn is the lacebark pine (*Pinus bungeana*; Zone 5). The wood is brittle and its single trunk had just grown stout enough to display the white-mottled steel gray bark when an ice storm broke off its top, leaving an ungainly shape I tried to correct by cutting side branches back into old wood. Few conifers put up with this treatment, and this one did not survive such drastic surgery. There's a youngster coming along, multitrunked this time, to better display the bark and to give the tree a better chance of surviving injury from snow or ice.

In cool regions white-trunked silver and paper birches (*Betula pendula* and *B. papyrifera*, respectively) have pride of place in the winter garden. They will not long tolerate hot and humid weather, but the river birch (*B. nigra*; Zone 4) takes both cold and heat in its stride. In the wild this species tends to grow in wet, low-lying places, but these conditions are by no means essential; river birch needs only a reasonably moisture-retentive soil. *Betula nigra* 'Heritage' is a fine selection, with shredding bark of cream, buff, and hints of apricot, glossy leaves small enough that they don't smother underplantings when they fall, and buttery yellow autumn color. I haven't yet been able to fit it in, but it is under my eye, well-displayed, as a solitary specimen in a neighbor's lawn. Lawns are too much like housework for me—endlessly repetitive labor merely to keep things as they are. Mine is a grassless garden, but I do covet all those expanses of empty lawn in my neighborhood, populating them, in my imagination, with the specimen trees and large shrubs I can't fit into my own 2 acres.

When waxing lyrical about trees and shrubs grown for their bark it is only fair to point out that the wait can be long, and the time span between planting and reward differs a great deal from one species to another. One of the river birch's good qualities is that the trunks gain in girth relatively fast and in scale with the leafy canopy. It is, in fact, at its most ornamental in youth. On old trees the bark remains attractively shaggy but loses the pastel colors.

River birch is usually grown as a triple-trunked specimen, often achieved by planting three striplings in the same hole, with trunks sloped out from each other.

"Oh well, it makes room for something else," said a friend consolingly when a dainty cherry tree, *Prunus incisa* (Zone 6), died, as cherries usually do in rather few years in borer country. What it made room for is *Pseudocydonia sinensis* (Zone 5), with pale pink flowers followed by large quincelike fruit that can be made into jelly. What moved the pseudocydonia to the head of the waiting list is its gray green bark, stripping down to silver and tan, a sight to make winter welcome. Five years after planting it, I'm still waiting.

The following are the trees and shrubs I grow mainly for their bark and colored stems that have proved the most rewarding.

Ulmus parvifolia

LACEBARK ELM, CHINESE ELM

Lacebark elm (*Ulmus parvifolia*; hardiness varies with cultivar) grows quickly in height but increases slowly in girth. My 10-year-old *Ulmus parvifolia* 'Drake', the only form I could find at the time I planted it 6 years ago, has a trunk circumference of only 15 inches, while the top has grown so tall and loosely spreading that it requires considerable prun-

ing every year. The bark, mottled in olive green, gray, and buff, with golden overtones and a sprinkling of orange lenticels (tiny warty protuberances), has been decorative from the start, but it will be many years before this tree becomes a striking specimen.

The flowers, tiny and likely to pass unnoticed, are followed by lacy sprays of seed wafers resembling rolled oats. This form keeps some or all of its neat little glossy leaves in mild winters, but Zone 7 is its probable hardiness limit. *Ulmus parvifolia* 'Allee' is hardier and highly recommended, but don't expect instant gratification. Gambling that I'll live another 20 years, I've planted that as well. Lacebark elm has so far proved resistant to Dutch elm disease.

Acer griseum

PAPERBARK MAPLE

At 20 years of age my paperbark maple (*Acer griseum*; Zone 5), with a trunk girth of 17 inches, is not yet at its prime, but its dual ornamental qualities of leaf and bark earn it a place even in infancy, at the same time presenting a bit of a placement conflict. Leaf color shows best backlit, but bark detail frontlit. I give myself only a passing grade for the spot I chose, facing north-east under the high shade of a pine. It likes it there, and sun from behind

adds backlit brilliance to the scarlet autumn coloration of the pretty, unmaplelike, trifoliate leaves, but sun from the front highlights the bark for little more than an hour each day. Autumn color is fleeting, while the beautiful bark is there all year, a shining reddish brown flaking and curling over hints of rust from the underbark. I've short-changed myself in not making that the primary consideration. I did plant it near the front of the bed, where the trunk is unobstructed, surrounded only by a ground cover of *Campanula poscharskyana* interplanted with snowdrops.

Acer palmatum 'Sango kaku'

CORAL BARK MAPLE

Of few plants can it be said that they never have an off moment. The coral bark maple, *Acer palmatum* 'Sango kaku' (Zone 6; synonym 'Senkaki'), is one of two plants in my garden that share the blue ribbon for minimal maintenance and year-round appeal. (I hear the question: the other is *Lagerstroemia fauriei*.) This time advantage is to the young, and trunk girth doesn't matter. Only wood of the current year's growth has the bright red bark, and keeping it at eye level calls for judicious use of a pruning saw. It is, however, a comparatively slow growing small tree, and if left unpruned it will be many years before you have

to crane your neck to see the new red wood against the sky.

Through summer the coral bark maple is a serene and shapely green presence welcome among the bright colors and lush foliage of the season. Perhaps it is in autumn that I enjoy it most. There are still a lot of flowers in the garden—late chrysanthemums and asters, camellias, Mexican bush sage (*Salvia leucantha*), *Hamamelis virginiana*, a few late clematis blooms, a sprinkling of flower on *Prunus* 'Hally Jolivette', and others. There's plenty to do, but the pressure is off. Autumn is our long Indian summer of relaxed, comfortable gardening in near-perfect weather. And now the maple turns glowing amber, a toasty-warm, golden retriever sort of color, touched some years with apricot or red. It will hold its leaves for 2 or 3 weeks more, and when they fall, they crinkle and pile up in a fluffy lightweight blanket that will not smother the snowdrops and *Campanula garganica* growing underneath. So weightless are the leaves that tidying away those that drift into the driveway is as effortless as scooping up foam.

The sales appeal of coral bark maple lies in the red winter bark. The colder the weather

LEFT *Acer palmatum* 'Sango kaku' (coral bark maple)

gets, the more the color intensifies and it has few midwinter rivals, especially when seen against a carpet of snow under a blue sky. Snow and ice storms see me dashing out into the garden to capture on film red twigs encapsulated in ice, or snow caught like fragments of drifting cloud in the upper branches. Ideally this maple should be placed where it is frontlit for at least part of the day, and if possible where it can be viewed from the warm comfort of the house. Visitors get that benefit from my tree. It was planted, fortuitously, where the young, red-barked upper branches are framed by one of the high awning-windows of a guest bedroom.

The names by which I identify various parts of the garden are seldom poetic: Wellhouse Bed, Spruce Bed, Back Berm, The Avenue, The Island, and beds designated by color. The coral bark maple is in the Septic Tank Bed, with most of its roots in the shallow layer of soil over the concrete tank. The water table is high, and during prolonged rain the tank (pumped out each year for obvious reasons) overflows. All this fazes the maple not at all. Pruned only to remove occasional wayward branches or bits of dead wood, it has attained 10 feet in 20 years and about as much across. Another specimen is coppiced each year to keep it no more

This sturdy crape myrtle, *Lagerstroemia fauriei*, has yet to be damaged by ice or snow.

than 5 feet high and to induce growth of colorful young branches, a process it has tolerated for about 10 years without protest.

Coral bark maple can be rooted from cuttings, but it is not easy. A few seedlings have appeared around the largest of my two trees and they have the typical red bark.

Lagerstroemia fauriei
CRAPE MYRTLE

Crape myrtles (*Lagerstroemia*) are among the bark elite, and none more so than *Lagerstroemia fauriei* (Zone 6), which attracts more compliments than anything in my garden except the coral bark maple. That its white flow-

Lagerstroemia fauriei (crape myrtle)

vase-shaped form and beautiful bark. Crape myrtles revel in heat and seldom bloom without it, but the bark is more than enough to earn this tree a place anywhere climate permits. Now nearly a quarter century old and a veteran of many winter ice storms and summer droughts, *Lagerstroemia fauriei* rises an imposing 30 feet, with a total chest-high girth of 7 feet for its triple trunks. In autumn its small, glossy leaves take on all the warm colors of the spectrum, striking on the tree and a carpet of color on the ground where, too small to look untidy, blow around, or damage the underplanting of shore juniper (*Juniperus conferta*), they can be left to decay. The tree needs brief valeting in high summer, when it sloughs off its old elephant gray bark in large paper-like pieces, revealing a strokably slick under-bark of cinnamon and olive with touches of brighter green. A serendipitous winter color echo occurred between the cinnamon brown of the trunk and the rust-brown-clustered seed chalices of the tall *Lilium formosanum*.

Pruning is the only other attention needed, and it involves removing superfluous branches that clutter the framework while they are small and avoiding as far as possible large cuts that would leave a scar. Pruning such specimen trees should be a slow and thoughtful process, with if-in-doubt-don't the guiding rule. One

day a neat little notice, hung on the doorknob of the house by contractors for the electricity company, threw me into a panic. "Please indicate your pruning preference," it said. On the other side were line drawings of atrocities abundantly in evidence in the neighborhood: the flat top, the lopsider, and the crotch. When my none-of-the-above preference was emphatically imparted, the crew foreman allowed that the tree posed no present threat to the wires, "but it will before we come again in 3 years." Compromise was reached, based on an old adage: I would pay the piper (pruner) and I would call the tune. Nowadays this means extensive annual pruning, but that is 20 years ahead for those who plant this species now, and the tree is picturesque from its early years.

Crape myrtles have dense and thirsty roots, but the list of plants that will grow under and around them is amply long. *Juniperus conferta* 'Blue Pacific' (Zone 6) seems to enjoy its rather dry quarters and has spread into an extensive carpet, surrounding without damaging a *Pyracantha* 'Navajo' sheared once a year in early spring to maintain it as a low mound. The juniper is one of the unsung stalwarts of the garden, its quiet presence calming among showier plants. Spearing through it in contrast to its flat form are clumps of gold-striped *Yucca*

ers are not flamboyant, noticeably scented, or followed by colorful berries makes manifest what we gardeners are often slow to grasp: foliage and form make a more lasting contribution than flowers. While many trees have showier flowers, and some a more pyrotechnic display of autumn color, no ornamental tree I have seen surpasses crape myrtle in its shapely,

'Golden Sword', to add a touch of winter color, and invincible scarlet montbretia. The montbretia's splash of summer color would soon become a lava flow but for sessions spent pulling most of it out.

Lagerstroemia fauriei was brought from Japan to the U.S. National Arboretum in the 1950s. It is somewhat hardier than the better-known *L. indica* (to −10°F) and resistant to the mildew that plagues some selections of that species. The two species have been crossed to produce a big range of colorful hybrids. One of these, *L.* 'Natchez', has cinnamon brown bark almost as beautiful as that of *L. fauriei*, good autumn color, and pure white flowers in 1-foot panicles. It is a winner highly regarded and already widely planted.

Cornus

DOGWOOD

Dogwoods (*Cornus*) and willows (*Salix*) with colored stems look so much alike that after years of growing them I still often turn to Hillier's *Manual of Trees and Shrubs* to jog my memory as to which is which. Potential size and spread are factors to consider. *Cornus alba* is a medium-sized, clump-forming shrub, and *C. stolonifera* is a similar size but (obviously) stoloniferous. *Cornus sanguinea* makes a small tree, and *Salix alba* a large tree. Al-

Red-stemmed dogwood *Cornus alba* 'Sibirica' with yellow-edged leaves of *Elaeagnus* ×*ebbingei* 'Gilt Edge' and straw-colored *Miscanthus sinensis* 'Variegatus'

though they are kept cut back for maximum production of colorful bark, their potential size is reflected in their speed of growth and spread.

Trudging through an unusually heavy fall of snow to visit the red-stemmed dogwoods, *Cornus alba* 'Sibirica' (Zone 3), I reflected that outside a house window would be a better place for shrubs with colorful winter bark. I pondered on where I might put another clump and concluded there was no suitable spot. My main windows face south; they'd need to face north to see the dogwood, lit from the south, at its brightest, and the shrub would need to be sited outside any shadow from the house. Are architects ever presented with such horticultural requirements when commissioned? And would they understand that shrubs like dogwoods and willows with red or yellow bark color poorly in shade and glow at their brightest facing the sun? My walk was amply rewarded by the drama of the dogwoods against the sparkling freshly fallen snow.

If properly pruned, red-stemmed dogwood is such a shapely shrub in winter, slightly vase-shaped with the slim, smooth stems sufficiently separated to reveal other plants behind, in this case a brightly colored silverberry, *Elaeagnus ×ebbingei* 'Gilt Edge', and red-berried *Ilex cornuta* hollies. Pruning three clumps occupies an hour and a half in early spring, before the shrubs leaf out, and another hour in autumn after leaves are shed. In spring some of the oldest wood is sawn off at the base. Low side branches growing horizontally are next removed. The remaining stems are then cut back to about 1 foot. Growth is rapid in spring and the bushes become an amorphous mass of green foliage about 5 feet high through summer, a restful background for brightly colored annuals and perennials. Such hard pruning reduces the likelihood of these shrubs bearing their small clusters of white flowers, but the flowers are of minor ornamental value. When the leaves have been shed and the shrub's

framework can be seen, any dead stubs or thin whiskery branches are removed to leave a clean skeleton through winter. Because only young wood is brightly colored, severe pruning is needed to maintain perpetual youth and to prevent the shrubs from growing out of proportion. In cooler regions where growth is slower, removing only 2-year-old stems is sometimes advocated.

A sunlit, south- and west-facing ell where these red-stemmed dogwoods grow, backed by evergreen hollies on one side and a massive *Magnolia grandiflora* on the other, has become a winter corner for shrubs with colored bark that lend themselves to annual coppicing. The scarlet willow, *Salix alba* 'Britzensis' (Zone 2), more pale orange than scarlet for me, grows to 8 feet in a year. The popular yellow-stemmed dogwood *Cornus stolonifera* 'Flaviramea' spreads rather fast, and I wanted a clump, not a grove or a thicket, so I passed on this shrub in favor of *C. alba* 'Bud's Yellow' (Zone 3), a newcomer that stays in its clump and also has brighter yellow bark. *Cornus stolonifera* 'Silver and Gold' (synonym *C. sericea*) merits the extra effort should it need control because of its dual assets of yellow bark and white-variegated leaves. It grows fastest in wet soil, but its corner in my garden

is only moderately moist, which seems to have slowed it down.

Propagation of these dogwoods and willows could not be simpler. A few 1-foot-long pieces of stem are pushed into the ground on the shady side of the parent shrub at pruning time in autumn or spring and left to get on with it. This hit-or-miss method always ensures a few spare plants.

In another part of the garden coral barked *Cornus sanguinea* 'Winter Flame' (Zone 2; synonym 'Winter Beauty') has proved to be the most flamboyant dogwood. Autumn leaf color of soft amber touched with orange is an asset, but stem coloration is a knockout, a conflagration of scarlet, orange, and yellow. Pruning has been less simple than with the others. "As the twig is bent, so is the tree inclined," goes an old saying. Well, sometimes. I'm bent on creating a multistemmed shrub, while 'Winter Flame' is inclined to be a tree. A compromise was reached, with the oldest branches removed from the base, the remainder cut back by half. The cut ones branch out into a larger, fuller bush than the other dogwoods do and by far the most spectacular in winter. If I could have but one dogwood with colored bark, 'Winter Flame' would be it.

Cornus sanguinea 'Winter Flame' at left with red-berried *Nandina domestica*, golden *Chamaecyparis pisifera* 'Filifera Aurea', green-stemmed *Kerria japonica*, and *Miscanthus sinensis* 'Zebrinus', still an effective screen from the road beyond

WINTER FLOWERS

Flowers need not necessarily be alive to add to the beauty of the winter garden. The seed plumes of such grasses as *Miscanthus* and *Pennisetum alopecuroides* make a big contribution, and so does *Sedum* 'Autumn Joy', with its rust-colored domes topping stalks sufficiently sturdy to stay upright through occasional light falls of snow. Fresh flowers are precious, though, for brightening both the garden and the house. A good many winter-flowering shrubs have fragrant flowers, and budded branches cut from most of them will open indoors.

Jasminum nudiflorum
WINTER JASMINE

Winter jasmine (*Jasminum nudiflorum*; Zone 6) never fails to cheer the coldest months with sunny yellow flowers for 6 weeks or more. It likes full sun and doesn't object to low-fertility soil that sometimes gets dry in summer. In sandy soils and warm climates it can become a

Sedum 'Autumn Joy', which holds its structure and dead heads through winter, with *Viburnum plicatum* 'Watanabe' in background

mess if left to its own devices, exceeding its allotted span and tangled with the weeds it is not dense enough to deter. A little attention at frequent intervals prevents this happening. Arching, evergreen stems root where they touch the ground, often several feet out from where the plant was sited. This trait makes winter jasmine a useful bank cover provided the plant doesn't become infiltrated by stoloniferous grasses from an adjacent lawn, and that weeds are promptly removed. In tighter quarters winter jasmine can be kept within bounds by pulling out and pruning back tip-rooted branches before they leapfrog on, and occasionally removing an elderly branch from the center.

By far the most effective way of growing winter jasmine is, however, against a wall, fence, or building, with lath, trellis, or wires behind which vining stems can be tucked or to which they can be tied. It will flower in shade, but not as fully as it will with sun for at least part of the day. I have trained winter jasmine on the south- and west-facing sides of a small wellhouse, a process begun by severing a dozen or so rooted tips from elsewhere and spacing them 6 inches apart along the base. Which side flowers best varies with weather patterns. Flowers facing south open earlier and are therefore more likely to be damaged by hard

Jasminum nudiflorum on a wall

frost. Crisscross lath, half an inch clear of the sidings, is all the support the jasmine needs, but it is a scrambler, not a climber, and can't manage by itself. I spend, at a guess, half a day each year taking care of it. In one main session in spring I cut some old stems out from the base and shorten side growths back to a few inches. Then I spend odd minutes from time to time removing the few stems near the base that

manage to arch out and root, and guiding slender new stems with their tiny leaves behind the lath as they elongate. In summer the jasmine provides support for a small-flowered clematis of the *viticella* group that doesn't mind being cut back hard when its season has ended and that of the jasmine is about to begin.

Young stems of winter jasmine stay green in winter, and the leaves are so tiny that the

Lonicera ×purpusii

change is almost imperceptible when they drop in late autumn. In *Jasminum nudiflorum* 'Mystique' a white edging makes the leaves more noticeable. That 'Mystique' has so far (2 years) been less robust in my garden may be the result of planting it out while only pint-pot size. Where summer heat is intense many plants need a substantial root system before they become self-sufficient. I've usually found it best to buy small plants, pot them on, and wait until roots start to appear through the base of a gallon container, at which stage they need planting out or moving into bigger containers. Otherwise the roots become congested and less than fully functional.

Lonicera ×purpusii
WINTER HONEYSUCKLE

Lonicera ×purpusii (Zone 5) is considered the best of three similar winter honeysuckles, the other two being its parents, *L. fragrantissima* and *L. standishii*. *Lonicera ×purpusii* 'Winter Beauty', raised at Hillier Nurseries in England, has larger flowers and is deemed the best of all, but I can find no source for it in North America.

Lonicera ×purpusii is more likely than *L. fragrantissima* to retain all or part of its leaves in winter. If used, as mine is, to screen a chain-link fence, leaf retention is an advantage; otherwise it is not, because the flowers show best on bare branches. The flowers are small and white, with flared petals and prominent yellow stamens, grouped in little bunches evenly spaced along the stiff straight stems. So pervasive is their fragrance that I usually catch the scent before noticing the flowers. Were I spartan enough to sleep with the window open on nights needing several blankets, it would be nice to have this plant outside a bedroom window. I am not, so I settle for sprigs picked in bud and brought indoors to open. This hybrid honeysuckle is a very reliable winter bloomer. If one lot of flowers gets frosted, the plant usually has more held in reserve.

Having made its presence smelt from midwinter to early spring, *Lonicera ×purpusii* lets other plants take the limelight. In summer as unprepossessing as forsythia, it is also as easy to please and with the same tendency for arching branches to root where they touch the ground. Unpruned it becomes ungainly in habit and as much as 10 feet high. It can be kept more compact by removing a few of the oldest stems in early spring, cutting them off close to the ground. New ones will soon develop.

Chimonanthus praecox

WINTERSWEET

I'm reluctant to chop down a healthy 10-foot-tall shrub and none too eager to face the task of hacking out its roots, but I really should bite the bullet with *Chimonanthus praecox* (Zone 6; synonym *C. fragrans*). Its fragrance cannot be faulted, but my plant was raised from seed and has the typical flowers of the species, small and of a needing-to-be-laundered white with maroon centers. I'd like to replace it with *C. praecox* 'Luteus', a better form, with slightly larger flowers of diaphanous pale sulfur yellow.

Old-fashioned popular names are so much prettier than most of those newly coined, and "wintersweet" is apt for a shrub that engulfs the garden in fragrance in midwinter. Wintersweet is a chancy thing. Some years it wafts its fragrance over the garden while the snowdrops are in bloom, other years it is earlier or later, and still other years it may be ruined by freezes. Once open the flowers can stand some frost, but they do not occur over so long a period as winter honeysuckle and are therefore more likely to be damaged. Were I planting one or the other, it would be the winter honeysuckle.

Wintersweet plants raised from seed or cuttings are often slow to flower, but because heat speeds the process, gardeners in hot summer regions need less patience. The little bud knobs don't form on new wood, so pruning, which can be drastic if necessary, should be done immediately after blossom time.

Hamamelis

WITCH HAZEL

One February an ice storm, beautiful but treacherous, encapsulated the flowers of *Hamamelis ×intermedia* 'Jelena' in a glassy coating for several days. When the weather's mood switched to warm and windy, crimped ribbon petals curled up protectively within the encasing ice unrolled again, unblemished by their week-long entombment, into flowers reminiscent of sea anemones, with twelve tentacles waving out from each group of three tightly clustered calyces. A long, cruel winter, which killed in turn the flowers of wintersweet (*Chimonanthus praecox*), the usually weather-resistant *Prunus mume*, and early camellias, left the witch hazels unscathed. They just

Hamamelis ×intermedia 'Jelena'

scrunched themselves up and waited until conditions improved, in a state of suspended animation that got me musing on whether some kind of cryogenic process might one day make hibernation possible for humans, turning the Rip Van Winkle story into reality.

On this February day *Hamamelis ×intermedia* 'Primavera' is the garden's shining star. Its flowers a luminous lemon yellow, radiant in sun and bright even in shade or under cloudy skies. Coppery flowered 'Jelena' starts earlier, some years in January, and stays in bloom the longest. The blood-orange colors of its spidery apricot petals stretched out from

Hamamelis ×*intermedia* 'Jelena'

crimson calyces bring a warm glow to the winter scene. *Hamamelis ×intermedia* 'Arnold Promise', another first-rate gleaming yellow, is the latest to bloom, stretching the season of the winter witch hazels to about 3 months.

The hybrid witch hazels I've grown have nearly all been shapely, sturdy, weatherproof, undemanding, and beautiful. Some kinds in some years and some climates display brilliant red and orange autumn color if they get sun for at least half the day. They have seldom done so for me, and fragrance from the flowers is faint and undefinable, but I am more than content with most of the witch hazels that I have grown. *Hamamelis ×intermedia* 'Diane', however, was put up for adoption and now has a new home. Seen frontlit, the ruby red flowers are dull; they need sun shining through from behind to light them into life. Poor placement was my fault and could have been remedied, and the rangy, wide-spreading framework might have been forgiven, but Diane's habit of clinging to its dead leaves (a tendency of its *H. japonica* parent) is a serious flaw in a witch hazel. Summer drought can cause witch hazel leaves to die before they are ready to abscise, and they then remain clinging to the bush. Of the forms I've grown only 'Diane' has done so every year. Its place has been given to yellow-flowered *H. ×intermedia*

Hamamelis ×intermedia 'Primavera'

'Sunburst', "which has caused much oohing and aahing," says the catalog of my supplier. Noting from its label that mine is a grafted plant, I hope I shall be oohing and not booing.

It is possible, but far from easy, to root cuttings of hybrid witch hazels. Cuttings taken at just the right stage of rather soft new growth in spring need the kind of high humidity conducive as much to rot as to rooting. Those that root then take as much as 4 years to bloom, an expensive process for nurseries, which therefore prefer to sell grafted plants. Once a grafted plant is in the garden, it must be watched for branches springing up from below the graft. Sometimes the scion (the grafted on bit) fails entirely. That's how I came by *Hamamelis virginiana* when I'd planted *H. ×intermedia* 'Arnold Promise'.

Hamamelis virginiana (Zone 4) has charms of its own and I am happy to have it. The source of the soothing witch hazel lotion, it grows rapidly into a large shrub or small tree. In autumn the leaves turn bright yellow for 1–2 weeks, then they drop, all at once, and there it stands with branches smothered in small bright yellow flowers with a faint but perceptible fragrance. It came by accident but stays by choice.

Grafting *Hamamelis* 'Pallida' onto *H. vernalis* (Zone 4) did not, however, meet with my approval and might well taint the reputation of a lovely, trouble-free shrub among gardeners who don't recognize what is going on. While better adapted to wet and alkaline soils than other witch hazels, *H. vernalis* has late autumn flowers with little ornamental merit and its vigorous suckering habit practically ensures that the rootstock will crowd out the grafted top if errant shoots are not promptly removed. Suspect any stems coming from the base of hybrid witch hazels that show unusual vigor. Some nurseries group 'Pallida' among *H. ×intermedia* hybrids; others consider it a form of *H. mollis*. Highly regarded for its large flowers of pale primrose yellow, 'Pallida' shares the elusive fragrance of *H. mollis*.

Witch hazels can be pruned or left alone as their place in the garden dictates. My oldest, 'Jelena', needed no pruning until, after 20 years, branches overhanging the drive became vulnerable to such large vehicles as the oil truck. 'Primavera', on the other hand, in retrospect planted too close to a path, needed annual pruning after its first 3 years. Cutting back the branches immediately after flowering, to within an inch or two of where they began the previous year, keeps it at about 7 feet. Annual rainfall, which averages 40 inches, has sufficed for these witch hazels. During summer drought they get such water as falls their way from sprinklers only when these are turned on for the benefit of thirstier plants nearby. They get a light mulch of shredded bark every couple of years, but I've found no need to apply fertilizer.

Prunus mume

JAPANESE APRICOT

I'm resolved to plant no more ornamental cherries, plums, peaches, or apricots, because sooner or later they succumb to borers, a major pest of this region. But an intensely fragrant white-flowered *Prunus mume* (Zone 6) is one of two long-term survivors I'll probably replace if their time comes before mine. (The other is *P.* 'Hally Jolivette'.) It was a gift from the late Henry Hohman of Kingsville Nursery, Maryland (famous in its time but long since

Prunus mume

closed), a quarter century ago and has bloomed unfailingly all these years. Some years the flowers begin in January and continue into March, while other years they start a bit later, but they always overlap with the snowdrops

(*Galanthus nivalis*) growing in the tree's shade. This tree has been attacked by borers but managed to live with the damage. Borers are now fended off with a bar of Octagon soap, an old-fashioned laundry soap that comes in dense, brownish bars with a satisfying heft in an age when packaging so often outweighs the miniscule contents. Hung in the crotch of the tree, in a plastic net bag that held a turkey, or oranges, or bulbs, it delivers a trickle of whatever-it-is (the label does not reveal) each time it rains, adhering to and staining the trunk. I don't guarantee that this folk remedy will work, but it costs very little and does no harm. One bar would last 6 months or more were it not that some creature—squirrel, possum, raccoon?—never caught in the act eats it now and then.

Japanese apricot grows fast and blooms only on young wood, which is green, canelike, and unbranched. To keep the tree shapely and floriferous, these green whips need pruning back. This job is usually done during the short period between flowering and leafing out.

Sarcococca

SWEET BOX

Sarcococcas are unpretentious small, dense evergreen shrubs of neat dignity and, provided they have shade from hot sun, a healthy and unmarred self-sufficiency that becomes increasingly endearing as weather extremes, pest, or disease take their toll of less adaptable plants. Ideally their soil should contain sufficient organic matter to retain moisture, but they tolerate quite dry shade, in foundation plantings under overhangs, for instance. I grow two species and like them so well I'll be adding more. *Sarcococca hookeriana* var. *humilis* (Zone 6) is a slowly spreading, stoloniferous ground cover of upright habit to 18 inches high, with shiny, lance-shaped, bright green leaves about 3 inches long. The flowers, in small axillary clusters partly hidden under the leaves, are plentiful but consist only of tiny tufts of white stamens, scarcely noticeable did not their lingering sweetness on mild late winter days draw one to investigate the source.

My 5 year-old *Sarcococca confusa* (Zone 7), growing in the summer shade of a large dawn redwood (*Metasequoia*) that sucks up a lot of moisture, is 3 feet high and 5 feet across. It is among the best plants for supplying cut foliage. The pretty leaves are a wavy oval with tapered tips, very dark green with the gloss of burnished leather. The wee flower tufts are borne at 1-inch intervals along the underside of the stem. A vase of cut stems will perfume a room. The beadlike black berries that follow the flowers have no ornamental value, but they are one way of distinguishing between this and the rarer *S. ruscifolia* var. *chinensis* (Zone 7), a similar shrub but with red berries.

Daphne odora

WINTER DAPHNE

As winter draws to its close, the winter daphne (*Daphne odora*; Zone 7) bathes the garden in fragrance. Most blossoms have some faint scent if one puts one's nose to them, but comparatively few are as pervasively redolent as this. As well as the green-leaved, pink-flowered species, I grow five other forms: white-flowered *D. odora* 'Alba', red-budded, pink-flowered *D. odora* 'Alden's Regal Red', *D. odora* 'Zuiko Nishiki', which is supposed to have pink and white flowers on the same plant but so far has borne only pink ones, *D. odora* 'Aureomarginata', with pink flowers and yellow-edged leaves, and an unnamed selection with white flowers and white-edged leaves. The unnamed daphne looks like *D. odora* 'Ringmaster' pictured in *Variegated Plants in Color* by Yoshimichi Hirose and Masato Yokoi, which also illustrates four other forms I've yet to see but long to get my hands on.

Daphne odora is evergreen, but the leaves may get scorched at temperatures below 15°F and it defoliates at its hardiness limit. Someone, somewhere, long ago said in print that *D. odora* 'Aureomarginata' is hardier than the

Daphne odora with ruby red *Helleborus abchasicus* in foreground

A form of *Daphne odora* with white flowers and white-edged leaves, perhaps *D. odora* 'Ringmaster'

others, a supposition promulgated ever since. My experience is otherwise. In my garden this cultivar, or form, has twice been winter-killed when the species and the white-flowered form survived. My longest-lived daphne, a 5-foot-tall *D. odora* 'Alba', was 12 years old when a pine branch heavy with snow crashed down and crushed it to death. No conclusions about comparative hardiness should be drawn from this, because longevity has more to do with soil and site than with a particular cultivar.

How often have you seen a daphne—any daphne—of obvious old age? I once saw a 20-year-old stand of the low and spreading

Daphne cneorum (Zone 5), but daphnes seem to be naturally short-lived, with 10 years a good life span for most of them. Why complain that they don't live into a decrepit old age? Would we wish it for ourselves? Ten years is longer than most of us keep our clothes, and one can have a dozen daphnes for the price of a new suit, and a single plant in a gallon container for little more than the cost of a hamburger, fries, and Coke. Death while young is another matter. Sometimes premature death is caused by disease or a quirk in the weather, but more often by mistreatment and frequently by waterlogging. Daphnes are very drought resistant and can't abide wet feet. Winter daphne roots readily from cuttings taken in early spring, and if there are spares on hand the loss is less grievous when an old bush departs.

The best site for winter daphne varies with where you live. In England, which is really too cool for the plant's liking, it is often given the benefit of reflected heat against a south-facing wall. Although it likes warm regions better than cool ones, such a site would probably be fatal in places where paving gets too hot in summer to be walked on barefoot. My plants have lived longest under high-branched, evergreen red cedars (*Juniperus virginiana*), which have flexible branches seldom brought crashing down by snow and ice as those of loblolly pines (*Pinus taeda*) often are. One of my plants receives sun for much of the day, but most for only a few hours. Even in deep shade, with sun for barely an hour each day, every branch tip is crowned with a tight cluster of flowers, and foliage suffers less winter scorch in the shade. Bloom time is longer as well, continuing for 6 weeks or more.

The adaptability of *Daphne odora* to varying degrees of sun or shade is apparent in the underplantings: hellebores with the one in deep shade; ferny, yellow-flowered *Corydalis cheilanthifolia* with those in part shade; and blue plumbago (*Ceratostigma plumbaginoides*) with the one in mostly sun. Maintenance of winter daphne amounts to little more than the occasional topping up of mulch and sometimes a light spring trimming. While it is not advisable to hard prune old wood, young twigs grown long and sappy can be cut back in spring to keep the bush compact and among the most shapely of broadleaf evergreens.

Viburnum

Viburnum tinus (Zone 7; synonym *Laurustinus tinus*), a good looking large evergreen, can be relied on to bloom in late winter—if it has survived. On the margin of hardiness in Zone 7, it is a long-term survivor in my garden only under the protective canopy of tall red cedars (*Juniperus virginiana*), with shade for more than half the day. Delighting in sun, it is at its superb best a zone warmer in South Carolina. *Viburnum farreri* (Zone 6) and *V.* ×*bodnantense* hybrids, such a joy in England, have been disappointing in Virginia, where the flowers invariably get frosted in winter and branches die out in summer. White-flowered *V. farreri* 'Candidissimum' did better than any other, but was still scarcely worth growing. I gambled that the sunnier climate would induce bloom on *V. farreri* 'Nanum', in England a shy bloomer. And lost. Out.

Chaenomeles

QUINCE

If ever there was a survivor it is the orange-red quince seen around many old homesteads in southeastern North America, presumably *Chaenomeles speciosa* (Zone 4). Although the color might make quince difficult to place if it bloomed in the spring rush, it is most welcome in February and March, when there's little for it to quarrel with. In several respects it is more garden-worthy than many vaunted hybrids. It is the first quince to bloom, wreathing its branches with bloom from base to tip before the leaves appear, and doing this furthermore with no maintenance unless an occasional shearing.

Chaenomeles ×superba 'Jet Trail'

Most quinces need annual pruning if they are to perform at their best, and the usual rules do not apply. Branches grow 1 foot or more after spring pruning, but flowers are formed on only the first few inches. A second pruning is needed. If this has not been done in winter, bloom time is not too late to remove the surplus, nonflowering wood obscuring the flowers. Quinces show at their best trained tightly against a wall, and were my walls a more sympathetic color than red brick I'd experiment to find out if they'd get sun enough to flower freely against north- or east-facing walls. In hot regions such as mine they'd be unlikely to thrive in the intense heat of unshaded south- or west-facing walls. If you think the color of this handed-down quince harsh, try *Chaenomeles speciosa* 'Moerloosii' (synonym 'Apple Blossom', which aptly describes the color of its pink and white flowers).

Hybrid quince, *Chaenomeles ×superba* (Zone 5), tends to be a smaller bush than selections of *C. speciosa*. Of the few I've grown the bright white 'Jet Trail', low growing though not prostrate as sometimes suggested, has pleased me most. Its bloom time overlaps that of the snowdrops.

Cornus officinalis and *Cornus mas*

CORNELIAN CHERRY

These two Cornelian cherries (Zone 5) are very similar. The exfoliating bark of *Cornus officinalis*, supposedly a distinguishing characteristic, never met my expectations in the 20 years I grew it, nor was there ever a sign of the fruits that give it its vernacular name. The little fluffy balls of yellow flowers were so plentiful each February that in its mature years the tree resembled a yellow cloud. It was a short-trunked, fan-shaped specimen, with heavy wide-spreading lower branches when snow and ice rent the trunk asunder. Knowing its vulnerability, I hesitated to plant it again. Then, browsing through a catalog, I spotted *C. mas* 'Pyramidalis', with "narrowly upright habit even in old age." A year after planting it bore its first flowers, in mid-March, nicely presented against a plum-purple background from *Cryptomeria japonica* 'Elegans' (Zone 6). Just the thing for gardeners wanting to squeeze a quart into a pint bottle, but don't hold your breath waiting for fruits. Alice M. Coats, in *Garden Shrubs and Their Histories*, reports that *Cornus mas*, the male cornel, got its name because it produces only male flowers for its first 15 years.

Rhododendron mucronulatum

An eminent horticulturist, who had best be nameless since I'm going to argue, informed me that while bloom time varied from region to region and from year to year, bloom sequence remained the same. Would that it were so, there wouldn't then be the color clashes most gardeners suffer once in a while when plants that usually bloom in succession become synchronized. Weather is the usual cause, though the age of the plant can have a bearing on such anomalies. After seeing winter hazel (*Corylopsis*) blooming at the same time as *Rhododendron mucronulatum* (Zone 4), I tried to emulate this combination, unsuccessfully. In my garden this deciduous rhododendron blooms at the tail end of winter, just before forsythia, and is about done when the winter hazels begin. Only one year in twenty have they overlapped. So utterly unlike the stolid large-leaved rhododendrons, it might be a mass of lavender-winged butterflies hovering over a rounded, twiggy, leafless bush. It recovered quickly when moved to partial shade and leafy soil, after almost perishing in sun and sand.

Spiraea thunbergii 'Ogon'

Suddenly in mid-March *Spiraea thunbergii* 'Ogon' (Zone 4; synonym 'Mellow Yellow') is in full bloom. A certain and instant success, and as undemanding as most of the genus, this Barry Yinger find is what color-conscious gardeners have long waited for, a spiraea that doesn't bear flowers of shocking pink along with its yellow leaves. Blue flowers would be even better and for 3 years I had this contrasting combination in *Caryopteris ×clandonensis* 'Worcester Gold'. It then succumbed to root rot, as has, after only a couple of years, every caryopteris I've tried save gray-felted *C. incana* 'Nana', a prostrate form that thrives and self-sows until we in Zone 7 get a Zone 6 winter, a not infrequent occurrence.

It was the bright chartreuse yellow of the slender leaves that attracted me to *Spiraea thunbergii* 'Ogon', and this feature remains its main asset. The cloud of tiny white flowers for 2 or 3 weeks in late winter was an extra as delightful as it was unexpected. Obscured by the wealth of flowers, leaves start bursting from their buds in late winter and last until hard frost, often as late as Christmas, disappearing as neatly as melting snow when they finally fall to earth. To suggest a potential size would be guesswork and it really doesn't matter. The wiry stems are easy to shear, and the plant has responded willingly to my wish for it to remain a buoyant knee-high mound. Shearing is done immediately after it flowers.

Helleborus

HELLEBORE

Hellebores are the current darlings of the gardening world, but one cannot yet go to a garden center and be sure of getting the finest selected forms. Hellebores cannot be grown from cuttings, tissue culture techniques have not yet succeeded, clumps are slow to reach dividable size, seed may fail to germinate unless freshly collected, and seedlings from hybrids cannot be guaranteed to replicate the parent plant. Therefore choice forms remain scarce, expensive, and so eagerly sought that American enthusiasts chase off to England in winter to hunt them down. Don't feel deprived if you're not up to this search—there are no worthless hellebores. Those mentioned here are obtainable, affordable, lovely, and easy to grow. All except *Helleborus viridis* are evergreen, and all prefer lightly shaded sites. The

Rhododendron mucronulatum in bloom with *Aucuba japonica* behind it, *Daphne jezoensis* left of tree, *Schizophragma hydrangeoides* 'Moonlight' on tree, *Arum italicum* 'Pictum' at tree base, and dead fronds of *Thelypteris kunthii* at bottom left

H. orientalis hybrids give everyone a shot at selecting plants the equal of many commanding a high price.

A plant sold as *Helleborus viridis* (Zone 6), though there's some doubt about this, seems bent on self-destruction when, around mid-winter, it pushes through the ground leaves as soft and tender as those of forced celery. It seems as unkind as putting a kitten out in the cold, but light freezes do no lasting harm. Before the calendar marks the end of winter, 2-inch flowers of palest, luminous green are presented over dainty 1-foot-high mounds of lacy leaves. My plants self-sow modestly in the leaf litter under a large oak that shades them from afternoon sun. In my garden this hellebore frequently deals with summer drought by going dormant, retaining its leaves if kept watered.

Despite its disparaging name my silver-medalist, the stinking hellebore (*Helleborus foetidus*; Zone 5), gives off no effluvia I can detect, not even from crushed leaves. There's a look of cut-leaf Japanese maples in the duskily iridescent, fingered, saw-edged leaves held out on arching petioles resembling the ribs of an umbrella. *Helleborus foetidus* 'Wester Flisk' is a particularly fine form. Young leaves are charcoal with the hazy sheen of gasoline on water, developing hints of garnet as they mature, matched to the deep garnet of petioles

A large-flowered strain of *Helleborus niger* that starts to bloom before Christmas and continues through to spring

and stout central stem. A candelabra of flowers rises in pale contrast above the leaves. Each of the multiple arched stalks bears a small bunch of nodding flowers with pale green, pink-veined bracts. Buds form early in winter, clenched like fists until coaxed by warmth into pendant green goblets that act as umbrellas to keep the stamens dry. With pollination effected, they open into shallow, maroon-rimmed green bowls resembling elegant porcelain cups. Torpedo-shaped pods, ripening within the sepal bowl, split by midsummer and give birth to the seeds of the next generation. Seedlings come up in dense clusters, and little bunches can easily be lifted for transplanting. *Helleborus foetidus* makes a large

Helleborus orientalis

nious with seedlings but usually bequeaths a few before its life comes to an end, prematurely brought about by a winter of more than average severity.

Helleborus niger (Zone 4) is the Christmas rose depicted on Christmas cards, and *H. orientalis* (synonym *H. ×hybridus*) is the Lenten rose, but in truth the two are often in a neck-and-neck race to produce the first flower. *Helleborus niger* survives colder winters than other hellebores can tolerate, but most of its forms are poorly adapted to extreme heat or drought, set little seed, and are frequently hard to please. Many a witches' brew have I poured on my plants in attempts to win their favor. Seaweed extracts and Epsom salts seemed to help, as did replacing the sand with heavier soil and keeping it moist, but real success came only with a heat-adapted strain. This strain bears very large flowers (one measured 5 inches across), sometimes singly and sometimes in pairs. They are pure white at first, fading to pale pink, raised well above the leaves, and facing out. Moist (not wet) soil and midday shade suit them best, and they flower most profusely where they get several hours of sun. Seed set is ample, and seedlings flower in their second or third year. When winter is mild I've had this strain in bloom from November to April. There'll be fewer disappointments now

plant, 3 feet broad and 2 feet high when in bloom. Gray- or gold-leaved hostas make good summer companions for it, as does the gray-fronded painted fern, *Athyrium niponicum* 'Pictum'. Best of all is the year-round presence of variegated sweet flags such as white-striped *Acorus gramineus* 'Variegatus' or yellow-striped *A. gramineus* 'Ogon'.

Helleborus argutifolius (Zone 7) is a very substantial plant, sometimes attaining small shrub proportions. The flowers are a lucent green, in such large trusses that they may weigh the sturdy stems to the ground. If it didn't flower, this plant would still earn a place in my garden with its clumps of large, three-lobed, saw-edged gray-green leaves with lighter veining. Needing a wind-sheltered site and a soil that does not lie wet, it is parsimo-

that nurseries in hot regions are beginning to sell such heat-adapted strains.

Welcome as all these hellebores are, few would dispute the gold-medal status of *Helleborus orientalis* hybrids. Cold hardy, heat tolerant, and long lived, they are remarkably pest-free.

Hellebores are poisonous to humans and apparently to such pests as rabbits and voles as well, for nothing seems to munch on their leaves or roots. They can be divided but seldom need it, and they self-sow by the thousand. My only complaint, in fact, about *H. orientalis* hybrids is that I need to spend many hours cutting off flowered stalks before the seed is shed if these plants are not to take over my whole 2 acres. There is no doubt about their preference for hot summer regions.

Remarkably adaptable, Lenten roses prefer a lightly shaded site and deep, humus-rich soil, but provided sun and moisture are there in winter and early spring, they will grow almost anywhere, though I counsel against full sun. I have one extensive planting under a large dogwood (*Cornus florida*) that overhangs a boundary fence with a drainage ditch outside. Content in this deep rooty shade through summer, and with flowering not at all diminished, they have also self-sown through the fence to cover the sometimes wet ditch bank. Another

A selected form of *Helleborus orientalis*

colony survived one of the hottest, driest summers on record after I chopped down the loblolly pine (*Pinus taeda*) hitherto shading them from overhead sun. Clearing up the nonstop mess from loblolly pines—pollen, cones, needles, branches—accounts for fully half of all my gardening chores so they are being selectively removed. The hellebores continued to live, but less than joyously. Overhead shade was restored within 2 years with a group of three Chinese parasol trees (*Firmiana simplex*; Zone 7), a remarkable fast-growing small tree, unbranched when young, which in winter looks like a green pole thrust into the ground. Through the growing season this tree is topped with an umbrella of colossal maplelike leaves on long stalks. Picking these up when they fall is a matter of minutes.

Lenten roses consort well with the varied textures of such other shade plants as hostas, ferns, arums, asarums, corydalis, epimediums, rohdea, sweet flags (*Acorus*), and sedges (*Carex*). Clump forming, strap-leaved *Liriope muscari* is a perfect partner, and together they make a handsome, weed-deterring carpet of contrasting foliage appropriate equally to a woodland setting or a shady town courtyard. For echo-minded gardeners there are hellebores to pick up the pink of camellias or *Daphne odora*, whites to combine with *D. odora* 'Alba', and, though rare and expensive as yet, yellows to keep company with yellow witch hazels.

No other hellebores have flowers as varied as these: snowy white, creamy or greenish white, pale yellow, pale or deep pink, ruby red, plum, and sultry purple. Some are solid colors, and some are freckled with red in various configurations. There even are some with anemone-form or fully double flowers. What more could one ask? Well, perhaps that they be less modest about their charms and hold up their heads so that their pretty faces could be admired and photographed without stretching out on one's stomach to do it. Breeders have been striving for flowers that droop less, but there's still a long way to go. Should you be so lucky as to have a shaded hillside or mound

viewed from below, such a site presents them extremely well.

There's no need to spend a king's ransom to acquire a good collection of *Helleborus orientalis* hybrids. My collection, which began with a handful of seedlings from the late Elizabeth Lawrence, now includes whites of varying shape and purity, pinks, plum purples, and some as beautifully patterned as expensive named forms. *Helleborus abchasicus* (now usually lumped under *H. orientalis*) self-sows true to color, a deep ruby red that matches exactly the buds of *Daphne odora*. Others throw up fresh variations year by year. Visit a specialist nursery when hellebores are in bloom and buy a few, as varied as possible, that take your fancy, then begin your own selection process by leaving only favorite forms to self-sow and removing spent flowers from the rest. As I go about this, I often wonder what potential beauty I am snuffing out, but abortion seems preferable to infanticide, and if all are left, most of the crowded seedlings will die anyway.

Lenten roses present one annual dilemma—whether and when to remove old leaves. They can be left to die away naturally later in the year, as nature intended, but survival and multiplication are nature's sole intent, with presentation of concern only in so far as it aids pol-

lination. Gardeners, on the other hand, want the flowers to look their prettiest, and winter-battered leaves aren't conducive to this, so they at least should be removed. Removing all the leaves stages the flowers best, but in regions where the temperature yo-yos from freeze to mini heat wave and back, removing the protective umbrellas of leathery old leaves exposes emerging flowers to frost, and tender new leaves just beginning to unfurl are also vulnerable. Deciding what to do is an annual guessing game and gamble, with but little help from long-term weather forecasts.

Galanthus
SNOWDROPS

Could there be a lovelier herald of spring than the snowdrop *Galanthus nivalis* (Zone 3)? So frail, it seems, to survive the frosts and snows of winter, yet survive it does and triumphs. It is a tough and accommodating little bulb for tucking in handfuls under shrubs or planting in drifts in summer-shaded sites. William Wordsworth wrote a poem to the common snowdrop. He knew it, as first did I, in the cool of ivied English woods. Failure with snowdrops is much commoner than success in hot summer regions and why it has chosen to naturalize for me I cannot say. From a modest beginning of a dozen bulbs for $1 twenty years ago, there now are thousands, apparently impervious to the voles, squirrels, and rabbits that destroy so many bulbs.

Most newcomers to my garden get a dowry of decent soil mixed with the local acid sand in their planting hole, a mixture concocted by eye, feel, and experience from such ingredients as peat moss, perlite, coarse sand, leaf mold, alfalfa meal, sewage compost, cow manure, rock phosphate, greensand, crushed oyster shell (for supposed lime-lovers), and calcined clay (Turface granules) for lasting substance. In the absence of manure, maybe a handful of 10–10–10 or a sprinkling of Osmocote 14–14–14 to a barrowful is added. Still I claim no special credit for the snowdrops; they simply like it here. Inexplicably, success with the common double form sold as *Galanthus nivalis* 'Flore Pleno' has several times eluded me, yet the rarer double-flowered *G. nivalis* 'Lady Beatrix Stanley', a fairly recent addition, is already increasing. I lost a cherished clump of an autumn-flowering snowdrop to narcissus fly, a fat white grub that eats out the heart of the bulb. I found and squished it, but too late. This incident and repeated loss of the common double form have been the only fatalities.

Conditions that simulate thin woodland suit snowdrops best. Under my large wintersweet (*Chimonanthus praecox*), they jostle their way

Galanthus nivalis with leaves of *Cyclamen hederifolium*

up among green-ruffed, varnished yellow aconites (*Eranthis hyemalis*), as cozily crowded as a litter of newborn puppies, all somehow finding sufficient breathing space. Before the flowers of the aconites fade, my earliest daffodil, *Narcissus* 'Little Gem', joins them. At the front of an east-facing bed, with shrubs and trees behind them, snowdrops work a shift system with the Japanese painted fern (*Athyrium niponicum* 'Pictum'), which puts up new fronds as the snowdrops start going dormant. This time-sharing arrangement also works with hostas. More snowdrops stand out starkly white over a carpet of an ivy, *Hedera helix*

Cyclamen coum

'Spetchley', which has tiny, dark-green leaves plastered against the ground.

The snowdrops are at their most exquisite growing through the silver-marbled leaves of ivy-leaved cyclamen (*Cyclamen hederifolium*) beneath the bare branches of a doublefile viburnum, *Viburnum plicatum* var. *tomentosum*, interspersed with the brilliant pink chubby flowers of *Cyclamen coum*. The snowdrops multiply so bounteously, by bulb increase and self-sown seed, that here they must be thinned each year lest they engulf the cyclamen. They are easily divided in winter or early spring with instant gratification. In autumn, when most bulbs are planted, potential sites so obvious in winter have disappeared under lush foliage, along with the markers meant to serve as reminders. Snowdrops can be moved in full bloom. If clumps are kept intact or gently eased into smaller chunks, they look instantly at home in their new quarters. If the most rapid increase is sought, wait until they've finished flowering but still have their leaves, then divide them into individual bulbs or little clusters.

What affection and intimacy are revealed by old common names. "Snowdrops"—so evocative and so apt when the buds are white drops suspended from slender stalks like tears about to fall. Opened, the buds reveal green horseshoes on the scalloped edge of the inner segment underskirt. Only if you lift a flower or put a few of them in a vase and stand it on a mirror, as suggested by the late Beverley Nichols, do you get a glimpse of the heart-shaped green-striped lining of the petticoats. There are many named forms of *Galanthus nivalis*, with differences often so subtle they need a hands-and-knees approach to become apparent, a prayerful position entirely appropriate for such delightful harbingers of spring.

Galanthus elwesii (Zone 5) is a bit taller than the common snowdrop, with bigger flowers and wider gray-green leaves. It has been in my garden for many years, growing through *Campanula garganica* (one of the few campanulas that doesn't seem to mind intense summer heat) under a coral bark maple. It has done well but cannot compare with the common snowdrop in length of flowering time or speed of multiplication.

Cyclamen coum

The leaves of *Cyclamen coum* (Zone 6) are often plain dark green, but in selected forms they are brightly patterned with white and very decorative. Flower color varies from white through pinks progressing from blush to carmine. There can be cyclamen flowers for more than half the year when *C. coum* is mixed with *C. hederifolium*, and each seems able to hold its own in such a mixed planting. Braving winter and often flowering through the snow, this species usually peaks with the snowdrops but is more under the weather's control. There may be blooms for 3 months when winter is mild, but the buds stay hunkered down and wait until March if winter is severe. Expensive only when getting started, and well worth every dollar, *C. coum* self-sows fairly generously when settled in.

Eranthis hyemalis

WINTER ACONITE

Aconites, tucked under deciduous trees and shrubs where they don't get in the way of anything else during their long dormancy, deserve their brief, bright shining hour in the sun more often than they get it. They suffer badly from being lifted and stored; therefore only a fraction of the aconite tubers sold will survive. A healthy, hardy bulb, corm, or tuber planted in well-drained, friable soil may not be a long-term survivor if the climate doesn't suit it, but if a plant doesn't appear in its first year, assuming it wasn't eaten by rodents, it was probably dead on arrival. When the little aconite tubers arrive, soak them overnight, then cut one in half. If all that's there is brown mush, ask for a refund and use a different bulb merchant next time. Better yet, don't order any aconites. The best way of getting started is to beg a growing plant or two, or a smidgen of seed, from a friend. My aconites self-sow generously, with a marked preference for the gravel driveway. Winter aconite is hardy to Zone 4.

Scilla mischtschenkoana

Snowdrops and cyclamen are mutually enhancing, but the silvery blue of an early squill looked wan and washed out in the company of snowdrops and they've been moved apart. *Scilla mischtschenkoana* (Zone 2; synonym *S. tubergeniana*) is a pretty and sturdy bulbous plant, quite readily available, yet little known. The latest sneezelike name isn't likely to enhance the plant's marketability, and it has no

Eranthis hyemalis (winter aconite)

common name. Its milky blue flowers with darker veining are very much like those of the wee *Puschkinia scilloides*, which is so humble in size and coloring that it needs a rock garden setting to display it effectively. The scilla is bigger in bulb, leaf, and flower, and its color, though pale, is luminous and very apparent in a winter landscape of greens and browns. It is already in bloom as it pushes through the

Scilla mischtschenkoana

ground in February, with an ultimate height of about 6 inches.

Narcissus

DAFFODIL, JONQUIL

It feels like spring when the daffodils start to bloom, concurrently with the first roadside dandelions and a few weeks before the forsythia, but the calendar says winter still and the weather may yet ram it home with snow or an ice storm. Daffodil bulbs are poisonous and rodents do not eat them. Many of the daffodils I have planted have, nevertheless, petered out within a year or two. Still, there are plenty of stayers that flourish in moderately fertile, moisture-retentive soil with a generous ration of sun, without demanding the costly nourishment of special fertilizers.

Narcissus 'Little Gem' (Zone 4), a perfect miniature trumpet, 6 inches high, can be counted on for February flowers in all but the worst winters. The somewhat similar *N.* 'Cedric Morris', worth its king's ransom price if you can find it, is even earlier, sometimes for Christmas. The somewhat bigger *N.* 'February Gold' (Zone 5) is still of less overblown proportions than most hybrids, its *N. cyclamineus* ancestry apparent in perianth segments swept back a little, as if they faced a gentle breeze. I have pictures of 'Little Gem' and 'February Gold' blooming through the snow. *Narcissus* 'February Gold' came to me as *N.* 'Peeping Tom' (not a reliable daffodil for me), a common mistake in books and catalogs. The trumpet of 'Peeping Tom' is slimmer than that of 'February Gold'. I can never find enough places for daffodils where they get their needed quota of sun without being an eyesore while the leaves are dying away, but I found the perfect spot for 'February Gold' under a wisteria trained as a large shrub. Here it gets full sun from autumn through early spring, then the wisteria leafs out and hides the daffodil's withering foliage.

No sooner does 'February Gold' get going

Narcissus 'Tête-à-Tête' under *Chionanthus retusus*, with an early seedling camellia in background

than it is joined by the Lent lily (*Narcissus pseudonarcissus*; Zone 5), a native of Europe. What I am growing is the form known as 'Early Virginia' or 'Trumpet Major'. This daffodil seems to walk with the wind at its back, sweeping the perianth segments forward. By early March N. 'Tête-à-Tête' (Zone 3) is usually a sheet of bright green foliage and warm yellow flowers under a Chinese fringe tree (*Chionanthus retusus*) not yet in leaf. As well as being a stayer of quick increase, 'Tête-à-Tête' gets bonus points for managing to be both dainty and dashing, quite a trick to pull off. The name 'Tête-à-Tête' comes from this daffodil's tendency to bear some flowers in pairs, as if they were chatting to each other. Only about 6 inches high, 'Tête-à-Tête' is less messy than big daffodils when dying away. Far removed from grace is 'Erlicheer', purchased for its early blooms, then discarded as hideous. The flowers are packed into globs lacking clarity of form and too heavy for the stalks to support if wetted by the lightest rain.

Most early daffodils last for several weeks but not all. Hot on the heels of my mentioned medalists comes a daffodil of rock garden proportions, *Narcissus romieuxii* 'Julia Jane' (Zone 7). Less than 6 inches high, with threadlike leaves, 'Julia Jane' doesn't stay long enough to get high marks, seldom lasting as much as 2 weeks, but what a little show-off while it lasts. Its frilly, chiffon-textured, hoop-petticoat corona of luminous, pale lemon yellow swirls flirtatiously around exerted stamens.

Crocus

No matter what the calendar says, *Crocus tommasinianus* (Zone 3) in bloom marks the end of winter. It may be cold, there may even be snow on the ground, but this sprightly little bulb is a true herald of spring. Crocuses have always been "iffy" things for me: in England a network of black thread was needed to discourage sparrows from pecking out the buds, and in Virginia rodents polish them off in short order. When voles ate the corms, I started planting my crocuses in sunken pots. Then, when my cats took early retirement, rabbits moved in and razed the foliage as soon as it appeared. Despite attempts to ward off rodents with sprinklings of sewage compost, dried blood, and used kitty litter, the only species to survive in quantity is *C. tommasinianus*, aided, perhaps, by a covering carpet of creeping raspberry (*Rubus pentalobus*; synonym *R. calycinoides*), with interlacing stems that make digging and burrowing less easy. I take the time to spray on a concoction of Tabasco sauce and eggs to make the foliage unpalatable to rabbits, cussing a bit but counting the blessing that I don't have to contend with deer.

Brent Heath of Brent and Becky's Bulbs recommends mixing rodent-vulnerable bulbs with those they avoid: tulips among daffodils, for instance. Some of my biggest surviving clumps of crocuses are crowded in among a solid sheet of starflower (*Ipheion uniflorum*) under a star magnolia (*Magnolia stellata*). Perhaps the faint onion smell of the starflower's foliage deters the rodents, or perhaps its prodigious increase sates their appetites before they get to the crocuses. One way or the other this combination seems to work.

Rapid increase of *Crocus tommasinianus* bulbs is reflected in the price. With bulbs costing ten for $1, gardeners can afford to be generous and should be. A hundred bulbs will get this crocus off to a flying start, though a thousand would be better. Splurging with the white form, *C. tommasinianus* 'Albus', is comparatively costly. I indulged myself with fifty bulbs anyway, justifying the extravagance by mentally trading it off against the cost of dinner in a good restaurant. Tidbits for voles instead of a luxury dinner for me was not the trade-off I had in mind, so I planted the bulbs in a tall courtyard tub.

Other tubs house little snow crocuses, *Crocus chrysanthus* (Zone 3), in assorted colors: white 'Snow Bunting', yellow and violet 'Advance', creamy 'Cream Beauty', blue 'Skyline', bronze-feathered yellow 'Gipsy Girl', and straw yellow 'Brass Band'. When they flowered, one tub had a lopsided look, marking my failure to pay attention to flowering times, which can differ by 2 weeks or more. By chance I had planted three early forms on one side and three late ones on the other.

Planting bulbs in containers raises them out of the reach of wildlife and domestic dogs, but not, however, cats, which like a raised perch, especially a forbidden one. Safe in containers, crocuses can multiply undisturbed until there are enough to risk a few in the ground, as I did with pure white 'Ard Schenk', now looking bridal growing through a white-edged ivy, *Hedera helix* 'Glacier'. When the bulbs are dormant the tubs are filled with annuals that require infrequent watering: pelargoniums, annual periwinkle (*Catharanthus roseus*), and *Portulaca oleracea* have been among the best.

Iris histrioides 'Major'

Iris histrioides 'Major' (Zone 4) has violet-blue flowers similar to those of *I. reticulata*, but blooms earlier and has persisted in my garden for 20 years, while repeated plantings of *I. reticulata* have come and gone. So why is this species so scarce? American gardeners may have to order it from English bulb growers. My plants grow through a mat-forming variegated sedum, *Sedum lineare* 'Variegatum', which marks the spot all year and prevents me accidentally digging up the bulbs.

BROADLEAF EVERGREENS AND CONIFERS

In cold winter regions conifers play a bigger role than broadleaf evergreens. The only broadleaf evergreen I can think of that actually prefers cold regions to hot ones is the mountain laurel (*Kalmia latifolia*; Zone 4). Where summers are hot and winters relatively mild, the reverse is the case, with broadleaf evergreens an important component of the garden. Some are as colorful as flowers, and all contribute year-round shape and texture that are most appreciated when winter has stripped much else away.

Ilex aquifolium 'Myrtifolia Aureomaculata'

In my garden's early stages a knowledgeable friend told me that English holly (*Ilex aquifolium*) wasn't suited to the region. It took me many years to find out that he was wrong. Although our gardens were only 20 miles apart, his was on clay, mine on sand, and that makes all the difference. Dainty, small-leaved, yellow-variegated *I. aquifolium* 'Myrtifolia Aureomaculata' (Zone 6), a non-berrying male, is the form I'd choose if I could have only one holly. It isn't easy to find, but it is well worth the search, and only if enough gardeners ask for it will it become more plentiful. Small and slow growing, it has 2-inch leaves of brilliant green with a yellow central blaze, on the lines of 'Goldheart' ivy (*Hedera helix* 'Goldheart'). Well-drained soil, kept moderately moist, and a site out of the afternoon sun meet its moderate requirements.

Ilex vomitoria 'Pendula'

WEEPING YAUPON

Because I planted its male mate too far away, the small-leaved evergreen *Ilex vomitoria* 'Pendula' (Zone 7) has never managed more than a handful of berries, which doesn't matter a lot because this holly is grown mainly for its fine texture and narrowly weeping form. By no means new, rugged in all respects for Zone 7 and warmer, and for me pest-free for a quarter century, it remains too little applauded. Snow tends to slide off its weeping branches and for 20 years it suffered no damage and required no maintenance, attaining a 10-foot height in its poor, dry site and almost full sun. Then a week-long ice storm left it so badly damaged that it had to be cut back hard. Within a year it had regained its height and neat appearance. A bitter tea can be brewed from its leaves, but reflect on this holly's specific name before you sample this.

Ilex cornuta 'O'Spring'

CHINESE HOLLY

Ilex cornuta 'O'Spring' (Zone 7) cheers winter days not with berries but with variegated foliage. All Chinese hollies have lustrous leaves, but where those of Burford hollies are high gloss, those of 'O'Spring' have a satin finish. Patterned in gray-green and primrose yellow, they have the filmy look of a scene viewed through muslin curtains, bright enough to stand out in winter, then blending peacefully with brighter colors in the summer scene. Rounded to irregularly pyramidal in form and very dense, it takes many years to grow head high and can be kept that height, or shorter, indefinitely with an annual spring pruning. It is at its best with protection from hot afternoon sun.

Ilex crenata 'Yellow Helleri'

JAPANESE HOLLY

Japanese hollies (*Ilex crenata*; Zone 5) are the bread-and-butter of the southeastern landscape industry. They are not grown for their small black or occasionally creamy white berries, but for their fine texture, controllable size, and serviceability—qualities suiting them well to foundation plantings and as alterna-

Ilex aquifolium 'Myrtifolia Aureomaculata'

Ilex cornuta 'O'Spring'

tives to boxwood. They are structural plants in the main, but some are also colorful. *Ilex crenata* 'Yellow Helleri' is indistinguishable from green *I. crenata* 'Helleri' if grown in shade, but in sun it is a subdued chartreuse through winter, becoming much brighter in spring and then nicely matched to an underplanting of golden thyme. It is among my most valued shrubs, forming dense inverted bowls of tiny leaves, 3 feet wide in two decades. Unfortunately, the wholesale nursery that introduced it has dropped production. If 'Yellow Helleri' cannot be found, the alternative is *I. crenata* 'Golden Gem', which, though a brighter gold, needs more frequent clipping to keep it shapely.

My three specimens now need an annual trim to prevent them overgrowing the path they flank. This job takes only minutes with the electric hedge saw, and because the leaves are tiny, pruning does not leave the neat domes disfigured. With such relatively slow growing shrubs, bare earth (and the temptation to fill it with something else) can be avoided by planting a group of three shrubs initially, first positioning the one that will be there permanently then adding the other two to form a triangle. When they start to crowd each other, the two spares can be moved elsewhere.

Three bushes of *Ilex crenata* 'Yellow Helleri' with white-flowered *Hydrangea arborescens* 'Annabelle'

Aucuba japonica

I've never liked the jaundiced and spotty foliage of the ubiquitous *Aucuba japonica* 'Variegata', commonplace, I suppose, because it was the first aucuba introduced from Japan and has been passed along for more than two centuries by cuttings rooted in water, a no-fail method of propagation. It tolerates deep shade, poor dry soil, and root competition, but there are prettier forms equally able to triumph over adversity. All are hardy to Zone 7.

If a berrying display is the main object, choose *Aucuba japonica* 'Rozannie', which is to aucubas what *Ilex cornuta* 'Burfordii' is to hollies—a self-fertile plant in a genus usually dioecious. 'Rozannie' has the largest and prettiest berries, acorn shaped and at first a blend of red and yellow similar to a Fuji apple, eventually becoming scarlet. The leaves are broad and very glossy on a rounded bush that takes many years to attain a height of 4 feet. My plants self-sow in embarrassing abundance.

For brightening shade all year long, I'd choose *Aucuba japonica* 'Picturata'. Each leaf has a bold yellow central splash, though a proportion of the leaves regresses to speckling as the bush grows bigger. Being male it could serve as stud for such female selections as *A. japonica* 'Fructu-albo', a compact form with leaves blotched in green and gold and berries of pale greenish yellow, or *A. japonica* 'Salicifolia', with willowy dark green leaves.

Aucuba japonica 'Sulphurea Marginata' has leaves edged with a creamy yellow that mixes agreeably with any other color and particularly well with purple. One of my plants is growing near an evergreen azalea called 'Koromo Shikibu', with strap-petaled pale purple flowers, and underplanted with a dark purple periwinkle (*Vinca minor* 'Atropurpurea'), which in turn is interplanted with cream and yellow forms of the English celandine (*Ranunculus ficaria*).

Aucubas make long-lasting cut foliage, and chances are good that they'll root in the vase ready for potting up. My aucubas have been trouble-free when grown in shade, but I've had stem die-back and necrotic leaf spots on some plants exposed to afternoon sun. A site facing north or east suits them well, ideally in humus-rich soil, though they'll put up with anything.

I find the sex life of aucubas a bit mysterious. There are both male and female plants among the multitudinous seedlings that spring up around my 'Rozannie', as well as some with yellow-freckled leaves. 'Picturata', a male, has sported a branch heavy with berries, and 'Sulphurea Marginata', supposedly female, has been an unwilling mother despite the close

Aucuba japonica 'Picturata'

proximity of male forms. Plants do not always fit themselves into the neat categories we devise for them, so expect some surprises.

Osmanthus heterophyllus 'Goshiki'

Osmanthus heterophyllus

HOLLY-LEAVED OSMANTHUS

I have already raved about the fragrance of holly-leaved osmanthus (*Osmanthus heterophyllus*; Zone 6). Purple-leaved *O. heterophyllus* 'Purpureus' also has fragrant flowers, so I'm assured: rabbits ate my plant down to the ground its first winter and it never recovered. I just read that varmints avoid prickly plants. That writer wasn't the first to fall into the trap of surmise. It seems reasonable to assume that spiny plants would be eaten only as a last resort, but my experience has been just the opposite, so young osmanthus, hollies, and barberries get a protective ring of chicken wire for their first few years.

The merit of several osmanthus lies mainly, if not entirely, in their striking foliage. My plants have never yet flowered. *Osmanthus heterophyllus* 'Variegatus' (Zone 7) was in the garden (more appropriately described, at that time, as a yard) when we came. Having been moved twice since then, which no doubt slowed its growth, it is now about 6 feet high and loosely pyramidal. The spiny, hollylike leaves have a crisp, clean variegation that appears to be sparklingly white, but on close inspection proves to be creamy. This very pretty form, slightly less hardy than the species, seems entirely content in an open spot under a tall red cedar (*Juniperus virginiana*) that gives it some protection from intense overhead sun. Camellias, *Illicium anisatum*, and *Daphne odora* 'Alba' are its companions.

Now, how can I make you want to grow *Osmanthus heterophyllus* 'Goshiki' (warmer parts of Zone 6)? It is compact for a start, a dense mound taking several years to attain a 2-foot height. The leaves, typically spiny, are in proportion at roughly 2 inches long. The older leaves are dark green and liberally spattered with lemon yellow, while the young ones are yellow and lightly freckled with green. It may sound like a virus infection, but the overall effect is, I promise, extremely appealing.

A scarce form with all gold leaves remains on my wish list, as does *Osmanthus hetero-phyllus* 'Aureomarginatus' with yellow-edged leaves. The little *O. heterophyllus* 'Kembu', a recent addition to my garden, is described thus by Heronswood Nursery, from which it came: "An interesting and pretty, variegated cultivar with very narrow puckered leaves blotched and streaked with white, forming a dense and textural low, rounded shrub." Looks good so far.

Elaeagnus ×ebbingei 'Gilt Edge'

The tantalizing fragrance wafted towards drivers approaching Virginia's historic towns of Yorktown and Williamsburg in autumn emanates from *Elaeagnus pungens* (Zone 6) along the highway center strip. Even at touching distance the small brown-freckled white flowers are scarcely discernible, tucked as they are under the leaves, but they dispense a powerful aroma. From the olive-shaped pale orange fruits flecked with silvery scales that follow the flowers come the names autumn olive and silverberry. For years I assumed that "pungens" referred to the fragrance, when in fact it means piercing and describes the slightly thorny twigs, hence another folk name, thorny elaeagnus. Dense enough to cut dazzle from headlights, massive enough to cushion the occasional skidding car, and quick to recover from damage, this large shrub is often used as a barrier on the center strips of double highways. Vine-like in the speed of growth of its long whippy branches, wind and salt tolerant, and drought resistant, *E. pungens* makes massive thickets that provide screens and cover for birds on large properties, but it is not sufficiently decorative and needs too much pruning to merit space in most gardens. Selected forms and hybrids are another matter. In England I grew *E. pungens* 'Maculata', a large and handsome shrub with dark green yellow-splashed leaves.

Now I prefer the hybrid *Elaeagnus ×eb-bingei* 'Gilt Edge' (Zone 7), a dense, upright

Elaeagnus ×ebbingei 'Gilt Edge' with red-berried *Ilex cornuta*

evergreen shrub with large, oval, bright green leaves silvered beneath and brilliantly edged with cowslip yellow. It has the same pervasive fragrance as *E. pungens* but not the thorns. Pruning once a year, an uncomplicated task involving only the cutting off of branch wands extending beyond the desired height and width, maintains it at about 7 feet. As with all variegated shrubs, branches reverting to green must be removed: this has so far happened only once. Full sun is best, though light shade is acceptable, in any decent soil that does not get sodden. My plant is in a sunny corner devoted to shrubs that are colorful in winter: hollies for berries, and dogwoods and willows for their colored bark. The soil is an acid sand that is somewhat enriched by years of mulching. No fertilizer has been needed. Rabbits haven't bothered it so far, but I did lose one shrub when voles ate off its roots, so I try to have a spare coming along as insurance against future mishaps. Cuttings of young wood root quickly in a peat-sand mix if kept moist and humid in a propagator or covered with clear plastic.

Euonymus

Evergreens with golden or variegated foliage become prominent in winter when color from flowers is lacking. Ivy (*Hedera*) has the most variations on this theme, but the genus *Euonymus* is a close runner-up and among its numbers are some of the most attractive and versatile evergreen shrubs. *Euonymus japonicus* and *E. fortunei* are the species with most to offer. Oddly, *E. japonicus* 'Silver King', commonplace in North America, is seldom encountered in England, while *E. fortunei* 'Silver Queen', commonest of all in England, is seldom seen in North America.

Where winter lows seldom drop below 15°F *Euonymus japonicus* (Zone 7) is one of the toughest broadleaf evergreens available, and its variegated forms are among the most eye-catching. Two in particular will dominate the scene: *E. japonicus* 'Ovatus Aureus' and *E. japonicus* 'Silver King'. Both are chunky bushes with oval leaves margined respectively in yellow and white. I'm more drawn to the less ostentatious, tiny-leaved *E. japonicus* 'Microphyllus', so like boxwood that many southeastern gardeners think that's what they are growing, and especially to *E. japonicus* 'Microphyllus Variegatus', a dwarf rounded bush with each little leaf neatly edged in white. It is marginally hardy in Zone 7, and it constantly throws green reversions, so when I lost the gamble to winter I seized upon *E. japonicus* 'Silver Princess' as an alternative. Introduced by Monrovia Nursery of Azusa, California, in 1994 and given a Zone 6 rating, it is almost as dainty but more vigorous and robust, slowly becoming a 3-foot rounded bush with narrowly spatulate, inch-long, dark green glossy leaves brightly edged in white on slender upright stems. It is a neat little shrub for brightening a shady courtyard garden or woodland walk and very undemanding. The latest addition to my euonymus stable, *E. japonicus* 'Microphyllus Pulchellus' (more likely to be sold as 'Microphyllus Aureus' or 'Butterscotch'), is a chipper little bushlet of manicured appearance, with shiny, toothed leaflets, bright green edged with yellow, arranged in a spiral around stiffly upright stems. Now in its third year, it has grown more rapidly than *E. japonicus* 'Microphyllus Variegatus'.

Euonymus fortunei (Zone 5) is hardier than *E. japonicus*, equally heat tolerant, and more versatile. This species has an ivylike ability to climb, but can also be grown as a free-standing bush. Its many forms vary in size and habit from the tall, bushy, large-leaved, free-fruiting *E. fortunei* 'Vegetus' to the tiny-leaved, green carpeting or climbing *E. fortunei* 'Kewensis' and *E. fortunei* 'Harlequin', with leaves blotched and bordered with white. On nonlingering, finger-tingling days, star status goes to *E. fortunei* 'Emerald Gaiety' which, with a little urging, will bend itself to the gardener's whim, as bush, ground cover, or self-clinging vine. Two of my plants, one on either side, mark the entrance to a pathway off the drive. Maintaining them as mounded bushes requires only the occasional removal of branches heading for the sky and removal of layered side branches that spoil the rounded outline. The patterning of the inch-long oval leaves with finely toothed or scalloped edges resembles that of many ivies and consists of a central patch of green and gray, often lobed in shape, on a background that is creamy in young leaves, white on older ones, and touched with pink in winter time. With its smaller leaves and less rigid form, 'Emerald Gaiety', while still prominent in the landscape, has more charm and grace than the chunky *E. japonicus* 'Silver King'.

With my runner-up, *Euonymus fortunei* 'Sparkle 'n' Gold', there's never a dull moment from leaves edged with brilliant chartreuse-yellow becoming touched with orange in winter time. It is allowed to layer itself and clipped once or twice a year to keep it no more than 1 foot high. 'Sparkle 'n' Gold' is one of the evergreen gold-foliaged plants spaced along the front of my hot color border for continuity. *Euonymus fortunei* 'Emerald 'n' Gold' is similar but lacks the orange winter tints. My third choice in this species is *E. fortunei* 'Moonshadow', a pretty name for a pretty selection

Euonymus japonicus 'Silver Princess'

softly colored in primrose yellow on green, with a rambling habit suiting it for ground cover use.

Propagation is a nursery owner's dream, or maybe not given that all but the purple-thumbed cut into nursery sales by rooting euonymus and passing it on. Cut off 6-inch-long pieces, remove the lower leaves, insert them in a mixture of peat and sand, cover the pot with a plastic bag if the weather is hot and dry, stand it in a shady place, say, "Hey, presto!" and you have more plants. All right, I exaggerate, but not by much. If you are after quick results the whole potful can be planted as a single clump.

Perfect shrubs? Not quite. Euonymus scale can scurf the stems and kill the plants if protective measures are not taken. Once a year, in late winter or early spring, all the euonymus in my garden are sprayed with dormant oil. With a well-designed sprayer this job doesn't take long, but with a poor one it is a lengthy and frustrating chore. The quality of my sprayer, a plastic 2-gallon pump type of French manufacture, makes it a pleasure to use, but many others have found their way into the garbage can. The challenge with dormant oil is guessing when to use it, days being few and far between when conditions are ideal, namely, no wind, no tender young growth, and no rain, frost, or high temperature present or impending. One has to seize the moment.

Yucca

My parents taught that if anyone sought to please—with a meal, a compliment, or whatever—one had a duty to BE pleased, or at least to put up a good pretense, early training that perhaps exacerbates my disgruntlement with plants that don't respond to my overtures. In England heathers headed my list of favorites, but in Virginia they aren't even on it. One can go off plants if their behavior repeatedly disappoints. The other side of that coin is affection for plants that are easily pleased, always provided they don't travel at such speed that one must be forever reining them in.

Several yuccas measure up, gaining high marks for combining long-lasting good looks with minimal demands for maintenance. Come heat, drought, or cold, they have flourished, in sun or light shade, good soil or poor, sand, clay, and purchased "top soil" that set like concrete, tested high for salt content, and looked suspiciously like mud dredged from the creek. Heavy rain doesn't bother them provided it drains away fairly quickly. One clump did rot out when a nearby soaker hose was left running for several days during a summer drought. A snag with soaker hoses is that the soil immediately alongside becomes saturated before moisture has percolated out to plants 1 foot away. Yuccas, which manage nicely with what the heavens send, should be planted 1 foot away from soaker hoses, which is easier said than done. In 20 years that's been the only mishap.

Cutting off flower stalks, removing offsets that detract from the symmetry of the clumps, and cutting off dead basal leaves in early spring have been the only attentions needed until recently. Then there arrived the yucca bug, a small brown insect that sucks and saps the leaves, leaving them yellow-speckled and drained of vitality. Like invading armies, these insects come in hordes and are highly visible as they scuttle over the leaves, which is their

undoing: one good dowsing with whatever killing chemical is currently permitted usually suffices to exterminate them, though they'll probably be back the following year. Frequent drenchings with miscible oil is an alternative control.

Yucca flowers, waxy white and lilylike in conical clusters atop stiff, woody stalks, contribute spirelike elegance to beds and borders, but the flowers are secondary to form, and yuccas hidden behind other plants are a wasted asset. Yuccas such as Joshua tree (*Yucca brevifolia*) and Adam's needle (*Y. gloriosa*) become small trees and look most at home in desertlike surroundings (both Zone 5). Those I grow sit trunkless and V-shaped on the soil, a firm, neat outline that adds structure to softer plantings. They can anchor the corners of beds and punctuate borders, and triangles of three bring permanence to their patch of ground while seasonal plants (early crocuses, perhaps, followed by annual portulaca, then such late crocuses as *Crocus goulimyi*) come and go around them. Many evergreen shrubs, especially conifers, are permanently damaged if other plants are allowed to sprawl over them, but yuccas suffer no long-term harm.

Filaments along the margins of the graygreen, broadly swordlike leaves of *Yucca filamentosa* (Zone 5) glisten in the sun, especially when backlit. Though the leaf blades of other yuccas may be showier in color, none has filaments as long and curly. The broad stripes on the leaves of *Y. filamentosa* 'Variegata' (synonym 'Sunburst') start off creamy and become white, sometimes pink-tinged following a freeze. It is the best yucca for pink and blue color schemes, while yellow-striped yuccas excel in hot color plantings of orange, scarlet, and sunny yellow. The finest in this category is *Y.* 'Color Guard', with a gold center that takes on orange tints in winter. The yellow stripes of *Y.* 'Golden Sword' do not take on this warm tint. Both of these yuccas have broad, slightly lax leaves. *Yucca* 'Bright Edge' has narrower, more stiffly upright leaves edged with bright yellow. These three have been shunted back and forth from one species to another, so until they come to rest I'm dodging the issue.

The needlelike tips of yucca leaves look fierce, and they can be. The leaves of *Yucca glauca* (Zone 4), for example, are rapier stiff and sharply pointed. Weed close to this plant and some bloodletting is likely to ensue. The chubbier leaves of *Y. filamentosa* 'Variegata' also remind me to keep my mind on the job with an occasional jab. If you don't think yuccas worth the shedding of blood (which may depend on whether it's your blood or some-

×*Fatshedera lizei* 'Annemieke'

one else's), opt for 'Color Guard' or 'Golden Sword', which are less likely to wound.

×*Fatshedera lizei*

This hybrid between a shrub (*Fatsia*) and a vine (*Hedera*, or ivy) makes a garden talking point. Known to English estate gardeners as fatheaded lizzy, it lacks an American common name. Within its hardiness limits it is an at-

tractive, tough, accommodating, and versatile evergreen. In leaf and flower ×*Fatshedera lizei* (Zone 7) is a scaled-down version of fatsia, while from ivy it got lankiness but no ability to cling. Adapted to sun or shade, including dry shade, and to most soils, it can be fastened to a wall or fence to head height or more, or kept cut back as a medium-sized shrub. Winter-scorched plants recover quickly if cut back hard.

Ligustrum sinense 'Variegatum' with *Hedera hibernica* 'Deltoidea' on siding and *H. helix* 'Glacier' in container

I grow three variegated forms. "Try to grow" would be more truthful with ×*Fatshedera lizei* 'Variegata', which has leaves broadly edged in white. It is considerably less hardy than the others and I can barely keep it alive. The other two have long been reliably hardy. ×*Fatshedera lizei* 'Pia Variegata' is much smaller than the species, with undulating leaves narrowly edged with white. It makes an at- tractive ground cover for a shady bank. ×*Fatshedera lizei* 'Annemieke' (synonyms 'Lemon and Lime', 'Maculata') is more flamboyant, brightest in spring and summer but a colorful asset in winter as well. The leathery, slightly wavy leaves look as if Clorox has been poured along the central veins, fading them and their tributaries to cream and seeping out to bleach random portions of the dark green leaf to lime.

These variegated forms tolerate full sun but do best in sites with afternoon shade.

Ligustrum sinense 'Variegatum'

CHINESE PRIVET, JAPANESE PRIVET

Privets have long been gardening's whipping boy and recommending any of them is likely to draw flak. W. J. Bean (*Trees and Shrubs Hardy in the British Isles*) considered *Ligustrum sinense* the best of the deciduous privets, but read on and there's a warning note when he added, "It is now naturalized in parts of Australia and of the U.S.A." Local guidance should be sought, for whether a plant is inva- sive depends on where you live and, to some degree, on where you put it. If every plant in- vasive anywhere is to be forbidden, our gar- dens will be the poorer and our lives more ha- rassed. I am constantly pulling out seedlings of *L. japonicum* but have yet to find one of *L. sinense*.

Ligustrum sinense 'Variegatum' (Zone 7), the daintiest variegated privet, lightens a sun- less courtyard corner. It is in a narrow bed be- tween house and paving, partly under the eaves and therefore pruned every other year to restrict its height to about 8 feet. Its haze of small gray-green leaves edged in creamy white, on slender, graceful stems fanned into mesmeric movement by the slightest breeze, is a daily source of pleasure from inside or out-side the house all year long but especially in winter. In this shady corner it does not flower and fruit, and its roots cannot compete with other plants for moisture. In sun it bears a pro-fusion of sprays of creamy flowers, fragrant if you like the smell of privet, smelly if you don't. It roots very quickly from cuttings, and sev-eral cuttings in a container soon make an at-tractive small bush for plunging into tempo-rary gaps in flower beds. A friend has planted one on either side of a wide path and pruned them to form an archway.

Agarista populifolia

FLORIDA LEUCOTHOË

Surprisingly, for a Florida native, *Agarista populifolia* (synonym *Leucothoë populifolia*) was one of only two broadleaf evergreens (the other was *Viburnum ×pragense*) in my garden to come unscathed through two consecutive winters cold enough to wipe out *Pittosporum tobira*, most *Raphiolepis*, a variegated *Vibur-num tinus*, many camellias, and much of the *Ligustrum japonicum* ubiquitous in my re-gion. It has now been in perfect health for more than two decades. What I didn't know when I planted that 6-inch baby evergreen was that its speed of growth would rival that of Leyland cypress.

Agarista populifolia

Agarista populifolia (Zone 7) is a back-ground shrub or small tree for a spot where it gets shade during the hottest hours of the day and the soil doesn't get bone dry. Multi-stemmed, with loosely arching branches, it can easily become 10 feet high and as wide in a few years. It can be hard pruned, but several strong shoots spring from any pruning cut and put on 4 feet of growth in a year, so one is soon back where one began. Fortunately, its mildly suckering habit provides a ready source of plants for relocation, so all is not lost if you put it in the wrong place.

Specific name notwithstanding, Florida leu-cothoë looks more like an evergreen weeping willow than a poplar. It looks even more like what it long was called, a leucothoë. Glossy elfin-ear leaflets are laddered along lax

Hedera colchica 'Dentata Variegata'

branches that are green in their first year, then oxblood red. Racemes of small, white, delicately scented tubular flowers dangle from the leaf axils in spring.

Hedera

IVY

In my ivy-collecting heyday I had well over a hundred kinds, and several overgrown neighborhood yards testify to my generosity in sharing them! I did caution about putting ivy on house walls, but I make two exceptions myself. *Hedera hibernica* 'Deltoidea', which used to be considered an English ivy (*H. helix*) but is now considered an Irish ivy (a change of some significance in that Irish ivy is considerably less hardy than English ivy), has been growing for 20 years in a northwest corner where the red brick house meets the wood siding of the garage. Slow growing and dense, it is free of the characteristics that caused me to discard most of those ivies I once grew: rampant growth and the tendency to revert from named form to common ivy. It took many years to climb the 8 feet to the roof overhang, and half an hour twice a year spent removing tip growth suffices to keep it under control. Young plants of 'Deltoidea' have heart-shaped leaves and are often called sweetheart ivy. Mature leaves assume the shape of an heraldic shield, and the plant is then called shield ivy. The confusion is aggravated by the change of species name, so watch that you don't buy the same plant twice.

Persian ivy (*Hedera colchica*; Zone 7), on the east-facing brick wall of the house, grows relatively slowly and adheres less firmly than most ivies, making it easier to remove unwanted strands. The leathery, dark green, heart-shaped leaves can measure 6 inches or more across. The leaves of *H. colchica* 'Dentata Variegata' are prettily appliquéd with a maple-leaf shape in gray and dark green on a creamy yellow background. I had hoped this ivy would brighten a shady wall under a wide roof overhang, but it grew out towards the light and refused to take hold. Most ivies make good container plants, and this one now covers the surface and drapes the sides of a tall, round courtyard tub that houses *Salix caprea* 'Weeping Sally', a pendulous willow adorned with silvery catkins in early spring. *Hedera helix* 'Glacier' (Zone 6), its triangular leaf patterned in cloudy green and pewter, spills from another container. Ivies along with the dainty variegated privet, *Ligustrum sinense* 'Variegatum', the obstreperous greater periwinkle, *Vinca major* 'Variegata', evergreen azaleas, and a ground cover of *Ophiopogon japonicus* around a large oak tree keep the courtyard clothed through winter with minimal maintenance.

To my surprise many ivies have preferred sun to shade, even in my region's hot climate, including the one that takes center stage in winter, a form of Persian ivy, *Hedera colchica* 'Sulphur Heart' or 'Paddy's Pride' (Zone 7). My plant is highly visible, climbing the tall trunk of a pine near the house, where I see it every time I go up or down the drive on foot or in the car. The leaves are similar in size and shape to those of *H. colchica* 'Dentata Variegata' but more wavy and pointed and with reversed patterning: bright yellow in the middle, merging into light green, then darker green. Young leaves have the biggest proportion of gold, while on old ones the creamy yellow veining is pronounced against a green that becomes almost black around the edges of the leaf. The plant is vigorous when established but a bit slow getting started.

My other ivies are all forms of English ivy (*Hedera helix*; Zone 6 as evergreens), but that's about all they have in common so greatly do they vary in color, shape, size, and habit. One of the endearing traits of ivies is the lopsidedness of the leaf, which is seldom entirely symmetrical or in direct line with its petiole.

An unattractive feature of many neighborhoods, including mine, is electric, telephone, and cable television wires strung along streets and garden boundaries. One cannot do much about the overhead wires, but their accompanying poles can be put to use. I grow annual vines on pole stays, and 'Goldheart' ivy has finally taken hold on a pole erected some 30 years ago and now sufficiently free of creosote that the ivy tolerates it. This ivy, with a bold bright yellow flash on the dark green leaves, is deservedly popular, but it does have a regrettable tendency to produce strands of all-green leaves. Growing it in a conspicuous place makes it more likely that such strands will be spotted and removed before they take over. 'Goldheart' does not branch sufficiently to be a good ground cover ivy.

Although ivy is not parasitic and does no harm on the trunks, it can smother the canopy of a tree. *Hedera helix* 'Glacier' has done this on what used to be a pine but is now an ivy pillar, 20 feet high and 6 feet across, of arborescent flowering form in its upper reaches. Soon it must be cut down, before the roots of the dead pine rot and snow, wind, or heavy rain topple it. The ivy has a successor, cascading down from a decapitated red cedar. This second ivy gets afternoon sun from the west, while *H. helix* 'Bruder Ingobert', streaked and dappled with white, climbs a sunless trunk and spreads in a pool around its base.

Hedera colchica 'Sulphur Heart'

I would not put any ivy on a small ornamental tree, but I have two others growing on old pines with 20-foot branchless trunks. *Hedera helix* 'Harald', with small, shallowly lobed leaves patterned in cream, gray, and green grows on a tree in full sun. Every few years, when it gets near the canopy, it is cut through at about 10 feet. Everything above that then dies, browns, and looks messy, but one seldom looks up beyond head height to see it. *Hedera helix* 'Spetchley' (synonym 'Gnome') has triangular, slightly wavy leaves no bigger than a fingernail when young. They get bigger on old

and boulders." It survives but doesn't prosper at this extreme where summers are so hot that an egg could be baked on paving, but given some relief from afternoon sun and soil that doesn't become completely dry, it is very tolerant and among the best evergreens. For those who garden under pines the "rake-ability" of its slender leathery leaves is a big asset.

When one finds an easy-care plant that looks good for all or most of the year, it makes sense to use more of it. Sweet flag is so easy to propagate that doing so is quick and inexpensive. Well-rooted outer fans can be pulled off with the fingers, or the whole clump lifted and divided. Landscapers make bigger drifts, while plant collectors seek out other forms. I did both. *Acorus gramineus* 'Variegatus', white striped and 15 inches high, is used as a continuity plant on both sides of a mulch path. The clumps are spaced about 6 feet apart. For several years *Oenanthe javanica* 'Flamingo', a low-growing plant with divided leaves marbled in green, pink, and white, mingled prettily with one clump, but it is stoloniferous, with invasively rapid spread once settled in, and has now been evicted—I hope. For the continuity planting large clumps were divided into smaller ones of more or less even size. Then, needing a few more plants, I assembled additional clumps from a pile of leftover pieces,

gathered into higgledy-piggledy bunches, a sloppy piece of work for which I was later punished by the ragged, uneven look of fans growing haphazardly. Sweet flag grows from slender rhizomes, with a fan of foliage at the tip, and when several rhizomes are planted together, fans that face each other have no place to go. They sort themselves out in due course, as the strong kill off the weak. Meantime they shamed me.

Clumps widen so fast that nowadays I close my mind to the waste-not-want-not dictum of childhood and throw quantities away. Giving plants away is one of gardening's pleasures, but some restraint is needed: potting up all the spares from a mature garden consumes a lot of time, pots, and compost, and then the pots take up space and must be kept watered until adopters come along. Common sense dictates that surplus sometimes be discarded unless there are actually friends-in-waiting. Garden centers may call me blessed for not, in this instance, diminishing their customer base.

The dense arching clumps of *Acorus gramineus* 'Ogon', the yellow-striped counterpart of 'Variegata', are among the showiest plants in the winter garden. They are a splendid foil for the purple foliage of *Ranunculus ficaria* 'Brazen Hussy' and, later, the perfect companion for golden hostas. The cheerful summer

presence of 'Ogon' compensates for the absence of *Hakonechloa macra* 'Aureola', perhaps the most exquisite of all grasses, but one with which I have failed, failed, and failed again.

Everyone who sees it wants a bit of *Acorus gramineus* 'Minimus Aureus' and usually gets it right then and there because the miniature tuffets of chartreuse leaves scarcely 3 inches high increase fourfold each year if the soil is moist, and small fans are easily wiggled off with the fingers. This sweet flag I've used as an underplanting for *Lonicera nitida* 'Baggesen's Gold' (Zone 7), a bushy honeysuckle of matching color but contrasting texture that grows in full sun where summers are cool, but prefers light shade in hot regions. The diminutive sweet flag needs little maintenance, but because it is so tiny, with roots to match, it is a kindness to give it water during periods of drought. If there haven't been enough giveaways to do the job, I thin the plant every other year. It makes an attractive alternative to golden Scotch moss (*Sagina subulata* 'Aurea'), or golden creeping Charlie (*Lysimachia nummularia* 'Aurea') as small-scale ground cover for moist and shady places.

One learns not only from one's own mistakes but also from those of others. The maintenance crew in a garden I was visiting had mistaken sweet flag for liriope and shaved off all the foliage in early spring. When I saw the plants in midsummer they were picture perfect, while back at home my plants hadn't fully recovered from the scorching wrought by an unusually cold winter. Routine late winter shearing isn't essential, but it does rejuvenate plants in less than pristine condition. Rabbits, which often do the shearing of the liriope, have not as yet touched the sweet flags.

CONIFERS
×*Cupressocyparis leylandii*
LEYLAND CYPRESS

Many years ago this transplanted English gardener put in an experimental group of Leyland cypresses (×*Cupressocyparis leylandii*; Zone 6) in front of red cedars (*Juniperus virginiana*) in a corner of my 2-acre lot. Leylands hadn't then incurred the widespread disapprobation of England's gardening press. Virginia wasn't England anyway, and Leylands hadn't been tried here. Furthermore, there was plenty of room in my garden, and a Leyland sold here, ×*Cupressocyparis leylandii* 'Silver Dust', was new to me and very pretty. A goldthread cypress (*Chamaecyparis pisifera* 'Filifera Aurea') joined my Leylands for no better reason than that a bare patch of earth stood waiting to be filled when it was given to me. The Leylands went when I wearied of watching them turned into a bagworm bed and breakfast. While one cannot but marvel at the way bagworms protect themselves from predators by going about their business encased in the needles of their host, a conifer festooned with these hanging cone-shaped structures is not a pretty sight, still less one stripped to a skeleton.

Two Leyland cypresses are back, 'Silver Dust' and 'Golconda', a recent introduction with bright yellow foliage, supposedly a dwarf, with pruning into conformity in store for it should it prove otherwise. Both are well away from the bagworm-harboring red cedars (*Juniperus virginiana*) from which this pest migrated to the Leylands planted earlier, but there's been an interesting development. For years the junipers formed a screen down one side of the property, their branches dense to the ground. As they progressed toward becoming trees, the lower branches died and they were then limbed up to 7 feet and subsequently to 10. And now, no bagworm. Coincidence, or do the moths not fly high? Whatever the reason, I am grateful.

Chamaecyparis pisifera '**Filifera Aurea**'
GOLDTHREAD CYPRESS

The goldthread cypress (*Chamaecyparis pisifera* 'Filifera Aurea'; Zone 5), apparently not to the bagworms' taste, continued in its original spot until a year ago, untouched by pests all those years and one of my top ten for year-round, maintenance-free good looks. Shapely without being stiff, its conical shape and threadlike foliage help it shed snow and ice when other trees and shrubs are being flattened or emitting ominous creaking sounds under the strain. The largest splash of yellow in the winter garden, it got enough sun year-round, mostly from south and east, to retain its bright color, much of which would be lost in shade.

In summer the goldthread cypress played a subordinate but no less important role anchoring one end of a hot color border. The marginally hardy gloriosa lily (*Gloriosa rothschildiana*), with roots under the goldthread's protective skirts, climbed 5 feet into it, clinging by tendril-like leaf tips. Yellow striations in the leaves of *Canna* 'Pretoria' picked up the color and line of the conifer's stringlike foliage, while the size and form of the leaves was in marked contrast. The canna's orange flowers played well against the gold and kept coming all through the season.

A succession of other plants come and go in that border in a changing panorama: scarlet-and-yellow columbines, lily-flowered 'Queen of Sheba' tulips, yellow irises, orange butterfly

Chamaecyparis pisifera 'Filifera Aurea' (goldthread cypress), ice coated

winter, a protracted and neck-aching job done with a pole and rope pruner. Too little, too late. A quarter century is a good life for a conifer in this fast-growing climate. I thanked it and bid it goodbye. I miss its cheerful presence while waiting for its successor to grow.

Chamaecyparis obtusa 'Crippsii'

A question that gauges the worth of a plant is this: "If it died, would you plant another?" With the goldthread cypress my answer was "Yes." I did just that, though for a little while it was touch and go, because all these years I've hankered to have an old love under my eye again, *Chamaecyparis obtusa* 'Crippsii' (Zone 5), a golden cypress of similar shape and size but with foliage in fans instead of threads. This popular pyramidal shrub was the first conifer I ever planted in my English garden 40 years ago. Growth is slower in England, and there my conifer has remained through three tenancies and four ownerships, getting little if any care and still as handsome as ever. I have it again now, in another part of my Virginia garden, where it is proving every bit as lovely and trouble-free as it was in England, but much faster growing. I now nibble at this and the goldthread cypress with scissors at frequent intervals to keep them youthful longer.

weed, yellow rudbeckia, orange-and-yellow *Lantana camara* 'Miss Huff', feathery scarlet-flowered *Ipomopsis rubra*, and the red-flowered, purple-leaved *Dahlia* 'Bishop of Llandaff'. In winter the goldthread cypress was accompanied by the chartreuse foliage of *Euonymus* 'Emerald 'n' Gold' now touched with orange, the red berries of nandina, and

the cardinal red branches of *Cornus sanguinea* 'Winter Flame'. All these plants benefited from the color and stability of the 10-foot golden pyramid the conifer became. But, after 20 years of carefree existence, it became a bit threadbare, with its trunk visible through the thinning foliage. In attempting to rejuvenate it, it was given a light trim each year in late

Chamaecyparis pisifera 'Boulevard'

Another false-cypress just replaced is the feathery blue-gray *Chamaecyparis pisifera* 'Boulevard' (Zone 4), for there is none lovelier. The first one grew a foot a year and after 10 years became too big for its ill-chosen spot. I can do better by it now, in placement and in pruning. Prune, prune, prune—little and often —is a lesson I've been slow to learn, but one that is a necessity where heat and rain result in junglelike speed of growth.

Thuja occidentalis 'Smaragd'

This densely conical arborvitae, now in its fifth year, came with outstanding credentials and is living up to them, having so far received no maintenance whatever. Though sentinel stiff, *Thuja occidentalis* 'Smaragd' (Zone 4; synonym 'Emerald') does not look out of place in informal surroundings. It faces into baking western sun without protest, and its crowded fans of foliage remain bright green summer and winter alike.

Thujopsis dolobrata 'Nana'

FALSE ARBORVITAE

False arborvitae (*Thujopsis dolobrata* 'Nana'; Zone 6) is of altogether softer mien than *Thuja occidentalis* 'Smaragd'. The friend who gave me cuttings said she had grown it for many years and it had been self-sufficient. My experience echoes hers through two more decades, the only damage being foliage scorch during winters of exceptional severity; refurbishment was rapid when dead sprays were cut off. When in full sun the foliage took on a tarnished look, I decided to move my two bushes and did so with no setbacks. Both are now in east-facing beds, with bright light but little direct sun, where they've formed lacy flattened mounds 3 feet high and 5 feet wide. This size is suited to foundation plantings, which makes it the more surprising that false arborvitae should be so uncommon. Perhaps that is in its best interest. Heaven forbid that it should be sheared into balls and boxes!

Suspecting the potted plants in restaurants and airport lounges of being artificial, I often give them a surreptitious squeeze. Presented with a cut spray of false arborvitae, lying as flat as a lace doily, I might guess plastic, so leathery does it look and feel. H. J. Welch, in *Dwarf Conifers*, published in 1966, likens it to arborvitae (*Thuja*) foliage put through a mangle, "becoming thereby squashed out very thin and much wider." He found it indestructibly hardy in England. But between us, we've made it sound stiff and formal, when in fact the much divided foliage fans have frondlike grace. The surface of the leaves is glossy green, and only when a breeze riffles the leaves does one see the silvery underside. This conifer makes a good companion for evergreen azaleas.

Finale: Transition to Spring

Forsythia

When dandelions begin to brighten roadside verges at the tail end of winter, forsythias start to open their flowers of matching yellow, epitomized by *Forsythia ×intermedia* 'Spectabilis' (Zone 4), an indisputably first-rate shrub except where bitter winters destroy the flower buds. Does a touch of snobbishness creep in that I nix this selection and grow instead the primrose yellow *Forsythia* 'Winterthur'? The latter certainly combines more agreeably with the pink camellia bloom so plentiful at this time of year.

There are two other forsythias in the part of my garden reserved for hot colors. *Forsythia* 'Fiesta' (Zone 5) is grown mainly for its gold-variegated foliage but also contributes a generous quantity of early bloom. It manages, like most of its clan, to elbow itself some space in a crowded corner, interweaving its supple branches with those of a neighboring kerria. *Forsythia ×intermedia* 'Gold Leaf' (Zone 4) is grown solely for its bright yellow foliage. Marrying winter to spring, these two forsythias, with *Euonymus fortunei* 'Sparkle 'n' Gold' and the Japanese azalea *Rhododendron* 'Girard's Hot Shot', are key components in a gorgeously vulgar combination of hot colors that will shortly follow

An end, and a beginning. It is spring again.

LEFT *Forsythia* 'Fiesta', at center, starts to bloom at the divide of winter and spring, with *F. ×intermedia* 'Gold Leaf' just starting to leaf out at left, first flowers of *Kerria japonica* 'Pleniflora' at right, and white *Arabis procurrens* on ground

SOURCE LIST

In assembling the following necessarily limited list of mail-order nurseries the aim was to include at least one source for every plant mentioned. There are, of course, hundreds of other excellent nurseries, and with shipping now so costly it is sensible to buy from local nurseries when they have what you seek. Pacific Coast gardeners can pinpoint some sources in *The Pacific Northwest Plant Locator* by Susan Hill and Susan Narizny, and Barbara Barton's *Gardening by Mail* should be on every gardener's bookshelves. Most of the plants mentioned are available in Britain and can be located in the *RHS Plant Finder*. Many nurseries make a charge to help cover the cost of their catalog. Please inquire.

Arbor Village, 15604 County Road "CC," P.O. Box 227, Holt, Missouri 64048

Asiatica, P.O. Box 270, Lewisberry, Pennsylvania 17339 (Asarums and other rare Asian plants)

Avant Gardens, 710 High Hill Road, North Dartmouth, Massachusetts 02747

Benner's Gardens, P.O. Box 875, Bala Cynwyd, Pennsylvania 19004 (Plastic mesh deer fencing)

Blue Meadow Farm, 184 Meadow Road, Montague Center, Massachusetts 01351

Kurt Bluemel, 2740 Greene Lane, Baldwin, Maryland 21013 (Grasses specialist)

Brent and Becky's Bulbs, 7463 Heath Trail, Gloucester, Virginia 23061

F. W. Byles, P.O. Box 7705, Olympia, Washington 98507 (Japanese maples)

George C. Bush, 1739 Memory Lane Extended, York, Pennsylvania 17402 (Irises)

Camellia Forest Nursery, 125 Carolina Forest Road, Chapel Hill, North Carolina 27516

Clematis Specialty Nursery, 217 Argilla Road, Ipswich, Massachusetts 01938

Coastal Gardens, 4611 Socastee Boulevard, Myrtle Beach, South Carolina 29575

Eco Gardens, P.O. Box 1227, Decatur, Georgia 30031

Eastern Plant Specialties, P.O. Box 226, Georgetown, Maine 04548

Evergreen Nursery, 1220 Dowdy Road, Athens, Georgia 30606 (Liriope and ophiopogon)

Fairweather Gardens, P.O. Box 330, Greenwich, New Jersey 08323

Fancy Fronds, P.O. Box 1090, Gold Bar, Washington 98251 (Ferns)

Forestfarm Nursery, 990 Tetherow Road, Williams, Oregon 97544

The Fragrant Path, P.O. Box 328, Fort Calhoun, Nebraska 68023 (Seeds of fragrant, rare, and old-fashioned plants)

Garden Vision, 63 Williamsville Road, Hubbardston, Massachusetts 01452 (*Epimedium* specialist)

Geraniaceae, Robin Parer, 122 Hillcrest Avenue, Kentfield, California 94904 (Geranium specialist)

Girard Nurseries, P.O. Box 428, Geneva, Ohio 44041

Glasshouse Works, P.O. Box 97, Church Street, Stewart, Ohio 45778

Goodness Grows, P.O. Box 311, Highway 77 North, Lexington, Georgia 30648

Gossler Farms Nursery, 1200 Weaver Road, Springfield, Oregon 97478

Greer Gardens,1280 Goodpasture Island Road, Eugene, Oregon 97401

Hansen Nursery, P.O. Box 1228, North Bend, Oregon 97459 (Cyclamen specialist)

Heronswood Nursery, 7530 N.E. 288th Street, Kingston, Washington 98346

Iris City Gardens, 502 Brighton Place, Nashville, Tennessee 37205 (Irises)

Joy Creek Nursery, 20300 N.W. Watson Road, Scappoose, Oregon 97056

Klehm Nursery, 4210 North Duncan Road, Champaign, Illinois 61821

A. M. Leonard, 241 Fox Drive, P.O. Box 816, Piqua, Ohio 45356 (Garden supplies)

Louisiana Nursery, 5853 Highway 182, Opelousas, Louisiana 70570

McClure & Zimmerman, 108 W. Winnebago Street, P.O. Box 368, Friesland, Wisconsin 53935 (Bulbs)

Niche Gardens, 1111 Dawson Road, Chapel Hill, North Carolina 27516

Nuccio's Nurseries, P.O. Box 6160, 3555 Chaney Trail, Altadena, California 91003 (Camellias)

Old House Gardens, 536 Third Street, Ann Arbor, Michigan 48103 (Antique bulbs)

Park Seed, 1 Parkton Avenue, Greenwood, South Carolina 29647

Pine Knot Farms, Rt. 1, Box 146A, Clarkesville, Virginia 23927 (Hellebores)

Plant Delights Nursery, 9241 Sauls Road, Raleigh, North Carolina 27603

The Primrose Path, R.D. 2, Box 110, Scottdale, Pennsylvania 15683

Reflective Gardens Nursery, 24329 NE Snow Hill Lane, Poulsboro, Washington 98370

Robin's Nest, 7802 NE 63rd Street, Vancouver, Washington 98662

Singing Springs Nursery, 8802 Wilkerson Road, Cedar Grove, North Carolina 27231

Siskiyou Rare Plant Nursery, 2825 Cummings Road, Medford, Oregon 97501 (Alpine and dwarf plants)

Southern Perennials and Herbs, 98 Bridges Road, Tylertown, Mississippi 39667

Trennoll Nursery, 3 West Page Avenue, P.O. Box 125, Trenton, Ohio 45067

Twombly Nursery, 163 Barn Hill Road, Monroe, Connecticut 06468

Viette Farm & Nursery, P.O. Box 1109, State Route 608, Fishersville, Virginia 22939 (Perennials)

Wayside Gardens, P.O. Box 1, Hodges, South Carolina 29695

We-Du Nurseries, Route 5, Box 724, Marion, North Carolina 28752

Wilkerson Mill Gardens, 9595 Wilkerson Mill Road, Palmetto, Georgia 30268

Windrose, 1093 Mill Road, Pen Argyl, Pennsylvania 18072

Woodlanders Nursery, 1128 Colleton Avenue, Aiken, South Carolina 29801

Woodside Nursery, 327 Beebe Run Road, Bridgeton, New Jersey 08302 (Daylily specialist)

Yucca Do Nursery, P.O. Box 104, Hempstead, Texas 77445 (*Zephyranthes*)

HARDINESS ZONE MAPS

AVERAGE ANNUAL MINIMUM TEMPERATURE

Temperature (°C)	Zone	Temperature (°F)
-45.6 and Below	1	Below -50
-45.5 to -40.0	2	-50 to -40
-40.0 to -34.5	3	-40 to -30
-34.4 to -28.9	4	-30 to -20
-28.8 to -23.4	5	-20 to -10
-23.3 to -17.8	6	-10 to 0
-17.7 to -12.3	7	0 to 10
-12.2 to -6.7	8	10 to 20
-6.6 to -1.2	9	20 to 30
-1.1 to 4.4	10	30 to 40
4.5 and Above	11	40 and Above

0   200   400 km

design: D. Schreiber
courtesy of Verlag Eugen Ulmer

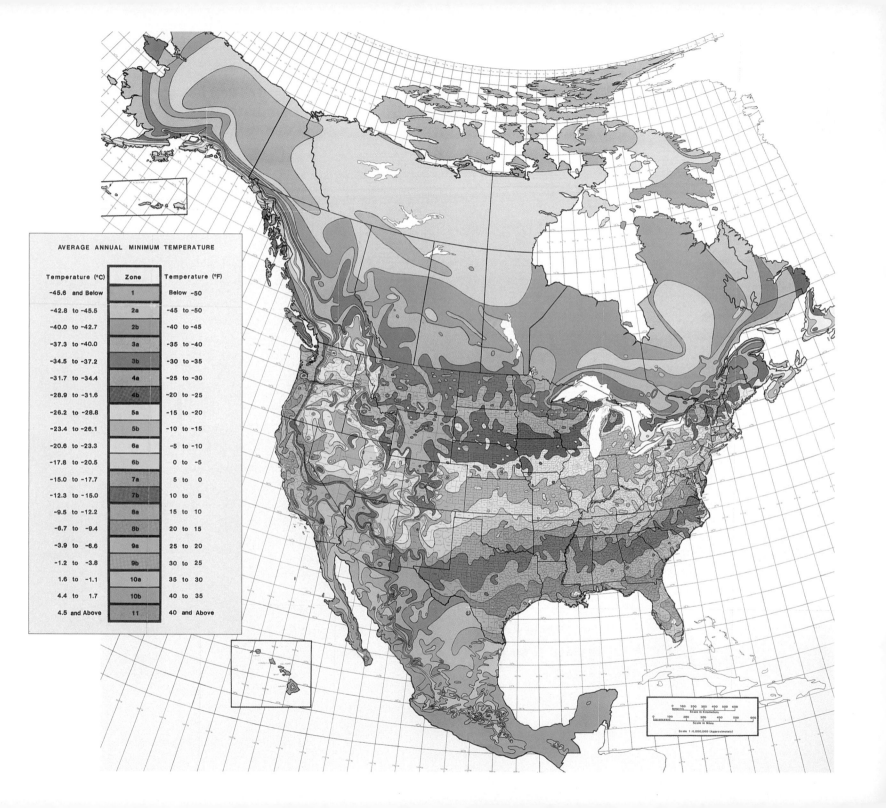

AVERAGE ANNUAL MINIMUM TEMPERATURE

Temperature (°C)	Zone	Temperature (°F)
-45.6 and Below	1	Below -50
-42.8 to -45.5	2a	-45 to -50
-40.0 to -42.7	2b	-40 to -45
-37.3 to -40.0	3a	-35 to -40
-34.5 to -37.2	3b	-30 to -35
-31.7 to -34.4	4a	-25 to -30
-28.9 to -31.6	4b	-20 to -25
-26.2 to -28.8	5a	-15 to -20
-23.4 to -26.1	5b	-10 to -15
-20.6 to -23.3	6a	-5 to -10
-17.8 to -20.5	6b	0 to -5
-15.0 to -17.7	7a	5 to 0
-12.3 to -15.0	7b	10 to 5
-9.5 to -12.2	8a	15 to 10
-6.7 to -9.4	8b	20 to 15
-3.9 to -6.6	9a	25 to 20
-1.2 to -3.8	9b	30 to 25
1.6 to -1.1	10a	35 to 30
4.4 to 1.7	10b	40 to 35
4.5 and Above	11	40 and Above

Scale in Kilometers

Scale in Miles

Scale 1:6,000,000 (Approximately)

CONVERSION CHARTS

FAHRENHEIT	CELSIUS
0°	−18°
10°	−12°
15°	−9°
20°	−7°
75°	24°
80°	27°
90°	32°
100°	38°

INCHES	CENTIMETERS
¼	0.6
½	1.3
1	2.5
2	5
3	8
4	10
5	13
6	15
7	18
8	20
9	23
10	25
11	28
12	31
13	33
14	35
15	38
16	40
17	43
18	45
19	48
20	50

FEET	METERS
1	0.3
2	0.6
3	1.0
4	1.2
5	1.5
6	1.8
7	2.0
8	2.4
9	2.7
10	3.0
11	3.3
12	3.6
13	3.9
14	4.2
15	4.5
16	4.8
17	5.0
18	5.4
19	5.7
20	6.0

FORMULAS

$$°C = (°F - 32) \times \frac{5}{9}$$

1 inch = 2.5 centimeters

1 foot = 0.3 meter

1 yard = 0.9 meter

1 acre = 0.4 hectare

1 gallon = 3.7 liters

1 cubic yard = 0.8 cubic meter

REFERENCES

Bean, W. J. 1970–1980. *Trees and Shrubs Hardy in the British Isles*. 8th ed. London: Murray.

Bir, Richard. 1992. *Growing and Propagating Showy Native Woody Plants*. Chapel Hill: University of North Carolina Press.

Brickell, Christopher. 1989. The American Horticultural Society *Encyclopedia of Garden Plants*. New York: Macmillan.

Coats, Alice M. 1992. *Garden Shrubs and Their Histories*. New York: Simon and Schuster.

Cumming, Roderick W., and Robert E. Lee. 1960. *Contemporary Perennials*. New York: Macmillan.

Dirr, Michael. 1990. *Manual of Woody Landscape Plants*. 4th ed. Champaign, Illinois: Stipes Publishing.

Dobson, Beverly, and Peter Schneider. 1984. *Combined Rose List*. New York: B. R. Dobson.

Eddison, Sydney. 1997. *The Self-Taught Gardener: Lessons from a Country Garden*. New York: Viking.

Galle, Fred. 1987. *Azaleas*. Rev. ed. Portland, Oregon: Timber Press.

Griffiths, Mark. 1994. *Index of Garden Plants*. Portland, Oregon: Timber Press.

Grimm, William Carey. 1968. *Recognizing Flowering Wild Plants*. Harrisburg, Pennsylvania: Stackpole Books.

Haworth-Booth, Michael. 1984. *The Hydrangeas*. 5th ed. London: Constable.

Hay, Roy, and Patrick M. Synge. 1969. *Dictionary of Garden Plants in Colour*. New York: Crown.

Heath, Brent and Becky. 1995. *Daffodils for American Gardens*. Washington, D.C.: Elliott and Clark.

Hillier, Harold. 1973. *Manual of Trees and Shrubs*. Newton Abbot, U.K.: David & Charles.

Loewer, Peter. 1993. *The Evening Garden*. New York: Macmillan.

Macoboy, Stirling. 1981. *The Color Dictionary of Camellias*. Sydney: Lansdowne Press.

Mallet, Corinne. 1992. *Hydrangeas: Species and Cultivars*. Centre d'Art Floral.

Mickel, John. 1994. *Ferns for American Gardens*. New York: Macmillan.

Odenwald, Neil, and James Turner. 1996. *Identification, Selection, and Use of Southern Plants for Landscape Design*. Baton Rouge, Louisiana: Claitor's.

Ogden, Scott. 1994. *Garden Bulbs for the South*. Dallas, Texas: Taylor.

Picton, Paul. 1999. *The Gardener's Guide to Growing Asters*. Portland, Oregon: Timber Press.

Rix, Martyn, and Roger Phillips. 1981. *The Bulb Book*. London: Pan Books.

Royal Horticultural Society. 1998. *The RHS Plant Finder 1998–99*. London: Dorling Kindersley.

Sheldon, Elisabeth. 1997. *The Flamboyant Garden*. New York: Henry Holt.

Smith, A. W. 1972. *A Gardener's Dictionary of Plant Names*. Revised and enlarged by William T. Stearn. London: Cassell.

Sunset Editors. 1995. *Sunset Western Garden Book*. Menlo Park, California: Sunset Publishing Corporation.

Thomas, Graham Stuart. 1992. *Ornamental Shrubs, Climbers, and Bamboos*. Portland, Oregon: Timber Press.

Van Melle, P. J. 1943. *Shrubs and Trees for the Small Place*. New York: Charles Scribner's Sons.

Welch, H. J. 1966. *Dwarf Conifers*. Newton, Massachusetts: C. T. Branford Company.

Wyman, Donald. 1996. *Shrubs and Vines for American Gardens*. New York: Macmillan.

Yoshimichi Hirose and Masato Yokoi. 1998. *Variegated Plants in Color*. Japan: Varie Nine.

INDEX